Beyond Hegel and Dialectic

SUNY Series in Hegelian Studies
William Desmond, Editor

Beyond Hegel and Dialectic

Speculation, Cult, and Comedy

William Desmond

State University of New York Press

Published by
State University of New York Press, Albany

© 1992 State University of New York

For information, address State University of New York
Press, State University Plaza, Albany, N.Y., 12246

Production by Diane Ganeles
Marketing by Theresa A. Swierzowski

Library of Congress Cataloging–in–Publication Data

Desmond, William, 1951–
    Beyond Hegel and dialectic : speculation, cult, and comedy /
William Desmond.
        p.   cm. — (SUNY series in Hegelian studies)
    Includes bibliographical references and index.
    ISBN 0-7914-1103-6 (alk. paper). — ISBN 0-7914-1104-4 (pbk. :
alk. paper)
    1. Hegel, Georg Wilhelm Friedrich, 1770-1831.   I. Title.
II. Series.
B2948.D47   1992
193—dc20   91-26541
                                                       CIP

10 9 8 7 6 5 4 3 2 1

For George L. Kline

Ó táim dom chur amach
's nach ligthear dom istigh,
buíochas le Rí na bhfeart
nach féidir mé a chur amach amuigh!

Old Irish Epigram

He who hurries cannot walk with dignity.

Chinese Fortune Cookie

O sages standing in God's holy fire
As in the gold mosaic of a wall,
Come from the holy fire, perne in a gyre,
And be the singing-masters of my soul.
Consume my heart away; sick with desire
And fastened to a dying animal
It knows not what it is; and gather me
Into the artifice of eternity.

W. B. Yeats, *Sailing to Byzantium*

Contents

Contents

Preface

We live in a time of rush. This is reflected high and low. Low: contemporary societies have little or no time for metaphysical pondering. High: even the privileged, academic philosopher is often caught in the hurry, too harried by professional obligations to have enough time or inclination to think. We risk the seduction of what I will call "thought-bites": positions ready prepared for speed reading, prepackaged for mental digestion. Our quick attention to ideas, more or less familiar, offers a satisfaction but this is short-lived. Little nourished, we seek the stimulus of more quick "thought-bites" to keep the hunger of spirit at bay.

A philosopher has to be prepared to stand aside in the rush—and to let that hunger of spirit speak. The willingness to think long, with a discerning taste for what sustains thought—these are necessary for philosophy. To have the freedom to think one must have the time to savor thought. There is no quick or easy solution to philosophical perplexity that would give to the mind an undemanding rush of conceptual ecstasy. Philosophy can be urgent but need not be hurried. Philosophy requires the patience of thinking. Patience of thought is especially required when, as we often find, philosophy does not dispel our perplexity but deepens it.

I claimed in *Philosophy and its Others* that philosophy must acknowledge its own plurivocity. It does not just have one voice, say, that of a dominating univocal logicism. My other works reflect this openness to the possibilities of plurivocal saying. *Art and the Absolute* was a somewhat more scholarly effort to think through some of the major questions at issue in Hegel's aesthetics. *Desire, Dialectic, and Otherness* was a systematic development of the metaxological sense of being, articulated through a hermeneutics of desire in quest of ultimacy. *Philosophy and its Others* developed this metaxological sense, relative to the aesthetic, the ethical, the religious, and to

xi

philosophy itself, each as crucial ways of mind and being. That book had a systematic side, but as taking thought to the limit of system, it also had an essential poetic side. It is the most plurivocal of these three works.

The present work is different again. In the main, it is a dialogue and confrontation between the metaxological sense of being and the dialectical sense, especially Hegel's. It is not concerned only to interpret or comment on Hegel. Hegel will be very important, but so will major figures from the tradition of philosophy, as will some influential contemporary thinkers. Not studies, or systems, or poems, I think of its chapters as ruminations, metaphysical meditations. These are efforts to think patiently, to think long and hard. They ask a similar thinking from the reader. They eschew the "shot from a pistol" style of journal articles. They cross and crisscross a terrain from a plurality of angles, back and forth, stating themes and restating them, thinking and thinking again, thinking otherwise again. They look at different landmarks from different angles and directions, approach old landscapes with new viewings or with old viewings deepened. They are not simply linear, though they are generally linear. Each section within each essay might be read as a essay in itself. The matter itself demands more than one formulated thought, shows itself demanding a plurivocity from the philosopher.

Some parts of the present essays appeared in significantly different form in studies written over a number of years.[1] In rethinking the themes of those studies, I found that the matter took on an essentially new shape, consistent with developments in my own thought. I found that there is never an absolute finish to a philosophical thought. There may be an exhaustion or abandonment of some thoughts; there may be a renewal of thoughts that, in being renewed, become significantly other to their previous form. But whether in exhaustion or abandonment, renewal or tranformation, the restlessness of thought returned, unasked, to trouble and to disturb.

My gratitude goes to my wife, Maria, for unfailing support, to my children, William, Hugh, and Oisín for disturbances that do not disturb but delight.

As with two previous manuscripts of mine, George L. Kline has commented and made suggestions with exemplary judiciousness and attention to detail. In gratitude for his encouragement and friendship, and in admiration of his contribution to philosophy and scholarship, I dedicate this book to him.

Introduction

In this work I offer a number of meditative essays, all on themes related to the limits of philosophical thought. By limit I do not mean a mere line that is the negative demarcation of a confined zone for philosophy. I mean the place of meeting where philosophy encounters and opens up to what may be other to its own familiar categories. A limit in this sense is affirmative: it articulates a space of significant betweenness, wherein philosophy might come to intermediate with what is not reducible to its own categorial self-mediation. Moreover, in this liminal middle and in encounter with what is other, philosophy might find that its own distinctive modes of thinking must be reformulated under the impact of such otherness. Hence my chosen themes: time and its other, speculation and cult, representation, evil, comedy. Cult as enacting our community with the divine other, comedy as the mocking other of logos, each of these takes speculative thinking into this space of the intermediate. So also does representation as the imagistic other of the logical concept, as does evil as a recalcitrant negative otherness. The thought of eternity as the other of time carries speculative mind into this limiting between.

All such themes tax the conceptual resources of philosophy. They require more than scientistic univocity or scholarly exegesis. They call for metaphysical meditation. By such meditation I mean an extended reflective discourse which mingles expository, interpretive, critical and speculative thinking. A philosophical meditation requires a patient dwelling with a matter at issue. Such patient thinking must try to stay true to the intricate contours of the matter itself. That mindful dwelling may find that the matter at stake demands a plurality of articulations, ranging, as I say, from the expository to the speculative, perhaps even letting ring out on occasion the philosophical laughter that mocks the pretension of abstract analysis.

1

Throughout the work there recurs an affirmation of the indispensability of speculative philosophy. Sometimes this is in a spirit sympathetic to Hegel and against speculation's post-Hegelian detractors. Sometimes I defend speculation in a form that is not at all Hegelian and with recognition of the genuine concerns raised by philosophers after Hegel. After Hegel speculative philosophy has been subject to onslaughts of criticism, whether of the Marxist sort, or of the Nietzschean or the Heideggerian, or of the positivistic/scientistic kind, or the deconstructionst type. Since these onslaughts have often been provoked by Hegel, inevitably, and in a variety of ways, one must return to Hegelian philosophizing itself, with special reference to the issue of speculative reason. But this is not simply a book on Hegel, though I will say a lot about Hegel. My turn to Hegel is with the aim of thinking the matter anew, thinking otherwise than in terms of Hegel's dialectic, not with the aim of historical exegesis or reactive *apologia* for the Hegelian style of speculation.

So I do not aim to present a systematic reconstruction of the entirety of Hegelian philosophizing. There is a reason for this, besides diffidence and the daunting nature of such a reconstruction. I find a certain logic in Hegelian thinking that repeats itself throughout the entirety of the system; this is the logic of what I call "dialectical self-mediation." The logic of dialectical self-mediation includes a reference to what is other, but also always ends by including that other as a subordinate moment within a more encompassing self-mediating whole. This dialectical inclusion precipitates one of the chief questions that occupies me: the issue of the limits of systematic philosophy itself, relative to its claims to comprehensiveness. The question has haunted Hegel in the past, and still continues to haunt any serious dialogue with his thought. My own thought has always been drawn to modes of meaning that, certainly on first glance, seem to be other to or outside system. I particularly mean art and religion, both as mode of mindfulness that carry their own distinguishing marks apart from philosophy, but both also as explicitly singled out by Hegel himself for special inclusion at the apex of his system.

Here Hegel is accused of a hubris of reason, a disrespect for what is other to thought, and a will to subordinate all being to philosophical speculation. Yet the Hegelian idea of philosophy is most deeply articulated in relation to absolute spirit. This is the consummating thinking wherein the various oppositions of subjectivity and objectivity, self and other, freedom and necessity, time and eternity are said to be overcome. Here philosophy shares the spotlight with art and religion, both of which are also said to be modes of absolute spirit, that is, concretions of self-knowing spirit in which the alienating dualism of finite experience and thought are overcome. The accusation of reason's hubris reappears even here in that philosophy ultimately subordinates art and religion and thus shows its failure to respect their otherness as other, that is, as intrinsically justified in themselves and not merely in terms of their dialectical interplay with and preparation for philosophy.

The conviction that speculative philosophy has ended—embraced for instance, by Marx, Kierkegaard, Nietzsche, though not only them—is not unrelated to this. The matter is equivocal in that many philosophers who reject Hegel actually practice modes of thinking that have some precedent in Hegel; Marx and Kierkegaard immediately come to mind. What presupposition flowers into this hesitation before, indeed recoil from speculative philosophizing? I suggest that one important presupposition concerns a failure to think through crucial implications of the *proximity* of art, philosophy, and religion. Hegel is seen as a systematic, scientific philosopher. In contemporary philosophy, the image of the philosopher as a mathematical technician or a kind of scientist has often been to the fore. Alternatively we find the image of the scholar. Hegel is famous for his claim that he has succeeded in making philosophy into a science. This claim is articulated in the context of Hegel's own debt to the tradition of transcendental philosophy. Hegel tries to bring this tradition to a completion with a self-justifying doctrine of presuppositionless science, or a logic that is also a transcendental ontology.

I am not denying this. I am denying that this is all. So I am asking: How then do we take seriously the proximity to ultimacy shared between art, religion, and philosophy? If we ponder this proximity a different face of Hegel must emerge. This other Hegel shows continuity with the metaphysical tradition prior to transcendental philosophy, shows also, let us say, a postmodern promise, in being concerned not to deny philosophy's bond with its significant spiritual and cultural others. Philosophy must be science, Hegel says; it must not be edifying. Kierkegaard will denounce him for betraying something essential to edifying thought. But the tale ends with a twist that is in tension with this contrast. Philosophy is systematic, yet at the apex of the system the deepest definition of philosophy is in terms of its interrelation with two modes of mindfulness that are at the edge of system and that resist the pretensions of analysis to reduce their richness to a catalogue of univocal concepts. If systematic philosophy must take account of the proximity of art and religion, proximity to philosophy in their proximity to ultimacy, then what we mean by philosophical science is itself made problematic.[1]

I find a challenging paradox here that I need to state at the outset. This paradox not only draws our attention to thought provoking ambiguities in Hegel; it draws us to fundamental tensions inherent in the philosophical enterprise itself. It also provides us with some basis for trying to interpret Hegel differently, indeed to think otherwise than Hegel did. I mean particularly a reinterpretation in terms of what I call a "metaxological understanding" of the interplay of philosophy and its others. I return to this below.

The paradox is the following: In Hegel himself we find the coexistence of an inexorable will to systematic reason *and* philosophical respect for modes of mind that normally are taken as recalcitrant to rational systematization. Hegel wants to think the dialectical togetherness of philosophical reason and its recalcitrant others. The paradox consists in the tense coexistence of systematic philosophical completeness and philosophical openness to what is other to philosophy. To claim the first seems to deny the second: if thought is systematically complete in principle, there is nothing other and essential to which it is to be open. To assert the second seems to deny the first: if one continues to be open to otherness, one necessarily seems to grant something other than, or essentially outside of, systematic completeness.

To think this togetherness is a potentially explosive project, since this togetherness, if thought of dialectically, seems to subordinate the very otherness that is allegedly to be respected. The will to systematic science seems intent on subordinating all others to the self-mediation of philosophical thought; philosophical openness to modes of mind other than system seems to undercut this very will to systematic inclusiveness. At once philosophy seems to be the imperious superior of its others and the patient servant of the inherent meaning of these others as others. This paradox seems to show that philosophical thought is in contradiction to itself. Either it pursues its will for systematic completion through to the end, and then it will inevitably subordinate all others to itself. Or, if it tries to exhibit this patient openness to otherness as other, it must give up at the outset its will to systematic completion. It seems we cannot have both.

In my view Hegel rejects this either/or. The daring of his philosophical ambition, which might on occasion also be called "humility," is the desire to respond to both these requirements. That is to say, the paradox above outlined reveals what in *Philosophy and Its Others* I claim is the *double* requirement of philosophical thought; namely, that it not only be thought thinking itself, but that it be thought thinking its others. I want to ask how Hegel's dialectical way of philosophizing lives up to this double requirement of thought. Does

Hegel tend to reduce this double requirement to a singular, all-embracing process of dialectical self-mediation? If he does, and I think he does, and if the result is identified with the completion of speculative philosophy, as most post-Hegelians seem to think, do we not here have a major source of the ambiguous status, not to say always threatened position, of speculative philosophy ever since? One cannot deny that Hegel invariably gives philosophical priority to *thought thinking itself*. Nevertheless, the stated paradox forces us to rethink what it is to think philosophically. It forces us to rethink the others of philosophy, not only in their continuity with philosophy, but also in their discontinuity.

The element of continuity is the side most frequently stressed by Hegel's admirers. The element of discontinuity, as attenuated by Hegel, is the side most loudly protested by his detractors. The complex togetherness of the two needs to be explored. I will stress this togetherness, and do so, both to Hegel's credit when praise is appropriate, and to Hegel's discredit when criticism is in order. This requires something like the double reading of Hegel that I had already recommended in *Art and the Absolute*.[2] In that work the element of discontinuity was subordinated to continuity. This was a strategic muting to allow us to hear Hegel's complex voice above the post-Nietzschean and poststructuralist pandemonium of voices. Some of my critics thought I was too Hegelian, others thought I was not Hegelian enough, others again thought I got the balance right. Be that as it may, though the element of continuity will be stressed in this work also, the element of discontinuity will be allowed more prominent place. This is entirely appropriate, given my concern with what is other to system at the limits of philosophical reason.

I need to spell out a little what I see as the double requirement of philosophical thought. Elsewhere I have given an account of this in its own terms and independently of Hegel, terms that have led me into disagreement with Hegel.[3] I ask the reader's attention to these remarks, since they indicate my proximity to dialectical thought and yet also my disquiet with its characteristic ways of giving an account of what is other to thought. This doubleness will crop up throughout these meditative essays, since even granting my desire to read Hegel with a generous hermeneutic, suspicion cannot be entirely laid to rest about Hegel's dialectical relation to otherness. In this I agree with a pervasive unease that has not yet been dispelled in the aftermath of the Hegelian system. Hegel occupies a certain intermediate position between continuity and discontinuity, identity and difference. What is the nature of this middle? Hegel's answer is: the middle is dialectical. The answer I suggest is: the middle is metaxological. This answer takes us beyond Hegel and dialectic.

This metaxological view informs the present work at a deep hermeneutical level. Sometimes it is more explicitly to the fore, sometimes it is an undercurrent, not stated at the level of thematic objectification. To articulate the relation of thought and what is other to thought, we need a certain complex balance of unity and plurality, identity and difference, sameness and distinction. How does the metaxological sense of being answer this need? I derive the term from the Greek *metaxu*, meaning "middle," "intermediate," "between," and *logos*, meaning "discourse," "speech," "articulate account." The metaxological concerns a *logos* of the *metaxu*, a discourse of the between, the middle. We find ourselves in an intermediate place, inadequately interpreted either by totalizing holisms of the sort attributed to Hegel, or by the discontinuous plurality we find in deconstructive thought, indeed in Wittgensteinian pluralism. My concern for this "middle" acknowledges the contemporary concern with difference and plurality. But it dissents from any sterile obsession with discontinuity. Otherness itself asks us to think through the meaning of the community of being. A community of being that sustains otherness distances us from merely asserted difference, as well as from any equally unfruitful sense of totalizing unity.

I define the metaxological sense of being in its dynamic inter-relation to three other senses; namely, the univocal, the equivocal, and the dialectical senses. The first sense, the univocal puts the stress on simple sameness, hence on the unmediated unity of the self and the other. The univocal sense has its hermeneutical place in any interpretation of being, but its unmediated sense of unity does not do justice to the complex *differences* we also need to acknowledge. The equivocal sense, by contrast, is at odds with univocity and tends to call attention to aspects of unmediated difference between the self and the other. Instead of a reductive univocity, a sense for the equivocal helps us recognize a certain rich ambiguity in the intermediate being of things. The difficulty is that we can remain mired in an equivocity that reneges on the appropriate mediation of difference. Ambiguity is not merely to be asserted; it is to be mindfully mediated. If we remain with a merely asserted equivocity, we produce a form of pluralism devoid of a sense of any deeper relatedness of things. Plurality becomes indistinguishable from a dispersal of being that is merely fragmenting. Deconstructionist thought risks this kind of equivocal thinking in its critique of univocal unity.

The dialectical sense of being is more complex than univocity and equivocity. Like deconstructive thought, dialectical thinking is critical of the finality of univocal unity and any simple unmediated sameness. But dialectic, which is not merely negative, is also diffident with respect to any merely equivocal thought. As I said, ambiguity is not only to be acknowledged, it is to be mediated, thought through in as mindful as way as is possible. Unlike deconstructionist thought, the dialectical sense suggests the genuine possibility of mediating equivocal difference. One reason that we cannot rest with unmediated difference is that such difference engenders a sense of alienating antithesis or dualistic opposition. Dualistic opposition and equivocal difference subvert themselves, as does mere univocity, if we think the matter through. The possible togetherness of the opposites is opened up by the dialectical sense.

The issue at stake here is the nature of this togetherness, for this togetherness defines the community of the self and the other in their likeness and in their difference. The limitation I find with the dialectical sense, and this I find in Hegel, as will become evident in a variety of ways, is that it shows an equivocal tendency to interpret *all* mediation primarily in terms of *self-mediation*. The togetherness of the self and the other and their intermediation is, in the end, seen in the light of a certain privileging of self-mediation. Though the need to mediate equivocal difference is granted, the danger here is that of reducing *all otherness* to a form that must be subordinated to the putative primacy of such self-mediation. The doubleness of the self and the other is not fully recognized as the basis of a togetherness that is irreducibly plural; it becomes dialectically converted into a dualism that is to be mediated and included in a higher and more embracing process of self-mediation. Then dialectical converts the mediation of self and other into two sides of a more embracing and singular process of total self-mediation. The thought of everything other to thought risks getting finally reduced to a moment of thought thinking *itself*.

The metaxological sense of being is not so much hostile to dialectic as it is to any such reduction of otherness, and to the reduction of a pluralized intermediation to a singular self-mediation. It wants to articulate the togetherness with a different accent on otherness. This fourth sense articulates the space of the middle as open to a double mediation, a double that is no dualistic opposition. The middle is plurally mediated: it can be mediated from the side of the dialectical self; but also it can be mediated from the side of an otherness that is not to be reduced to a moment of self-mediation. I note that Hegel also believes that the other mediates the middle; but we will have many occasions to note that this mediation from the side of the other invariably turns out to be a penultimate, hence subordinate moment of a more ultimate process of dialectical self-mediation; mediation from the other and by the other turns out, in the end, to be a mediation of the self in the form of *its own* otherness, and hence not the mediation of an irreducible other at all.

The complex "between" as articulating a metaxological sense of the togetherness of self and other is not to be understood in terms of such an encompassing dialectical self-mediation, even in all its internal complexity. The "between" grants otherness its irreducible otherness. If otherness is to be mediated, and it is, it must be mediated in terms other than dialectical self-mediation. The latter risks saying that the plurality of forms of mediation all in the end come down to one essential form that encompasses all the others. But metaxological intermediation is itself plural. There is an affirmative sense of the double that cannot be spoken of simply as a dualistic opposition. Nor is the other simply the self in the form of its own otherness: there are others to the self that are not the self again in its own otherness. Our intermediation with these others cannot be included in dialectical self-mediation. The mediation of the metaxological between cannot be exhausted either by the mediation of the self or the mediation of the other. Neither side can claim entirely to mediate the complex between. The "whole" is not a whole in the sense of a conceptual monologue with itself; it is a plurivocal community of voices in interplay just in their genuine otherness.

The double mediation of the metaxological means that genuine speculative mind must be both self-mediating and also open to the intermediation between thought and what is other to thought, precisely as other. One does not reject the univocal, equivocal, and dialectical senses of being. Each has its contribution to make, albeit in the sense that requires our attentiveness to the dangers above suggested. The deepest openness of speculative mind is the impossibility of the ultimate closure of thought by itself and in itself.

Here we see how this fourfold sense of being relates to the task of speculative thought. Speculative philosophy is concerned with the mindful thought of being, and if the mindful thought of being must be metaxological, speculative mind is charged with a *double imperative.* First, it cannot betray the inherent exigency of its own form of mindfulness. Perhaps this is rendered by Aristotle's description of the ultimate *energeia* of being as *noēsis noēseōs*, thought thinking itself. Hegel's absolute Idea answers to this requirement. Genuine thought mediates with itself, must be as internally coherent and consistent as possible. Relative to the fourfold sense of being this means that speculative mind is dialectically self-mediating in thinking through the apparent equivocality of being in search of a community of meaning more complex than univocal identity.

The fundamental tension for speculative mind emerges here, in line with the paradox I noted with respect to Hegel between systematic completeness and what is other to system. When thought thinking itself privileges only its own internal self-coherence, it is tempted to renege on potentially dissident forms of otherness that resist complete conceptualization. I think that in modern philosophy this temptation to renege on dissident otherness follows from Descartes' formulation *"cogito me cogitare."* This might be seen as a subjectivistic version of Aristotle's *noēsis noēseōs*, answering in its own way to the requisite self-mediation of thinking. The difficulty is that when we elevate this into *the* essential form of thought, we produce a contraction of metaphysical openness to otherness. This we see in the subsequent history of modern philosophy, endemic to which we find a sense of mind's alienation from being's otherness. Because of the absolutizing of self-mediating thinking, the otherness of being is now reduced to a mindless dualistic opposite; or alternatively it is dialectically dominated by an idealistic self-mediation; or it is simply mindlessly let be in its unmediated thereness, or irrationally celebrated in its brute facticity by post-idealistic philosophy.[4]

Against the attempted closure of thought on itself in seamless self-mediation, speculative mindfulness must recall us to this *second exigency* of thought, beyond dialectical mediation. Self-mediating thought must be genuinely open to the otherness of being, even in all its forms dissident to complete conceptualization. Speculative thought as metaxological is charged not only with the self-mediation of thought but with the intermediation between thought and what is other to thought. Some of the post-Hegelian accusations against traditional speculation perhaps originate in a tendency of metaphysics to give unbalanced stress to the first exigency of thought thinking itself. Therein lurks the danger of a certain logicism: speculative philosophers create grand structures of conceptual abstractions, but because they have neglected the second exigency of thought's openness to otherness, the grand conceptual structures have too tenuous a connection with being in its otherness. Speculative mind as metaxological demands of philosophy a self-mediating openness to otherness where the second exigency breaks open the tendency to closure on the part of self-mediation. This second exigence is so important that honest speculative reflection may find its self-mediations broken or ruptured on forms of otherness that its categories cannot entirely master.

Speculative philosophy must be mindful of the voices of such others. The different chapters of this book try to reach this mindfulness. Since speculative mindfulness cannot be the conceptual monologue of thought thinking itself, it must let the impact of otherness strain its own voice into a saying that takes us to the edge of dialectical logos, and beyond. The limit then ceases to be the negative line of demarcation but that place of meeting, where speculative mind genuinely opens itself to what the voices of these others bring, on their own terms, to the metaxological between.

If I reject the closure of self-thinking thought, I do not blankly repudiate the notion of wholeness, as does deconstruction. This again relates to the complex togetherness of self and other. A metaxological web of relations articulates their differences but also holds them together. Being held together, holding together points to a sense of "wholeness" that is not closed. I suggested in *Art and the Absolute* that the art work is such an open whole.[5] I suggest that the mindful human being is such an open whole: it is not *the* Whole, nor does its philosophical thinking completely overreach all being in its otherness; as intermediate it is other to closed totality and to sheerly indefinite incompleteness. The openness of every whole is precisely the eruption of the metaxological charge of otherness, either within that whole itself or at its utmost limit where it faces what is not itself.

This metaxological sense of being, as not hostile to such an open wholeness, is in this regard closer to Hegel than are deconstructionist thinkers who all but automatically, I almost said mindlessly, disdain any suggestion of wholeness. Any suggestion of wholeness is immediately identified with a closed totality. The metaxological sense tries to articulate dialectical self-mediation itself with sufficient qualification to avoid the kind of totality that Hegel celebrates and that deconstruction excoriates. That said, we must also be attentive to neglected spaces of openness within Hegelian dialectic itself to which the deconstructionist can be blind. The metaxological sense of being tries to give a different modulation to the *dia* of *dialectic*. This *dia*, this dyad, this twosomeness recalls us to a doubleness, recalls us to the middle as itself plural. One way to open the dialectic, and move beyond the closure of self-mediation, is simply to become mindful again of dialectic's own doubleness. This reminder of doubleness makes us less impatient, after Hegel, to reduce the double intermediation to a singular process of total self-mediation. The dialectic must become dynamically dyadic because ultimately it finds itself in the interplay of the middle as metaxological, and its demand of pluralized mediation.

I suggest that Hegel can be fruitfully reinterpreted as trying to stand dialectically in the middle, the best articulation of which would be metaxological. But partly because of the legacy of the traditional privileging of thought thinking itself, partly because of the residues of the Cartesian *cogito* and the idealism of the transcendental ego, Hegel's inhabitation of the middle inevitably gives stress to self-mediation. The metaxological middle is turned into the Hegelian whole whose complete dialectical self-mediation results in the subordination of being's otherness to thought thinking its own categories. The double exigency of thought in the true middle is collapsed into the first exigency of thought thinking itself. The second exigency of thought thinking its other is distorted by being dialectically domesticated. This dialectical domestication within the Hegelian whole does not do justice to the overdetermined power of being as agapeic origin, nor to all of the complexities of our own intermediate being.

I underline that the point is not to deny an interplay of self and other in Hegel, nor to deny that Hegel interprets community in terms of spirit. The point is that this interplay and community and spirit are understood on the model of a dialectically self-mediating whole, and this means the placing of otherness in a finally subordinate position. Hegel's system evidences more and more inclusive self-mediating wholes, which progressively incorporate all otherness as a necessary moment of the whole's own self-development. Hegel's whole is an infinite self-mediating whole. Nor is this infinity understood as an unmastered agapeic otherness, but simply as the purest, most ultimate self-mediation, that is to say, the circular process by which infinity passes into finitude and finitude passes into infinity. I dissent from this understanding of infinitude, both with respect to the unmastered infinitude of the divine and the inward infinitude of the self, that is also not mastered by dialectical self-mediation.[6]

I put the question this way: Aristotle says that "the least number, strictly speaking, is two" (*Physics*, 220a27), but can Hegel really count to two, or count to a real two? This seems a ridiculous question since Hegel is notorious for his stress on the number three, and all its trinitarian implications. I ask the question in all seriousness. I also ask for a mindfulness larger than univocal literalness. If what I said about the double mediation of the metaxological in contrast to the singular process of dialectical self-mediation has been understood, then we can say this. Hegel counts to three, but in dialectically counting to three, he is finally counting to one; the third turns out to be the first; for the second, in dialectically turning into the third, also turns out to be the first; three turns out to be one, two turns out to be one, hence Hegel does not finally count beyond one at all.

How then do we count to two, really count to a two? Must we not actually count to four to be able to count to a real two? Or count to two one's that are themselves doubles? This is suggested by the metaxological sense of being: if we can count two wholes as each dialectically self-mediating in an open way, then the intermediation *between* these two cannot just be dialectical self-mediation or any singular process of self-mediation. We have the basis of a between that is genuinely non-reductive of plurality, even while it allows the intermediation between the one and the other. In this account of things, every one or whole or integer is itself double, doubly mediated. If we can count this one as two, and count another one as two, and if it is the case, as the metaxological sense suggests, that two such doubly mediated ones cannot be reduced to or encompassed by each other or by another one, a further singularly self-mediated one, then I say we can count beyond one to two. Then we can count to three, to four. . . .[7]

The tension between dialectic and the metaxological, the sense of the intermediate and the doubleness of mediation it requires, will be variously seen in the chapters to follow. The themes which will occupy us forces us into interplay, not only with Hegel, but also with thinkers like Plato, Socrates, Saint Augustine, Saint Thomas Aquinas, Kant, Kierkegaard, Marx, Nietzsche, Heidegger, to name some of the major figures that will be important.

Apropos of Hegel's relation to pre-Hegelian and post-Hegelian philosophers, I find myself again in a middle position. On the one hand, I think that Hegel is far richer than many of his overcomers acknowledge. The effigy of the "ontotheologian" has become a bogey-man brought out on occasions of ritual polemic to terrorize the opponent, namely, those who do not buy the hermeneutical line that philosophy went disastrously off the ontological tracks with Socrates. Dialectical thinking offers a powerful mode of philosophizing. Part of its power is the power of the tradition itself in this sense: the ideal of univocity may indeed drive the reduction to logicist unity, but this ideal is *already* transcended by any mode of dialectical thinking. Such thinking thrives on its acknowledgement of the dynamic interplay of the self and other, unity and difference, sameness and otherness. This power of dialectical thinking is not something that Heidegger or Derrida have overcome. Its power is not completed or exhausted, but still stands before us a promise. The suggested opening of dialectical to metaxological thinking is part of that promise. Hegel's thought makes its own efforts to stay as close as possible to the concrete *Sache selbst*. This is the middle itself, whether dialectically or metaxologically articulated. Hegel is not a mere abstract thinker. If Hegel is an abstract thinker, then all philosophy is mere abstraction.

On the other hand, Hegel is not immune from severe question. There is a drive to systematic science which the darkness of being checks. Hegel himself is selective is his own interpretation of the tradition of philosophy, and ultimately opts for the superiority of post-Cartesian, post-Kantian systematic science. There is the risk of neglecting other aspects of the tradition which resist this scientific mold—I think of his unsubtle dismissal of Platonic myth, or his contemptuous remarks on Diogenes for whom philosophy was a way of life, not systematic science. I have already noted his development of dialectical thinking such as to subordinate the interplay of being and thinking to an *Aufhebung* that is not called for by the interplay, conceived as metaxological. Against his privileging of self-mediation as *the* form of mediation, which subordinates being's otherness to self-thinking thought, there are forms of otherness and intermediation that disrupt this hegemony of self-mediation. There is in Hegel a dominance of the language of the whole, expressed in a pervasive metaphorics of circularity, that is not compatible with the notion of agapeic infinitude and its unmastered otherness. Because of such matters, I take seriously the ideas of otherness and difference that post-Hegelian and anti-Hegelian thinkers press on us. In a word: I am "dialectically" ambiguous about Hegel's own dialectical ambiguity. But to deal with this dialectical ambiguity we must go beyond Hegel and dialectic to the metaxological sense of being.

The following meditative essays address this dialectical ambiguity. They metaxologically hover between a yes and a no to Hegel: a yes, more sympathetic than his critics; a no, more nuanced, I hope, than the no his detractors pronounce.

In the first chapter, I reflect on speculative mind and history. I address the post-Hegelian reduction of philosophical reason to a historicism that takes no account of what is other to time, traditionally called "eternity." I reflect on the dialectical mediation of these two in Hegel, not their dualistic reduction either to complete temporal or eternalist terms. I remark on the historicism pervasive in post-Hegelian philosophy, whether in Marx, or Nietzsche, or Heidegger, and the accompanying critique of speculative philosophy. I find much greater internal complexity in Hegel's mediation of speculative philosophy and history than do his critics. While finding myself at odds with these critics, nevertheless I criticize the internal logic of Hegel's dialectical mediation as inevitably attenuating the otherness of the eternal. A metaxological understanding of that otherness asks

of mind that it speculatively re-raise the question of time's other. This
is a justified speculative question, not to be pushed to the side by easy
disposals of Platonic transcendence and medieval otherworldliness,
whether in the name of Hegelian dialectic, Marxist history, Nietzsche's
contempt for "afterworldsmen," or Heidegger's destruction of metaphysics. The resistance of time's other to philosophical system must
be raised, just in its resistance either to such dismissal or to definitive
univocal resolution.

In the second chapter, I turn to Hegel's own understanding of the
kinship of philosophy and religion. I meditate on his strange saying:
Philosophy too is cultus, *Gottesdienst*. This is a saying we find used
early in the *Differenzschrift*, and repeated in both the lectures on
religion and aesthetics. I ruminate on it as a speculative provocative,
all the more provocative given the many antagonisms of philosophy
and religion after Hegel. I will suggest a metaxological interpretation
of cultus in terms of a togetherness of manifestation and sacred
otherness, and the irreducible sense of the double indicated above.
I will find in Hegel a subordination of otherness to manifestation,
the reduction of the metaxological double of the human and divine
to a dialectical self-mediating unity. This I find even in his
confrontation with the negative, relative to the unhappy consciousness
and the "death of God."

I read Hegel's concern with this "death" without being cowed by
a Nietzschean trumpeting of the event, the long term cultural effects
of which have been to dilute the spiritual seriousness of the issues
at stake. I will say that Hegel has his finger on the pulse, though he
does dialectically miss the metaxological beat. This missing has
results in the very understanding of philosophy and the task of speculative mind, especially relative to its thinking of the transcendent
otherness of the divine ground, its dark manifestness even in the
immanent inwardness of worship itself. There is metaxological
otherness even in such inwardness. It is there even in the meditations
of philosophy, even in, so to say, the speculative prayers of thought
trying to think itself alone.

In the third chapter, I attempt an interpretation of the relation
of speculation and representation, which is continuous with the
tension between dialectical self-mediation and metaxological intermediation. I look at Hegel's recognition of a certain doubleness in
religious representation. This issue of representational thought and
philosophy is also a strong concern of contemporary Continental
philosophy in its desire to develop an approach to otherness that is
non-objectifying. I agree with the latter *desideratum* but disagree with
the mode of its contemporary implementation. Hegel's acknowledg-

ment of the doubleness of representation is done dialectically, which implies its subsumption in a more inclusive speculative unity. As such it does offer some basis for the reductive charge, but it must also be re-thought in a more open way, in the spirit of a certain hermeneutical generosity.

There is something very untrue to Hegel when his concern with religion is reduced to Marxist or Kojèvian terms. The persuasiveness of these latter is parasitical on the atheistic ethos of post-Hegelian culture. Hegel himself is a Janus figure: in some ways he anticipates his descendants; he also recalls us to what was profoundly positive in pre-Hegelian speculation, still not marked by *de rigeur* ideological aversion to things religious. As Hegel himself says: Religion is possible without philosophy but philosophy is impossible without religion. We post-Hegelian philosophers are strange split creatures. On the one hand, we are overwhelmed by Nietzsche's passionate no to religion; on the other, we are still conditioned to epistemological squirming by the toxic residue of the positivistic mentality. Nevertheless, the kinship of religion and speculative philosophy shows them to be not just strange opposites but intimate, familial others. Speculative philosophy is defined by familial interplay with this other. Nor is this interplay devoid of discord. Familial mutuality is often the most contentious.

Any thinker without an ideological axe to grind immediately should suspect an affinity between the nonrepresentational thinking of the non-objectifiable (espoused by some Continental thinkers) and what used to be termed the "mystical." This word "mysticism" itself seems to have the mystical power to make many philosophers squirm. But squirming is not a philosophical response. The "shocking" sentences that pepper Hegel's writing about the mystical are politely avoided, when the term "mystical" is not conscripted as a jargon word to abuse the thought of Hegel. I will not deny that Hegel did not philosophically squirm in his own way in the face of the "mystical." But it is always relevant to ask about the *silences* that mark a philosopher's thought or scholar's commentary.

In the face of the conceptual silence of the "mystical," the silence of commentators tells us something about the philosophical silences about religion generally in post-Hegelian thought, apart altogether from the scholastic etiquette of analytical distaste. The same studious silence, trepidation, has attended the enigmatic and provocative utterances of Wittgenstein about the mystical and indeed about silence itself. The other of univocal analysis is skirted with wide distance. But I find strength in philosophical thought in the measure that it has the courage to try to think such otherness, no doubt in terms that transcend univocity. Even in Hegel's perhaps disingenuous use of the "mystical," we will find a dialectical preference for manifestation over otherness. From the metaxological point of view, there are ambiguities here in Hegel, not to say equivocations with respect to the speculative attenuation of otherness, equivocations I think Hegel did not truly think through.

The fourth chapter is concerned with the enigma that evil presents to philosophy. Do we here have a negative otherness that humiliates all speculative thinking? In the course of addressing this question, I analyze and criticize Hegel's dialectical interpretation of evil. Do we submit to Adorno's order: not only no poetry, but no speculative philosophy after Auschwitz? I say no to this no. There is a speculative thinking whose conceptual maneuvres do domesticate and neutralize the horror of evil. There certainly are modes of philosophizing that allow mind to sleep through the horror. But I say that speculative mind as metaxological, as genuinely open to otherness that may resist total conceptual encapsulation, such mindfulness is made sleepless by the thought of evil. Evil incites speculative mind to incessant wakefulness by disturbing it with a metaphysical insomnia that will not let it lie easily. Instead of the speculation that domesticates its other, we need a speculative vigilance that tries to last its watch on the Gethsemane night of thought.

The fifth chapter addresses the issue of the failure of logos and a different mockery of philosophy. Can a certain speculative laughter ring out in the night of failure? Has not speculative philosophy always meditated on its own possible failure as logos? Did we have to wait the revelations of deconstruction to know this? In post-Hegelian philosophy we sometimes find a substitution of aestheticism for scientism. So also we find a reluctance for the religious producing a certain readiness for the aesthetic. This is glaringly evident in Nietzsche. The coupling of the aesthetic and philosophy is also evident in Nietzsche's deconstructive offspring. In both the father and the offspring, we find the imputation that speculative logos is a failure that tries to conceptually mask its failure. In turning to speculation and comic art, I am not really reversing Hegel's progression from art to religion. Comic art has its own sacred dimension, in fact. The possible comedy of failing logos is at stake in both dialectical and deconstructionist thinking. There is, I say, a certain philosophical mockery of philosophy implicit in the tradition of speculative thought. Speculative philosophy masks its secretly laughing side as one way of dealing with the comedy of failed logos.

Dialectical and deconstructionist thinkers are aware of laughter's connection with negativity and otherness. This is related to the debunking of univocity: if we reflect on rigid univocity it will, willy nilly, lose its fixity, and, despite itself, falls apart into equivocity. All we have to do is keep thinking and mind will find the ground or pretext to dismantle this fixation. Can anything stand up in the face of this dismantling power of mind? I will say that there is a generous laughter and a merely debunking laughter. Deconstruction, I think, itself equivocates in its debunking of univocal fixations. Dialectic points us towards a more speculatively generous laughter, in that the dismantling of fixed univocity does not serve mere dismantling; it serves the reconstruction of a more complex, dynamic and fulfilling whole.

The speculative generosity of dialectic, though, does not get us to the agapeic energy of festive being that the metaxological allows us to see in laughter. There is a speculative laughter that issues from the festive celebration of being by agapeic mindfulness. This speculative yes to the community of being in no way subordinates the otherness of being to any conceptual whole constructed by the philosopher's mind. The yes of this laughter is a festive gesture towards the metaxological openness of agapeic being.

In the last chapter, I ask again: But can philosophy laugh at itself? Again the limits of speculative philosophy are at stake. Laughter seems to be outside system, seems to explode any logicist bias of speculation. Nor is the religious here out of play, for there is a sense of the comic that brings to mind a sacred folly. This is very evident with the ancient comedy of Aristophanes, one of the most profound mockers of philosophy in his caricature of Socrates. Hegel's attitude here is actually much more rich than is allowed by the caricature of Hegel himself as Dr. Panlogos. I will not exonerate Hegel entirely. But he does show an astonishing delight in Aristophanic laughter in preference to Socratic dialectic.

How can we make sense of this? Is there a secret side to Hegel that loves a clown? I will not ask this question in the spirit of post-modern frivolity but with the irreverent reverence of Aristophanic sacredness. The theme of dialectic and its other, the theme of the dialectical one and the metaxological double will appear again in this sacred folly. How will speculative mind relate to this alogical folly? Will the system, in the end, work a certain deformation? Will it be at a loss as to why there is a certain laughter that is other than, outside world-history? Will it be at a loss as to why we need a different speculative mindfulness to listen for this sacred laughter?

Our coupling of speculation with cult, evil, comedy—these undomesticated couplings—will cause the panlogist Hegelian to shudder at the impertinence to the logical concept. Perhaps not a few philosophers who pride themselves on being non-Hegelian, or anti-

Hegelian, will shake and shake their logicist heads. And in their shaking heads they will show themselves to be the unwitting blood brothers of the logicist Hegel himself. The logicist philosopher reminds one of the dutiful son who stays at home to meet his domestic responsibilities. But there is a prodigal son, and a prodigal philosopher. There is a prodigal Hegel. Were there not, we would have done with him long ago. I think that, finally, one has more respect for Hegel, the plurivocal Hegel, by letting the voices of these insubordinate, dialectically dissident others speak to philosophical dialectic, challenge it to think again, to think otherwise. After all, it is the prodigal son who, after wandering and venture and loss, really comes home, truly knows home, by knowing the heedless generosity of the agapeic father.

Chapter 1

Speculation and Historicism:
Between Hegel and Eternity

Speculative Mind and the Middle:
Between Time and Its Other

What, however, the age *needs* in the deepest sense can be said fully and completely with one single word: it needs...eternity. The misfortune of our time is just this, that it has become simply nothing else but "time," the temporal, which is impatient of hearing anything about eternity; and so (with the best of intentions or furiously) would make eternity quite superfluous by means of a cunningly devised counterfeit, which, however, in all eternity will not succeed; for the more one thinks oneself to be able, or hardens oneself to be able, to get along without the eternal, the more one feels the essential need of it.

Kierkegaard, *The Point of View for My Work as an Author*

When Kierkegaard said this, he sharply saw through his own era and was clairvoyant as to what might succeed it. The ambiguities of time and eternity still persist, as does our impatience with anything other than time. In reflecting on these ambiguities, I want to think against this impatience. Hegel dominated the intellectual milieu of Kierkegaard's time, but he, too, incarnated these ambiguities. Some of them he understood, others he misunderstood and perpetuated. Any rethinking of speculative philosophy, and not necessarily in an Hegelian sense, demands attention to these ambiguities.

One finds today a tendency to enlist Hegel as an ally for an essentially historicist conception of philosophy. Such an historicist Hegelianism is one shorn of the absolute, shorn, too, of any daring claims made for philosophy as an absolute knowing. The historicist Hegel is one stripped of the speculative dimension. This dimension

19

recalls Hegel's continuity with the entire metaphysical tradition and its respect for *theōria* as the highest mindfulness. This continuity is now broken by many thinkers after Hegel and for reasons connected to historicism. With this break the very identity of speculative philosophy is put in question.

This break is not only an intraphilosophical affair. In our post-Hegelian times, the corrosion of traditional religious and ethical values, coupled with the skeptical legacy of positivism in relation to metaphysics, coupled, too, with the instrumentalizing of being by technicism and scientism—all these induce a certain amount of epistemological squirming, when words like "absolute" are uttered. Those who hold that reason is essentially instrumental especially reject speculative philosophy, since traditionally the speculative required a mode of contemplative mind that transcended instrumentalization. If all reason is instrumental, inevitably the speculative must be empty for reason.

There is a philosophical irony here. Not a few critics of instrumental reason are in agreement with the advocates of instrumental reason in regard to just this suspicion of speculative philosophy. We find a startling agreement between positivism and various forms of post-Nietzschean thought, vis-à-vis the critique of traditional metaphysics. For example, Heideggerian hermeneutics is anathema to positivistic philosophy. Yet Heideggerians, strong critics of technicist thought, do agree with technicist thinking in calling speculative philosophy into question under the rubric "metaphysics of presence," "ontotheology." In their "destruction of metaphysics," they are surprisingly at one with the positivistic scorn.

Nietzscheans and sundry post-structuralists offer variations on the theme: speculative mind is rejected as the "phallogocentric" *theōria* of Platonism. Negative dialecticians, like Adorno, also strong critics of instrumental reason, are similarly suspicious of speculative philosophy. Indeed when Adorno says: After Auschwitz, not only no poetry, but no speculative philosophy—it is as if speculative philosophy was in complicity with this horror. This suspicion, indeed reduction of the speculative, tends to be a pervasive feature of forms of Left-Hegelianism indebted to Marx. What all these share is an unprecedented accentuation of the importance of time and a correlative depreciation, if not outright rejection, of any appeal to the transtemporal, to eternity. Hence Kierkegaard's clairvoyance.

This suspicion of speculation exerts its influence on the self-understanding of philosophy itself, as is reflected in one of the more discussed current issues, namely, that of "foundationalism." It is not always univocally clear what this issue is. But among a number of things, foundationalism implies the desire for some indubitable and incorrigible standpoint, or beginning or principle or ground, relative to which all meaning and knowing may be subsequently derived and legitimated. The incorrigible foundation will present itself to philosophy with a self-evidence and immediate transparency, and hence will be the court of first and final appeal in the adjudication of rational disputes.

Modern philosophy since Descartes is often presented as implementing such a foundationalist project, understood as the epistemological validation of claims to rational knowing. And there is little doubt that major strands of modern philosophy have sought the requisite foundation in the *cogito*, in human subjectivity itself, or the transcendental ego or its derivatives or surrogates. Hegel has been located in this tradition, and many aspects of his thought are continuous with its project. While he modifies the Cartesian foundationalism of the *cogito*, absolute spirit seems to serve a similar role, albeit complexly qualified. Absolute spirit reveals the first and final principle, the Idea relative to which everything is derived, relative to which everything is developmentally and teleologically oriented, relative to which all claims to know being are to be authenticated.

Today this aspect of Hegel's thought is understressed and a more historicist interpretation found more congenial. By contrast to foundationalism, historicism tends to deny any ultimate principles of intelligibility that remain constant throughout time's flux. It denies any claim to absolute knowing, precisely because every such claim is dependent on a host of historical relativities and contingencies. If we take these seriously, and the implied finitude of understanding, any claim to absolute foundations must be given up. Rather than a foundationalist view, we find a hermeneutical view which runs: Hegel was one of the first to underscore the intertwining of history and knowing, including philosophical knowing; philosophy is its own time comprehended in thought, he says, and thereby excludes any leap to an extra-temporal perspective; and though he spoke the idiom of classical metaphysics, in that very speaking, the metaphysician's proclivity to see things *sub specie aeternitatis*, in effect, is being dismantled and undermined; there are no trans-temporal foundations; the "foundations" are epoch-relative constructions of *Geist* as it historically unfolds.[1]

I will argue that these alternatives are not adequate to untangle the issues at stake, nor Hegel's views. A defense of speculative mind, which is historically self-conscious, need not be intended in any normal historicist sense. Nor need we appeal to a static, substance-like foundation, dualistically the opposite of becoming and history.

The issue is not a static eternity opposed to time, nor an Archimedean point outside history, but a hermeneutical mindfulness of the emergence of ultimacy within and through time, an emergence that is not a reduction to time *simpliciter*. Hegel himself develops a *dialectical middle* between an ahistorical foundationalism and an historicist anti-foundationalism. He suggests a hermeneutics of time wherein what we comprehend is not just time. His famous statement—philosophy is its own time comprehended in thought—is endlessly reiterated by those wishing to bolster the historicist conception. But we must ask with even more persistence: What does philosophy in time comprehend in time? Is it just time? Or is it the ground of temporal becoming that itself cannot be called a product of temporal becoming? Time's own other might be comprehended through time itself.

Since my interest is not simply with an exegesis of Hegel but with the matter itself, the major questions we must ask include: What would time's other be? Would it be what the ancients called eternity? Is this why Hegel offers a doctrine of absolute spirit and not just a hermeneutic of historicist rationality? Is there such a thing as a dialectical middle between time and eternity? What would this be? What follows from this middle for philosophical reason? Are there ambiguities about Hegel's dialectical middle that prepare the ground for a more thoroughgoing historicism, perhaps against Hegel's own intentions, or rather in line with one set of intentions but at odds with another set? Do we find a double set of intentions in Hegel, distributed between a logicist and a hermeneutical understanding of reason? Does this doubleness of intention show up in the task set for philosophy itself? And do the ambiguities of the dialectical middle undercut the ostensible purpose to mediate between ahistorical foundationalism and hermeneutical historicism, with the result that eternity is reduced to time in the final dialectical reckoning? Is time's other then collapsed into time? What then, with this collapse, would the properly speculative dimension of philosophy be?

The many sides of the matter demand that I take a kind of serpentine route. The middle asks for metaphysical meditation; with these questions it must be crossed and crisscrossed. With the serpentine Hegel as my interlocutor (but also others like Plato, Marx, Nietzsche, Heidegger), my reflections below will mix the expository, the interpretative, the critical and the speculative. First, I will speak of the fate of speculation after Hegel in the light of history's perceived relevance for philosophy. Marx will here be important. Second, I will focus on some important general characteristics of historicism. Third, I will situate Hegel's speculative response, in contrast to the widespread instrumentalization of reason we find in modernity, both before and after Hegel. Fourth, I will develop some implications, including some pertaining to Heidegger's attitude to the history of philosophy. Fifth, I will remark on the issue of philosophical contemporaneity in relation to what I call speculative timeliness. Sixth, I will turn to the above questions about Hegel's dialectical middle between eternity and time, between speculative logicism and hermeneutical historicism. In some final reflections I will argue that, regardless of Hegel's intent, or rather because of ambiguities in the plurality of his intentions, the dialectical middle is to be criticized for collapsing time's other into time. This collapse calls for a rearticulation of time's other in such a manner that its otherness as other is not dialectically reduced. This would be to reaffirm the need for speculative mind, but in a sense not exclusively determined by Hegelian dialectic.

All this will become more intelligible as we proceed but it is consonant with the position I develop throughout; namely, that Hegel does stand in a complexly articulated middle where his intention is not any univocal reduction of otherness to sameness; standing in that middle, nevertheless, he does claim to mediate all otherness, which becomes a moment of the dialectically self-mediating whole. This, I hold, does result in subordinating otherness to dialectical self-mediation. I, too, want to stand in the middle but there the crucial question is: Can the middle be articulated entirely in terms of dialectical self-mediation? I grant that dialectical self-mediation is indispensable to the articulation of the middle, but if it makes claims to *mediate totally* that middle, it closes thought off from forms of otherness which, if they are to be mediated, are to be mediated in terms other than dialectical self-mediation.

We must dwell in the middle dialectically, but this dialectic can never be closed. For we must also dwell in the middle in a different non-dialectical way, the metaxological way. This way articulates a logos of the *metaxu*, the middle, but in such a manner that it points to an *inter*mediation with otherness that cannot be reduced to dialectical self-mediation. Hegel, I grant, does inhabit the complex middle. To the extent that the claims of dialectical self-mediation are total, he is reductive of otherness. To the extent that he is open to otherness in the middle, Hegel's own thought, often against the grain of its explicit intentions, is the carrier of traces of otherness that are not and cannot be dialectically domesticated. Hegel is often both these sides. And even though he is predominantly the first, his dialectical dwelling with the middle opens up *for us*, unavoidably, the possibility of the second intermediation, the metaxological way.

Speculation after Hegel:
Modern and Postmodern Historicism

The issue of historicism has haunted Hegelian thought and
thought after Hegel. Moreover, it is very wrong to confine the issue
to nineteenth-century philosophy. I find it helpful to distinguish a post-
Hegelian and a post-Nietzschean historicism. The first is a logically
optimistic historicism, the second a hermeneutically suspicious
historicism. The first is logically optimistic: history reveals the
progressive unfolding of reason towards its *telos* in time. The second
is hermeneutically suspicious: in history we see the consolidation of
reason, as the repression of alogical energies of being which in
themselves have no inherent or rational *telos*. The first is dialectically
constructive or reconstructive, the second is deconstructive in an anti-
dialectical manner. For instance, Marxist historicism is a mix of
suspicion and optimism: it reveals itself as *hermeneutically suspicious*
in its revolutionary critique of capitalist society; but it is *logically
optimistic* in relation to the dialectical necessity of historical progress
and the coming communist utopia. By contrast, Heideggerian
historicism and post-Heideggerian deconstruction dominantly show
suspicious historicism in their attack, not only on Platonic eternity,
but also on any logically optimistic historicism: if there is here any
logic to history, it is the tale of the superimposition of logic on the
alogical powers of history by ontotheological metaphysicians. I will
have more to say about Marx, Nietzsche, and Heidegger below.

Hegel's thought, precisely because of his dialectical middle, has
been subject to vagaries of historical interpretation. Considering his
fortunes since his death, philosophers periodically have seen fit to
announce what they claim (in Croce's now hackneyed words) is dead
and what is still living in Hegel. As a dialectical middle offers a
mediated unity of opposites, from this middle Hegel's successors have
often picked and chosen what they deem suitable to their own
purposes. What is dead for one commentator miraculously comes alive
for another, and vice versa. Since his individual death, Hegel has had
many subsequent deaths, and also many resurrections. The strife
between right and left Hegelians was only the first battle over what
was vital legacy and what superseded refuse in the remains of the
Hegelian middle. Hegel returned to life in Anglo-American thought
in the latter half of the nineteenth century, only to suffer an inevitable
crucifixion, by philosophers suspicious of speculative metaphysics, like
Moore and Russell. Hegel has always been a presence in contemporary
European thought, recently as representative of everything that has
to be "overcome." The father Hegel has to be repeatedly killed by

his anti-Hegelian sons. But he must also be kept alive or brought to life again. If Hegel lacked this posthumous life, he could not be the antagonistic other to be repeatedly opposed. Hegel has to be repeatedly resurrected to be repeatedly crucified.

The crime of philosophical parricide is not common in academic studies of Hegel. We find family squabbles or logical bitching or textual *apologia*—a tame contrast to the ideological wars that in the past have swirled around Hegel's name. Instead of the civil wars, even world wars of ideological struggle, the "Hegel revival" means the civilized scholarly war of textual contestation. Many still revile Hegel and the type of philosophy he epitomizes, but the unavoidable fact is that he is still a living presence in contemporary philosophy. Even if the sophistication of our abuse only reaches the level of the jeer, this is only to confirm his tenacity as an enemy who resists being dispatched. Moreover, we cannot jettison Hegel because the fate of philosophy is also bound up with political history since Hegel. Without Marx's influence, Hegel's shadow would not be cast so long. While that influence is now in a drastic decline, still Hegel's ghost is not laid. Nor will the downfall of Marx necessarily inter Hegel. It may perhaps resurrect his ghost one more time, the ghost of an other Hegel.

The issues of "postmodernity" take shape here. Postmodernity is bound up with the notion that we are in a period of post-history. This, in turn, is connected to the Hegelian idea of the end of history. The thesis of the end of history implies that the modern age articulates all the essential possibilities of spirit in its dialectical realization of freedom; in articulating them temporally, modernity has exhausted the repertoire of possibilities. What remains disputed is the full actualization of the possibility, the worldly embodiment of the spirit of freedom.

In the past, the Left-Hegelian, especially the Marxist, claimed to be Hegel's rightful heir. The worldly embodiment of freedom in history is to be concretized in the Communist state. This state is the end of history—the society of social freedom beyond the dialectical war of master and slave, exploiter and exploited. The undermining of the credibility of totalitarian communism now has offered the opportunity to Western conservatives to appropriate the Hegelian theme of the end of history. Liberal democracy is extolled as the end of history. Hegel in his grave would turn uneasily at the apotheosis of the instrumentalized spirit, contained in the elevation of consumerist culture into the absolute. This end of history would be the end of philosophy in the dissolution of speculative mind into the means/end system of instrumental consumerism.

Marx's relevance to the issue of speculation and history is almost exemplary in this sense. His thought strips the dialectic of all speculative dimensions; speculation is reduced to history, now considered as the temporal self-production of the human. Hegel's successors, and Marx very explicitly, do him the honor of first discovering the historical character of the human being's self-creation, albeit, it is quickly added, in a manner "mystified" by his religious concerns. Many thinkers, not necessarily Marxists, share such a view which broadly runs: Though indeed Hegel spoke of absolute spirit, and with a mystical bias emphasized the intimacy, indeed identity of man and God, he nevertheless places strong stress on becoming, process, development. All such ideas bind us to the historical. The intimacy between the human being and God is historically revealed in the Christian religion, where Hegel sees the dialectical identity between the human and divine. Hegel correctly identified the human and divine, but wrongly hypostatized spirit into some power transcending man. The human is identical with the divine because the divine is identical with the human, namely, an alienated projection of human power, which now must be restored to its true human source and hence to its non-alienated form.

This view asserts indeed a dialectical middle between the human being and *Geist*, but only because spirit is the human spirit, not some other power. In fact, *Geist* is nothing other than, nothing but, human activity developing itself and coming to determinate articulation through the dynamism of the historical process. Though Hegel implies a *Weltgeist* transcendent to the human spirit, by articulating the dialectical middle between the human and the divine, he really shows that there is no *Weltgeist* other than the human. Rather humanity is just the *Weltgeist* of the historical world in that human power brings history into being and moves it as a meaningful world. History is the production of human and not divine power. The progressive development of humanity towards emancipation from all alien powers becomes synonymous with historical progress.

It is generally admitted that Hegel took history seriously, and in terms close to the above characterization. I think, however, that the difficult questions only now begin. What does it mean for philosophy to take history seriously? Hegel's answer makes no sense without philosophy as a venture of speculative mind. Relative to this venture, the seriousness of time is to be thought, but this seriousness is manifest from a standpoint not itself identical with time as normally comprehended. It is not too wrong to say that history for Hegel is ultimately devoid of seriousness if divorced from the speculative. History is not just farce, though it has its comic deflations and tragic resonances. To take history seriously is to determine the intelligibility it discloses. But the ultimate principles of temporal intelligibility are not exhaustively characterized as but the *products* of temporal genesis. Temporal genesis is the production of eternity, and is intelligible as the disclosure of this.

Much more needs to be said on this, and will be said. For now we recall that Hegel wanted to avoid those extremes that subsequently defined the left and right Hegelians. The left Hegelians reduce eternity to history. To reject this reduction is not, contrariwise, to advocate the negation of history, its dissolution into eternity, a view sometimes imputed to the right Hegelians. Hegel is neither right nor left. These extremes play one side of Hegel's complexity against another. The real issue is neither the reduction of eternity to time, nor the annihilation of the historical in the trans-historical. It is to comprehend what it is that ultimately grounds the conjunction or intermediation of the two. This is the problem of the middle.

While Hegel's intent was to articulate this middle, does his working out of this intent lend itself to the extremes just noted? I think that it does, and mainly because of ambiguities generated by the dialectical middle in relation to time's other. I return to this question below: Namely, even if history is intelligible as the production of eternity, does history so exhaustively determine the dialectical unfolding of eternity that any other, transcendent to history, becomes completely mediated by history, and hence immanent to history? Hegel, I believe, answers in the affirmative. But we are not yet in a position fully to understand this view which, in claiming to retain the speculative dimension, sets him at a significant distance from the simplistic reduction of Marx.

"The immediate *task of philosophy,*" Marx says ". . . is in the service of history. . ."[2] This service makes him rethink the inner essence of Hegelian dialectic but by turning it to economic, social, and political history and hence shearing it of all its speculative dimensions. So Marx accuses Hegel of reducing the history of alienation to a history of alienated thought: history becomes the production of abstract thought, which Marx identifies with logical and speculative thinking. For Hegel true mind is logical, speculative mind; hence the human character of production, its historical character, is reduced to the production of abstract mind.[3] While Hegel's "outstanding achievement" is the "dialectic of negativity," which allows us to understand the "self-creation of man as a process," nevertheless Hegel's speculative philosophy is a *masked* vision, which in its speculative hiding ends up as a "mystifying criticism."[4]

Like many critics, Marx judges the speculative philosopher to be an alienated thinker, with all the idealistic embarrassments Hegel had with the transition from Logic to Nature. It is as if the eternalist mind cannot reconnect with history: the logician, as the voyeur of time, cannot be incarnated in its concrete body. I am reminded of Aristophanes suspending Socrates in a basket above the stage of drama: the speculative philosopher dangles in the empty air of alienated thought. Aristophanic comedy debunks the emptiness of abstraction in terms of the alogical laughter of the body. Historical materialism shares a not dissimilar debunking attitude to speculative mind. Aristophanes would also have mocked at the risible pretension of historical materialism to have the master key of history.

There is here an interesting congruence between the Christian and atheistic critics. Kierkegaard's critique of Hegel is not at all unlike Marx's; both claim he is an abstract, alienated thinker. Kierkegaard sees Hegel as a pure eternalist, eternalist in the sense in which logical truth is necessarily true, *sub specie aeternitatis*. This is the abstract logical eternity of the philosopher, the philosopher's God that can be thought in abstraction but to whom one cannot pray. Kierkegaard, not without ambiguity, invokes his own notion of eternity, dependent on Christian revelation. Kierkegaard, like Marx, wants to refuse to the philosopher the alienated luxury of abstract thought and to reveal his logical eternity as a sterile ideality. Both make Hegel a logical eternalist, though their respective senses of the *concreteness* of history are radically different.

Marx wanted to re-ground knowledge and action upon a nontraditional basis. Hegel completed and exhausted the contemplative task of thought. It remained to displace philosophy from contemplation to action, from speculative thought to historical praxis, and so to institute knowledge as an instrument of revolution. The metaphysics of eternity must be replaced by the revolutionary reason of concrete history. Philosophy must cease to wonder and its thought be reversed into a weapon. A different reversal can here occur. Marx may do Hegel an unwitting favor: He becomes less a decisive break with Hegel as a pointer back to him, and so indirectly to the entire tradition of speculative philosophy Marx claimed to surpass. Instead of an indirect confirmation of Marx via Hegel, we discover the revolutionary Marx as a truncation of the speculative Hegel. I say "truncation" with all its connotation of a violent cutting. At a time when we have done with worshipping Marx, we must ask if his excision of speculative philosophy has produced a diminished body of thought that in the long run, if untreated, will die from the wound it believed it had inflicted on the speculative other. This wound on thought seems really self-inflicted.

Marx's truncation reduces speculation to purely historicist thought by collapsing Hegel's absolute spirit into objective spirit: the historical realms of morality, economics, civil society, politics. "Hegel has merely discovered an *abstract, logical* and *speculative* expression of the historical process, which is not yet the *real* history of man as a given subject but only the history of an *act of creation,* of the *genesis of man.*"[5] The speculative absolute is really only an aftereffect of concrete history, mistakenly identified by the idealistic philosopher as its ground and origin. German philosophy is merely the *ideal prolongation* of German history.[6] So we must invert the origin and the aftereffect. ". . .We Germans have lived our post-history in thought, in philosophy. . ." In the collapse of absolute into objective spirit, the denigration of speculation is its supersession by historical praxis. "Real" history is tied up with the realization and abolition of philosophy; speculative philosophy is resolved only by means of practical activity. . .[7] .

When Hegel keeps open the difference of objective and absolute spirit, he wants to preserve speculative mind as not entirely reducible to the historicity of objective spirit. Absolute spirit articulates the speculative sense that reason is at work in forms of being, nature, and subjectivity included, that seem the work of what is outside reason. The three forms of its activity are art, religion, and philosophy. Certainly these are made possible by processes of historical unfolding, development, and support. But for Hegel they give articulation to *Geist* as a dynamic power not reducible to any one time, since it cuts across time as the ultimate generating basis of time's own intelligibility. Art, religion, and philosophy are those forms of activity that most deeply express the human condition and its mediated relation to the ultimate generating source of time itself. They are historical products in one sense, yet they mediate what for Hegel cannot be reduced to a mere product of historical production, namely, *Geist* itself as the actively *producing* power of history. History ultimately gains its intelligibility only in relation to absolute spirit as the trans-temporal dynamism of being, articulated in determinate form in time. Art, religion, and philosophy are each different articulations of the middle, each implicated in different ways with the speculative dimension of being. In the middle of history, each of these as a historical production of *Geist* serves to remind us that *Geist* itself is not just a historical production.

Relative to historicism this implies: Intelligibility is not exhausted by humanity's historical constitution, but rather this constitution is made possible by more primordial principles of intelligibility. If so, philosophy not only needs to be properly cognizant of history, and of its own history, but relative to the middle, it must confront a dialectic between an excess of history and an absence of history. The philosophical middle must avoid two extremes: on the one hand, an approach so ahistorical that it lacks concrete insertion in the historical world wherein we become and find ourselves; on the other hand, an approach so historicist that we fail to find significant constancy of intelligibility in being, as the mind staggers directionless from relativity to relativity. The speculative middle, whether dialectically or metaxologically conceived, seeks an equilibrium between the demands of history and what Dostoevski called those "accursed eternal questions."

Marxist history violently represses these accursed questions. They are repressed as metaphysical distractions from an historical *praxis* that would absolutize itself. These accursed questions make us skeptical of any absolutization of the historical. They condemn us to irremediable exile from the historical complacencies of every temporal home. They keep us off balance with the radically unsettling thought of time's other. Post-Hegelian history itself shakes asunder all historical complacencies. These accursed questions not only shake the foundations of historical complacencies, but also make it incumbent on us to ask if there are any such foundations in history at all.

In modernity's amnesia of time's other and its hollowing out of all trans-temporal grounds to time, the Marxist anti-speculative truncation reduces God to man as the maker of history. But after Marx we find the further reduction: instead of being the maker of history, the human being becomes the victim of history. The repudiation of the human absolute quickly follows that of the divine absolute. God is said to die with the unfolding of the dialectic of post-Hegelian history, but so also does man, so say Nietzsche and Foucault. And now in the iron age of post-history, postmodernism still twitches with all the anxieties of time to which modernity previously had been prone. Its response seems to accentuate these twitches of time, accentuate them as if this were to celebrate the Nietzschean innocence of becoming. After Hegel, and more so after Marx and his progeny, we cannot be innocent, least of all about time, and the slaughterbench that modern history has produced. These twitches are, so to say, the afterlife of modernity's corpses—the ghost of its dead spirit, wandering in the contemporary *Zeitgeist* without grave or rest in a hallowed ground.

The question then is: Does postmodernity, as post-history, merely prolong the proper disenchantment of later modernity with history? Is the postmodern celebration of the innocence of becoming just a sly Nietzschean dissimulation of its spiritless weariness with history?

Are its calls for otherness the most effective way of perpetuating the *same* modernity, without a philosophical bad conscience vis-à-vis modernity's anxieties about time? Or does the true need of time's other ask us to radically rethink the speculative? Must we become speculative philosophers again, perhaps of a different kind? Does Hegel offer us a genuine option between the haunted afterlife of postmodernity and the living spirit of speculative mind? Or does his own version of speculative mind, and his rendition of the dialectical middle between time and time's other—do these sign for modernity the remote death warrant of deathless eternity?

Radical and Moderate Historicism

The serpent turns. Before we can address such questions, we need a fuller understanding of historicism itself. Historical consciousness is generally taken to be a relatively recent innovation in Western culture. Essential to this innovation is the belief that human affairs must be understood on a developmental model. It is sometimes implied that the Greeks had no such concept of history. But Plato and Aristotle were by no means unfamiliar with the dynamic nature of things, were indeed acutely aware of genesis. Yet their interpretation of change circled around the possibility of an ideal stability. The genesis of a thing manifests its nature in so far as the thing is in process to be itself. The ideal or *eidos* is that *telos* to which the genesis of a thing is directed, at which telic point the individual thing becomes identical, or approximates identity, with its essence. *Phusis*, nature is essentially purposive. In that sense, the nature of a thing is its purpose. Form and finality cannot be sundered.

History implies reference to human acts, *rēs gestae*, and not just to the dynamic nature of all things. For the Greeks human events were themselves natural, with the proviso that human nature has its own specificity and difference. The modern historical consciousness, by contrast, tends to be marked by a sense, not of the human being's difference *within* nature, but of its difference *from* nature. This view secularizes the religious ascription to the human being of sovereignty over a created nature, itself set off from God. From this sense of difference, scientifically secularized by Cartesian dualism, springs the disjunction between nature and history, or in the cognitive sphere between the *Naturwissenschaften* and the *Geisteswissenschaften*.

The rise of historicism in the nineteenth century was motivated, in part, by reaction to the positivistic reduction of the specifically human to the rest of nature, nature conceived here not in Greek terms but in terms of mechanistic science. One can understand, indeed subscribe to this affirmation of the difference of the human over against the mechanistic. The result, however, has sometimes been a *new dualism* of the human being and nature. Far from resolving the problem, this dualism initiates a new one. How far do we go in the assertion of the difference of the human being? If we push this assertion in a certain direction the outcome might be that splintering of "the two cultures," the scientific and humanistic. Pushed further, the assertion of difference can splinter the integrity of the human into a disseminated diversity of fragments. Can we situate deconstructive *différance* here, as a masked rejoinder to a disguised dualism?

The dualism of nature and history helps us highlight two related responses. One response reduces the historical to the natural, such that human action is understood in terms not essentially different from what makes any natural process intelligible. This is a *naturalistic reduction*. The other response harbors the *historicist reduction*. Then we claim a freedom for the historical, a freedom that might take different forms. For instance, we might hold that the developmental dimension of the human being is decisive for all its knowing. Even natural science is itself the product of a development of reason, historically determined. Then we are tempted to invert the positivisitic reduction of the historical to the natural, and claim comprehensiveness for the historical. We cannot uphold the independence of nature to the human being, since we cannot abstract from the human being. In history, it is said, we come to knowledge of human events. In nature, it also seems, we come to know *ourselves* in the end, and not some cosmos abiding in inviolate otherness or objectivity.

Consider the point this way. One of the chief characteristics of the human being is its active nature. We are not passive before an otherwise ready-made world. We are agents. Or as Nietzsche says: Man is the unfinished animal. Through this our agency we constitute a human world; without it, what is before us sinks into dull unintelligibility. We do not possess a ready-made identity, but come to be a self in an open process of making ourself. History, it is said, is just this process of humanity's self-making. History is the articulation of the unfinished animal, or if you like, a sequence of drafts by the human being whereby it essays to portray the power of its activity and so define itself. History is the humanization of the unfinished animal.

As I understand it, the issue is not the defense or denial of our active nature, but rather the interpretation of its significance. Historicism is one such interpretation. For our purposes we might distinguish a moderate and a more radical historicism.[8] The moderate sense claims that even if nature is independent of history, nevertheless, our comprehension of it is conditioned by historical circumstances. A distinction between nature and history is admitted. Though the emphasis falls on the historical, nature subsists as a limitation, despite the fact that everything we say about it is irremediably conditioned by history. This limitation may be differently interpreted, yet any recognition of it prevents history from becoming the *inclusive* context of all meaning. Something may still lie beyond history, though for our access to it, history must always function as gateway. In granting man's active power, we must acknowledge boundaries that restrain its absolute self-assertion. History is circumscribed by an otherness. Human freedom, though real, is not absolute; it is constrained by necessities, albeit opaque and difficult to determine.

The second, more radical historicism interprets our active power as a drive to the extreme of absolute autonomy. Wherever possible, this stronger historicism will eradicate every restraining heteronomy. As with any historicism, this second view claims that the human being produces itself, coming to recognize itself in its productions. But carrying this to the extreme, it is asserted that *all* we recognize, *all* we can recognize, is the human itself. A total claim is made here. Anything other than the human is not to be acknowledged as finally other. Indeed if anything intimates its otherness, nature for instance, this is not taken as refutation. Any such intimation of resistant otherness becomes rather a spur pricking the strong self to place *itself* in that space of otherness. Here we have a *program* for the historicization, humanizing of such otherness, such that once again man can be said to recognize nothing but himself, even if sometimes, as here, this self-recognition is mediate and indirect.

This radical historicism obliterates the difference between the human and nonhuman in the very historical process of mediating that difference. Its eradication of this difference is effected by means of the self-assertion of the absolute difference of the human being. Its mediation reduces the difference, not by reducing history to nature, but by subsuming nature into history. Nature is absorbed into history as itself simply one more of humanity's historically conditioned perspectives. The truth of nature, then, is not nature's truth but man's truth, and so itself a historical construction. The upshot is that history closes in upon itself and becomes the *only horizon* of significance and intelligibility.

The historicist Hegelianism I noted at the outset, though it might employ categories that serve to qualify or disguise its implications, seems to me to be underpinned by presuppositions such as I have just outlined. The anthropological counterpart to this historicism is an anthropocentric humanism wherein man is the beginning, middle and end, wherein his active power is dedicated to the task of humanizing whatever is. *The human being claims to be the absolute middle.* Since through the medium of historical self-production, humanity produces *itself*, it claims to be the beginning of history. Since it produces itself *for itself*, it claims to be the end of history. Thus, this anthropocentrism tries to produce the closure of historicism, closure in these three senses: closure of the historical in itself as putatively a completely self-mediating realm of meaning and being; closure of the historical to any putatively radical otherness, whether of nature as a limiting otherness, or eternity as an irreducible other to time; closure as completion of the historical in the project of the human being to be a completely self-mediating power.

With respect to the last closure, any non-historical limit becomes a barrier that the human being, in principle, can surmount. Similarly any constraint on human freedom is said to be only provisional. Freedom rather defines its own limits, indeed defines itself in the surmounting of limits, which on reflection turn out to be merely self-imposed. The human being is not limited by a human nature which intrinsically defines it, one which, though capable of different manifestations in different times, still is constant as a principle of continuity across different times. On the contrary, the human being has no abiding nature; its nature is itself a historical product, and as such infinitely malleable, as Nietzsche and Sartre assert. The human being is not defined by an intrinsic humanness that sustains continuity. Rather its plastic power is the possibility of radical discontinuity.

So it is not surprising that this radical historicism coexists with a will to *revolution*, that is, the faith in man's capacity to institute radical discontinuity. Marx's view of history clearly points in this direction. The name "historical materialism" indicates just that sublation of nature into history, mentioned above. As Marx puts it, except maybe for a few coral reefs, nowhere does nature exist in a purity untouched by human hands. What we find in nature is historical, the intervention of the human. We need only recall Marx's infatuation with *industry*. Industry, he proclaims, is the open book of human powers. Industry is that material appropriation of human power, which allows us to appropriate the power of material nature. The record of history is the tale of industry through which human beings become free of natural, and indeed supernatural necessities. History is the history not of God's grace but of man's work. For Marx the dialectical middle of history will be the site of struggle for the completely autonomous self-mediation of human society. There will be no absolute other.

Historicism and the
Instrumentalization of Speculative Mind

Where does Hegel stand? Clearly Hegel is deeply attentive to the active, historical nature of the human being. One way he puts this is: The human being cannot be fully understood as substance; it must be grasped as subject, that is, as self-conscious, self-determining being. But despite this stress on humanity as historically self-determining, Hegel cannot be unequivocally assimilated to historicism in either of the two senses delineated. Let us take the first moderate sense.

Hegel distinguishes nature and history, and admits that our knowledge of nature presupposes the development of certain historical conditions. Similarly, history itself cannot be totally abstracted from natural necessities. Yet the human knower can have a true knowledge of nature. One can come to know nature as nature, and not just as a categorial grid, subjectively constructed, that we impose on an otherwise unintelligible nature. Human reason is articulated through historical development; but in its coming to articulation, reason can free the human knower from the limitations of self-enclosed subjectivity, and from the constraining particularities of historical conditioning. Reason opens out to what is, regardless of whether it is nature or history. True knowledge of nature is true of nature; it is not just a reflection of the subjective knower taken as totally opposite to nature. On this point a careful reading of Hegel will show that his idealism is an uncompromising realism.

There is no absolute barrier separating the knower from nature's intelligibility. But if there is no such barrier, do history and nature collapse into each other, forcing us to claim Hegel as a historicist in the second sense? In this more radical sense, nature is subsumed into history, any radical distinction between them disappears, and history becomes the only and ultimate horizon of meaning. I do not think Hegel intends the disappearance of this distinction. It might seem so, in that Hegel certainly holds that reason can appropriate the truth of nature. But to appropriate the truth of nature can mean to understand nature as it is. This need not imply any obliteration of the distinction between nature and history.

There is, however, a more fundamental reason why we cannot assert univocally that history is the one and ultimate horizon of intelligibility. There is a third term besides nature and history, necessary to the determination of the intelligibility of both. As Hegel puts it in his philosophy of nature: "God reveals himself in two different ways: as Nature and as Spirit. Both manifestations are temples of God which He fills, and in which He is present."[9] The reference to God may be here taken as a representation that points us to the ultimate ground of intelligibility. Following traditional usage, we can call this third term (which is really the first), eternity. Without this third first, we could not ultimately ground the openness of reason (that is, its orientation to truth), nor prevent the collapse of nature into history, nor put any limit to the assertion of the absoluteness of the historical, taken alone.

The idea of eternity is not a univocal concept. It allows a plurality of possible interpretations, including the static eternity of Parmenidean being with its long influence on Platonism and Christian theology, the logicist eternity of necessary, trans-temporal truth, the agapeic eternity of some theistic views, the eternal recurrence of Nietzsche. One must also include what I call an "erotic absolute": an eternity in process of striving to become itself, in process of determining itself fully in the productions of time which are its own self-production. I would include Schelling, Whitehead and process philosophy, as well as Hegel himself, as proponents of such an erotic absolute. This matter will be addressed further below, particularly the difference between an erotic and agapeic absolute, since this reflects a crucial difference between the interpretation of being in terms of dialectical self-mediation and metaxological intermediation.[10] But we must dwell further on speculative reason and historicism.

The question we recall is: Are the grounds of temporal intelligibility exclusively the products of temporal genesis; if not, is there a sense of speculative mind that, while capable of offering a philosophical hermeneutics of the historical, is not itself simply historicist? The following, additional considerations are significant for the modern, historicist consciousness. They cast light on what I see as a widespread but essentially wrong *instrumentalization* of speculative mind.

Reason for the historicist is not a given, just there, outside of any development in time. Reason is something historically constituted. As a construct, it must be determined by more primordial principles that generate it. But if so, reason must become dispossessed of any sovereignty, even in fields where its exercise seems paramount, for instance, in the mathematical sciences. Consider here how sometimes the mathematical sciences are described as theoretical *constructions or created systems.* A crucial implication of this description, one not always drawn, is the necessity of some constructing, creating power that itself cannot be absolutely identical with reason in use *within* the constructed system. Should he admit such a principle of construction, the mathematically bent philosopher turns out to be peculiarly akin to thinkers who appear to be his antithesis, thinkers like Nietzsche, for example.

For Nietzsche too reason is not sovereign; it is derivative; it is a creation, an expression, an instrument of the will to power. To illustrate this kinship of the mathematician-philosopher and the thinker of the will to power, we need only mention Descartes. Descartes was one of the first moderns who explicitly coupled knowing and power, despising as useless ancient speculative metaphysics, desiring a new science which would make man, in his famous phrase, "the master and possessor of nature." On the matter of reason and power, the mathematical technician, Descartes, is not entirely different to Nietzsche, the poetic rhapsode.

If there is a more ultimate source of reason that itself cannot be said to be rational, then the use of reason within a historically constructed system must become essentially instrumental. Action becomes more fundamental than contemplation, will comes to dominate reason, praxis provides the justifying end of theory. On this view, any speculative claim to reason's sovereignty must be an inversion of the true state of affairs. The hermeneutics of suspicion will suspect such claims as merely more idealistic, but masked instrumentalizations of a source that is not itself rational. Thus, Marx will condemn Hegelian reason as idealizing a state of affairs that in its true reality is irrational: the Hegelian rationalization of the real is the idealistic mask of its real irrationality. Thinkers like Nietzsche will indict reason as a comforting illusion that protects us from the Dionysian darkness at the basis of all being, what in relation to Schopenhauer's will I termed the dark origin.[11] This, too, is said to be beyond the principle of sufficient reason; thought through to the proper conclusion, it must topple reason from its throne.

When we put the question to this historicist intrumentalization of reason, What distinguishes good reason from bad? very often the answer given is *success*. Good reason works. Reason tends to be instrumentalized not only in its origin and operation, but also in its end. As a means to an end, reason is directed to goals that are not themselves the outcome of reason but the product of some extra-rational source of valuation. There is nothing intrinsically valuable about reason as an instrument. When reason is thus instrumentalized, it becomes the handmaid of the powers that be, if you happen to be a conservative, and of the powers that will be, if you happen to be a revolutionary. Especially in the latter case, philosophy ceases to be *theōria*; the tool of history it now becomes is, as we saw before with Marx, a weapon. Not metaphysical astonishment, Plato's wonder, but ideological war in history's service becomes the work of the philosopher.

This instrumentalization of reason is pervasive in modernity. Its pervasiveness in presupposition and praxis makes us take the matter as self-evident. But such self-evidence is not at all evident. Suppose reason is to be defined as nothing but a product of historical process; can we then, strictly speaking, give any reason for the historical process itself? This question returns us to the issue of the seriousness of time. In trying to answer it in present terms, we confront peculiar consequences. Since reason is a product of history, this other reason of history (in the sense of ground) cannot itself be reasonable. If reason is only a product, it would seem that the *producing* ground of the historical process cannot be anything but irrational. We must admit also, it seems, that this irrational ground is more ultimate than the rational, and that the ultimate basis of intelligibility is itself unintelligible.

But then reason becomes the product of the irrational. And since what the irrational produces, the irrational may also destroy (with or without reason!), reason cannot be said to possess any intrinsic worth. This entails that reason may be brushed aside without reason. Reason becomes all but indistinguishable from unreason, as but another fortuitous formation of the irrational. Since all history seems to have a nonrational ground, and since reason seems to be but one of history's products, reason itself cannot have a rational ground. As grounded in the irrational, reason is not rationally grounded at all. Reason is another form of unreason, which some accept only because of taste or convention, while others do so just out of plain timidity to risk the disruptive power of a more uncompromising irrationalism. In a word, reason is only the *temporary sobriety* of unreason.

This issue centers on the question: What, if anything, is there absolute about reason, and what, if anything, does reason reveal as absolute? This question reveals the unavoidably speculative nature of the issue. Despite the bar by Kant, or Marx, or Nietzsche, the speculative springs up again. For the historicist there can be nothing absolute about reason, for the reasons just adumbrated. If reason is just a result of the historical process, by that fact, it is less absolute than this its generating source. The implication must be that the irrational, or let us say the arational, is absolute, if anything is. The difficulty, however, is that we are compelled to but cannot give a philosophically satisfactory rational justification of this view. We find ourselves with a peculiar "absolute" that cannot stand to reason. Perhaps we are then driven to "prove" this absolute by other means; for example, by revolutionary praxis, or by heralding the advent of the superman, or by invoking the all comprehensive success of global technology. Can we rest satisfied with this? I think not. All such appeals to success, praxis, the coming age or hero, technological domination of the earth, simply beg the question.

Take the answer already cited: good reason is distinguished from bad by success; good reason works. This, however, explains nothing, unless we can already distinguish between worthwhile and worthless work. If we cannot presuppose this power of distinguishing, that is, presuppose the very discriminating power of reason, this criterion of success is ultimately vacuous. It cannot allow us to distinguish between success and failure, and so in fact is no standard at all. Put differently, we cannot justify the instrumentalization of reason if we cannot presuppose already some justified reason for such an instrumentalization. It is not the instrumentalization that justifies reason, but reason that justifies the instrumentalization.

Here we must think seriously about the comprehensive intent of speculative thought. In saying this, I do not defend any "panlogist" pretensions of Hegelian reason. Regardless of "panlogism," reason need not be confined only to something conditionally generated. One might argue for a sense of reason as a generating energy of being (energy as *energeia*, at-work [*ergon*] as a *Verwirklichung*), a sense of original mind more primordial than a mere product of historical process. Hegel here does echo the great thinkers of the tradition of speculative metaphysics, like Plato and Aristotle for whom reason does possess some speculative freedom. It has its own unconditional power of activity, and especially in certain of its theoretical exercises, most notably philosophy itself, gains its greatest range of liberty. Instrumentalized science is not reason's fulfillment but metaphysics in the older nomenclature, speculative philosophy in Hegel's usage, reason's inquiry into the first and most ultimate principles of intelligibility.

Such a sense of speculative reason might rise above the historically contingent, or alternatively, delve hermeneutically into its deepest depths. Reason in its speculative enjoyment is not exhausted by its instrumentalized use. There is about such an enjoyment something other than will to power. Nor can a more normal sense of what "works" provide the ultimate standard. In itself reason reveals something absolute, which reveals the human being's metaphysical capacity for and kinship with what is absolute. Hegel, of course, will try to articulate this capacity and kinship in terms of the categorial intelligibility of a dialectical logic. Without metaphysics, history proves to be devoid of ultimate intelligibility. Nor should we be surprised at what has followed the repudiation of metaphysics after Hegel. Initially, history without metaphysics translated itself into history with ideology. In the end, history with ideology surrenders to history as a handmaiden pliable to power and might.

Of course, to speak of reason's *sovereignty* is clearly to invoke a political idea, with ineradicable connotations of authority and power. This is explicitly stated by Aristotle and reiterated by Aquinas.[12] It is not that the sovereignty of reason has nothing to do with power. Recall the wider sense of the "work" of reason implied above. Inevitably the question of sovereignty, including any claim made on behalf of reason, must be related to the legitimate use of power, the authority of power. But again the point is: the work of reason can command authority, not because of power, but because of its justified openness to truth. Instrumental reason imposes an unjustified narrowness on this openness. True: this "openness" makes us ask if "sovereignty" is the best word—too easily this degenerates into "dominance," "mastery," "tyranny." But the sovereign openness of reason, I think, is exactly other to such tyranny—it is justice. To speak of reason's sovereign openness as justice is to use language that already opens reason's self-understanding beyond univocity—the ideal of the dominating mind that reduces otherness to sameness. Instrumental reason can be dominating in just this bad sense, but speculative mind is not. It transcends instrumentalization. Ultimately power does not justify reason; reason justifies the use of power. Legitimate power cannot be itself justified without at some point invoking the authority of reason in a sense more comprehensive than instrumental reason.

Indeed the reason why instrumental reason itself can be criticized is because at work within its unjustified narrowing of the scope of philosophical mindfulness is a more comprehensive sense of reason that it tries to stifle—without success. Instrumental reason is parasitical on the power of a more comprehensive sense of reason to which ostensibly it denies legitimacy. When Hegel speaks of speculative reason I take him to be recalling to mind this more comprehensive sense of philosophical mindfulness.[13]

I endorse this needful reminder. This is not to say that Hegel's interpretation of the more comprehensive sense is not without its own difficulties. There is an interesting note in Nietzsche which reflects his debt to Schopenhauer in relation to the critique of Hegel: both excoriate what they see as Hegelian historicism for producing a *deification of success*. I will not deny an element of truth in this view, and will more fully return to equivocations in Hegel on this issue in a later discussion of dialectic and evil. I think it is true to say that for Hegel good reason works, but our notion of what truly works cannot be narrow. It must be grounded on a comprehensive sense of the community of being as a whole. Hence the reason that works has to be more speculatively generous than the more usual instrumentalized sense. There are workings of reason that transcend the work of instrumentalized reason. Hegel himself would confine the later work to the level of *Verstand*, while he would see the former work occurring at the level of *Vernunft*. The famous statement that called so much infamy upon his head "The actual is the rational, the rational is the actual," contains just that reference to the working (*Verwirklichung*) of reason (*Vernunft*), work beyond the instrumentalization of being and mind.

Here we can make a crucial point about historicism itself, deeply consonant with the point that the work of instrumental reason presupposes the being-at-work, the *energeia*, the *Verwirklichung* of a more comprehensive sense of mind. We can say that historicism itself has its own exigence for absoluteness, an exigence which its own incomplete self-understanding conceals, even from itself. The radical historicist will say: all knowledge is historical. How do we establish the truth of this assertion? It seems that its truth must be itself determined historically, that is, established in terms of its temporal genesis. But, then, we have the paradox of an assertion at once relative and unconditional. And it is unconditional: when we say "All knowledge is historical," we make a categorical statement that is putatively true trans-historically. We do not want to imply that *tomorrow* some knowledge will not be historical. Of course, we have no justification at all for foreclosing future knowledge on historical grounds alone.

At this point, we might admit that our assertion is not historical in the normal sense, but transcendental. It asserts that history is the ground of the possibility of all knowledge. Yet to justify this transcendental ground, we must resort to historical relativities themselves to remain in accord with our explicit avowals. Thus, at once, history seems to be an absolute presupposition and a conditioned product. What is the relation of unconditional presupposition and conditioned product? At best we might say that they mutually generate each other: history as presupposition generates history as product, which in turn generates history as presupposition and so on. History generates history, and to identify the historical, we must presume the historical. In fact, history in this transcendental historicism now seems to take on something of the character of a *deus ex machina*, a temporal rival of God as a *causa sui*. And as we saw, there have been those willing to speak of the self-creation of history in terms of the human being as absolute. Even Heideggerian philosophy will offer both a version of transcendental historicism and a tortured, because equivocal, effort to escape its implications.

But here always the very power of creation, the *energeia* of being as originative, is presupposed, and must be presupposed as already there regardless of historical development. What is this that is always already there, other than the dialectical circle of historical presupposition and product? Is history, or even nature, the right word for it? Is the irrational its proper name? Schopenhauer will call it Will, Nietzsche will to power, Hegel the Idea, I have called it the "absolute original." Thinkers will agree or disagree on the philosophical interpretation of what it is. But in their naming of it, in their efforts to interpret it, all show themselves as thinkers carried by a philosophical mindfulness more radical than instrumental reason. All are speculative thinkers, even though Nietzsche and Schopenhauer might shudder to be thus associated with Hegel. Historicism suffers from speculative amnesia with respect to this philosophical mindfulness. It is content to glide over this issue, because its admission must prevent history from closing in on itself in smooth self-justification. Is the supposed self-creation of history nothing but its unacknowledged, surrogate eternity? Does historicism here pay a wicked compliment to eternity?

In fact reason's exigence for absoluteness is inherent in the very articulation of historicism itself as a rational doctrine. For the doctrine that all knowledge is historical claims universal validity. It is not asserted as merely provisionally valid. Its assertion implies that it instances one truth not to be dissolved in historical relativities. It implies it is true now; it was true in the past; it will be true in the future. So to articulate the truth of historicism is already to surpass its explicit avowals. We must say that historicism makes an exception of itself; to be taken seriously, it must make an exception of itself. It applies its pronouncements to others claiming trans-historical validity and rejects their claims, but it evades the application of its pronouncements to itself. Should it cease to make an exception of itself, immediately we discern its inconsistency. To understand what it means to assert the historical character of all knowledge is to imply some sense of a more ultimate standpoint (whether explicitly articulated or not) in relation to all historical knowledge. But such an implied sense must transcend any particular instance of historical knowledge. It must be trans-historical. We must invoke what is other to history even to speak of history. The failure of historicism is a failure of self-knowledge. Historicism fails to account for itself.

This self-knowledge of reason is essential to philosophical mindfulness. Speculative mind radicalizes the inherent exigence of this self-knowledge in carrying thought to the extremities of origin, ground and possible completion. Nor must this philosophical self-knowing end in the closure of self-thinking thought: on the contrary, self-knowing may bring itself, or be brought to a limit where it knows that what reason asks of it is a radical surpassing of self, *a speculative openness to what is other to all self-thinking thought.* Nor is this enterprise devoid of its doubting, skeptical, negative side. On the contrary, the power of philosophical mind is just its ability to face squarely this negative side, even at its most extreme, and to try and stand its ground before it. This may mean the encounter with forms of otherness on which founder those claims of the philosophical mind to a self-sufficient, self-mediating cognition, to a completely secure science. At such limits the most reasonable thing reason may do is to debunk itself and its own claims to absolutely self-certain knowing. Strange as it may seem, this self-debunking may be an act of faith in reason, not the despair of reason.

What I have just said takes us to the edge of Hegelian speculation, if not over the edge. But it does not do away with speculative mind-fulness. I return to this. Does historicist reason have the philosophical courage to apply the self-debunking power of mind to *itself* rather than to an other? The cheapest debunking is of the other, the hardest debunking is of the self. What must follow when historicism does apply its doctrine to itself, that is, when it radically implements its rejection of any trans-historical validity, and turns this repudiation back on itself? The result must be the undermining, from *within*, of the historicist's confidence in the power of reason. *Historicist reason can give no ultimate reason for reason.* Radicalizing historicist reason means undermining ultimate confidence in reason. Historicism collapses into *nihilism*, the denial of any ultimate grounds of intelligibility. The power of reason dissolves into power—without reason.

This extreme result is revealing about the validity of making history absolute. Of course, one might consent to this nihilism, giving oneself over to irrational celebration of the absurd or to acquiescence in the merely factic. But this would be not to learn either from history or nihilism. One refuses the irrational consequences of making history the absolute horizon of intelligibility. One discountenances the task of thinking through that exigence for absoluteness inherent in philosophical mind. One eludes an unconditional requirement by the abortion of speculative mind. Nihilism then is the despair of reason that immolates on time's altars its unwanted offspring.

Heideggerian Historicism and Speculative Philosophy

The question is how we are to understand reason's nature, and its positive power even in its seemingly limitless capacity for debunking. Since I want to strategically stress certain key points, the following, including some pertinent remarks on Heidegger's historicism, must suffice.

If reason is a dynamic power, how are we to interpret this dynamism? As I implied, there is a philosophical mindfulness more fundamental than instrumental reason, one not confined to that calculative ratiocination that we utilize historically in the service of pragmatic desire. The dunamis of this philosophical mindfulness cannot be simply described in terms of the successive motions of temporal displacement. It articulates itself as a metaphysical self-consciousness of historical succession, and so itself is no longer merely successive. It returns upon itself, seeks to know itself in sequential unfolding. As such it is not restricted to what, for Hegel, is the "bad infinite" of endless succession.

Confronting this "bad infinite," philosophical mind faces the potential absurdity and nihilism of history. It knows itself as the impossibility to rationally rest content with this. It is driven to more. Reason's dialectical nature opens up with this its infinite restlessness. Reason is an infinite restlessness that is restless for the infinite. It is not linear in the successive sense but "circular," and not in a vicious way either. For Hegel, reason justifies itself, similar to the way that, for Spinoza, truth is the standard of itself and its opposite. It circles around itself in self-knowledge, discovering in its own dynamism both a standard of absoluteness and an orientation to the absolute. In Platonic terms, the dynamism of reason is an eros for eternity, an eros that articulates the transcendence of speculative mind towards the ultimate other.

I deliberately mingle Platonic and Hegelian stresses in a manner that would make Hegel uneasy. This Hegelian uneasiness will be made more clear as we continue. In no way do I want to say that the above "circularity" of reason entirely escapes its own dialectical ambiguities. In particular, there is always the danger that reason will completely *close in on itself*, making claims to be absolutely self-mediating, and in a manner that closes reason off from what is other to reason. Such a circularity of reason produces a questionable apotheosis of *thought thinking itself*, in relation to which all otherness is merely a subordinate moment in a dialectical unfolding. This claim to close the circle of thought's self-mediation provides a significant bone of contention about "panlogism" between Hegel and his successors. I do not think that Hegelian reason can be totally exonerated. Below I will look more closely (in the final three sections) at how the logic of a dialectical circularity, coupled with the primacy of self-mediation, leaves Hegel's position concerning history and speculation in a decidedly equivocal position. Hegelian circularity means that what is other to history, the trans-historical, becomes dialectically mediated by the historically immanent, and becomes so mediated that any otherness as an otherness is reduced. The transcendence of the trans-historical, dialectically mediated by history, is reduced to immanence.

Nevertheless, Hegel's non-historicist sense of reason is important for our understanding of philosophical tradition and contemporaneity. I will highlight some differences with Heidegger's attitude to philosophy's own history. The fact that reason issues in speculative mind, even within the relativities of history, implies that the metaphysical quest of ultimacy need not be unwarranted pretension or hubris. It may be a necessity imposed by the nature of mind itself and of being. Any rejection of this quest fails to meet Hegel's criticism of Kant: any imposition of a limit on reason is self-cancelling, self-refuting. To plot any such limit is already to have surpassed it. Reason is just this activity of surpassing, is the self-consciousness of transcendence.

An unlimited reach does not imply an unlimited grasp; nor does it imply an irrational leap into the void. Rather it reveals mind's possible openness to the qualitative infinity of being as present. It reveals reason as a self-transcending power in the middle between time and time's other. The question then is: Can this middle be entirely characterized as a dialectical middle? In Hegel's case, this means closing the gap between reason's reach and reason's grasp. Hegel's makes this claim. But one can take a stand in the middle without granting this claim, without granting that the middle is to be entirely characterized in terms of dialectical self-mediation. An affirmation of speculative mind need not commit one to the Hegelian sense with all its claims. But in either case, it will not do to label, indeed libel speculative metaphysics as "onto-theology," in the Heideggerian manner.

I noted before this irony: Heidegger as critic of technicist mind, instrumental reason, is deeply in agreement with the same technicist in his suspicion of traditional metaphysics. Metaphysics is unfairly totalized as "metaphysics of presence," which is seen, in the terms I use, as only another expression of a reductive *univocal* sense of being, which, in turn, is absolutized in technicist mind. But there are deeper ironies, even sinister ones. Heidegger strongly emphasizes the historicity of thought. He offers an ontologizing of history; so much so that the inseparability of being and time makes one wonder if time is now doing the work of eternity. It is as if he cannot quite get out of the hearing of Nietzsche's shouting down of Plato's eternity, and yet his own post-Nietzschean "time" works like a surrogate eternity. Feeling the hot vehemence of Nietzsche's denunciation of Platonism, Heidegger cancels out the language of eternity, which seems to be identified with the rigidified univocity of the Platonic *eidos*. There is something disingenuous in this, since the withdrawal of Being even in its historical manifestness, which Heidegger does want to espouse, cannot be approached without the thought of the other of time, whether explicitly named as eternity or something else.

Of course, Heideggerian historicism has not escaped the charge of nihilism, indeed the charge of crassest subservience (Croce called it "the prostitution of philosophy") to the idol of the National Socialist State.[14] In his Rectoral Address, his three services to that idol were: *Arbeitsdienst, Wehrdienst, Wissensdienst*: work-service, military-service, science-service. These remind one of Plato's three classes in the *Republic*: the workers, the warriors, the philosopher-statesmen. But unlike the Platonic hierarchy, Heidegger says the three "are equally necessary and of equal ranking," indeed "equally primordial."[15] Heidegger will later try to fudge this in the *Spiegel* interview. His statements are studies in ambiguity, but given many other statements of obeisance to the reigning powers, it is hard to shake the suspicion that this is consistent with (and here is the sinister irony) a *total instrumentalization of philosophy* in the service of the idol of the state. Philosophy's service is in league with the "military-industrial complex" of the state, the service not only of being, but of war and death and murderous death. Heidegger will deny this (again in the *Spiegel* interview), but his own originally equivocal language trades on the possibility of such a service to the state. This is an instrumentalization of philosophy from the Right, a kind of ideological twin to the instrumentalization from the Left. The critic of instrumental reason offers a new "higher" instrumentalization of philosophy —*Wissensdienst* in obedience to the "highest" historical fate of the fascist state. The *Führer* taking the victory salute in a black military sedan replaces Hegel's Napoleon as the *Weltgeist* on horseback.

If this is Heidegger's "lower historicism," we also find a "higher historicism." The first raises tormenting questions for philosophy, and in my later discussion of evil, I will have something to say about the seductions of the world-historical universal, whether of the Right or Left. When the philosopher places himself unreservedly in the service of such putative universals, he risks a treason to philosophy, not to mention elementary ethics. Heidegger himself seems to have had no embarrassment in admitting to Karl Löwith that his political commitments followed from his views of the historicity of Being.[16] That is, the "lower historicism" follows from the "higher historicism."

Heidegger's "higher historicism" relates to his concern with the contemporary task of thinking at what he claims is the end of philosophy—an old story that goes back to Hegel and claims made on behalf of the system. As permeating his view of the "history of Being," this "higher historicism" helps account for his suspicion of traditional metaphysics, his critique of technicist mind and yet his proximity to technicist mind just in this suspicion of the tradition of speculative philosophy.

Thus, in "The End of Philosophy and the Task of Thinking," much of what he says in critique of Western reason is not beside the point *if* reason is exclusively instrumental. But in the form of a "higher historicism," Heidegger totalizes the Western tradition as an epoch of Being, a totality whose end, namely, completion, appears in the global dominance of cybernetic thought. Here by a "higher historicism" I mean a certain acceptance of the sequence of philosophical possibilities articulated in the history of Western philosophy, acceptance of this sequence as a kind of metaphysical destiny. One might want to speak more neutrally of a "transcendental historicism." This expression is perhaps less charged, yet no less speculatively problematic. Nevertheless, it is Heidegger himself who obsessively invokes destiny (*das Geschick*), and not just transcendental conditions of possibility.

I note the language of historicist totalization: "All metaphysics, including its opponent, positivism, speaks Plato."[17] Notice how Heidegger gives us a synoptic overview of the historical totality, ironically reminding us of Plato's philosopher—the spectator of all time and all eternity (cf. *Republic*, 537c). Thus, to the metaphysical question about the ground, Heidegger answers in terms of the history of putatively epochal answers: "...the ground has the character of grounding as the ontic causation of the real, as the transcendental making possible of the objectivity of objects, as the dialectical mediation of the movement of the absolute Spirit, of the historical process of production, as the will to power positing values."[18] What we have here is a kind of historicist slide show of the epochs of Being, from precritical metaphysics, through Kant, Hegel, Marx, to Nietzsche, the inverted Plato and last metaphysician.

This is my point: the slide show is so smooth and continuous that overall we seem to have one overarching snapshot of a totalized tradition. The philosophies in sequence are all reduced to different expressions of the same ground—"The ground shows itself as presence"[19]—as if they followed each other by an inherent necessity, without radical ruptures. It is as if we were looking down from such a great height, looking down at things from such a distance, that fundamental discontinuities are flattened and radical ruptures are smoothed over. But how can we look down from such a height if we are caught up in the historical flux or in one of the epochs of Being? Is not Heidegger subject to the previously noted difficulty of all historicism: How can he say that *all* being is historical, if he does not somehow transcend history? Again to speak of the *withdrawal* of Being, as he does, certainly implies some such transcendence. Is this a pointer again to an unnamed eternity? If the historicist claim (even a "higher historicist" one) is made totalistically, is it not self-deconstructing? If the claim is not made totalistically, what then is the *other to time* that we must acknowledge?

From Heidegger's height all systems of metaphysics are lumped together as the oblivion of Being, and Heidegger become oblivious to those possibilities of thought in some philosophical views that are not oblivious of Being. Not surprisingly, in this historicist totalization Heidegger treats instrumental mind as the destiny of speculative mind, without any adequate acknowledgment that the latter is not at all reducible to the former, that the former in fact is blind to the interests of the latter and, if totalized, produces just that oblivion of Being that Heidegger himself laments. The sickness is attributed to the cure.

In search of the contemporary task of thought, Heidegger claims that philosophy ends in cybernetics: its proper completion is thus really the reduction of speculative mind to instrumental reason. This may have some truth if, in the terms I use, both speculative mind and instrumental reason are each reducible to the univocal sense of being. But this is not true of speculative mind. I say the difference must be kept open, as it is, for instance, in Hegel's distinction between *Vernunft* and *Verstand*. Heidegger comes perilously close to acquiescing in this reduction, as if it were some historicist fate. Ironically, we are reminded of the charge against Hegel as offering a quietist canonization of the Prussian status quo. If the cybernetic age is the destiny of Western metaphysics, one bows one's historicist neck before the brute power of what is. Or rather one celebrates the power of the seemingly winning side, with a clean conscience that the destiny of Being has fated it so. Others, the other becomes the victim who must bow before the power of history's winning side. But history proved to be a fickle bitch and the winner later lost. What does this say about historical destiny? What does it say about Heidegger's hermeneutical judgment about history and the ethical? Heidegger's Nazism is an indelible stain that warns us of daimonic surrender to the evil powers of history. The speculative light of the "higher historicism" collapses into the political darkness of the "lower historicism."

Heidegger strategically blurs philosophical differences. The Nazi blurred difference by murder of the other. I confine myself to the blur in philosophy. I agree that in modernity we find a reduction of speculative reason to instrumental. One need only think of Descartes' rejection of Aristotle and Plato: their speculative metaphysics is literally useless. Descartes sought a new science that would confer practical benefits and make man "master and possessor of nature." Descartes is perfectly right: speculative metaphysics is useless. But speculative philosophers always knew it was useless, for it was an employment of mind, an enjoyment of mind beyond pragmatic concerns: it was an activation of the energy of mind beyond the instrumental. Plato knew this, Descartes knew this, but they interpret the uselessness differently.

Heidegger fudges this absolutely crucial difference in his will to straitjacket the philosophical tradition into one mould. The charge against the metaphysics of presence becomes an instance of that same metaphysics, in its reduction to a univocal category of a complex, often duplex and ambiguous heritage. The non-instrumental mindfulness of speculation is obliterated. Indeed I think that an instrumental mind, which totally forgets the speculative, is ultimately murderous, since it turns everything into a means to an end, including the ethical and the other. The greatness of speculative mind is that it does not turn the middle into such a mere means, for it is ever watchful for being that is intrinsically worthy, original for itself, an end in itself in the middle itself. Speculative philosophy demands this vigilance of mind to being that is *essentially other* to instrumental reason.

In the Heideggerian totalization consider some of the blurred differences with respect to philosophical possibility. Consider that Husserl and Hegel are two major figures often linked to Descartes' legacy. Yet Husserl is a trenchant critic of historicism.[20] Hegel is also not a historicist in the senses previously delineated. Both are "Cartesians" in their quest of self-determining, purely autonomous thought. They might also be called "Aristotelians" in the emphasis on thought thinking itself. These emphases, deeply consonant with the philosophical tradition, might offer *some* basis to the description of that tradition as "metaphysics of presence": thought totally transparent, absolutely present to itself. But these emphases do not exhaust either of these thinkers, certainly not Hegel, or the tradition of philosophy.

Consider the sense of *metaphysical otherness* we find in Plato. This gets blurred in the reduction to Cartesian subjectivity. This is important because Platonism as speculative metaphysics always implied the possibility of *thought thinking its other*, not just thought thinking itself. The other is not to be reduced by thought. I will refer again to the Platonic sense of metaphysical otherness in relation to Hegel's dialectical reduction of eternity as other to history as self-determining. But these are just a few essential differences. Heidegger's synopsis flattens them into a univocal historical totality. We are supposed to think "difference as difference," he says. But it seems we are not to think deeply enough the differences of philosophical possibility. I note also Heidegger's awed reference to Parmenides' well-rounded truth, *eukukleos Alētheia*.[21] The irony here is that the image of circularity and its closure on itself is the most used traditional representation of the perfect movement and of eternity, as well as the thought that thinks itself, whether in the majestic solitude of Empedocles' circle, or in the self-circling thought of Aristotle's God, or the self-thinking Idea of Hegel's absolute, each the speculative acme of absolute self-presence.

Hegel, it must be said, also totalizes the history of philosophy as telling the dialectical tale of progressively unfolding thought—thought that completely determines itself, up to the acme of pure thought thinking itself. Heidegger makes claim to be open to the other as other; and yet all he seems to see is what he wills to see. Hegel is less disingenuous in his totalizing: he unabashedly wants thought to think itself, and so is philosophically frank about the dialectically subordinate place of the other to thought. For Hegel the history of philosophy stammers to be Hegelian; for Heidegger, the tradition does not stammer to be Heideggerian because it supposedly stifled the pre-Socratic truth of being, the *alētheia* that Heidegger now stammers to resay. But—strange to say—in the intervening silence of the metaphysical millennia, the philosophical tradition takes on the distinctive accents of Heideggerian saying, or perhaps, not-saying.

Heideggerian saying exhibits its own strategic silences. In accusing the tradition of oblivion to the other of thought, he is conveniently mute about the otherness of the thinking of speculative metaphysics, especially *its otherness* to instrumental reason. He calls this other, the unthought. I prefer to call it the other of thought. This seems to me a more coherent locution. For Heidegger does want to think this unthought. If we simply say, there is an unthought, then our thought risks incoherence. We mitigate this incoherence if the unthought is the other of thought, to which we are philosophically unfaithful if we conceive of philosophy as exclusively thought thinking *itself*.

In the end, Heidegger is again a strange twin of Marx: the end of philosophy yields an instrumentalization of philosophy. Marx applauds this, and wants to further this instrumentalization in the direction of revolutionary praxis. Heidegger the Nazi also ardently pursued a revolutionary praxis.[22] Heidegger the thinker equivocally acquiesced in the instrumentalization as a destiny of the history of Being. Though he may not be entirely at home with it, the fact that the oblivion is a destiny of Being makes him accept the instrumentalization in a manner much closer to Marx than to Hegel. His not being-at-home with the outcome, his spurious claim that the outcome is the result of speculative mind, does make him call for a different thinking. But the promise of that other thinking was always there in the despised tradition of speculative thinking. Speculative thinking was *always* other to instrumental mind.

Heidegger tries to recover the difference, I think, in his later notion of *Denken*—but supposedly *outside* philosophy. In earlier writings (e.g. the 1929 lecture "What is Metaphysics?") he seemed more willing to acknowledge the hidden power of this other thinking as already there in philosophy. Even in the Rectoral Address some remarks about Greek *theōria* are equivocal on this score. I think that this recovery of an other thinking is really a renaming. *Denken* is old speculative vintage poured into the new bottles of post-philosophical philosophy. Heidegger comes across as downplaying this in order to play up his own putative "difference"—the radicality that supposedly gets behind speculative thinking to the so-called unthought. Despite the explicit claims of respect, one senses a reluctance of generosity towards the great speculative ancestors, as if Heidegger were too infected by the hermeneutics of suspicion of his sometime mentor Nietzsche. Heidegger's echoing of Nietzsche is nowhere more evident than in his will to be a radical other to the philosophical tradition. This is his *accentuated modernity*: the revolutionary will to be an absolute original, even while claiming to pursue a different patient, humble, will-less thinking.

I do not underestimate Heidegger's complexity as a thinker. Heidegger is a philosopher of transcendence, and not merely human self-transcendence. The heritage of his Catholic upbringing resounds in his thought, and even his use of the word Being echoes back to that heritage and the name that cannot be finally silenced: God. Nevertheless, Heidegger's path to transcendence was blocked in at least two crucial ways. The first block comes from Kant's critique of traditional metaphysics and the replacement of metaphysical transcendence by a transcendental philosophy. I call this a block because Heidegger is penetrating enough to see that transcendental philosophy, whether Kantian or Hegelian or Husserlian or even Heideggerian, ultimately defines the other in terms of the *for-self*, and hence produces the oblivion of Being in its otherness to the knower, produces the eclipse of transcendence in its final grounding ultimacy. I cannot here make any further point about Kant who, while ostensibly a debunker of metaphysical transcendence, is yet a tortured thinker of transcendence, hidden in all the scholastic casing of transcendental jargon.

I refer below (*The Dialectical Reduction . . .*) to my discussion of what I call the double vision vis-à-vis the preservation of transcendence in terms of the irreducibility to time of eternity as time's other. Kant can be reread as a double thinker in the sense intended, as potentially a tortured metaxological thinker who yet cannot shake off the scholastic chains of philosophy as a science. Heidegger, at his best and as a thinker of transcendence, might also be seen as a tortured metaxological thinker, as concerned to think the other of thought.

Though transcendence as other to human self-transcendence seems blocked by the Kantian critique of traditional metaphysics, nevertheless, the desire for transcendence persists, regardless of the Kantian prohibition on speculation. This desire continues to ferment in the middle between beings and Being. Thus, Heidegger's ontological difference between the being of beings and the being of Being testifies to the continued persistence in the middle of this desire for transcendence. Such a desire for transcendence in the middle is simply our being, and hence is ineradicable, hence, too, will surface inevitably in the thinking of any philosopher worthy of the name. Without subscribing to the details of Heidegger's formulation, I would grant that something like the ontological difference is necessary for any genuine metaxological thinking. The transcending movement of thinking finds itself in the middle between the being of being and the being of Being. This is close to an ontological reformulation of the metaphysical difference of time and eternity (not time in Heidegger's sense) in the metaxological space wherein the philosopher thinks.

By the second block on transcendence I mean the Nietzschean bar. There is no question that the Madman's howl "God is dead" deeply affected Heidegger. Nietzsche enjoins a return to the pagan earth, in opposition to the Platonic and Christian flight to eternity. Yet here, too, the desire for transcendence still ferments in the middle, but now it is redirected back to this world of time. I also suspect that Heidegger was quite influenced by Nietzsche's critique (in the *Birth of Tragedy*, for instance) of Socratism as the apotheosis of "theoretical man." With Socrates begins rootless thinking, rational, placeless Enlightenment. Whether this is a caricature of Socrates is not now the issue. The point is that Nietzsche redirects the eros for eternity back to the earth. In Heidegger this redirection gets reinterpreted in terms of the historicity of Being. The ineradicable eros for eternity in the middle means that this historicity of Being functions as *both* time and eternity, as a surrogate eternity. The historicity of Being is made to do the work of transcendence. Add this to the Nietzschean emphasis on the pagan earth, and it is conceivable why historicity as a surrogate eternity might now be seen as erupting in time. In times of crisis, of *kairos*, the trans-temporal cuts into and across time, rupturing the domestications of being in which we have grown stale ("inauthentic" is Heidegger's word). It erupts in privileged peoples, like the Greeks and the Germans. It erupts in privileged individuals, like the poet, or the great statesman, or the great thinker. Hence the triad: Hölderlin, Hitler, Heidegger himself.

The issue is related to what I call the religious urgency of ultimacy in *Philosophy and its Others* (chapter 3). Heidegger's sense of the people, of origins and belonging, are bound up with the idea of home, the metaphysics of home. I do not dismiss this metaphysics of home as some sentimental nostalgia, as do some post-structuralist thinkers. The metaphysics of home has to be thought through far more radically. Neither the braggadocio of the avant garde nor the sentimentalized nostalgia of the rear guard will do. Heidegger's own Nietzschean sense of the Dionysian origin is an effort to think the earth as home: the origin is a root of being deeper than Socratic rationality. We cannot stifle our eros for eternity; but this eros will fill itself with substitutes when transcendence as other is blocked off; eternity or its substitute will interrupt our metaphysical slumber. In the gap, in the middle between eros and ultimacy, we will fill up this middle with our own constructions, if transcendence as other is barred to us, or if we refuse transcendence as other. To the extent that modernity is in flight from eternity, its tale is one of false absolutes, false eternities, false gods.

One can see why National Socialism might serve, did serve as an idolatrous surrogate for transcendence. One suspects that Heidegger saw it as the eruption of the urgency of ultimacy, of the promise of a religious renewal of the people, but not from a putatively empty transcendence above, but from below, out of the roots, the origins, the heritage. Heidegger's politics are sacral politics, a form of cultus in the widest sense. The great difficulty is how this cultus produces the oblivion of the proper otherness of eternity to time. This cultus is already the eclipse of eternity. For Heidegger transcendence from above is blocked by the Kantian and Nietzschean prohibitions, and Plato is seen as a bad dualist. And yet there is a torturous ambiguity in Heidegger's sense of Being as origin: concealing in self-revealing. My sense is that Heidegger is trying to keep, in a very equivocal way, a version of what I call the double vision. This is not thought through enough, not metaxological enough; hence the danger again of the collapse of the "higher" into the "lower" historicism.

Compounding this danger is the way the thought of the early Heidegger is saturated with the language of will, violence, self-assertion. In terms I will use below, Heidegger's sense of Being as origin is an erotic absolute (evident, for instance in "The Origin of Art Work"). This language of self-assertion evidences the urgency of ultimacy in the perilous form of an impatient will to transcendence, as if one could command the ultimate, take it by the scruff of the neck and dictate to it. This is not only impossible; it is laughable. But it shows Hedeigger infected with the will to power of modernity that he will later subject to such severe criticism. Later in trying to escape the degeneration of the erotic absolute into this will to power, the ambiguity of his language of the origin becomes even more tortured: the doubleness of revealing and concealing becomes more pronounced. In certain respects, this is all to the good; but the ontological perils of equivocity are not thought through metaxologically.

As a privileged thinker, Heidegger was not immune from the temptations of monstrous arrogance. He showed a strange inability to confess the elemental. Why, for instance, could the sorrowing clown Charlie Chaplin see right through the *Führer* in the *Great Dictator*, while the world-historical philosopher not merely could not see through the *Führer*, but joined the infamy? World-historical importance produces a blindness to the truth of the elemental, world-historical importance incapable of mockery of itself, laughter at itself. There is spiritual freedom, the seed of it certainly, in this laughter.

Consider how that most human of thinkers, Nietzsche, the suffering, laughing Nietzsche, is all but turned by Heidegger into one of the voices of Being: a nameless placeholder for an anonymous power. The elemental Nietzsche who in *Ecce Homo* reminded us of the relative merits of coffee or tea or cocoa in the morning—this Nietzsche now a last nameless voice of Being in the history of metaphysics! Is this related to Heidegger's anonymous way of naming mass murder, when comparing it to modern agriculture? He seemed unable to assume the elemental I in his writing; hence we find a stiffness in the rhetoric of the master thinker that verges on the portentous and pompous. Heidegger could not *confess*—something radically particular and elemental. Farias recounts the story: after the war Rudolph Bultmann said to Heidegger that like Augustine he would now have to write his retractions (*Retractiones*). Bultmann recalls: "Heidegger's face became a stony mask. He left without saying anything further."[23] His stature would have been greatly enhanced if he had honestly, elementally, without subterfuge, made National Socialism an explicit theme of *Denken*, after the horror was manifest in its indescribable monstrousness.

Heidegger, I grant, was a dark philosophical genius. His *devotees* follow him in attacking the tradition of speculative metaphysics for speaking logocentrically. Yet the voice speaking through the follower is not that of the other of thought or the unthought. It is the voice of Martin Heidegger himself. The devotee, and recently the post-structuralist, repeats such labels as "onto-theology," "metaphysics of presence," and so on, like a kind of magical refutation of speculative thought. Reiterated incantations of "onto-theology," "logocentrism," and so on, become a post-Nietzschean exorcism of the unholy spirit of traditional metaphysics, that demon Platonism. But naming, rather renaming a philosophical position is no solution to a perplexity. For free thought the perplexity remains open, the question remains to be thought or rethought. With the follower the thinking of the unthought remains, alas, an unthinking.

Even if something like "onto-theology" and speculative metaphysics can be tied together, this need not surprise or daunt us, since philosophy and religion may have a deep affinity. This may be a source of strength, not a weakness. I return to this in subsequent chapters. Again the Heideggerian resort to ritual terms like "onto-theology" reminds one of the Marxist's distaste for Hegel's concern with religion as "mystifying." Thus, too, the Marxist is not unlike the analytic philosopher: for both, terms like "mystical" are uncritically used as jargon words of abuse. All of this, however, merely gives expression to a philosophical difference; it does not settle it.

If we refuse to compromise the transcendence of God, then we are *always* on our guard against *every absolutization of any historical formation*. Every one of the latter is a human construction, some perhaps with a greater claim to truth and ultimacy; none the truth, none the ultimate. Their absolutization always yields a false absolute, an idol, not a saving god. The preservation of transcendence as *other* precipitates in us an *ineradicable skepticism*, religious, metaphysical, ethical, about every absolutization of history, and *all* of its powerful formations. The absolutization of history is a metaphysical lie.

Speculative Timeliness: Untimely Thought

How do these remarks bear on the issue of philosophy's contemporary task in the light of its heritage. First, the question of speculative timeliness must take on a complex modulation if our interlocutor is Hegel. I agree that there are urgent questions for post-Hegelian philosophy in relation to Hegel's dialectical middle and the tradition of speculative metaphysics as tempted to privilege thought thinking itself. In my view, philosophy always thinks the middle. The question is whether dialectically self-mediating thought can completely account for it. I do not think so, for the middle is metaxological. Therefore, it is timely to think through the dialectical middle, in light of the philosophical tendency to subordinate the other of thought to thought's own self-mediation, to thought thinking itself. However, Hegel is not to be "overcome" but rather thought through. This language of "overcoming" actually is parasitical on the dialectical language of Hegelianism that it supposedly claims to "overcome." Its comical end-result is a line of philosophers leapfrogging their predecessor towards a claimed absolute originality. And, of course, it is always easier to leapfrog by belittling your predecessors, rather than by really thinking through the matter more profoundly.

The historicist parochialism of the twentieth century resides in the conceit that thought is better because it is contemporary. This remark is not said in any reactionary spirit, but in skepticism of the idols of the time. The skepticism we direct on our predecessors could be creatively directed on ourselves. The results can be liberating: we are allowed to see *their otherness* with respect, while we become disquieted about the pressing noise of proximate debates. Honest thought is often out of joint. Thus so the Heideggerian rhetoric of logocentrism and ontotheology has bred a kind of scholastic stultification. The rhetoric masquerades as thinking for itself but we find a wearying sameness in the practitioners. The proclaimers of difference turn out to be clones of either Heidegger or Derrida—hoist with an irony to which their own allegiance to irony seems blind. It is easier to take the speck out of the eye of sober ontotheology than the beam from the manic eye of deconstruction. A lot of what now is touted as postmodernism smuggles back some old wine in new looking bottles, all the while congratulating itself on its "creative advances." We may be at the end of the modern age, but we also ought to be honest. The real otherness of the philosophical tradition ought to be granted. Only thus can we gain real distance on ourselves. We must stop reading the Western tradition univocally and stop charging *it*, like ungrateful heirs who reverse the charges, with reductive univocity.

Second, speculative timeliness requires an untimely thinking, which transcends any univocal relation to history. In some ways Hegel is unmatched for historical sophistication. Some have seen his thought as but the summation of past philosophy, the very hyperbole of a philosophical postscript. But philosophy is most deeply tied, not only to religion, but also to art, and not to historical erudition. Hegel would agree with Aristotle when he said that poetry is more philosophical than history. This tells us as much about philosophy, as about art. The timeliness of a great work of art, as of philosophy, is a certain untimeliness that cannot be reduced to historical information. The other of time comes to timely/untimely manifestation in time itself. Time itself, as timely, manifests its untimely other.

Third, the philosopher does not turn to past philosophers to dazzle others with the virtuosity of his scholarship. He does so because he finds philosophy there—flesh of its flesh, spirit of its spirit. He discovers a speculative kinship across time, a kinship often timely for him in revealing thought that is other to his own time. The stress falls not on the *history* of philosophy but on the history of *philosophy*. I recall here Hegel's disparagement of certain historically minded theologians. These busy themselves about the convictions of others. They are like clerks in a mercantile house whose task it is to keep the accounts of wealthy strangers, and who act only for others without ever obtaining any wealth themselves. They know as little of God as a blind man sees of a painting, even though he handles the frame.

Fourth, though philosophy is not reducible to history, knowledge of its history can give a ballast, indeed weightiness to living philosophical reflection. The untimeliness of thought consists, as it were, in the fact that there are no philosophical *fashions*. On the essential speculative issues, the truly timely philosopher does not date. To know what philosophers have done is to know what philosophy can do. Yet there is this sting. We need a certain double attitude to the tradition of philosophy, a middle between excessive memory and excessive forgetfulness. A false timeliness can be produced by excessive forgetfulness, a false untimeliness by excessively epigonal memory.

On the one hand, remembrance can burden thought with the weight of its own past. Thought can become paralyzed by excessive historicist memory. In remembering everything historically, we remember nothing philosophically, for our discernment of the memorable may be feeble, because merely epigonal. On the other hand, if we lack recollection of philosophy's heritage, a bland contemporaneity will brand the latest fashion as absolute novelty—until the next pretender leapfrogs to absolute originality. Forgetfulness will preen itself with the illusion of newness. We unwittingly reduplicate the positions of the past, albeit with a contemporary coloration. We claim to be radically new, but in fact our philosophical amnesia lacks the skepticism needed about its own contemporary importance. We also lack the hermeneutical generosity towards the great philosophers that rediscovers the basis of their greatness; we fail to think their otherness, because we miss the sources out of which their greatness grew.

In one case, memory loses itself in unphilosophical immersion in the past whose speculative *timeliness* it forgets; in the other case, forgetfulness excites itself with an unphilosophical rejection of tradition, failing to remember its still powerful *untimeliness*. These extremes are related offshoots of historicism, one turned towards the past, the other towards the future. Both glide over the astonishing present of being and the ontological perplexity it occasions, as something to be surpassed, though in different directions. Both glide over the greatness of prior thought in its grappling with this perplexity. For one, philosophy's heritage is the tired history of what is true; for the other, it is the tedious history of what is false, and the present is just a mere means to the unprecedented post-philosophical future. In one, antiquarian reverence mummifies philosophy's past; in the other, the negativity of thought turns against this past, repudiating any preceding claims to greatness, as the hermeneutics of suspicion unleashes an orgy of deconstruction. One is a scholarly latecomer, tired with heavy historical memory; the other is a lightheaded youth, infatuated with futurity, but in the innocence of its becoming, ever in danger of being dazzled by every groundless happening, simply because it is new.

In this tension between the old and new, one side seems reactionary, the other revolutionary. But each dialectically implies the other, and neither is adequate to the middle. The old guard of scholarship may kneel in the church of spirit whose crypt contains the corpus of tradition; the *avant garde* of post-philosophical philosophy may shoot its manifestos from the postmodern barricades at any last stray thinker from the past. But for all that the historicist grey elder and the Nietzschean post-metaphysical child are quite similar. The question is: Do they have sound judgment as to the metaphysically essential, robust philosophical memory that discerns the speculatively memorable? Can this judgment or memory be derived from historicist concerns alone? If it were, would our problem be only pushed one stage further back? Does history abandon us at a certain point?

Speculative thought asks: What things of metaphysical worth are preserved in the flux of historical relativities, what memorable things preserve themselves? There comes a point when we grow surfeited with history, whether reverencing the dead days gone, or announcing some glorious state coming. In Hesiod we find this prophesy: one day men will be born grey-headed, and as soon as this generation appears,

Zeus will erase it. Does historicism bring to birth such grey-headed infants, that is, the unity of the above extremes, the living contradiction of too much indiscriminate memory and no memory at all? Or does time bring to birth, as Plato thought, children with the promise of philosophical memory?

What of speculative timeliness in Hegel? Is there not here, too, a sense of the untimely? As I said, to justify an historicist view, Hegel's saying—philosophy is its own time comprehended in thought—is endlessly quoted. But in honesty we cannot silence Hegel's crucial addition: "...the great thing is to apprehend in the show of the temporal and the transient the substance which is immanent and the eternal which is present...." Hegel says: the great thing.[24] The great thing for philosophy is to apprehend time as the show of the eternal. Is this great thing related to the metaphysically memorable? Must it not also be the great difficulty? Is it like Spinoza's great thing: as difficult as it is rare? How would such greatness, difficulty, rarity fit with the so-called pervasiveness of the "metaphysics of presence"? Would it not be conspicuous by its absence? Would it not be invisible to an exclusively historicist philosophy? Or silenced, like Dostoevski's "accursed, eternal questions"?

And what, in any case, is the show of the eternal in the transient? Is this the conjunction of the untimely and the timely? What is this immanence in time of eternity? What has this to do with the middle? The Hegelian middle claims to mediate the transcendence of the transhistorical in terms of its completely immanent appearance in time, and in a form said to overcome the traditional, Platonic dualistic way. Does the untimely here conjoin with the timely with too much equivocal historicism? We must reconsider Hegel's dialectical middle, asking if it articulates the show of the eternal in time with a significant equivocation, one on which historicism itself is parasitical. The serpent turns again.

Speculative Logic and World-History

I now come to a significant wavering in the Hegelian middle. I have repeatedly said that Hegel wants a dialectical mediation of time and eternity. I ask: Does this dialectical mediation reveal ambiguities that provoke serious questions about the entire Hegelian project and its success? I will say: With respect to the logical Idea, Hegel wants clearly to put to rest any suspicion of historicism; and necessarily so, for if Hegelian logic is infected by historicism, then its claims to lay bare the ultimate grounds of intelligibility will be fatally undermined.

Here again Hegel has strong affinities with Husserl, the most vigorous proponent of philosophy as *strenge Wissenschaft* in the twentieth century, and also an unrelenting critic of historicism. Hegel insists on philosophy as systematic science and in a manner which distances him from historicism in the senses I have adumbrated. Just as Husserl was frequently dismayed at what passed for his authentic successors, so Hegel would have been dismayed were philosophy as science to be repudiated or reduced, in the name of the same history to which he also called attention.

   That said, Hegel also claims that the logical categories, while not simple historical products, manifest themselves in time. One sees why this is to the point. Hegel, as it were, wants to reject any Leibnizian disjunction of truth of reason and truth of fact, wants to cross Lessing's broad ugly ditch between reason's necessary truths and the contingencies of history. If the logical categories do not manifest themselves, they fail precisely in their central function of making intelligible to us the being of what appears. Without some appearance of the intelligible in what appears, the appearance is unintelligible. The intelligible makes intelligible what appears to mind. So without some appearing, the intelligible is itself unintelligible. Without some appearing, the logical categories fail, not by their redundancy, but by their impotence. The further issue then is: Whether the appearance of the categories in time is the complete dialectical self-mediation of eternity, or whether there are modes of appearance in which the otherness of eternity is reserved as other, even while it appears? Is all appearance dialectically self-mediating in Hegel's sense? I deny this, as will appear.

   We must say that Hegel has a double intention in this sense. The categories are not temporal products simply and hence philosophy cannot be reduced to historicism. But while the categories are not temporal products simply, they render possible the temporal production of historical intelligibility. This double intention stands on a necessary difference between logic and history, trans-temporal categories and temporal intelligibility. Philosophy must do justice to both. I see this as a reminder that philosophy is always in-between. Yet that difference must also be mediated, if the logical is to be intelligible to us in time, and if the temporal is to be intelligible in rational terms.

   How does Hegel respond to the between? He responds to the difference by claiming that history progressively mediates the manifestation and appropriation of the logical categories. Indeed it so completely mediates them that any otherness of the trans-temporal seems to be finally overcome by the complete self-mediation of historical *Geist*. Hegel interprets the between in terms of history as the dialectical self-mediation of eternity: history is the medium by which eternity comes to mediate with itself and to knowledge of itself in its complete temporal self-realization. I defend a different way of being between. The middle is not exhaustively characterized by Hegel's dialectical middle. This other way is the metaxological between.

Before explaining how this doubleness will be reduced to a dialectical self-mediating whole, I will first sketch the double intention in Hegel's view of the *history of philosophy*. Then I will look at a somewhat different face Hegel shows when he turns to *world-history*. There we find far less ambiguity. We find less equivocal evidence that Hegel does dialectically reduce eternity to time. In the logic of philosophy, Hegel *does want* to preserve the eternity of the Idea; in history as more normally understood, that eternity seems to be entirely mediated by the progress of world-history.

With respect to the first point, at the end of the *Phenomenology* Hegel contemplates the possibility of a double vision. He grants a difference between history as seen from without, history as a succession comprehended in time by the historian, and history as having passed into the recollection (*Erinnerung*) of philosophy and there being appropriated in the interiority of self-mediating mind that is not dispersed on temporal succession. In the second case, the self-externality marking successive time (as one thing after another) is cancelled and *aufgehoben*. Hegel talks about this second view as "cancelling time." The philosophical comprehension of history somehow cancels time.[26]

Hegel's *Logic* systematically follows the attainment of absolute knowing in the *Phenomenology*, but here too we move in a domain that seems other to time and history as normally conceived. This is implied by the famous, to some the infamous metaphor of the *Logic* as the eternal thought of God before the creation of nature and finite spirit. The *Phenomenology* brings us to the standpoint where we can begin to understand the intelligible structure of the eternal logos. The *Logic* dialectically unfolds the intelligible categories of this logos, categories which in turn are absolutely indispensable to making intelligible sense of what is manifest in time, history. The logical structure of eternity makes rationally intelligible the productions of time. This has to be maintained.

I previously noted Marx's difficulty with the transition from these categories to nature, hinting that here might be occasion for Aristophanic laughter: the laughing body returns abstracted thought to concreteness from the alienation of thought's pure ideality. There will be a time yet for more philosophical laughter. But this notorious transition recalls Parmenides asking the younger Socrates: Are there *eidē* of things like hair, mud, dirt? Socrates the idealist is clearly uncomfortable with the thought of dirt (*Parmenides*, 130c–e). In his *Lectures on the History of Philosophy*, Hegel praises Plato's *Parmenides* for dispensing with myth, and for taking flight into the pure thought of thought.[26] This is right but very incomplete. The exchange between Parmenides and Socrates is a clear caution concerning the pretensions of "pure thought." This *Caute* is all the more powerful coming, as it does, from the mouth of a philosopher whom we revere as the original father of all pure speculative thought. Dirt is the reviled other. Parmenides, the father of speculative logos, asks whether logos must take this, too, into account. Socratic philosophy may claim to be inspired by the Delphic command: *gnothi seauton*. Yet self-knowledge cannot forget the other. Philosophical honesty cannot forget the dirt. Parmenides is said to be the logical defender of pure eternity, of being beyond all becoming, closed in the security of its own well-rounded sphere. And yet seemingly anomalously, Plato—supposedly a son of the eternalist Parmenides—is reminding Socrates not to forget the otherness of dirt.

The issues at stake here will return in later discussions of evil and laughter. On a more general level, the question of otherness forces us to ask about the ontological status of the Idea or ideas. Hegel emphasizes the dialectical self-mediation of the logical categories, and this includes a certain relation to otherness. The logic offers the original ground of intelligibility, but for Hegel origin in the truest and fullest sense means the self-generating Idea. We might say that the Hegelian Idea as original being tries to unite the Platonic *eidos* and Kant's transcendental ego. With the Platonic *eidos* it shares an ontological character and an emphasis on determinate structure. With the transcendental ego it emphasizes the active subject as self-articulating and self-relating. There are also relevant differences with Plato and Kant. For Hegel's Idea articulates itself in time, hence breaking with the Platonic dualism of time and eternity. History tells of the emergence of *Geist*, which becomes free in its dialectical overcoming of otherness: spirit becomes at home with otherness by recognizing *itself* in otherness. The Hegelian Idea breaks with Kantian categories as subjectivistic constructs of *Verstand*, which are arrested before appearances, without access to the ground of appearance or the thing in itself.

Platonic dualism make metaphysically problematic the ingression of the eternal Idea into time; Kantian dualism places us finitely in the sphere of time and cuts us off epistemologically from any justified access to eternal Ideas. Hegel's Idea is said to overcome both these dualisms: With Plato the eternal nature of the essential structures of intelligibility are affirmed, with the qualification that eternity manifests itself in time. With Kant, the active power of the mind is affirmed, but far from being cut off from the essential structures of intelligibility, the active self-development of mind is just the mediation, the dialectical self-mediation of these intelligibilities in the temporal process itself.

This dual requirement, answering to suitably modified versions of "Platonism" and "Kantianism," is nowhere more evident, I think, than in Hegel's introduction to the *Lectures on the History of Philosophy*. This is appropriate, for philosophy as Hegel sees it, namely, as thought thinking itself, is already relatively free of the clutter of contingencies that besets history as concretely lived. Philosophical thought does not simply reduplicate this contingency on the more abstract level of thought. On the contrary, it more clearly shows forth the progressive grasp of philosophical mind of the inherent intelligibility of the Idea in all its sides.

The Idea that philosophy grasps is not simply temporal. Here is just a brief sample of relevant citations that show Hegel repeatedly insisting on this point. Thus, Hegel implies a basic similarity between the systems of philosophy in historical sequence and the sequence in the logical deduction of the conceptual determinations in the Idea. Historical succession in systems mirrors logical progression towards the full determination of the Hegelian Idea. Here he also says that you need philosophical logic to be able to comprehend the history of philosophy as *philosophy*.[27] I take the implication to be that there is a trans-historical sense of the Idea that is always necessarily pre-supposed in our hermeneutical approaches to the manifestations of the Idea in history. Hence, also Hegel demands a certain freedom from the hurry of lived history relative to the slowness of the *Weltgeist*: it has no need to hasten. Why? "It has time enough just because it is itself outside of time, because it is eternal. . ."[28] Hegel alludes to Jesus' image of the kingdom of heaven in speaking of philosophy's relation to the eternal: Philosophies have no sensuous medium, "but they do have Thought, Notion and the Eternal Being of Mind which moths cannot corrupt, nor thieves break through and steal. . .the history of Philosophy has not to do with what is gone, but with the living present."[29]

This is the same emphasis on the living eternal present in the *Philosophy of Right*, contiguous to the famous passage about philosophy being its own time comprehended in thought. Historicist Hegelianism is conveniently silent about this glaring emphasis. It finds it best not to notice it, or quickly explains it away as an embarrassing metaphorical lapse or metaphysical flourish. I insist on both sides, even if it is not clear how you can have both sides together. To notice both sides is to be honest about the tensions in Hegel's position that are not necessarily put to rest by hurrying on and speaking more quickly about dialectical mediation. Regardless of the final adequacy of his mediation, Hegel is entirely superior to his historicist interpreters because he is willing to put the double requirement right up front, great difficulty and all.

The same tension and doubleness in the *Philosophy of Right* pervades the *Lectures on the History of Philosophy*. Every philosophy is a child of its time. The philosopher "cannot escape out of his time any more than out of his skin, for he belongs to the one universal Mind which is his substance and his own existence. How should he escape from this? It is the same universal Mind that is embraced by thinking Philosophy; that Philosophy is Mind's thought of itself. . ."[30] Here we find, on the one hand, resources for an essentially historicist interpretation. But then, on the other hand, Hegel's talk about a universal, hence eternal spirit, recalls us to the entire tradition of speculative philosophy, which is significantly at odds with historicism.

Inevitably we ask: Can one, how can one, hold these two together? Is there a danger of the complete logicization of the tradition of philosophy, with Hegel and Heidegger then agreeing on the nature of that tradition, but disagreeing in their evaluation? Is the individual philosopher the puppet of the *Weltgeist*, the particular philosophical mind an historically contingent expression of the universal, eternal spirit? Do we here have uncanny anticipations of the Heideggerian view that the great thinker is the privileged communication of the proper mittence of Being for his own epoch? Is the Hegelian philosopher the mouthpiece of *Geist*, as the Heideggerian thinker is the shepherd of Being? In the pursuit of the double intention, do we not find here an equivocal wavering between time and eternity? Does Hegel waver between our being bound as philosophers to our time and yet participant in what transcends time? How do we quieten the suspicion that if world-historical individuals are *instruments* of the *Weltgeist*, the philosopher himself can hardly expect to escape a similar instrumentalizing? Hegel may present his view as the logic of Providence, but is it perilously close to the destiny of Being in Heidegger? Is philosophy instrumentalized as much by *die List der Vernunft* as by Marx's necessity of History, as by *das Geschick des Seins*?

Other relevant citations from the *Lectures on the History of Philosophy* and other Hegelian writings could be adduced, but these would be redundant to the major point. The crucial question is: Whether a dialectical account of the relation of eternity and time has the result not only of mediating their dualistic opposition à la Plato and different forms of supposedly religious dualism (Judaism and Catholicism), but also has the effect, in the final reckoning, of emptying the very otherness of eternity into time, without remainder.

This emptying of eternity into time might be spoken of as its *kenosis* or its dialectical disappearance. Does Hegel sufficiently guard against the latter outcome? I think not. That is, if we start by granting the normal dualism of time and eternity, dialectical thought will claim to show the untenability of the dualism, because the show of eternity in time must be granted even to affirm the dualism. Having undermined the dualism, dialectical thought will proceed to sublate the difference by claiming the dialectical union of time and eternity. But this union is effected by the developmental process of time itself. So the net effect will be to see time itself as the dialectical self-mediation of eternity in which the original otherness of eternity is progressively appropriated by an historically immanent process. The relation of time and eternity and the developmental process of history simply concretize the dialectical process of the whole.

World-History and the Logic of Dialectical Self-mediation

To see how this is worked out, I briefly glance at Hegel's philosophy of world-history in terms of his three epochs of *Geist*: the Oriental, the Greek and the Germanic/Christian. His famous schema states: in the Orient, only one is free; in the Greek world, some are free; in the Germanic world, all are free. The Oriental world corresponds to the immediacy of spirit; spirit has not yet risen above nature: it is submerged in the sensuous otherness of nature; the One who is free is the Emperor or Patriarch who alone stands out of the homogeneous mass. This stage of immediacy corresponds to the abstraction of the Idea in itself, or God the Father as a self-enclosed eternity in transcendence. True, the latter aspect only properly comes to light in what for Hegel is the dualism of Judaism in which the absolute transcendence of the One is set in opposition to finite, de-divinized nature and the human being in its condition of essential estrangement. We need not dwell on the particularities of Hegel's view of Persia and Israel and so on. The point is that the thought of eternity as an irreducible transcendence is seen as a merely abstract, immediate, undeveloped beginning. It is not the truth in its complete articulation. If it is taken as the truth of the whole, the result must be an alienating dualism of eternity and time.

Now this alienating dualism *can* function affirmatively for Hegel, but only in the light of its dialectically *provisional* character. Thus, in distinction from Oriental immediacy, Hegel claims that spirit emerges from and wrests itself free from nature in Jewish religion, as is reflected in their sublime poetry (e.g., the Psalms). God as spirit is elevated absolutely above nature. Through God's otherness as a radical "beyond," nature as an external otherness is de-divinized. Hence the human being, as the bearer of a higher spiritual destiny, itself promised by the transcendent God, can assert its superiority to nature. Jewish sublimity allows the human self to assert its superiority to nature as an otherness, but still for Hegel, *God's otherness* is such as to diminish the human spirit to a subordinate role. It is not nature's transcendence but God's that prevents the more complete self-mediation of the human spirit. Dualism may develop our difference, but we cannot remain at the level of opposition to the otherness. Then the human being becomes a servile, alienated thing opposed to a godless nature over against it, and threatened above by the towering transcendence of a majestic, powerful God.

I do not endorse these Hegelian views of transcendence. I am just underscoring how Hegel sees world-history as relentlessly working according to the logic of dialectical self-mediation. This logic is reiterated again and again. It informs the development and teleology of all Hegel's hermeneutical efforts. Thus, not surprisingly, in the second epoch of world-historical *Geist*, with Greek religion and art, we move beyond the above dualisms and the striving for eternity as a beyond. Spirit emerges from nature, comes into its difference as other to spiritless nature, yet retains its continuity with the sensuous beginning out of which it emerges. The harmony between the human spirit and its *this-worldly* embodiment is clearly of great value for Hegel. What we might call the principle of *immanent wholeness* shows itself in the Greek world, albeit in the form of *aesthetic self-mediation*. The otherness of Jewish transcendence has diminished relevance here.

The movement beyond the doubleness of the Jewish view to what Hegel sees as the dialectical self-mediating harmony of the Greek world is reflected in his discussion of its art. Greek art expressed the Greek sense of the absolute; it was then historically the supreme mode in which the absolute was articulated. Let me dwell on this. In Hegel's view of Greek art, we find a confluence not only of logic (the structure of the concept as dialectical self-mediation) and history (as the progressive dialectical self-mediation of reason and freedom), but also of aesthetics and religion. Art and religion coalesce in Greek history but all exhibit the dynamic structure of the logical concept as dialectical self-mediation.

In the classical art of Greece the Ideal is attained, for here we find dialectical self-mediation in the most consummate aesthetic form. True, this acme of Greek art is itself a mediated result—behind it is a history of struggle; what precedes harmony involves struggle with what is other to spirit. The indeterminate Oriental One must become dialectically self-mediated before the result can be aesthetically articulated in consummate form. But in the latter case, nature, and especially the human body, become the body of the gods, themselves seen as personal powers, not subpersonal savage forces (captured in the Titans). This is, so to say, the aesthetic *Aufhebung* in Greek history of the Oriental otherness. For instance, there is an *Aufhebung* in *myth* of the Symbolic (Hegel's aesthetic category for the Oriental) into the Classical, in the battle of the chthonic and Olympian gods, and in the Olympians' victory, which yet preserves something of the chthonic powers.

Thus, Hegel's second epoch of world-history dialectically overcomes the alienating otherness of the Jewish divinity. Spirit mediates with itself by idealizing the sensuous otherness of nature, most particularly the human body. Hegel agrees with Hölderlin when he called the Greek world *"ein Reich der Kunst."* The Greeks are *the aesthetic people.* Their way of being exhibits the logical structure of the concept as dialectical self-mediation, but their self-mediation predominantly takes an aesthetic form. Art was the privileged mode of the absolute's articulation, hence their religion is called the "religion of art" (*Kunstreligion*). Their beautiful gods expressed a union of nature and spirit, a union that itself is spiritual and not sunk in nature's otherness, as is the Oriental beginning. Spirit knows itself to be fundamentally dealing with *itself* in its dealing with nature: the sensuous self-knowledge of *Kunstreligion* is the aesthetic self-mediation of spirit.

The logical dynamism of the absolute is the process of dialectical self-mediation. This logical dynamism will be evident everywhere, in art, in religion, in nature, in society, in history, in philosophy itself. Thus Hegel speaks of Greek art as articulating the "eternal powers that hold sway in history."[31] Greek art sensuously mediated the temporal manifestness of the eternal. What is salient is the *anthropomorphic* self-mediation of original *Geist*. Surprisingly for the "panlogist" Hegel, the Greeks are not the people of philosophy but of art. Philosophers, like Plato, would be *anomalies* to Greek aesthetic being, as Nietzsche claimed about Socrates. In his way, Hegel would agree with Nietzsche. It is as artists, not philosophers, that the Greeks expressed their sense of the ultimate, and for Hegel in threefold fashion: as the subjective, the objective and the political work of art.[32] Each is a different manifestation of what above I called the "principle of immanent wholeness."

First, the Greeks cultivated the human body, the only truly proper vehicle of spirit in nature for Hegel. Here we find the subjective work of art: the bodied subject shapes itself as a living organic work of art; nor is this reverence for the body opposed to religious reverence. I take it that a point of great attraction about the Greeks for Hegel and his contemporaries is that their aesthetic religion enjoined no shame with respect to the body, a shame associated with otherworldly forms of ascetical religion. This is reflected in the second point: the Greeks objectified their sense of the ultimate powers in the statues of the gods that are beautiful spiritual individualities. In the artistic idealization of the human body, and in opposition to the formless indeterminacy of the Orient, we are confronted with defined, determinate, indeed radiant individual wholes. In the religious statues, the objective works of art, the Ideal is attained and every indeterminacy overcome.

Third, the same sense of immanent wholeness is at work in the Greek polis, the political work of art. Here we find the ethical, legal and political self-mediation of the Greek people. The polis was like an ethical, religious whole, shaped by its citizens as if by a community of artists. It is self-mediating, not at the level of some solitary individuality, but in terms of the community as a whole; for in the assembly, the customs and laws, in the games and festivals, the people came to recognize themselves in the social otherness. The polis overcomes the otherness of the social world for the citizen and so, like a communal work of art, was a dialectical whole wherein the people found themselves again.

Inevitably one asks: If this principle of immanent wholeness is so pervasively at work in the Greek world, overcoming the alienating dualisms of prior historical stages, why do we not attain the end of history here? The answer for Hegel is that the immanent wholeness of Greek absoluteness is only an aesthetic absoluteness, a balance of mediated spirit and immediate sensuousness. It is not the absolute totality, for an *otherness remains* that is not completely mediated. Just because of the otherness of the aesthetic immediacy, the limit of this mediation of absoluteness appears for Hegel. Dialectical self-mediation can never be historically complete for Hegel if it remains tied to a sensuous other that remains an other. There will *always* be some such a remainder in the aesthetic.

The third epoch of Hegelian world-history testifies to a more thoroughgoing self-mediation and a more radical turn to inwardness.

Philosophy itself comes on the scene. Its elevation of *thought* marks a break with the sensuous otherness of Greek aesthetic being (again consider Plato). I see Hegel as implying that Socrates is the beginning of the end of the Greek world and hence as marking a break with Classical art. Hegel displays some sympathy for Aristophanes' attack on Socrates, a sympathy that should astonish those who simplistically bandy about the charge of "logocentrism" (on the difference of Socrates and Aristophanes regarding the end of antiquity, see chapter 6). The relevant point now is that for Hegel philosophical thought does insist more uncompromisingly on dialectical self-mediation, the constitution of a self-grounding knowing.

Philosophy mediates for the few, not the many. For the many the Christian religion is crucial. Here Hegel sees a decisive overcoming of the dualism of time and eternity in the claimed entry of divinity into history. Hegel sometimes speaks almost rhapsodically of the completion of time: the end of days is here; the dialectical union of time and eternity is historically effected in Christianity. The Christian religion (passing through the Roman world) articulates and world historically consolidates a sense of spirit as an infinite inwardness that can never be adequately mediated in an aesthetic way. It is not only the dialectical union of time and eternity in history that we find in Christianity, but also a sense of spirit as the power to overreach all sensuous otherness, because it knows itself to be always and in principle in excess of sensuous mediation.

In Hegel's third epoch of *Geist*, dialectical self-mediation must now take place in inwardness. Here both conceptual thought and religious representation are more adequate than art. The opening of inwardness gives rise to a sense of the transcendence of spirit to any sensuous manifestation. This is reflected in the Christian emphasis on the infinite worth of the individual. This emphasis on the individual as individual will be developed further by the immanentization of the Christian standpoint in modern secular society. This transcendence for Hegel is not to be an otherworldly transcendence, but an immanent historical one.

From the end of the Greek world to our own time, the historical formation of spirit is dominated by a sense of the self's infinite inwardness and the working out of its implications. Otherness does not vanish but its dialectical overcoming is effected in a new context. The Greek acme was itself sustained by slavery, but in the Germanic/ Christian world freedom is universalized, although not immediately. Hegel details the protracted dialectical process of historical development that is necessary to bring this principle of universal freedom to proper light. The historical process dialectically overcomes otherness.

The Roman emphasis on the legal person's universality is important,[33] as is the anguish of a godless world driving the self into itself. Medieval dualism projects the self's transcendence into a supersensuous beyond. The Reformation emphasis on the individual, the subsequent secularization of selfhood that transforms worldly life— Hegel sees all these as facilitating the final reconciliation in his own time. In that time there is the completed mediation of an unsurpassable return to self.

For Hegel the Protestant self-mediation in inwardness is a significant break with the religious otherness of Catholic heteronomy, whether the external authority of the Roman Church or the external transcendence of eternity in medieval otherworldliness. The Lutheran reformation effects the revolutionary return of self-mediation to inwardness, free of such constraining heteronomy. For Hegel this self-mediation in inwardness, though a form of spiritual being-at-home with self, becomes a form of not-being-at-home with the *world*, if it does not embody itself outside the privacy of spiritual inwardness. Self-mediation, autonomy, seeks its worldly embodiment. Luther and Descartes are thus twin heroes for Hegel—one in relation to faith, the other in relation to thought. The renewed freedom of secular thought in Descartes, and later in the Enlightenment, will liberate us from otherness and merely inward spirituality more completely than religious faith alone. This is why the French Revolution, and its inauguration of the modern state as the social embodiment of worldly freedom, is for Hegel the secular completion of the religious revolution of Lutheran Christianity. The limit of religion as spiritual inwardness is dialectically overcome in philosophically mediated politics, the Revolution prepared and mediated by rational philosophical Enlightenment.

I stress in all of this the overcoming of the otherness of the transtemporal, the secularization of the eternal, in a complete self-mediation or process of autonomy of putatively rational history. True, Hegel was a critic of the shortcomings of Enlightenment reason and the excesses of the French Revolution in its effort to give a worldly embodiment to an *abstract* rationality and freedom. Nevertheless, Hegel sees himself as completing the essential point that they bring to historical light, albeit inadequately; namely, the secular overcoming of otherness in the rational self-mediating state, the historical state that embodies the this-worldly freedom of rational autonomy. Autonomous secular history is teleologically bound to overcome the heteronomy of religious eternity.

In an early writing, Hegel lays this out with a Marxist, indeed Nietzschean bluntness: "Apart from some earlier attempts, it has been reserved in the main for our epoch to vindicate at least in theory the human ownership of the treasures formerly squandered on heaven; but what age will have the strength to validate this right in practice and make itself its possessor?"[34] Admittedly Hegel becomes more qualified in stating the essential point, and did feel that the abstract reason and freedom of the Enlightenment and the French Revolution led to failure and to moral horrors like the Terror. He came to feel that religion deserved a more complex respect. Speculative reason will allow the ultimate truth to be present in representational form in religion. But the essential point remains, namely, the historical necessity of the dialectical transition from religion to philosophy, or in terms of politics, from religion to the state. The dialectical supersession of the heteronomy of eternity in history remains at the center of Hegel's later philosophy.

The above compressed summary of Hegel's view of historical development indicates that at the end of the unfolding we find the full articulation of all of the essential possibilities. This *telos* itself reiterates the structure of historical origination, namely, dialectical self-mediation as spirit recognizes itself in all otherness. What was implicit in the beginning at last comes out of its hiddenness. The indefinite Oriental beginning, with its enigma, mystery, yearning for elusive "beyondness," has now been entirely mediated, as have also the two major forms of transcendence we find in monotheistic religion, namely, Jewish and Catholic otherness. In overcoming the otherness of eternity, history has fulfilled its task of entirely mediating the Idea as the dialectical origin. Hegel's view of the end of history can be fully understood only if we understand this sense of historical origination. This end is the entire self-mediation of what was implicit in the origin and its being brought out into the light of spirit. The end is the origin again, in the sense of a return to what was implicit there but in a manner that shows the origin to have been *articulated completely* by dialectical self-mediation. Perhaps we should not say that history overcomes the otherness of eternity, but that eternity overcomes its own initial otherness through history, such that history is simply its dialectical self-mediation.

So when Hegel talks about reason in history, the accent falls on the *self*-realization of reason. The ultimate goal of history is the *self*-knowledge of spirit. Hegel's teleology of history is not unreminiscent of Husserl's: the latter sees reason in Western history and its *telos* as the attainment of *strenge Wissenschaft*. Hegel is less "transcendental" than Husserl in being more attuned to lived history, and knowing the double requirement I mentioned above.[35] That the goal of history is the self-knowledge of spirit is most clearly reflected in the history of philosophy itself: the injunction *know thyself*! is given pride of place by Hegel. Reason as abstract immediacy creates its own other—which is itself again—hence reason knows *itself* in the other. Thus, reason is essentially determined as *thought thinking itself in its other*; even this "other" is reason's own self-creation, self-realization. This throws further light on the cunning of reason (*List der Vernunft*): in lived history we seem to be scattered abroad on an otherness that resists our comprehension or mastery; but the cunning of reason always works behind our back to restore reason in the otherness, to make manifest over huge stretches of historical development that it labored all along to bring reason back to *itself* from its other. Thought thinking *itself* always has the final word for Hegel.

This is not unrelated to Hegel's commitment to the sense of progressivism of modernity. Hegel does not privilege futurity, as modern progressivism generally does. This is so, however, because of his belief in the *already effective* accomplishment of the secular eschatology of history in the modern state. Futurity is not privileged, because already the present fulfills the past by bringing to light all the essential possibilities of freedom in history. Eternity finds its goal, produces itself temporally in this profane teleology. Kojève, for all his one-sidedness as a commentator, grasps the result of this, namely, a finally homogeneous history.[36] Time completed dialectically mediates the triumph of the identical, the same.

So Hegel's modernity consists not so much in his emphasis on inwardness (this is an Augustinian, Kierkegaardian theme too), but on inwardness understood as a dialectical self-relation, which is entirely self-mediating. The greatness of our time, Hegel says, is that freedom is recognized. How is freedom described? Freedom is the *spirit at home with itself in itself*.[37] This is the idealism of self-relation in which thought thinking itself always dialectically obtains the final and privileged position. The absolute privilege of dialectical self-mediation extends to the whole historical process itself.

When we understand this, we have to ask: What has become of the speculative? Is the speculative any longer the opening of philosophical mind to time's other, an opening marking the *noesis* of the Platonic philosopher or the *theōria* of the Aristotelean metaphysician. Or does speculation, as dialectically self-mediating thought, become the mind's *mirror play of self-thinking*, for which there is no real other. The *speculum* literally is a mirror. But now the *speculum* is no longer a glass in which we divine the other darkly, but a reflecting "other" that is bright but in itself empty, an empty middle or medium that serves the self as a dialectical means for returning back to itself. The *speculum* becomes an emptied glassy other in which the mind, seeking enlightenment, sees only itself. Enlightenment is simply the speculative seeing of the self, by the self, in the other that is not other, that is itself.

"*Die Zeit ist der Begriff selbst der da ist. . .*" *Time is the concept that is there*, as Hegel provocatively suggests in the *Phenomenology*[38]— a saying that Kojève exploits to the hilt. What does the *da*, the "there," mean? Must we interpret it dialectically or metaxologically? If the dialectically self-mediating process of history reduces speculation to this mirrorplay of self-thinking in the empty mirror, must not the other in the middle become a subordinated means? Does Hegel not land back in the view of history as the transcendental process of the self-validation of reason (as in the *Phenomenology*), and with the difficulties mentioned above (in "Radical and Moderate Historicism"), most acutely concerning history as the *causa sui* of a surrogate eternity: the *causa sui* history that would do away with eternity, close in on itself by closing out eternity as other, by presenting itself as eternity's temporal surrogate? The historicist self keeps polishing the mirror in the belief that thus only will it continue to see itself, or see itself better. In fact, its polishing of the mirror serves, not so much a more penetrating self-knowledge, but the reiterated rubbing out of the faded traces of the radical other. The self-knowing that seems to shine so bright in fact produces a reflecting void, empty of the true other. This shining void is the dark night of history, without the radical other.

In sum: When time is completed dialectically, the upshot is that history mediates the triumph of the identical, the same. Every otherness, including the most mysterious otherness of all, the transcendence of eternity, is said to be behind us. It is against this belief, all pervasive in historicist modernity, that Kierkegaard protests in the epigraph I cited at the outset. We now can see more clearly how Hegel incarnated the ambiguities of his own time concerning time and eternity. His understanding of these ambiguities shows him also as their captive. Relative to this captivity, every effort to safeguard eternity as time's radical other protests passionately against the historicist complacency of Hegel's famous judgment: *Die Weltgeschichte ist das Weltgericht*. This judgment risks the hubris of immanence that preens itself on its rational superiority to all transcendence. This supposed speculative superiority is really founded on nothing but the dialectical hollowing out of eternity as time's other, a hollowing performed by this judgment itself. And yet this judgment is not the last judgment. Not touched by eternity, it does not touch eternity. Its hollowness rocks the cradle of the void negativity of historicist hubris. And after Heidegger's fall from grace, when Hegel says we must venerate the state as an "earthly-divinity (*Irdisch-Göttliches*),"[39] can we suppress the shudder of unease that passes through us?

The Dialectical Reduction of the Double Vision

We have seen how history as the progressive realization of reason follows the logical structure of Hegel's concept. Reason's historicization takes the form of a dialectical movement from the immediacy of the Oriental to the totally self-mediating freedom of the modern world, a dialectical movement that is hard to distinguish from a historical reduction of eternity to time. The logic of Hegelian history offers a secularized version of the religious representation of original unity, fall into division and doubleness, progress to mediated reunification. The *Vorstellung* of sacred history is transformed into the *Begriff* of secular history. Existentially put, Hegelian history reveals the final overcoming of the unhappy consciousness—the epitome of the dualistic opposition of time and eternity.

Can this dialectical reduction of the eternal be sustained, especially if it involves a complete exhaustion of its otherness to time? One can claim that eternity is the other of time, but with Hegel eternity becomes time's own other in such a dialectical manner that time seems only to recognize *itself* once again. What more can we say of the eternal as other? I alluded to Hegel's categorization of Jewish and Medieval transcendence as dualistic alienations. One has to ask: If eternity exhaustively determines itself in its historical self-manifestation, does it not make itself *redundant as other*? Must time's other be collapsed into time? Is there a transcendence that is not entirely mediated by history?

Consider here three of the major relevant options. These are: (*A*) What I will call a *double vision*, where eternal reason is still different from historical reason, such that a gap of otherness remains between them, even in their dialectical mediation, or perhaps metaxological intermediation. (*B*) One might have a *singular vision* in which history is the dialectical self-mediation of eternity. In this second case, history is swallowed in eternity; this singular vision gives to eternity the ontologically privileged position. (*C*) One might have another *singular vision*, but in this case one in which eternity is dialectically self-mediated by history, such that *history* has the privileged position. In this third case, eternity is understood in terms of an abstract reason that is made determinate *and* appropriated by dialectical reason in history; eternity is dialectically incorporated into time.

Where do we locate Hegel relative to these options? The double vision of *A* is rejected by Hegel. I qualify this: the double vision is rejected as the final view. The double vision as an initial dualism is granted by Hegel in this qualified sense, namely, as an abstract starting point to be surpassed or transcended, not only by logic but also by concrete history. In Hegel's scheme, any form of the double vision is rejected as an end. Such a double vision for Hegelian dialectic is always an oppositional otherness that is to be overcome, mediated in a higher *coincidentia oppositorum*. In fact, the progressive realization of spirit and reason in history shows just this dialectical rhythm of the mediation of all such doubles, double visions (again see Hegel's responses to Judaism, Catholicism, Platonism, Kantianism, to mention some major doubles). The Hegelian middle that results is never a simple return to an immediate unity, but always an advance to a self-mediating totality. Indeed, this is what the modern state is for Hegel and there is much at stake when Hegel speaks of the state as God's march through history (see above on the "earthly-god"). In brief, we can locate Hegel in relation to double vision of *A*, only to the extent that *A* is seen as *the problem* to be overcome dialectically.

If *A* is where Hegel is not, can we locate him more affirmatively relative to the singular visions of *B* and *C*? The singular vision of *B* would correspond to a variation on Neoplatonism, but one filtered through modernity, in the sense of trying to give due weight to historical consciousness. By contrast, the singular vision of *C* would correspond to a modern version of what we might call "post-religious reason," a version which, as stated, already contains anticipations of thinkers like Marx. In Hegel's own case, post-religious reason is defined in terms of the speculative *Aufhebung* of religion into philosophy in absolute spirit. What this essentially means is that post-religious reason will have to overcome dialectically any trace of the *double vision* in religion.

There is a difficulty here in that even in *B* itself (Neoplatonism qualified by some sense of history) certain traces of the double vision are inevitable. The only way to make the singular vision of *B* intelligible to temporal reason is to grant time and eternity as other to each other; for only thus can time be grasped as other to eternity. So while this single vision denies any radical other to eternity (since eternity in *B* is the self-mediating totality), in fact we philosophers have to appeal to an other to eternity to make good the claim that eternity is the dialectically self-mediating totality which includes time within itself. This inevitable appeal to some sense of eternity's other, however minimal, reinstates something of the double vision and hence of transcendence. As I claimed above, in his pursuit of a singular vision, even Hegel has to grant some version of the double view as a starting point.

The real question is the persistence of this double, its rightful and inevitable persistence, against the claims of the dialectical middle to mediate completely the otherness of eternity. I suggest that though claiming to take his stand in a dialectical middle, Hegel actually wavers between the speculative univocity of *B* and the historicist univocity of *C*. This is a major reason why, after Hegel, his dialectical middle is split so radically by the divide between Right and Left Hegelians. The Right Hegelian incorporates the double vision of *A* and the singular vision of *C* into the singular vision of *B*: time becomes ultimately unreal because the otherness between time and eternity is dialectically incorporated into the self-mediation of eternity. This entails a dialectical reduction of time to *eternalist univocity*. I think this is the kind of Hegelian eternalism that Kierkegaard so vehemently protested as falsely attenuating the finitude of the particular "I," called upon to decide its ambiguous existence in the test of sometimes equivocal time. Moreover, Kierkegaard protests in the name of a different eternity.

By contrast, the Left Hegelian reduces the dialectical middle from the other side. Instead of the dialectical reduction of time to eternalist univocity, we find the dialectical reduction of eternity to *historicist univocity*. Any transcendence as implied by the double vision of *A* is radically rejected: eternity as other is rejected as the self-estranged power of humanity projected into transcendence. Such eternity is said to be equivocal, duplicitous: it is an other that is no other, since it is only the power of time itself projected into an alienated otherness. We can say that Marx reduces the speculative vision of *B* to the historicist univocity of *C*: the alienating equivocalness of Neoplatonic eternity, all eternity, is debunked by the post-religious reason of the revolutionary philosopher whose only element is time.

I am not just saying that Right and Left Hegelians split the Hegelian middle, albeit in different directions, such that neither does justice to Hegel's complexity. This is true, but I also think that Hegel is inclined in the same direction as Marx, namely, to reduce *B* to *C*, albeit in a more dialectically rich, yet more ambiguous form, than in Marx. For Hegel it is not that Neoplatonic eternity is *debunked* by post-religious reason: more complexly, Neoplatonic eternity is *aufgehoben* by post-religious reason. Hegel will claim that essential to this *Aufhebung* is the moment of preservation. His continued insistence on this moment of preservation accounts, I believe, for his wavering relative to the singular visions of *B* and *C*.

I know that Hegel would reject the implication that there is any wavering in the *Aufhebung*. Why? Because wavering implies that the double vision is not entirely transcended. Yet if Hegel inclines to the singular vision of *C* with respect to *concrete history* (as we saw above with respect to world-history), he inclines towards the singular vision of *B* with respect to the *Idea* as an eternal self-diremption and self-reunification of the absolute (as we saw above with respect to logic and the history of philosophy). The wavering might seem to be merely the dialectical interplay of the two sides. Yes and very well; but the question is whether that interplay allows the otherness of the other side, namely, the transcendence of eternity to be in its otherness. If there is to be this continuing interplay, then the otherness of eternity as transcendent has also to continue. Hegel seems to say something like this (in part anyway) at the logical level of the Idea (though even here one wonders if eternity is just logical possibility, albeit in the dynamic Hegelian sense of power to self-actualize in time). But at the concrete historical level, the interplay is finally resolved from the side of history. The dialectical wavering is overcome in the realization of reason in history, a realization which, in principle, is complete. This realization must imply the claim to have surpassed all wavering, and hence the surpassing of all double visions into a singular, self-mediating totality.

Let me put it in terms of the fourfold sense of being outlined in the introduction. A difficulty with any defense of eternity as other, with any version of the double vision, is that it bogs down in a dualistic opposition, which yields the *equivocity* of a difference between time and eternity without the possibility of their mediation. Often this equivocity results from thinking of eternity in *univocal* terms: eternity is said to be a static univocity of being, beyond the equivocal mutability of time. Eternity simply is, hence it is univocal being; time both is and is not, hence it is equivocal becoming. Becoming's doubleness is duplicitous; in opposition to this we seek, say, the univocal eternity of Parmenides, or the Platonic *eidos* as the univocal unit of immutability.

I think we need to avoid any double vision which is a mere equivocity without any mediation of difference. The systematic view developed in *Desire, Dialectic, and Otherness* goes beyond this wavering between equivocal becoming and static univocal eternity.[40] This is related to the metaxological between as pointing, through becoming as openly self-mediating and intermediating, towards the absolute original as an agapeic other. The agapeic other, even in mediating the between, lets the other be as other; hence its intermediation never reduces the double to a singular process of self-mediation. Hegel also wants to avoid such dualistic equivocity between time as equivocal becoming and eternity as univocal stasis. But in mediating the difference, he dialectically produces his own peculiar univocity in finally privileging *self-mediation.*

This *dialectical univocity*, as we might term it, in turn, produces its corresponding *dialectical equivocity*. This is the wavering between the singular visions of *B* and *C*. Hegel's dialectical equivocity is his wavering between two dialectical reductions: on the one hand, the dialectical reduction of time to eternalist univocity; on the other hand, the dialectical reduction of eternity to historicist univocity. But just in that dialectical equivocity we discover the *non-dialectical* persistence of the doubleness, against the claim of dialectical speculation to have produced the *Aufhebung*, hence complete mediation, of the two by reduction to a single self-mediating totality.

Does Hegel really work out a satisfactory relation of eternal concept and concrete history. I do not think so. I suspect that any effort to do so, which also wants to preserve the difference between time and eternity, must at some point bring us back to some version of the double vision of *A*, hence to the ultimate otherness of the eternal. This might bring us to a metaxological intermediation of the two, rather than the dialectical self-mediation of time in eternity or eternity in time. Hegel's whole account of the realization of reason in history corresponds to what in *Desire, Dialectic, and Otherness* I have called an erotic absolute in contrast to an agapeic absolute.[41] An erotic absolute is one that is initially marked by a certain lack or indeterminacy; to complete itself concretely and overcome its initial lack, it must articulate itself in time; time is hence the necessary process of articulate self-development by which the absolute mediates with itself and brings itself to completion. Thus, in Hegel, eternity in itself becomes a mere abstraction. Hence inevitably any claims to transcendent otherness are for him merely abstract and in themselves empty. As this abstraction, eternity inevitably is lacking concrete determination and needs history to effect the process of the absolute's own self-determination and completeness.

This is why Hegel concludes the *Phenomenology* with the citation and alteration, not to say disfiguration of Schiller's lines:

> From the chalice of this realm of spirits
> Foams forth for Him his own infinitude.

Without history absolute *Geist* would be a lifeless solitary (*leblose Einsame*), Hegel says. This is how Schiller's lines run:

Though the highest Being (*das höchste Wesen*) found no equal,
From the chalice of the whole realm of souls
There foams to him—infinitude.

It is significant that Schiller's poem is entitled Friendship, *die Freundschaft*. Any hint of the agapeic otherness of the ultimate will be transposed by Hegel into an erotic conception of a dialectically self-mediating absolute. This is why Hegel excludes the line just preceding the ones he cites. The line is very clear: The highest Being found no equal (*kein Gleiches*). I read in this a suggestion of the unequalizable being of the transcendent, in my terms the agapeic absolute relative to which every concept of ours in unequal. By silencing this inequality, and by altering the last two lines in conformity with an erotic absolute, Hegel wills to silence every inequality of the absolute. By this silence he claims to think the absolutely circular absolute, the seamless whole wherein all otherness, including the ultimate otherness of the Unequal, is conquered as a subordinate moment in a process of dialectical self-mediation.

With respect to Hegel's absolute as erotic, we must say that an absolute that in itself is merely abstract and empty and a lifeless monad seems like no genuine absolute at all. Consider these two ways in which Hegel describes his *Logic*: on the one hand as the "exposition of God as He is in His eternal essence before the creation of nature and finite spirit"; on the other hand as "the kingdom of shadows." A few pages separates these two descriptions. But let us perform a little non-dialectical logic on them, and we reach this conclusion: God in His eternal essence is identical with the kingdom of shadows! The eternal excess of God's light is indistinguishable from the kingdom of shadows. Eternity in its essence becomes the darkness of a lacking abstraction. How then is it possible to understand whence, in the first place, comes the energy of being in the indeterminate lack that supposedly necessitates the drive of the abstract absolute into time?

The only way I know how to approach the problem is to try to think, in contrast to an erotic absolute, what I call an "agapeic absolute." The very lack driving erotic articulation is itself only possible on the basis of the prior original energy of being which in itself is plenitude rather than lack. The negative self-determination of an erotic absolute through time points to a more fundamental affirming of being as plenitude, to the original energy of being as agapeic creation. Here one might argue against Hegel's understanding of being as the emptiest, most poverty-stricken of categories. What is at stake in the plenitude of the original energy of being is not a category at all. One might metaxologically read the affirmation

"Being is," as deeply other to this indigent being of the Hegelian category. One might read the affirmation "Being is" as a doubling of the original energy of being as plenitude, as a redoubling which grounds the basis of a real two. Doubling, redoubling would be the creative generosity of the ultimate origin as an agapeic absolute.

By contrast with an erotic absolute, an agapeic absolute in itself is absolute: in itself it is not lacking indeterminacy, but a plenitude that is more than any determinate being, a plenitude that is over-determined and infinite. Hence, its relation to time is not that of a necessary determination to fill up its own lack. An agapeic absolute is not initially the indeterminacy of lack, but the affirmative indeterminacy of inexhaustibility, that is, the overdetermination, more than determinacy, of plenitude in itself. An agapeic absolute allows the absolute to be absolute in itself, allows it to be other to finitude; and also allows finitude to be other in itself.

For this is what agapeic creation would be: the giving of being to the other that lets that other-being be as other. To be *itself*, agapeic eternity does not have to recover finite being; hence finite being can be let be as irreducibly other. Yet this double otherness does not preclude mediation, or better intermediation. But the *inter*, the between can never be entirely mediated in terms of self-mediation alone, whether from the side of the eternal or the temporal. Even if we say that God is the privileged mediator, the supreme mediator, the freedom of the other as finite in the context of agapeic creation could not be reduced to God's own dialectical self-mediation. Agapeic creation gives an irreducible otherness to the being of finite creatures. This is an ontological freedom that may always shatter the dialectical claims of a singular, totalized self-mediation. Another expression of this irreducibility concerns evil and dialectic, to which I will return.

Thus, I argue for the continuation of the double. The double for us is ineradicable. I do not say that the double is necessarily a dualism. For dualism begets an essentially oppositional relation between two terms or realities, and in the long run an oppositional relation generally tends to undercut itself. Hegel is right to draw attention to the way dualistic opposition, carried forward by the flow of becoming or thought through by the dynamism of mind, tends to deconstruct itself dialectically as an opposition. The opposition opposes itself. Hegel reads the self-opposition of dualism in terms of the reinstate-ment of unity. In *some* cases I read it as the reinstatement of a mediated unity, but in *other* cases it must be read as the restoration of a *different double*—in this sense of a restoration of positive interplay between two terms irreducible to each other. This interplay is not simply dialectical self-mediation. The preserved double that is not a dualistic opposition points to a sense of otherness that is not the dialectically self-mediated otherness of Hegel. It is the otherness of *community*, but again not in Hegel's sense of a dialectically self-mediating whole.

I argue that the double is irreducible when the two terms in interplay are themselves dialectically *self*-mediating beings. The mediation between two beings, each of which is dialectically self-mediating in a non-closed way, is not itself just another form of dialectical *self*-mediation. If it were, this would be to reduce the double to a unity. This cannot be, because a being that already is dialectically self-mediating is so internally complex as to constitute an entire world unto itself. Such a world would be a kind of "open whole," a description that itself is double or paradoxical from the standpoint of closed totality.[42] Hence an open whole contains its own inward otherness that is never simply available as a moment for the self-mediation of some other being, nor indeed for *its own* complete self-mediation. If this non-availability is then double, that is, if we have more than one open whole, we have a redoubled recalcitrance to any *singular* dialectical self-mediation. Doubleness appears and reappears. The redoubling of doubleness would be the openness of actual infinitude. Plurality itself becomes the generosity of creation, the irreducible gift of the agapeic origin.

We have to resort again to metaxological intermediation. None of the beings that are dialectically self-mediating are closed on themselves; their own internal dialectic is open. Moreover, their inward self-mediation is also open to the otherness within the self itself; the self is marked by its own *inward* otherness. Hence its own dialectical self-mediation can never be elevated to any putative closure of complete self-transparency. This is the resistance to closure only from one side. But if the other side is also an open dialectical self-mediating being, the same inherent recalcitrance to dialectical totalization prevails. Metaxological intermediation is simply respect for the richness, complexity and community of ownness and otherness that is going on, always and already. Ownness and otherness and metaxological community escape beyond final encapsulation. But such an "escaping" can be acknowledged as such. Nor is this an escape from mediation; the task of self-knowledge and knowing the other is not short-circuited or put aside.

On the contrary, we are driven in further ceaseless search. But this is now marked by humility before such otherness, whether inward or transcendent. The other of time escapes speculative totalization. But one does not, one cannot cease, one will not cease to think speculatively. Philosophy's reasonable dream of the ultimate otherness renounces all totalizing hubris. In this renunciation, speculative philosophy is renewed as thought's restless exigency to still think otherwise what is other to thought, to think what we can hardly think: the absolute original as the absolute other.

Chapter 2

Speculation and Cult:
On Hegel's Strange Saying:
Philosophy is God-service

Philosophy, Cult, and the Instrumentalization of Mind

Hegel's philosophy presents a progressive dialectical *Aufhebung* of all otherness. It attenuates the otherness of the trans-historical, leading to its appropriation by the secular mediations of profane history. I claimed a significant equivocity in Hegel's speculative thought of the dialectical reconciliation of time and eternity. I do not now retract this claim but neither do I say that Hegel is a simple reductionist. One cannot gainsay that he presents his philosophy as speculative and hence as non-reductionist in intent. Yet precisely his equivocity makes available the dialectical means that might be used for the reduction not only of religion, but also of philosophy itself. Instead of retracting the claim of Hegel's equivocity, I explore further (in this chapter and the next) its manifestation in the relation of philosophy and religion.

We must counter the instrumentalizing of philosophical reason and rethink the speculative sense as naming a non-instrumental mindfulness. A like instrumentalizing can happen with religion. I cite Marx and Nietzsche as paradigmatic, though in very different ways. Both instrumentalize philosophical reason to undermine its putative "sovereignty"; both reformulate its task in the services of something other to reason. Marx instrumentalizes mind to make philosophy an ancilla of the proletarian revolution; Nietzsche instrumentalizes mind to debunk reason's claim to sovereignty, to unmask it as in the service of powers other than rational, namely, a secret will to power—the debunking and unmasking are now to serve a less dishonest, a more artistically affirmative manifestation of the same will to power.

83

With both the instrumentalization of philosophy and religion proceeds in tandem. In Marx's case, religion is said to be exploited by the ruling powers to make more manageable those whom they exploit. The real truth of religion is not in religion itself but in the more basic operation of political and economic power that uses and manipulates the religious as its own strategic tool. The opium of the masses serves to anaesthetize the oppressed to their own alienated condition and hence perpetuates it. Religion is instrumental—the altar is ancilla to the throne, the priest is tool of the king. (Here Lenin is more extreme, cruder than Marx.) Cunning priestcraft makes use of superstition, instrumentalizes the holy as a means to an end outside of itself. Since religion is the most powerful instrumentality of the ruling powers that ideologically masks the truth of exploitative power, the critique of religion provides the basis of all critique. The whole alienated system of means and ends—religion as the means, exploitation as the end—must be destroyed. The destruction of the religious will serve the construction of the revolution. Thus, the Marxist critique—especially evident in the criticism of Hegel—is essentially dependent on this *double instrumentalization*, that is, of both philosophy and religion.

Nietzsche's purposes are deeply at odds with Marx's, but he essentially shares this instrumentalizing of religion (its sources in both are in the French Enlightenment). For Nietzsche, everything is a means to an end, an instrument of the will to power. Religion is simply the most historically influential instrumentality of the will to power. In Nietzsche's view, it is the instrumentality of a group the *opposite* of Marx's rulers, namely, the powerless: the religious is a means to an end, the tool by which the *slaves* try to give the masters a bad conscience about their otherwise guiltless expression of will to power. Nietzsche particularly wanted to destroy Christianity: while it was an instrument of the will to power, it was a perverse, indeed inverse instrument of that will, since it infected the will to power with a bad conscience about its own natural expression. The critical task of Nietzschean thought is to expose the perversion; the affirmative task is to redirect the guiltless will to power towards its affirmative concretion, a new Dionysian art of life. While not directly tied, as Marx is, to the critique of Hegelianism, Nietzsche, too, performs the double instrumentalization, of philosophy and religion. The philosopher evidences only a more rationalized expression, that is, a more secret and cunning form of the priestly will to power.

I argue against this double instrumentalization. While obviously open to instrumentalization, philosophy and religion are not necessarily and essentially instrumentalities in the above senses. Both are

what I would call finalities or integrities: finalities, not in any sense
of bringing the dunamis of mind or being to a dead closure, but modes
of mindfulness that engage what is ultimate, ways of being mindful
that themselves try to approximate ultimacy; integrities, as embodying
something of the realized, yet open promise of human wholeness. Both
may struggle to break free, so far as this is possible, from falsifying
instrumentalities. Both may struggle for a spiritual honesty, an
ethical and intellectual integrity, beyond the means/ends system of
instrumental life. Each may be beyond instrumental subordination
and exploitation, each a free integrity of being and mind.[1]

I say, so far as is possible, since this is the essential ideal.
Undoubtedly the practice is always impure, mixed. But this is no
argument against the essential ideal. Every genuine ideal has to deal
with the reality of mixture; its genuineness as ideal is not necessarily
compromised by that mixture; the ideal comes to its genuineness in
the metaxological middle in which we find ourselves. My refusal of
the double instrumentalization will be continuous with Hegel's
assigning of both religion and philosophy to absolute spirit. In so far
as this term tries to name the ultimate, in so far as it transcends the
sphere of objective spirit where the system of instrumentalities reigns,
I take it that Hegel wants to call our attention to modes of mindfulness
that free themselves from the system of instrumentalities and that
hence are intrinsically self-justifying.

Relative to this double instrumentalization, I will reflect on a
startling assertion in Hegel's *Lectures on the Philosophy of Religion*:
philosophy is worship, God-service (*Gottesdienst*).[2] This sounds strange
today, exotic even, given philosophy's long infatuation throughout
modernity with science. True, the ideal of philosophy as science has
recently been attacked. Still philosophy, it is said, requires the
analysis of concepts: its spirit is critical, not reverential. The philosopher is a conceptual technician, not a priest. Did not Hegel himself,
well before Husserl's ideal of philosophy as *strenge Wissenschaft*, insist
that philosophy must not be edifying, and must always present itself
in the shape of systematic science? What could be further from
worship? What God then could Hegel serve? What could be the cult
of Hegel's God-service?

This is not the only count on which Hegel and worship seem
peculiar partners. Hegel, it is said, carried rationality to the verge
of absurdity. His system is said to be reason's tyranny over the
irrational, an announcement of art's death[3] and religion's completion
and supersession. The religious person is wont to protest that Hegel
invades the transcendent and reduces it to immanence, storms

eternity and relocates it in the flux of time. We have looked at this
issue ourselves and have not held Hegel guiltless.

There is more. Hegel—it is said—is a philosopher of power: he will
let nothing be, but will swallow all within the Leviathan of the system.
He is the type of the rationalist blasphemer, as if to enter his system
were to go through Hell's maw. Does he not epitomize the philosopher's
pride in daring to compare his *Science of Logic* to God's thoughts before
the creation of nature and finite spirit? Is not this to run roughshod
over humble finitude and ill conceal one's hubris? Does not Hegel,
as Kojève implies,[4] arrogate for himself the title "wise man," one for
whom the distinction between man and God is naught? Hegel's God-
service would then be the cult of his own mind, thinking itself
absolutely, like Aristotle's *noēsis noēseōs*. But such hubris, in Hegel's
case, is not merely theoretical, as in Aristotle, but is said to reflect
the modern will to power. So Hegel becomes a father of fascism.
Disrespect for limits, lack of moderation, will to power, excess spilling
over into violence: these become the legacy of Hegel, this Hegel.[5]

How then can one possibly say: Philosophy is God-service? Is Hegel
sly? Is Hegel slippery? Is he mocking those who would sew him within
his system? What God is served? *Geist? Vernunft?* Jesus? Apollo?
Humanity? Did he not concur in the *Aesthetics: Humanus heisst der
Heilige?* Our god—logos: so said Freud, and thus signed himself a late
heir of Socrates. Does Hegel too adore logos? Is he secretly baiting
his religious readers, as Kierkegaard suspected? Or is he more
cunning than his commentators, and in his own way open to otherness? Does not the assertion conceal much? What then does it mask,
perhaps dissimulate? Does it not also reveal much, for those who have
ears to hear?

Suppose we read it in the way Nietzsche recommends we read his
own aphorisms, namely, as overdetermined condensations of a whole
world of concentrated thinking? To read such an aphorism, as
Nietzsche says, one must not be a modern man, but a kind of cow—
rumination is necessary.[6] If we ruminate on Hegel like a cow can we
chew some non-modern nourishment from the suggestion of
Gottesdienst? I take comfort in the thought of the post-Hegelian
philosopher as a speculative cow. In the night wherein we think, contra
Hegel himself, all cows are not black. Can we post-Hegelian cows find
secrets in Hegel? Must we quietly pause in indicting philosophy as
reason's tyranny, or as the logical consolation offered by the conceptual
negation of finitude? Must philosophy not entail a different affirmation of finitude in relation to finitude's own ground? Must it not point
to a certain relativity of finitude and its ultimate other, the infinite?

Might not Hegel, too, be dialectically subtle, a masked thinker, intimately cognizant of the pathos of distance?

Suppose we recall a remark attributed to Hegel: reading the newspaper is the morning prayer of modern man. A Marxist would like this, I suppose, this invocation of instrumental history. In modernity newspapers are like the oracles of world-history, wherein we hermeneutically divine the political noise of the day, rather, the political noise of yesterday as prophetic of the world-historical noise of tomorrow, the day after tomorrow. But Hegel's statement is often taken much too solemnly, for instance by Hyppolite. Can we not conceive of Hegel with a sense of humor? Is his tone ironic, at least half ironic, sardonic perhaps? In this ironic reference to the journalistic God-service of utilitarian modernity, might one not sense a bitterness about the spiritlessness of the age?

Think here of the implicit contempt in Hegel's vehement claim: A nation without a metaphysics is a like a temple without a holy of holies. This means—the political state is spiritually bankrupt because it is oblivious to the sacred truth of Hegel's metaphysics. Think of the speculative disdain in: Philosophy now goes in its morning dressing gown, instead of wearing the robes of the high priest. Listen again: Philosophers are like a consecrated priesthood, set apart and offered up as a sacrifice to spirit.' When we ruminate like a speculative cow on these statements, this old question keeps coming up: Is Hegel canonizing the status quo or is he trying to transubstantiate it, consecrate its promise of divine truth? The latter would mean distance from, disquiet with, its profane reality. It would mean war with the idols of the time—in the name of the spiritual promise of the time. Is it the cultivation of this promise that secretly nurtures, inspires the cult of philosophy?

These questions require us to go beyond the Hegelian letter to the secret sources out of which a philosopher thinks. We need to do this because a truncated Hegel is too easily available today. The kinds of criticisms first patented by a Kierkegaard are easily repeated without any struggle with the enigma of Hegel. Interestingly, quasi-Kierkegaardian criticisms of philosophy have been formulated by thinkers who are hostile to the religious alternative that Kierkegaard himself recommends against Hegel. Again I think of Nietzsche. Nietzsche is hostile, not only to speculative metaphysics, but also to religion, which is the exoteric complement of metaphysics: Platonism is metaphysics, as Heidegger reiterated, while Christianity is Platonism for the masses. This view is pervasive in European thought in our century, as my invocation of Heidegger makes all too plain. It claims to go to the secret sources of philosophy but only to expose its bad complicity with religion.

There is a line of appropriating Hegelian thought that would exploit it for a similar debunking end. Again the Left Hegelian line of Feuerbach, Bauer, Ruge, Stirner, Marx himself, comes to mind. The irony here with respect to Kierkegaard is that Hegelian thought is not only full square in the tradition of speculative metaphysics, but it is not unequivocally a hostile debunking of religion. Kierkegaard is not always generous enough to the piety of philosophy itself. From the standpoint of those who, in post-Nietzschean fashion, execrate religion, Kierkegaard and Hegel turn out to be much closer than Kierkegaard himself might like. Both claim to be some kind of Lutheran. Perhaps it is too strong to say that all post-Nietzschean thought execrates religion. Sometimes the execration itself evidences just that spiritual seriousness of passionate inwardness that Kierkegaard himself admired. We should say, in a nasal metaphor of which Nietzsche himself made excessive use, that post-Nietzschean thought does not execrate religion but sniffs at it. But to sniff is not to think a source, and we must think as well as sniff.

Philosophy is *Gottesdienst*. This may have the sound of pious platitude, and perhaps it did for some of Hegel's hearers in his own time. I hear it not as platitude but as a provocative. There is also a species of Hegelian sniffing. This sniffing suggests: Why must Hegel embarrass us? Why is Hegel so wicked? Some post-Hegelian Hegelians will say: Hegel's statement is concessionary religious metaphor to be accorded no real philosophical significance. Hegel spoke the contemporary idiom of religion, in order to reach the speculative place where most of his audience lived. But *we* (who are "we"?), we are the intellectual beneficiaries of the superior enlightenment that post-Hegelian history affords, and *we*, of course, have been progressively liberated from that place of religious thrall. And so there is no need *for us* to take that language seriously. This is an Hegelian way of remaking Hegel to conveniently fit the secular mould of post-Nietzschean tastes. Kierkegaard the antagonist remakes Hegel into an abstract thinker in order to attack him. But here we have the Hegelian commentators who would remake Hegel in order to preserve him, or one suspects, preserve *themselves*, from the cultural embarrassments that religious language evokes for them in our more radically secularized time.

I demur. We post-Hegelian cows should not shirk such embarrassments, even if it means rubbing the grain of post-Hegelian history against itself. An honest philosopher, and especially any thinker who declaims the postmodern slogans of "openness to otherness," must take religion seriously, must give it the most serious thought, as did Kierkegaard and Hegel. Religion is a dissident other. So let us listen to the voice of its dissidence. We need to take seriously the interplay of philosophy and religion, as Hegel does. Indeed we need to take seriously the ancient proximity between philosophy and religion, a proximity that does not exclude the most profound tension and struggle. The most bitter quarrels can be family feuds.

This too applies to the "ancient quarrel" of philosophy and poetry. Art, religion and philosophy constitute a familial community of spiritual others. The affinities and struggles generated in that community are too nuanced to be articulated by the polemical vituperation of a Nietzsche (but he was only an heir of vulgar Voltaire and the Encyclopaedists on this point) that would lump priest and philosopher together, partners in a conspiracy to foist false ideals on the human race, ideals that are insidious because presented under the banner of truth. This is the hermeneutics of suspicion flattening the complex otherness of the religious and philosophical tradition. This is a kind of *niaiserie* that polemical philosophizing easily conjures up to make its own case easier. Let us not congratulate ourselves prematurely on our own hermeneutical superiority.

Philosophy is *Gottesdienst*. The most well-known utterance of this comes from the *Lectures on the Philosophy of Religion*. But the phrase or variants of it well up again and again throughout the Hegelian corpus. This welling up alerts us to a hidden source of thought. I take seriously the fact that Hegel's use of this word spans his *entire* career, from the *Differenzschrift* to the late lectures on religion. In his first major publication, the *Differenzschrift*, he says: Art and speculation too are *Gottesdienst*. The term also appears in his *Lectures on Aesthetics*.[8] Either Hegel was too lazy a thinker to worry about repeating himself, or else something important is here at stake, and hence the phrase returns again and again. I adopt this second alternative. Consider, too, Hegel's attention to devotion/worship in his introduction to the history of philosophy. The task of philosophy is repeatedly expressed in its dialectical kinship with and difference from its most important other, namely, religion. I repeat the point: religion is philosophy's most important other. If we do not grant this, we might as well junk absolute spirit entirely. Without this, Hegelian commentary simply mangles the spirit of Hegel.

Philosophy and Cult: The Return of the Repressed?

But perhaps I am too harsh in identifying post-Nietzscheans as ideological execrators or hermeneutical sniffers at the religious. For the kind of kinship that interests me percolates into post-Hegelian discourse, albeit betraying the bad conscience of intellectuals timorous lest they be seen as in any way sympathetic to religion. The anxieties of religious influence cannot mask the return of the repressed in the irreligious itself. Let me offer a few examples, all of which recall us to a sense of sacred otherness beyond the mastery of instrumental reason.

Consider the cultus of Nietzsche.[9] Descendent of a line of Lutheran pastors, son of a pastor, as a child Nietzsche was nicknamed "The Little Pastor." At twenty he wrote a poem "To the Unknown God," which ends with the hope: "I want to know you, even serve you." Later he became the philosophical devotee of Dionysus, in opposition to the *Gottesdienst* of Socrates who devoted himself to Apollo.

Remember that Socrates himself, in the *Apology*, obsessively insists on his own "service to the god." The god has given him a station in life which he cannot desert (*Apology*, 28e). He is in vast poverty because of this service of the god (*tēn tou theou latreian;* 23c). That Socrates was never paid for this service (31c) points to philosophy as a non-instrumental service: the agapeic act of a *philos* who *philosophizes for nothing*; his poverty issues from the fact that he gives of himself. He himself is a kind of gift of the gods (31b); no greater good ever happened to Athens (30a). Socrates is transubstantiated into a sacrificial victim: since he is the god's elected one (see 29d–e, 30d–e), his killing will be the violence of an impiety. His death will be a desecration, like the killing of the criminal as a sacred figure.

Sly Nietzsche said that Apollonian Socrates was himself sly: a secret, suffering worshipper of Dionysus, masking this dark, chthonic *mustērion* with the excessively bright face of the Sun god. Like Plato, too, Hegel's cultic observance would seem to bow at this altar of Apollo, the serene Sun god. We should say that Nietzsche will not bow at the altar of Dionysus, but would rather dance around this suffering, festive god. But here Hegel and Nietzsche approach the same essential perplexity: the relation of art, religion, and philosophy, their responsive power, even saving power in the face of the basic discords, disunions of being. Hegel sees art and religion as dialectically mediated in philosophy. Nietzsche sees philosophy as masking and finally falsifying the deepest articulated truth, that of art, tragic art. It is extremely important to remember that the tragic art of the Greeks was not the aestheticist art of modernity. Tragic art is religious art. It is included in what Hegel calls *"Kunstreligion."* We could say without distortion that the tragic art of the Greeks is a *Gottesdienst* of Dionysus.

So though Nietzsche is vehemently opposed to Christianity, hence unlike Hegel, yet the religious and artistic are unified in Greek tragic art, performed in honor of the god Dionysus, with the god himself in attendance with his cohort of priests and hieratic followers. Tragic art is sacrificial art. It is art that makes sacred (the literal meaning of "sacrifice": *sacer facere*). Socrates' *Apology*, as I suggested, seems to offer us a philosopher's version of sacrificial art. Tragic art is one that makes suffering sacred. Thus in *The Birth of Tragedy*, Nietzsche calls for "festivals of world redemption and days of transfiguration." His faith in an *aesthetic* theodicy is to be taken in this strong festive or cultic sense.[10]

Nietzsche is quite like Kierkegaard in thinking that there is a redemption of life, other than philosophy can offer, and in rejecting the Hegelian supremacy of philosophy. This redemption is ultimately religious—Christian in Kierkegaard's case, pagan in Nietzsche's. Nietzsche's religiosity differs from Kierkegaard's Christianity in not being radically other to the aesthetic, where this means the festive celebration of the pagan earth and body. For Kierkegaard the aesthetic is pagan. Indeed he sees it as part of his own tangled destiny to seduce his contemporaries to Christianity through the aesthetic (as he puts it in the *Point of View*). By contrast, Nietzsche wants to seduce us *away* from Christianity through the aesthetic, and this means pagan religion.

To see how knotted the issue can be, it is interesting that Kierkegaard makes the charge of *paganism* against Hegel's *Christian* philosophy: the speculative system is really only aesthetic—a playing with possibility, albeit logical possibility. Multiple crisscrossings are possible between the aesthetic, the religious, the philosophical. And when Nietzsche says art is superior to philosophy, whether Socratic or Hegelian, it is his *Gottesdienst* that makes him say this. It is his pagan piety, his cultus of Dionysus. I would even say that there is a kind of aesthetic sacramentality about Nietzsche. This would set him against Hegel who dialectically subordinates the sacramental, since this needs the sensuous, needs the body, needs art, needs pagan nature. The Lutheran *Gottesdienst* of Hegelian thought leads to withdrawal from the sensuous other to the inner word.

Nietzsche is actually closer to Aquinas who points to "sacraments of nature" other than socially ritualized expressions.[11] What is the Greek festival? It is the *communal sacrament of Dionysus*. (Aristophanes knew this, and presents his own *parodia sacra* of the anaemic logical service of Socrates; see below chapter 6.) The sacramental need of otherness is weakened in Hegel's Lutheran retreat into the inner word, whose self-return and *Aufhebung* of otherness is speculatively completed in the philosophical *Begriff*. Hence, Hegel's remarks on the

Mass are essentially derogatory of the sensuous as such[12]: exteriority as such tends to be identified with alienation.

I return to this below in terms of Hegel's movement to reason after the unhappy consciousness where we find the problem of suffering, division, evil, godforsakenness, all issues that concerned Nietzsche in relation to the tragic art of Dionysus. Hegel's *Begriff* claims to redeem logically all ontological and epistemological divisions through its own dialectical self-mediation. Nietzsche's *Gottesdienst* of tragic art as the communal sacrament of Dionysus comes somewhat closer to the metaxological affirmation of otherness, which dwells in tension with the ineradicable otherness of the sacred for which sacramental sensuousness can serve as a sign.

Let me mention some others in whom the issue of the repressed religious surfaces. In Heidegger we find a post-Nietzschean anxiety about religion. Thus in his *Introduction to Metaphysics*, he pontificates that a religious thinker cannot ask a philosophical question. A Christian philosophy is a round square, he says; philosophy is Greek.[13] True and yet not true. This is really the voice of Kierkegaard again, only the prohibition in Heidegger works in a direction opposite to Kierkegaard, due to Heidegger's deference to Nietzsche's anti-religious orders. Heidegger's decree puts Christianity in suspension, in *epochē*. And yet if philosophy is Greek, Greek *theōria* itself is not suspended in such an *epochē*: metaphysics as *theōria* shares in the festival of speculative mind. The deep affinity of speculative mind and the religious celebration of festive being is ingrained in metaphysical *theōria*. The fundamental ontologist can put up the categorial "No Trespass" sign between philosophy and religion. But *both* philosophy and religion, as each capable of dissident otherness, at some point will walk past the forbidding sign. Certainly the most interesting philosophers are those least daunted by such categorial "No Trespass" signs.

Is it irrelevant that Heidegger studied to be a priest? (The oracular Wittgenstein, supreme pontiff of the ordinary language sect of analytical philosophy, also seriously thought of becoming a priest.) Is it irrelevant that part of the power of Heidegger's ontology springs from the way the word "Being" rides piggyback on the unarticulated resonances of the word "God"? Should we be surprised that a kind of sacerdotal aura attaches to the sage utterances of the later Heidegger? Heidegger himself crosses the "No Trespass" sign in his dialogue with the poet, Hölderlin. The question of the Holy itself crosses this dialogue with the poet, which is not "aesthetic" at all, but essentially about the problematic presence or absence of the Holy in modernity.

When Hegel himself spoke of philosophy as *Gottesdienst*, was not he too concerned with the piety of thinking? Did the painful memory of his mad friend, Hölderlin, sometimes cross his mind? Is Hegel's silence about this madness a sign of incomprehension, or is it a respectful reserve before something incomprehensible? Did Hegel ever think that Hölderlin's madness was a sacred folly, what I call an idiot wisdom? Or is idiot wisdom a sacredness beyond speculative dialectics?[14] One can say at least that Hegel's *Gottesdienst* was never intoned as a call to fervent prayer, in the shadow of the Nazi *Zeitgeist*, and in devotion to the "psychopathic god," as Hitler has been called. Hegel's *Gottesdienst* was never Heidegger's unholy hosanna of *Arbeitsdienst, Wehrdienst, Wissensdienst*.

My general point is the return in post-Hegelian thought of the otherness of religion, even if sometimes masked in aestheticist disguise or idolatrously perverted. Consider here Bataille, an admirer of Nietzsche. He attacks Hegel in the name of the sacred. Bataille's sense of Hegel is heavily influenced by a Kojèvian reading, itself influenced by a mixture of Marx and Heidegger. A different understanding is possible. Nevertheless, Bataille's remarks on the sacred are relevant in that he sought to surpass the instrumentalization of the sacred, spoken of above, and of which, in effect, he accuses Hegel. While this is not entirely fair to Hegel, Bataille's atheological religion rightly reminds us of the sacred as an excess beyond the principle of utility that embodies the calculative reason of instrumental mind.[15] The sense of the speculative I am trying to think is also in excess of utility and instrumental mind, though more from above, than from the dark below of Bataille's sometimes excremental vision. I will mention Bataille again in relation to laughter and dialectic.

At the opposite extreme to Bataille's dark sacred excess of the body, we find the return of sacred otherness in Levinas. Levinas' thought reminds us of Lev Shestov's contrast of Athens and Jerusalem. Shestov is one of those profound, radical philosophers who refuse the "No Trespass" sign mentioned above. He is a brilliant thinker of the limits of philosophy in relation to religion as an other. He is more direct and spiritually serious than Derrida, with a sense of the great tradition of speculative metaphysics more profound than Levinas'. He is unjustly neglected today, perhaps because the spiritlessness of the times does not quite know what to do with the force of his spiritual passion.

The philosophy of Levinas himself, in contrast to not a few post-structuralist thinkers, has always been marked by a spiritual seriousness that refuses to playact with the matter itself. Levinas speaks of *liturgy*, and when he does, he reminds us of something that crosses the frontier of religion and philosophy. "Philosophy is never a wisdom, for the interlocutor whom it has just encompassed has already escaped it. Philosophy, in an essentially liturgical sense, invokes the Other to whom the "whole" is told, the master or student." Yet, one recalls, the liturgy in Greek civic life related to a communal celebration, a public festival: the service to the community of a rich patron which reminds us a little of the *potlatch* that Bataille extols: expenditure without return: the religious festival as a "consumption" that transcends the instrumentalized system of means and ends. Levinas's reference to liturgy should recall us to the origin of philosophy in a transubstantiation of Greek religion: speculative mind as theoretical is metaphorically parasitical on religion, for the *theōroi* were religious delegates at the religious festivals. Should we draw from Levinas the thought: philosophy too might be a liturgy, a public work of thought in the service of the festival? The liturgy of philosophy escapes totalizing thought. Would not this cultus be a *Gottesdienst?* There is little doubt in Levinas' *Totality and Infinity* that religion and metaphysics are inseparable. Religion is beyond the ontology of totality; as metaphysical, religion is "the ultimate structure."[16]

I have cited just a few significant thinkers relative to the return of sacred otherness. Let us be clear what is at stake in our struggles with Hegel and let us give up shadowboxing. Let us be honest that the differences are not always so clear. Nor is it always easy to fix a univocal identity on Hegel himself. Let us be willing to grant a porosity, perhaps at times promiscuity, of philosophy and its others, in the present instance, art and religion. I say this in respect of elemental philosophical perplexity itself. For it is in that perplexity that the piety of the philosopher is cultivated. In that perplexity philosophical piety finds its home, in not being at home with the idols of the time.

Cult and Community:
The Manifested Otherness of the Sacred

I now offer some general reflections concerning worship. In the next section I turn to a negative form of worship with reference to Hegel's famous figure of the unhappy consciousness. I also resume the theme of eternity and the double vision. For Hegel the process of *self*-recognition in otherness is really at stake in the unhappy consciousness. This process is the birthplace of reason and spirit. This emergence means: the cultus of philosophical reason for Hegel is really the *self-cultivation* of spirit, which again proves to be dialectically self-mediating. Hegelian cultus as spirit's self-cultivation will throw light on Hegel's idea of philosophy, its strengths and limits, its reverences and idolatries.

Religious cultus is a many-sided reality, open to a plurality of possible interpretations. At one extreme, the relation between violence and cultus might be noticed, in the sacred negation of the sacrificial victim.[17] At the other extreme, cultus might be seen as the cultivation of the human being towards the height of its own sacred ultimacy, wherein its sacrifice affirms its community with the ultimate. I will emphasize a certain doubleness between these two extremes. This will let us pose strategic questions to Hegel, particularly concerning the irreducible otherness of the sacred. If philosophy is a *Gottesdienst*, we must ask if cultus articulates a balance of community and otherness between the human and divine wherein otherness is not attenuated. We must ask if philosophy conceptually respects that balance. Does Hegel reduce divine otherness to a moment of a self-mediating process, even granting that he identifies the community of the human and divine with this self-mediating process? I deny that this community can be entirely articulated in terms of a dialectically self-mediating whole. The middle between the human and divine is metaxological.

We must take note of a complex balance of identity and difference, sameness and otherness in cultus. Worship is a comportment towards the holy, our submission to and celebration of what is more ultimate than ourselves. At once the holy is both other to us and intimate. Cultus implicates us in the holy, yet the holy is not simply our creation. Rather it presents itself for reverence and veneration. If the holy is other to the human, it need not be interpreted (though it can be) as a radically dualistic opposite. In cultus the divine in its difference is thought to manifest itself as addressing the human and inviting its free response. Worship can be our free answer, now externalized and formalized in ritual, now veiled in the silent movement of inward spirit. It can be our free participation, by exterior deed and interior prayer, in the drama of the divine.

Worship testifies to the belief that God's nature is never to be completely hidden. It testifies to the presence of the sacred, not its empty absence. It turns us towards the hitherto hidden but now acknowledged presence of the divine. It lives in this acknowledged presence. A significant consequence may be the affirmative festivity of the cultus. Such sacred festivity does not simply lament the human being's wretchedness as a creature. To be is to be graced with being a creature. We are privileged, not punished with creaturehood. To worship may be to celebrate the sacred ground of the universe. God is the ground of the world: the festivity of cultus may be gratitude for the gift of being this ground gives.

There is doubleness and ambiguity in this. Human relatedness to the divine is fraught with tension. As a free celebrating comportment, worship inevitably entails some *difference* of the human and divine. This difference offers the middle space of a possible bond, but the same middle also grounds the possibility of our fundamental estrangement. Our free difference reveals itself in its power of rupturing negation. As free the human being can disrupt the given order of being; disrupting this order, his own being is wrenched out of joint, he cuts himself from community from his fellows, becomes hostile to the holy. Worship makes claim to heal such hostility. Converting the self from refusal to assent, from being shut up to being open, it claims to restore the basic bond with the sacred. It claims to overcome the divisions rending the self; it claims to help reinstate the self within the community; it claims to return the human being to participation in the divine order of the cosmos.

The public nature of the cult is important here. Public worship symbolizes this healing power of the sacred. Binding the individual to the community, it seeks to restore human beings, as communal others, to the sacredness of all being. From this point of view, even solitary worship, as with the prayer of the anchorite, cannot be interpreted as merely private or subjective. There is a certain sense in which worship as such, even in the radical intimacy of the inward spirit, repudiates the merely private. For a pure monad cultus would be impossible. The human being is human by virtue of its relativity to others, and most especially by its relatedness to the divine other. Worship would be the cultic mode of the basic being in relation, always a comportment which relates. Even the anchorite, in withdrawal, breaks contact with others at the level of distraction, but does so in order to reconstitute communion at another, more ultimate level. The person praying alone calls *out* in the silence; his silence reaches out to the silence of the sacred. True, there is a religious posture that is simply in flight from otherness; being alone becomes a withdrawal in the spirit of negation, not an affirmation in spirit. There is a solitude not open to the sacred but bent on the void.

Cultus ritually embodies the claim examined in the last chapter: a *dualistic opposition* of time and eternity cannot be ultimately sustained. What is here at stake is an otherness that is a *manifested* otherness. Thus, God is said to be transcendent yet also said, from Plato on, not to be envious.[18] The implication is that divinity does not remain monadically alone, jealous watcher of a separated eternity, an aloof catatonic. Worship enacts the presence of its manifested otherness. For this to be possible, the transcendent is not emptily transcendent but comes to appearance. Since everything existing participates, simply as being, in the ultimate ground of being, all being may occasion the appearance of the divine. All being may be hierophanous.

In cult, then, the divine is said to be at once both present and other. In this sense, the hierophany can be interpreted as the manifest otherness of the divine. Such an apparition of otherness cannot be understood in terms of the nugatory otherness of an absolutely inaccessible beyond. The worshipper responds to the hierophany as the embodiment of the divine, its incarnate revelation. This is why, as Hegel says, some notion of incarnation is necessary to all religion.[19] Nor need incarnation be a reduction of otherness; it may be a rich modality of the very being-there of the other. The necessity of incarnation is a condition of the possibility of cult without which every sacred gesture would be hollow. In this sense, the manifested otherness which is there but not reduced by being-there is the basis of the cultus as a communion. For the manifestation does not reduce the other in its appearing; the manifestation absolves the divine other from reduction in the appearing. The hierophanous manifestation guards, safeguards the divine mystery. A manifestation of otherness that is not reductive and that is also absolving is a metaxological relativity.

I hear a growing post-Nietzschean grumble in the background. It growls: please, please spare us; all this is just the old religious nostalgia. I start at the dread word "nostalgia," for it carries the skeptical contempt for all "*afterworldsmen*" that comes to us from the Nietzschean inheritance. Zarathustra's dismissive voice booms across our profane century. Nostalgia: desire to be unified with the divine, fear of one's finitude, rage at one's finitude, rancor at one's becoming, failure to dwell with its otherness. Nostalgia: metaphysical cowardice, corruption by the Platonic eros for eternity, absorption, forgetting in the *lēthē* of the afterworld. Ugly nostalgia: the ontological regression to sameness that the philosopher falsely presents as metaphysical progression to otherness and oneness with otherness. Must I go on?

But I must go on. I am momentarily transfixed by this boom of Zarathustra's voice, but the word "cultus" snaps the spell. There passes away from me that fear and trembling before the sacrifice of eternity that Nietzsche, religious Master of religious suspicion, tries to exact. The voice of Zarathustra rushes past, and now I hear the multiplied doppelgängers of his camp followers, the sound and the fury then fading away to a ghostly whisper of platitude. So I say: If the afterZarathustrians cannot bear this thinking on worship, let them skip the pages that offend their atheological pieties!

In the silence I would say that worship integrates the self with the sacred order, but I am no fool. With a bad Dionysian conscience

I realize that the word "integrate" will too easily fall to the withering charge of "nostalgia." I instead will venture to say, with a chastened but good Apollonian conscience: cultus necessarily cannot reduce the manifested otherness, because this otherness reveals the metaphysical dependency of finitude and the ultimate excess of infinitude. Metaphysical dependency? But is this not the very rancor against finitude? I cannot see why. It can be, as I will indicate below in discussing Hegel's unhappy consciousness and its characteristic devotion. But it need not be. It is possible to see the dependency on otherness that cultus celebrates as very different to the reductive sense of finitude as mere lack. In worship finitude is richly other; otherness is the gift of the agapeic origin.

I take this to be the metaphysical promise of phrases like: worship *consecrates* finitude, consecrates the ordinary by showing forth its extraordinariness. The "con-" (Latin, "*cum*") of "consecration" is always the bond of a difference that remains in the community wherein the otherness is manifested. The promise of the sacredness of finitude, the "*cum-*" of community—both are metaphysical bulwarks against "nostalgia" in the sense of reduction to simple, univocal sameness.

Thus in the sacred meal of the Eucharist, the ordinary things of our life, bread and wine, are transfigured. Bread and wine show the elemental necessities of our finitude: our need to eat and drink. (*Just eating and drinking and washing*, Feuerbach would say, in *The Essence of Christianity*.) Yet in the cultic consecration of finitude, bread and wine are liberated beyond finitude as merely lacking: they become the flesh of the God. The cult does not merely symbolize in the sense of represent a reality that is extrinsic to the cult. The cult does not extrinsically represent, but *performatively enacts* the presence of what the cult celebrates. In the feast of the agapē, bread and wine are *doubled*: themselves and yet other—the presence of a manifested other: flesh of the God.

In receiving this to his own flesh, the communion of the self cannot be an event of abstracted spirit. Cultic consecration is only possible for a bodied being. What is in play is the promised transformation of one's whole being. Far from the rancor of the "afterworldsmen," I take this as the sign of a mindfulness of being that in its promise is deeply affirmative of finitude. The divine is no longer to be seen as remote, jealously removed, but as moving within the finite world, at work and intertwined with its incarnate substance. Worship enacts this transfiguration of finitude. The cultus sings: God foments finitude from within. Being itself is and can be an agapeic feast.[20]

Worship often entails sacrifice. As I pointed out, etymologically sacrifice implies "to make sacred," "to do the sacred." It is true that the violence of the sacred can be connected with this in the destruction of the sacrificial victim or the scapegoat. But the doubleness in play can also mean a fundamental *reversal*: the negation may be in the services of an ultimate affirmation, the affirmation of the ultimate, as in the excess of destruction of the potlatch. Cultus may enact a certain *breaking through* of the sacred in the *breakdown* of all human mediations that claimed to be closed in on themselves in absolute self-sufficiency. The breaking through in this breakdown is a breaking open of a more ultimate participation in being. All claims to absolute self-mediation are ruptured by a more absolute otherness.[21]

In some religious traditions, even the god has to submit to such breakdown in order to be sacredly affirmed and for the breakthrough to be fully revealed. Thus in the Christian Eucharist, even God is said to be made sacred, sacrificed. God is said to sacrifice Himself, negate His aloofness in a jealous eternity, assent to the burden of finitude, and by assuming the suffering of time uplift time beyond its profanity. Such a kenotic God will be of importance for Hegel, as we shall see, in so far as he holds that the true God has to contain the negative within Himself. This is not the end of the matter. The "negative" can be said in many senses, and dialectical saying does not exhaust all the senses.

But from whichever side we look at it, cult implies a sense of being that transcends what is taken as the standard Platonic dualism, as it transcends the Nietzschean caricature of Plato that turns upside down that same dualism. Worship does not regard the merely "here and now," nor yet the merely "beyond," but the "beyond" in the "here and now," or alternatively, the "here and now" as the sacrament of the "beyond." In the performative making present of the otherness of the divine, the otherness, though manifested, is neither mastered nor reduced. Cultic celebration enacts a mode of being that surpasses the dualistic opposition of the sacred and profane. There is indeed a difference but not a dualism. Since the manifested otherness preserves the difference, worship is best called the "performative enactment of a community": a festive celebration of the community of being as metaxological.

If again we consider a consecration, there is indeed a "setting apart" of the sacred, but this "setting apart" is not dualistic abstraction from the profane. The holy place set apart for worship is consecrated ground *in the midst of* being as given. It is a "within" that is also an "outside"—the normal exclusive use of such categories is suspended. The space of the holy is a *"meta"* in the dual sense contained in the Greek word: both a "being in the midst," and a "being beyond." We find, as it were, a certain othering of being as given, which remains itself and yet is heterogeneous. The univocal sense of being is not sufficient. A thing here is not just univocally itself, and nothing more. A consecrated thing is truly itself only by being other than itself, is more fully itself only by being something more than itself. Butler canonizes this univocity of identity when he says: a thing is itself and not anything other. If the univocal sense of being exhausted actuality, acts of consecration would be impossible, except perhaps as fantastic excrescences of the imagination, that is, as lies of empty subjectivity, which is again to say, no consecration of being is possible.

Lest anyone think that the point at issue is some cheap sentimental piety, I mention again he who would be the kingly debunker of all such sentimentality: Nietzsche. When Nietzsche says that the only way in which life can be justified is aesthetically, through aesthetic illusion, he is dealing with the same matter at stake in what I am calling "consecration." The question is whether consecration is more than an aesthetic illusion, a noble lie, or a genuine letting come to presence of the deepest truth of being as sacred. Nietzsche could not always quite believe his own noble lies, hence the Dionysian consecration of being that he attempts in his aesthetic redemption finally falters.

One must here bear in mind the relation of cult and suffering. The univocal sense of being withers before both. Nietzsche's basic problem was the meaning of suffering; he offers a counteranswer to the Christian redemption in terms of sin, guilt and punishment. Tragic art, as the sacramental cult of Dionysus, is an affirmation of life in the truth of suffering. Tragic art is a cultic drama that deals with suffering, consecrates suffering, sanctifies suffering. Suffering is not redeemed in a Christian but a pagan way. Yet there is a link with Christianity in that tragic art transfigures suffering. When Nietzsche said: Dionysus versus the Crucified, the choice is between two different consecrations of suffering.

Nietzsche chooses the second. Hegel will choose the first in a qualified way, that is, to sublate it into speculative categories. Again the sacred and suffering invoke the pathos of the other, invoke intimacy and distance, in the sense of non-mastery of the other. In Nietzsche's sacred suffering, the will to power is transmuted into a metaphysical willing of being as being is, with all its darkness and destruction and anguish. The "aesthetic theodicy" of Nietzsche's *amor fati* has nothing to do with aesthetics. It is sacramental ontology. I will reinvoke the dying god below in relation to Hegel's unhappy consciousness.

The senses of being are not exhausted either by univocity, or equivocity, or for that matter, dialectic. The fullest sense of being is metaxological. Worship as the performative enactment of a solidarity between the human and divine is a festive celebration of the community of being as metaxological. This, coupled with the critical understanding of univocity and equivocity, means that the relatedness of the sacred and profane is neither a merely external relation, nor a merely internal one. It is beyond the dualism of the "internal" and the "external." As we shall see more fully, it is also beyond the dialectical sense of being in so far as dialectic, and especially in Hegel's hands, tends to favor finally the embrace of identity over the space of otherness. The other, though manifested in community, remains other: it is not just a moment in the dialectical self-mediation of Hegelian community, conceived as a closed totality or an absorbing god.[22]

God as the absolute original is not an absorbing god. The profane is not dissolved in the sacred: while remaining itself, it is manifested as more than itself. Nor is the sacred reduced to the profane, immersed in it without difference and so destroyed by absorbing homogeneity. The sacred as sacred enters into the profane: as the transfiguring power it both remains itself and communicates itself, broadcasts its reality as other to what is other to itself. Sacred and profane are bound together in a mutuality deeper than dualistic exclusion. Though consecration sets apart a place of worship, the transfiguration there effected returns us differently, newly, to the profane "outside." Worship stands in the space between sacred and profane: it endures the tension of their difference, yet mediates their reconciliation. This mediation is a metaxological intermediation of an open community, not a dialectical self-mediation of an absorbing totality. Worship purifies the space wherein the transfiguring power of the sacred is propagated into the profane. But the middle space does not mean that the two sides that bound it and enter it are then simply dialectical moments of a self-mediating totality whose process subordinates both sacred and profane to itself. So when Hegel says that the House of God is also the House of Man, the potential for dialectical equivocation is not immediately evident.[23]

In sum, worship involves the delicate balance of a dynamic equilibrium. In relation to God, it seeks to balance presence and otherness, manifestation and mystery, God's absoluteness in Himself yet His essential relatedness to the world. In relation to the human, it attempts to balance our greatness and nothingness, freedom and receptivity, proud dignity and humble place. These balances are precarious, hence permanently liable to distortion. Worship enacts a kind of proportion between the human and divine, but a proportion *in activity*, a proportion of dynamic relatedness, a proportion that does not deny the disproportion of God and man. So worship may degenerate into idolatry and fetishism. Here we find the reductive possibilities of the doubleness in play. Idolatry inappropriately endows the finite with a disproportionate absoluteness. The univocal sense of being rears its head here in religious, as opposed to secular form: the unappropriated otherness of the sacred is forgotten in relation to the consecrated thing, which now becomes a magically powerful thing, useful to appropriate all unmastered otherness.

The sacred cult then degenerates into a parody of itself in the religious fetishism which wills to possess God in possessing finite objects, the consecrated thing turned idol. Reducing God to manipulable proportions, this burlesque of the sacred turns God into human property, and in the process it diminishes the human itself. It univocalizes our metaxological doubleness in the middle. It separates our greatness from our nothingness, our freedom from our receptivity, puffing up our pride in trampling down the rough heterogeneities of our middle place in being. Thus, idolatry turns into a hubris that precipitates the human being into a void excess. But as freedom without receptivity is license, as greatness without the pathos of nothingness is itself the negation of greatness, the result is not pride with proper humbleness but in the end the humiliation of the human.

Idolatry is an ontological inversion that reduces the doubleness of the sacred middle to manipulable univocity. It cannot tolerate the constitutive ambiguity of sacred presence/absence, but substitutes a domineering univocity for what it sees as an intolerable equivocity. Then the occasion of veneration becomes a closed absolute end, instead of one offered opening, itself open to other such occasions of offering. The hierophany implies that God is not jealous, but the idolater is jealous of *his* gods. He himself is a jealous, orgic god that must usurp the hierophany as his own. Idolatry then becomes a closed, sacred *self-mediation* that inverts the relation of the absolute and relative, the infinite and finite. The idolatrous self claims to be both, a secular simulacrum of their dialectic. What he claims as his opening out to otherness dialectically masks the radical immanence of his closure on himself. His hubris of the whole is indistinguishable from a miserable guarding of exclusive gods, which on closer inspection evaporate into his own closed self. His "knowing" of "God" is really an intolerance to the threat of any heterogeneity that might prove to be beyond possession by his categories.

So idolatry congeals the dynamic nature of worship. The cultus becomes a univocal fixation with rubrics alone, the outward show of an empty ritual. The spirit has fled, and to call it back idolatry resorts to spells and magic incantations, all with the aim of demanding the divine presence. In demanding this presence, the idolater sets himself up as Lord and Master, God then being at his beck and call. Worship becomes will to power, will to manipulate and dominate the divine powers. Idolatry thus returns us to our opening theme of the instrumentalizing of religion. Properly speaking, the offering of sacrifice is not circumscribed by the spirit of calculation and its latent will to power. It is a gift, something "more" than narrow calculation, a giving over, a return, and not a return to or for the self, but to the other. It gives over all things, man included, as belonging with God. I say "belonging with," not "belonging to." The latter too easily conjures up the idea of God as a property owner who demands the return of the slavemaster. "Belonging with" signifies a mutuality, not to be expressed in the language of "ownership," "possession," "property." God is not to be likened to an absentee landlord.

Such offering transcends instrumentalization and the system of means and ends. Bataille's notion of the sacred as excess, as expenditure without reserve (I would say: motiveless offering, the thanking of metaphysical praise), while presented as a *ne plus ultra* of avant garde thought, is quite continuous with this old notion of the sacred gift. Bataille is "postmodern" because he realizes the archaic power of religious excess, excess that needed no justification in societies whose forms of life were not totalized in terms of the system of instrumentalities, that is to say, "premodern" societies. Bataille is a "postmodern" simply by virtue of listening well to the "premodern."

In the instrumentalizing of the religious, the sacred gift, however, is perverted into a bribe of God, a control of His favor. Instead of the festivity of participation in the excess of the sacred, idolatry reveals the will to totalitarian ascendancy over the infinite. Setting up man as the infinite, it manipulates stones, potions, bones, beasts' entrails— all dead things—thereby thinking to command what is beyond all the living and the dead. Our enlightened modern societies take respectable pride in the fact that, of course, we perform none of these superstitious rites in their archaic crudity. Modern rational enlightenment has demythologized idolatry. Should we congratulate ourselves? Alas, in an irony of the sacred, in an unwitting *parodia sacra*, our anthropocentric totalization of being offers simply another demythologized idolatry, namely, the demythologized idolatry of instrumental mind. But, of course, parody cannot really be unwitting. What we have here is another return of the repressed sacred, masquerading as its demythologization.

The god of idolatry, whether the archaic fetishism of premodernity or the instrumentally enlightened fetishism of modernity, is a dead god. (In attacking the fetishism of commodities, the idols of the capitalist marketplace, Marx was, in effect, a religious iconoclast.) For if the ritual, or let us say the technical process, becomes the dead product of a hierophany, now past, and if we cling to it, trembling before the absence of the vanished God, we merely succeed in realizing our suspicion. What suspicion? Answer: our subliminal horror at the emptiness of being without the divine. But, of course, we modern men have come of age and do not tremble—hence Kierkegaard's righteous wrath, and Nietzsche's passionate desolation. The dead ritual, or let us say the technical process, now blocks the divine instead of preparing the occasion of its new embodiment. Idolatry and sheer profanity thus come to the same thing. Both are related outcomes of the same collusion between an anthropocentric will to power over being's otherness and the will to univocalize being entirely. Both are indifferently different avenues to the same dead god, a god dead equally in time and in eternity, and dead whether we call this god, god or man.

The God-service of the Unhappy Consciousness

The sensitive reader may suspect the silhouette of Hegel, or perhaps a simulacrum of a Hegelian silhouette, in the above mask of the idolatrous self. Eric Voegelin sees more than merely a silhouette or simulacrum here: vying with what he calls Hegel's sorcery, he conjures up a Hegelian face, complete down to the little damning details.[24] I confess I cannot fix the face of Hegel with such cut and dried precision. In fact, there is no face of Hegel, no one univocal face. While not as multiply masked as a Nietzsche, there is still more than one Hegelian face. True, the silhouette of the idolatrous self sometimes does loom and dissolve in Hegel's self-presentation. It comes most clearly from the shadows when it is a question of, in the final reckoning, always dialectically subordinating otherness to sameness, difference to identity. But there are other, let us say, less impious profiles.

I now reflect on the community of cult relative to the figure of the unhappy consciousness. I sometimes will go beyond Hegel's text. I am not offering an *explication de texte*. I am thinking the matter at stake, sometimes in terms that may not be Hegel's. I believe Hegel would approve, certainly of the intent, perhaps not of the practice, since it criticizes Hegel. So do not say: Hegel did not intend to do this, as if his texts were sacred scripture. No interpretation is a reduplication of the text, and especially not a philosophical interpretation. A genuine philosophical response to Hegel is to respect his intentions but also to bring a question to his philosophical practice that may put it off balance. There is more philosophical piety in the latter than in the idolatrous hermeneutics that makes a fetish of the text. The latter is letter, not spirit.

The unhappy consciousness is central to the relation of religion and philosophy in the *Phenomenology*. I focus on a recurrent possibility of relatedness between the self and what is other. Hegel says that the thinking of the unhappy consciousness takes the form of devotion (*Andacht*): "Its thinking as such is no more than the discordant clang of ringing bells, or a cloud of warm incense, a kind of thinking in terms of music."[25] This thinking in terms of music is immediately criticized for not attaining the level of the concept, but nevertheless some connection with worship is implied. I suggest that Hegel sees in this unhappy devotion the epitomization of a cultus that elevates the divine into an absentee otherness, finally beyond all mediation, hence purportedly offering an endless perpetuation rather than cure of human estrangement. I want to emphasize Hegel's propensity to paint in dangerously negative hues the other that is recalcitrant to complete mediation, the other that remains other, no matter what.

I will say: Hegel exploits the fact that cultus implies the *manifested* other, but in criticizing the unhappy consciousness, he puts the primary emphasis on the manifestation, and only subordinate emphasis on the otherness as such. Then he claims to surpass the unhappy consciousness in the further drive to *complete manifestation*. The other becomes a moment in the dialectical self-mediation of the process of complete manifestation. The proper sense of religious mystery or transcendence or excess is then attenuated, dialectically domesticated. There is sufficient nuance in Hegel's account to make his treatment of the unhappy consciousness seem persuasive, and especially to the modern mind that prides itself in its preparedness for every critique of heteronomy, especially religious heteronomy. But what if we have now grown suspicious of the autonomy that establishes its own dialectical self-mediation by its inversion of such heteronomy and transcendence? We must also grow suspicious of Hegel, it would seem.

From his early theological writings onward, and throughout all his career, Hegel was concerned to overcome any division of the human and divine. Perhaps this showed more existential pathos earlier, becoming later more muted. Yet the pathos persists, as is evident in the late lectures on the philosophy of religion. The theme persists even under the mask of speculative logic. It is especially evident relative

to the unhappy consciousness. Some commentators have identified
this figure with the piety of Medieval Catholicism, its asceticism and
otherworldly dualism. Others find echoes of Hegel's various treatments
of Jewish religiosity, with its emphasis on the abnegation of the self's
will in submission to the might of the transcendent Lord.

More generally, the unhappy consciousness is a Hegelian figure
of the essential form of alienated selfness. It is a consciousness, and
in the *Phenomenology* all consciousness (*Bewusstsein*) implies *separation*: where there is consciousness there is the sense of difference. The
unhappy consciousness experiences this sense of difference but cannot
become at home with it. It is the quintessence of not being-at-home.
For Hegel it is divided on two fronts: it is divided within itself, and
divided from being other than itself. Its basic approach to being and
indeed the ultimate being is one of dualistic opposition: between the
self and the rest of reality there is a dualism; within the self there
is an internal rift. For it the very nature of being, internal and
external, is alienation, contradiction, disunion.

The unhappy consciousness, Hegel tells us, sets up a split between
itself, as changeable, and a "beyond," as unchangeable. Moreover,
there is no middle way between these extremes. Nevertheless, the
unhappy consciousness does desire contact with the unchangeable
"beyond" to redeem its own estrangement. But since this "beyond"
is itself strange, its effect can only be to increase the estrangement.
In contrast to the positive reality imputed to this "beyond," the
unhappy consciousness comes to see itself as merely accidental,
invaded by the sense of its own nothingness. Between the transcendent
other and the estranged self, there is a dualism of plenitude and lack,
but without the possibility of mediation and hence of reconciliation.
The unhappy consciousness craves intimacy with the unchangeable
"beyond"; but this "beyond" is foreign and extraneous to it; hence
it despairs of ever reaching the "beyond." At once it desires union and
reconciliation with the other and despairs of them both.[26]

What cultus would be consonant with this? Worship always
demands some surrender or submission or abandon to the ultimate
other, but here, it seems, this is carried to an extreme of prostration.
The human being feels itself a wretch, a worm, its worship reflecting
its needy selfness and indigent finiteness.[27] Worship is a punishment,
not a privilege: it is retribution for the Fall. Man falls, loses his
intimacy with God: the result is dissatisfaction. The unhappy
consciousness is this dissatisfaction in pure form. Existence itself is
exile, irremediable exile. Hence Hegel speaks of its infinite *yearning.*[28]
It hankers for what it never attains: its yearning is wispy and wistful,
a mere feeling.[29] I suppose this yearning would fit the bill of the

"nostalgia" denounced by the post-Nietzscheans. Hegel is their post-Hegelian cohort here: indeed he is intemperately contemptuous of such nostalgic yearning.

Consider why Hegel compares the thinking of the unhappy consciousness to a cloud of warm incense. When a cloud of incense ascends, it goes indeterminately upward, but goes nowhere definite. It ascends but dissolves. This is an image of vague longing that, because it would always be elsewhere, sorrows always over its present state. The unhappy consciousness, like the nostalgic exile, is neither here nor there. What is here carries the stain of the Fall: what is there is extraneous and inaccessible. Hence it is perennially frustrated both by the present and by the "beyond." Its own desire is vain; the world itself is vanity. In its worship the unhappy consciousness feels its degeneracy, not its dignity.

Something similar is noticeable relative to the dialectic of finitude and infinity, or for Hegel, the lack of such a dialectic. The unhappy consciousness feels the precariousness of its finiteness and the aspiration of infinity, but it separates finitude and infinity in a dualistic opposition. Torn apart by their opposed strains, its desire of infinity is evasive and unfruitful, its finitude is defeated. It wills to flee what is fleeting but brings its own transience with its flight. Thus, its hope of infinity is always an empty expectation.[30] But an empty expectation is hope's opposite: it is despair.

So the worship of the unhappy consciousness is both hope and despair. Perpetually it oscillates between these extremes: it simply *is* the suffering of this swing. Its worship is hence a poignant waiting for God that exposes it to the melancholy of distance. It is also the experience of the lack of God, God's absence whereby it is forsaken and orphaned. The unhappy consciousness is sorrow at its own transience and grief before a withheld, withdrawn God. In its banished heart it wishes for another existence to assuage its pain, another existence which its own despair makes impossible.

I am adding to Hegel's words, since what is at stake is not the letter of Hegelian writ, but the *spirit* of a crucial comportment to being. Let us say that there is a worship of assent and a worship of denial, a worship of reconciliation and a worship of rancor and resignation. We confront a strain of the second here. We find a way of being not at all unlike Nietzsche's slave morality with its subterranean rancor towards the superior other, the master. Here selfhood is tempted to efface itself.[31] Undermined within by a gnawing inferiority, it would abdicate itself to what is superior but in the abdication it substitutes self-humiliation for humility. Like Nietzsche's slave it turns against itself, turns its own cruelty inward and becomes a sick soul. The convergence with Nietzsche is quite understandable, since the unhappy consciousness continues to be infected with the dialectic of master and slave, treated earlier in the *Phenomenology*.[32]

So, too, it easily degenerates into a cult of degradation where prayer proves to be the slave's petition of the despot. Hegel is fond of reminding us of the Jewish wisdom that fear of the Lord is the beginning of wisdom.[33] Here, however, it also becomes the end. The slave fears the Lord because he has power over his life: fear of the Lord is fear of death. The slave's fear breeds a worship of death, a cultus of *mortification*.[34] Death is man's most uncertain certainty. The unhappy consciousness resigns itself to this certainty without being reconciled to it. It wills to do away with this uncertainty by reducing its own being to nothing, sanctifying itself by self-negation. It undergoes existence as shame, not as hierophany or good news. Its patience is really its despair of itself and God. Its praise of God takes the form of a groan. Its celebration of being is a ceremony of dejection, a feast of barren sighs.

Again I add to Hegelian writ with words Hegel did not write. Let us say that the central difficulty here is in making an idol of diremption. Itself the essence of diremption, the unhappy consciousness lacks self-knowledge and knowledge of its object. It knows neither itself nor God. Ultimately its outcome is, as it were, a war of contradiction. There is no peace between the human being and God, nor within the human being itself. Nor does God seem a God of peace: as Lord of death, He is wrath and destruction: as absconding, He is jealous of His prerogatives, arbitrary in His withdrawals. For Hegel mastery and slavery are permanent possibilities of being, and so also of worship. The contradiction here is between the human being as slave and God as master. Indeed this contradiction infects the conception of both sides: the human being is sundered from itself, God from the human being, and God Himself, arbitrary master, lacks self-consistency. The human being is diminished in this war: as slave it is a *thing* determined externally, plaything of an ambiguous God. The slave is separated from his own essence in confrontation with the external master. He submits, not to this, not to that, but to everything. God to him is simply the tyranny of things.

I suspect that much of this risks caricature of so-called "Medieval dualism," indeed of other so-called religious dualisms, like Judaism. While I do not accept the caricature, it has had a certain historical influence in this sense. One can make the case that such a tyrannical heteronomy in theological form inevitably inverts into an anthropocentric autonomy. One can also argue that this inversion (modern autonomy, fed on Cartesian dualism) *continues the tyranny*, in this case the tyranny of anthropocentric immanence. Human rancor at its own theological impotence before transcendence breeds in compensation an anthropocentric will to power in immanence. The religious slave in time will revolt. Hence, Marx's critique of religion as alienating merely wants to hasten this revolt of slaves and so takes place within the horizon of the unhappy consciousness. The secret source of its critical power in immanence is the rancorous passion of its powerlessness before transcendence.

In that sense, the worship of the unhappy consciousness can breed *sacrilege*. If its cultus is one of shame, and if shame involves an admission of our finiteness, yet if this finitude leads to despair, then such shame is really just a hostility to finitude. Its cultus cannot be the free release of finitude, but always simply entrenches the antithesis of the human and divine. Founded on misery, lowliness and prostration, it requires one's blind obedience. But since the divine is absent, this obedience is never given to something present: it is given to nothing. With respect to the manifested otherness I spoke of previously, the otherness here so swallows the manifestation, that there is no manifestation, indeed finally no otherness either. This cultus then becomes our alienation to nothing,[35] our giving of ourselves over to nothing. No wonder then that this feeling of nothingness reappears in human consciousness.[36]

Because this nothingness diminishes rather than elevates the human, makes unholy instead of consecrating, the sacred takes on an inimical look. The holy looks hostile because it makes the human being itself unhallowed. Hostile transcendence, in turn, may produce the sacrilegious backlash of hubristic anthropocentrism. Inevitably, as I said, the unhappy consciousness will be tempted to shake off its servility, to cease to be crushed. Instead of flight, it will fight. It will then will to be itself master, launch its offensive on the heavens.[37] For the master, obverse of the slave, wills to dominate, not this, not that, but everything: he wills even to dominate God. The unhappy consciousness is caught between abject submission and violent revolt. In both cases the risk is that the human being becomes reified, turned into a thing. Man as slave is an *insubstantial* thing, dissolving with trembling in the acid fear of the master. Man as master is an *obstinate* thing, inflexible in the unbending rigidities of domineering.

We can see here the beginnings of post-Hegelian religious nihilism with thinkers like Feuerbach and Marx who will to negate the Holy as the origin of man's misery. This religious nihilism is often a philosophical hope gone sour, the mutation of its disappointed piety into sacrilege. Nihilism is disillusioned religion, just as cynicism is acrid idealism, and fanaticism is frenzied faith. When frustration awakens the vague idealistic dreamer to his unhappiness, he rejects his dream and piety too, often with a brutality matching his prior ardency. Devoured by disillusion, the nihilist then substitutes sacrilegious politics for desacralized religion, seeking thereby a barbarous holiness. Then politics, conducted with religious passion, sets out to sanctify man, loathing his religious need with a perverse religious zeal. The connection with the unhappy consciousness reappears with Sartre. For Sartre man *is* the unhappy consciousness, his passion for God and the God he seeks both useless contradictions. Sartre sets before us this useless passion and contradiction of religion with a passion that, contradictorily, is all but religious.[38]

So the unhappy consciousness does not attain the overdetermined, festive intermediation of affirming cultus, in the form of the metaxological community of being. It is plunged alternatively into servility and despotism. It swings between these in despair and disappears in their rival nihilisms. For the truth of being human is bound up with God's truth: an empty sense of one goes hand in hand with an empty sense of the other. The unhappy consciousness produces this *double emptiness*: the human in a state of pitiable selfness confronts in opposition a nugatory eternity. Alternatively, in terms of the dialectic of master and slave, God falsely appears to our will to power in our image and likeness: as Himself a will to dominate everything. Thus, we cloak our secret sense that our own being, and ultimately all being, is will to power by imputing the tyranny to God, the ultimate being. But this is but our savage shadowboxing.

Nor is it, for Hegel, that the free human being does not know alienation. Rather he is marked by a different appropriation of it. Alienation is founded on the difference between the human being and God, but alienation is not identical with difference. Alienation is difference distorted, difference distorted into opposition. The unhappy consciousness is unhappy precisely because for it the difference of the human being and God is one of dualistic opposition. Thus, it twists the promise of their togetherness. Difference is inherent in the nature of things, so alienation is a recurrent possibility. To overcome alienation is not to destroy difference as such: this precipitates nihilism, the rival nihilisms of slave and slavemaster. It is to transcend difference as dualistic opposition, to recognize that there are differences grounded in a *mutuality* deeper than opposition. True difference entails articulated mutuality. To recognize this mutuality is to restore difference to true form. Nor is the dialectical way the only way to do this: the metaxological way insists on a stronger sense of otherness. Even the unhappy consciousness, in the travail of its despair, is itself struggling towards this mutuality. Its struggle not only entails recognition of what is other. It struggles to be recognized, as Hegel says.[39]

What is challenging about Hegel's account is its vision of affirmative possibility emerging in extreme negation. For despite its destitution the unhappy consciousness is still *capax Dei*. It comes to the limit and stares at death. It tastes the dregs of despair, but this is not utterly void. John of the Cross tells us that the soul is centered in its own nothingness. In some such sense the unhappy consciousness may know it is nothing. Its despair is essentially religious, as is its sense of nothingness. It brings before it forsakenness, abandonment, the numbing, bitter and bewildering experience expressed in the words "God is dead."[40] Nietzsche made this theme famous, but Hegelian dialectic had already tried to plumb this abyss.

Again there is an essential doubleness at work here. I find, for instance, an atheological version of God's death in Bataille's obsession with death and sacred violence. I find a celebration of a wanton sacrificial violence, an ecstasy of death in a kind of black otherness, a kind of atheological necrophilia. But God's death can be hope as well as horror, atonement as well as destruction. God's death is the sacrifice, what makes sacred: instead of atheological necrophilia, the violence on the sacrificial victim may release an affirmation of being beyond death. The speculative Good Friday may reveal the excess of the Sabbath of being, beyond dialectical negation. In knowing the death of God, the unhappy consciousness comes to know something more than death. To live one's being as plenitude is first to live one's nothingness, live through one's estrangement from God. One might even say that the grave and the womb here coincide. Even in this sacred tomb or burial place of the dialectic, for Hegel the unhappy consciousness is the center of the *birthplace* of spirit: its bewilderment, yearning loss, despair are the birthpangs of spirit's genesis.[41] Sacred nostalgia inverts itself and begins to be at home with being even in its not being-at-home with being. In a later chapter, I will speak of comedy in terms of this double: being-at-home in not being-at-home; and in terms intimately related to cultus.

With the cultus the eternal does not dwell away but erupts into time in the hierophany. With the death of God, we are exposed to hierophany in absolutely negative form. For the human being to be reconciled with death is for God Himself to be there, even in the ultimate negation of being. God must sacrifice Himself and not by remaining at a remove, on the outside. The manifested otherness means that the outside must also be within, which does not mean that it must be dialectically reduced. God must enter into the abandonment of the unhappy consciousness itself. This, I take it, is part of Christ's passion and agony when he cries out his forsakenness. The divine human is brought to despair, and so shares the deepest intimacy of human nothingness, freely giving himself over to death. Christ shares the wretched fate of abandoned finitude, and in his sacrifice manifests his solidarity with fallen humans. Christ is the image of God not as man's master but his brother: God's otherness is manifested here as brotherhood. As Whitehead put it: "God is the great companion—the fellow sufferer who understands." The divine solidarity with the human extends even to the extreme of plumbing absolute despair. Otherwise the redemptive sacrifice would be a hocus pocus show with no salvation from despair. To make the human holy, God exposes Himself to the unholy, exposes Himself to earthly execration.

The unhappy consciousness endures a trial of negation in which the human being and God both are tested. The human being is tested in its homeless sojourn in the world. God is tested and, as in the story of Christ's ordeal, literally put on trial.[42] Christ shares life and death with humans as himself a condemned human. His death returns God to the earth and the earth to God. In this trial of negation the human and the divine, even in their absolute opposition, are nevertheless present in their togetherness. Their mutuality is manifested, in death, beyond death, as more ultimate than their opposition. Thus, too, this trial releases the forgiveness of evil in which, as Hegel puts it, "what is absolutely in opposition recognizes itself as the same as its opposite, and this knowledge breaks out into the "yea, yea," with which one extreme meets the other." This "yea, yea" is not merely an indefinitely deferred enjoyment but the taste of eternity here enjoyed, the manifestation of the communion or the meeting of the human and divine. Hegel even says: This is the manifest God (*der erscheinende Gott*).[43]

The point for Hegel then cannot be any simple rejection of the unhappy consciousness. It is to see it dialectically as participant in the larger process by which the spirit mediates with itself in otherness. Modern enlightened consciousness might shallowly congratulate itself on its putative freedom from all heteronomy. Hegel too wants such freedom, but he knows that the price for it is not cheap. The *greatness* of the unhappy consciousness is its openness to the extreme possibility that itself and God are nothing. This anticipates the greatness of Nietzsche's Madman, the horror of whose sense of God's nothingness has since been cheapened into postmodern kitsch, not least by those professing their devotion to Nietzsche.

The Return of the Double

Let us take our bearings. I find a significant equivocity in Hegel's treatment of the unhappy consciousness, one which also appears in relation to evil and forgiveness, and in the connection Hegel notes between the unhappy consciousness and comedy. Cult and comedy are connected, in that there is a death of the divine in Greek religion too. To this I return. The equivocity in question relates to the double vision (see chapter 1) and Hegel's philosophical obsession to appropriate all heteronomy dialectically. My discussion above did not always separate my own views and Hegel's. These are not identical; they are significantly different with respect to the appropriation of otherness. This difference relates to the philosophical interpretation of doubleness.

I find much to the point in Hegel's account. Undoubtedly the unhappy consciousness seems infected with a wretched equivocity that cries out for further dialectical self-mediation. But can we think a less indigent sense of doubleness? Can we return to a different sense of the double? I suggest that hidden in this unhappy equivocity is a perhaps distorted expression of metaxological doubleness, and not just a mere failure of dialectical self-mediation. There may be a fundamental truth to the unhappy consciousness' sense of the "beyond" that is not to be just dialectically denied, or for that matter dialectically sublated.

Nor do I think that so-called metaphysical nostalgia intends a reduction of otherness to sameness. If there is nostalgia here, the metaxological preservation of an affirmative double is significantly less nostalgic than Hegel's speculative one. Most of the rhetorical charges of nostalgia are the diversionary tactics of shallow commentators who have not thought deeply enough about Hegel or the fundamental issues of the great metaphysical tradition. Hegel should be seen in the powerful light he deserves, even though that light has nuances, streaks of shadow, that are very difficult to detect. One suspects, too, that Hegelian "forgiveness" risks its own brand of dialectical hocus pocus which conjures away, in a conceptual sleight of hand, the negative otherness of evil. Then Hegelian dialectic sacrifices a significant otherness, but properly does not make sacred: dialectic inflicts its violence on the sacrificial victim. More is at stake between Hegel and Jesus than can be said here.

More generally, the dialectical appropriation of difference is not the only way to move beyond dualistic opposition. Hegel's intent is to attain that mutuality wherein "the I is We and the We is I." Yet in Hegelian *self*-recognition in absolute otherness, the otherness is not in fact absolute, since finally the other is the dialectical mirror which mediates *self*-recognition. By contrast, the ultimate mutuality, as understood metaxologically, is not simply self-recognition in otherness, since this would reduce the doubleness of mediation from both sides, to a singular process of dialectical self-mediation. Doubleness is always seen by Hegel as risking dualistic opposition and hence, as I put it above, the double emptiness of the unhappy consciousness. But metaxologically there is an affirmative doubleness, a double fullness rather than double emptiness, that resists reduction to a singular process of dialectical self-mediation. And yet like Hegel's dialectic, this affirmative doubleness is *beyond* the rival and mutually supporting dualistic oppositions, theological and anthropocentric, also mentioned above. Because Hegel does not adequately articulate this affirmative doubleness, his dialectical solution to the dualistic oppositions is always threatened with re-reduction, and re-reduction just to the dualistic oppositions and their reductions of the complex middle. This has happened again and again with those heirs of Hegel who are cruder practitioners of dialectical thought.

We need to stress that *for Hegel* the real unhappiness of the unhappy consciousness is its failure to absolutely mediate with *itself.* The deepest doubleness it experiences is its own self-division. It is the essential self-divided consciousness, and even the failure of its reference to the unchangeable beyond is its failure to recognize *itself* in this beyond. Hegel explicitly calls the unhappy consciousness, as self-contradictory and self-divided, the *double* consciousness.[44] If one reads Hegel's discussion carefully, one sees that the double relative to the unhappy consciousness is not a real plurality, a community of irreducible others, man and God. This double is ultimately the *self-division of a one.* The doubleness is the doubling (*Entzweiung*) of the one. The human and divine beings are set up as extremes of this one, that is unhappy precisely because it fails to *recognize itself* in the otherness. There is never any final doubt that for Hegel the persistence of transcendence as other will be marked down as a dialectical failure. Hegelian success would amount to the self-knowledge that the doubleness is really the self-division of a *dialectical one*, the self-knowledge of which returns the double to its mediated unity with itself. The double is unacceptable since it shows the failure of the figure to mediate its unity with itself.

As with any double vision, here we see Hegel's dialectical rejection of heteronomy as dualistic. But if there are doubles that are not dualistic oppositions and that cannot be reduced to dialectical self-mediation, then one must reject the rejection of heteronomy and the imputation that the result can only be the wretched being of the unhappy consciousness. I noted that the dialectical overcoming of the

double is for Hegel the birth of spirit. I would say that there is a
metaxological birth that overcomes dualistic opposition but not the
affirmative double. I agree with the search for the affirmative in the
negative, but the affirmative is not just dialectical self-mediation, nor
is negation identical with the sublation of the other. There is an other
affirmation and negation in metaxological being, less antagonistic
to heteronomy and the "unhappy consciousness."

There is also a being beyond death, what I call posthumous mind
in *Philosophy and its Others*, which preserves an intricately doubled
mindfulness, alert to the irreducible caesuras of being, and itself
irreducible to the unhappy consciousness or to any singular process
of dialectical self-mediation. Posthumous mind relates to the womb
and the grave, the here and the beyond, time and eternity, being and
death, in a manner to which dialectical self-mediation could not
possibly do justice. I can only suggest the point here, though I have
developed it elsewhere. Hegel is immensely suggestive in that if we
listen metaxologically to his dialectical discourse we catch in the ear,
sometimes faintly, the air of another music coming from elsewhere.
It is as if we hear a different song of otherness sometimes being
sounded or appearing in the interstices, or pauses, or silences, even
in the words themselves, of his dialectical discourse. So even the
musical thinking that Hegel attributed to the unhappy consciousness,
a thinking he is too quick to dismiss, carries echoes of this other music,
this music of the other.[45]

Hegel sees the unhappy consciousness, in the terms I use, as
vacillating back and forth between univocity and equivocity. The
divine transcendence is seen as a univocally unchanging beyond, a
rigid, static eternity, while the unhappy consciousness is the complete
other of this static eternity: complete other here means the complete
dualistic opposite. So we get an equivocal relation, or rather a lack
of relation between it and the beyond: between them is a dualistic
difference that allows no mediation. The univocity of static eternity
breeds the equivocity of a dualistic opposition of time and eternity,
and infects the inner reality of the unhappy consciousness itself as
an equivocal self, neither one thing nor the other, endlessly swinging
between desire and despair, willing to be univocally at one with itself
and always finding itself a failure, that is, finding itself as at odds,
at variance with its own self. This doubleness of the unhappy consciousness makes it for Hegel the figure of equivocal existence, whose
double duplicitous being Hegel then claims to mediate dialectically.

Static eternity here is more like the univocal immutable substance
of Parmenidean being. Static eternity is neither the erotic absolute
that Hegel presents, nor the agapeic absolute I defend.[46] In both the

latter we discover different dynamic forms of the energy of being. Hegel's unhappy consciousness fixates on static eternity and does not reach the erotic absolute. Relative to the latter, the self would come to itself, recognize itself in a dialectical process of overcoming the lack of the unhappy consciousness. But as I see the agapeic absolute, it grants the possibility, indeed promise of an affirmative double, a double fullness. It is not a One that has to surmount its own initial lack dialectically by means of the passage through dualistic opposition, overcoming that empty beginning in its own self-completion as a dialectically self-mediating whole. The agapeic absolute, out of its initial plenitude, grants the other its otherness in its own irreducible plenitude. Agapeic creating is not a fall into self-division of the erotic One, but the overfull generosity of the original power of being that grants plurality. With respect to the agapeic absolute, the otherness of the human and divine always remains irreducible, not in any negative sense that completely excludes all intermediation, but as grounding a metaxological community of real others. In fact, the intermediation necessary here has to be itself double in a positive sense.

Thus, too, the equivocity of the unhappy consciousness reminds us of the dualistic double of Kant. In response to this we find both Fichte's striving consciousness and its equivocal struggle to and fro between the ego and the non-ego, and Schelling's transcendental self that immediately would be at one, "like shot from a pistol," with the univocal eternity of the absolute *Indifferenzpunkt*. I see Hegel as trying to surpass dialectically the equivocity of Kant's dualisms and Fichte's striving, but also the univocity without difference of Schelling's *Indifferenzpunkt*. But Hegel's dialectic produces its own forms of univocity and equivocity. The Hegelian dialectical self as an absolute subject-object remains within the horizon of Kantian and Fichtean transcendentalism and gives a primacy to the subject (as Adorno, among others, believed). This is no simple reduction to immediate univocity, but Hegel does imply a dialectical reduction to the mediated univocity of absolute spirit.

Likewise Hegel's sense of the death of God seems to mediate the equivocity of immanence and transcendence, whether in Kantian, Jewish or Catholic "dualism." In fact, it ends in a dialectical univocity that attenuates transcendence as transcendence. Likewise it ruptures the inarticulated univocal eternity of Schelling's *Indifferenzpunkt*; it shows the absolute as intimately involved, indeed articulated by the process of history. Here is the erotic absolute again. But in Hegel's new monism of the whole—the higher, speculative univocity in which

Agapeic Absolute

history entirely mediates the inaccessibility of eternity—one is led to suspect that Hegel's affirmation of the eternal as eternal is finally equivocal.

In sum: The double as metaxological is not simply the equivocal double as played out by the unhappy consciousness. I quickly add that a generous reading of the unhappy consciousness will see in its equivocity, not the failure of dialectical-speculative univocity, but its improperly articulated quest of metaxological doubleness. Let us say that metaxological doubleness exhibits respect for real Secondness, in Peirce's sense. Metaxological doubleness is not to be identified with Peirce's Secondness; but both point to a similar problem in Hegel. It is not so much, as Peirce seemed to believe, that there is *no* Secondness in Hegel. It is more accurate to say that Hegel has a surrogate of Secondness, a dialectical simulacrum of real Secondness. Recall the question I put in the introduction: Can Hegel really count to two, count to a real two, the minimal number for Aristotle? Once again in Hegelian thinking such Secondness is seen as a *self*-division, hence a halving of the original unity. It is not seen as the basis of a metaxological plurality of irreducible wholes. Then for Hegel the double consciousness *must* be unhappy, as a one self-divided consciousness that misinterprets its own self-division as reference to an irreducible other (the unchangeable). For Hegel this must be a misinterpretation, because the other, dialectically understood, is merely *itself* in alienated form.

Dialectical philosophy claims to unweave the misinterpretation and this illusory fixation on irreducible otherness. In fact, dialectical doubleness is a misinterpretation of metaxological doubleness. If not freed from this misinterpretation, dialectic produces a simulacrum of real otherness, whether the metaxological double or Peircean Secondness, and circles around its own fetish of absolute self-mediation. The god the Hegelian philosopher then serves is the idol which dialectic makes of its own self-mediation.

Philosophical Cult and the Idolatries of Thought

I undertake another approach, this time in more conceptual terms, to Hegel's saying: Philosophy is *Gottesdienst*. Again I ask: What god does philosophical cultus seek, to what divinity is it devoted? Often the philosopher *does* provide the conceptual analogue to the unhappy consciousness. On this feeds Nietzsche's denunciation of philosophy as the nihilistic ascetical ideal masquerading in conceptual categories. When Socrates said that philosophy was a preparation for death, he reminded us of the unsettling experience of not being-at-home with being that haunts the philosopher. But can we ever entirely escape such disquietude? Can it be more than the metaphysical malaise that Nietzsche charges?

Speculation may well be a Socratic mask for suffering. But did we have to wait till Nietzsche to be reminded of this? Plato already knew this. Plato is the masked philosopher par excellence. Not only the logic of his arguments, but the creative dramaturgy of his philosophical impersonations, namely, the characters in his dialogues, are Plato's brilliantly multiplied masks. Hegel is generally given to prosaic directness, but he too said that philosophy is precipitated in the stress of bifurcation.[47] The word he uses is *Entzweiung*: division, being doubled, a one being two, cleavage. *Entzweiung*, endoubling, is the same word he uses in discussing the cleavage of evil. Philosophy has its origin in a sense of division, suffered as an evil. Philosophy suffers the pathos of distance. We begin in the middle, but the middle is double. What do we do with the distance, the middle, the suffering, the doubleness?

The philosopher is doubled in the middle: oriented to truth but by this very directedness cognizant of his distance, separation from truth. Such sunderance is never merely abstract but is concretely articulated in the thinker as himself, like the unhappy consciousness, marked by inner division. Philosophy is not exhausted by doubt, yet it is inseparable from doubt. To be thus in doubt, again like the unhappy consciousness, is to be neither here nor there. As we say colloquially, it is "to be of two minds," that is, to have one's mind divided against itself. The German for doubt, *Zweifel*, directs us to this double, *Zwei*. The philosopher undergoes the Fall as the despair of doubt.[48] Indeed if Hegel is right the quest for knowledge precipitates just that Fall (see chapter 4). Contradiction is not then a mere puzzle for intellectual tinkering, sparing us as essentially untouched. Contradiction is concrete, and philosophical thought is in the middle of its living stress. The philosopher is ordained, again like Socrates, by knowing that he does not know. Still, to acknowledge one's unknowing is not only the negative awareness of limitation: positively, as Hegel points out, to be aware of limits is already to be beyond them. The meaning of such "being beyond" in the doubled middle is the enigma at stake. Hegel will say, and not without justification: Acknowledgement of truth's absence implies truth's emergent presence. To be cognizant of absence is impossible without some sense of *what* is absent, which is to imply some presence of this absent thing. To be patient to the stress of contradiction is already to be guided by some norm of truth. The philosopher's doubt must have its ground in a prior fealty to truth.

So separation cannot be the complete disappearance of relation; it presupposes relation, it is itself a form of relatedness, albeit negative. Heidegger puts the point: Human existence is marked and directed by a prereflective comprehension of Being. In Platonic terms: We could not seek truth and recognize it on finding it, were we not already involved with it. The doubled philosopher is caught in the tension between contradiction and truth, separation and relation, doubt of cognition and recognition of what binds knowing to truth. As human beings we dwell immediately in this tension but philosophical thought brings the tension to mediated articulation.

Philosophical thought is an emergence of metaxological mindfulness from being itself. In the middle between our intimacy with truth and our distance from it, our ignorance cannot be a univocal blank. It is an intermediate condition, deeply stressed by the desire, hence anticipated presence, of what it knows it currently lacks. The fuller unfolding of thought is simply the mindful articulation of this intermediate condition of being. Is this mindful articulation entirely a matter of dialectical self-mediation? If it were, Hegel would be right and there would be no radical otherness. I think that the fuller unfolding is a matter of both dialectical self-mediation and metaxological intermediation with otherness. The philosopher in the middle experiences there the exigence of a double mediation: self-mediation and intermediation with irreducible otherness. The first mediation stresses thought thinking itself; the second opens up thought thinking its other. Does not Hegel privilege self-mediation, such that the second intermediation, thought thinking its other, becomes dialectically incorporated into thought thinking itself?

The double of doubt (*Zweifel*), the being in two minds of philosophical perplexity, seems to presuppose a prior unity with truth. I prefer to say metaxological community with truth. Hegel will say prior unity, yes; but this is only known in driving dialectically to the end, and erotically overcoming ignorance in knowledge of the whole. The true is the whole, he says; and this end is the completed dialectical self-mediation of the initially perplexing origin. Is not this Hegel's claim: that the double exigency of philosophical thought—the reflective analogue of unhappy consciousness—is incorporated into a *singular* process of total self-mediation? Hence the Hegelian philosopher totally overcomes the unhappy consciousness within himself, overcomes it through a complete process of conceptual manifestation in which no otherness remains finally mysterious?

Is this claim justified? Or is it so close to the truth, as to be extremely difficult to see in its untruth or infidelity to the doubleness? Again we ask: Must the doubleness within the philosopher, the need for double mediation, be identical with the unhappy consciousness, even though such an identification might be one possible ambiguous expression of the doubleness? Is the double mediation ever reducible to a singular process of total self-mediation? Do we not always remain in the middle whose double requirement thought must respect? This must be asked if the doubling is not the self-division of a one, but either real Secondness, or a metaxological community of irreducible others.

But for the present let us stay closer to Hegel's own discourse. Its resources allow us to speak of the doubleness, sometimes in terms that reflect Hegel, sometimes in terms that show through Hegel a sense of otherness that shadows his discourse and that is finally returned to the shadows when he privileges dialectical self-mediation as *the* singular process of mediation alone adequate to the fullness of being in the middle. I will now discuss sensation and analytical understanding in relation to philosophical reason. This will allow us to further articulate the middle, to develop the significance of its doubleness, and the power and impotence of Hegel's dialectical mediation of it.

With sensation we seem to grasp immediately the plenitude of concrete being, yet this plenitude is not full concreteness at all. Sensation shows the self as finite, facing and gazing at the infinite wealth of external otherness. Limited by perspective, the sensing self passively registers but a fraction of this external infinitude. For Hegel, as for Kant, sensation without thought is blind: without thought it sees everything immediately but discriminates nothing in what it sees, and hence sees nothing definite. To bind philosophical reason to such sensation is to court, as it were, a fetishistic concreteness, an idolatry of positivistic finitude.

To cling exclusively to sensation is to banish thought, and so to introduce disunion in us between immediate perception and mediated thought. This is not to resolve but to perpetuate dualistic opposition: between us and the external otherness, within our own being between our sensing and our thinking. Remembering the Medieval identification of sloth and despair, one might say that it is philosophical sloth to tarry thus thoughtlessly with the finite. Philosophy founded on such a sensationalism alone would be like worship based on the sentiments of subjectivity that takes pleasure in devotion to sticks and stones. It would be a blind cultic obeisance to an indifferent reality, an unthinking genuflection before immediate givenness. Such fetishistic positivism reminds us of the religious positivity the younger Hegel attacked.

If we take the second possible paradigm, the analytical understanding (*Verstand*), we avoid this idolizing of thoughtless concreteness. Analytical understanding abstracts from the immediate but does so in order to discriminate its undifferentiated givenness. It declines to make a fetish of the sensuously concrete. Quite the opposite, it constructs concepts through its own power, the power of subjectivity. It reveals that thinking is never totally dependent on the given of sense. Where sensuous concreteness is thoughtless, the thought of analytical understanding is abstract. Literally it "takes away" from the given: thus it is withdrawn into itself, at a remove from the real. One almost thinks here of a monastic withdrawal of philosophy from the promiscuous world of sensuousness, Hegel would call it a flight into the ideality of thought.

Any number of examples might be given, but I will just mention Descartes' methodical withdrawal from sensuousness into the thought of thought, the removed mind at home with itself in its own ideal inwardness. There is an air of, as it were, mathematical prayer in Descartes' methodical retreat from outerness. Here it it hard to forget that rhapsodist of Christian religion, Saint Augustine, and the commandment of his philosophical piety, which Husserl, the contemporary high priest of transcendental inwardness, also intones: *Noli foras ire, in te redi, in interiore homine habitat veritas*; do not go outside, return into self, truth dwells in the interior man.

After all, Descartes writes a *meditation*—in mathematical monasticism he becomes a cenobite of thought thinking itself. Descartes' philosophical meditations are, so to say, the analytical prayers of the abstracted intellect. These prayers also include an attempted logical exorcism of what Descartes calls the evil genius. The evil genius is the Luciferian night terror of skeptical thought. If the night terror cannot be transfigured into logical day, Descartes will be worse off than the divided self of the unhappy consciousness. He will be in the sin of unreason and not even know he is in this state of sin.

But Descartes believed that his philosophical thought held out, won through, in this dark night of the mathematical mind. Thought thinking itself emerges into logical day, reassured of its powers and its own self. It does so through an act of philosophical faith (posing as rational proof) in the ultimate thought that thinks itself, the divine mind. Descartes' *cogito* is the modern subjectivistic version of Aristotle's *noēsis noēseōs*. Hegel's logical Idea is a post-Kantian, post-transcendental heir of both of these: the Idea, in fact, logically reassures itself, renews its faith in itself, by actually constituting itself as the thought that thinks itself in its other. The other will be given a subordinate place in the dialectical self-mediation of the Hegelian Idea. The Hegelian Idea hence is more complex and rich than the abstract, analytical understanding. But the privileged philosophical prayer of *thought thinking itself* will be continued.

The virtue of the self-mediation of the analytical understanding, in comparison with sensuous concreteness, is its formal nature. But this is also its defect. It operates with the ideal of purely formal self-consistency, but this creates another dualism, in this case between abstract thought and real content. This difficulty of analytical understanding is the obverse of sensation: Sensation is thoughtless because of its idolatry of indifferent concreteness; abstractive understanding, closing in on itself in formal self-consistency, loses concrete content and so becomes empty thought, that is, thoughtless thought, that is, contradiction in the active being of mind itself. Sensation makes sense mindless, abstract analysis makes mind senseless.

Contrary to the specter commonly conjured up by Hegel's panlogism, for him abstract thought, strictly speaking, is always a contradiction: thought not concrete is not thought at all. In the measure that it cuts itself off from sensation's indifferent concreteness, abstractive understanding becomes itself indifferent to concreteness. This is one of the reasons why empiricism and formal logic often go hand in hand, namely, they feed on the same shared separation of thought and being. They can coexist in an indifferent juxtaposition, one specializing in abstract reflection, the other being impressed with the particularities of externality. In both cases mind's relation to being remains merely external, while the unity of mind is broken up into two separated functions. Philosophy based on this abstractive understanding again continues, rather than resolves, the external dualism of the self and the other, the internal dualism in the self.

Such abstract philosophy reminds us of the formalistic worship that meticulously respects the rituals, scrupulous about any slight deviation from the form. The rites of conceptual analysis are called the "logical method," or the "rules for the direction of the mind," or some such. Like formalistic worship, supreme emphasis on hygienic logic here provides a hint that living spirit has been dimmed, perhaps even put to flight. Just as sensation has its philosophical idolatry, that is to say, sophistry—the idol of the ideal—so also here. The philosopher now worships pure logical form. But this pure logical worship is the obverse side of the impure fear of the ontological recalcitrance of real concreteness—its heathen otherness to logic. In this fear of the heathen otherness a secret will to power may sprout in the ontological emptiness of abstract logical categories.

That is, abstractive understanding may react to the absence of given content by *itself* giving content to the real. Then the philosopher claims to bring his categories to bear on actuality, dictating them to being despite the resistance of its otherness. If abstract thought fails to conform to actuality, actuality must be made to conform to abstract thought. Then, as Kant says, we must put nature to the test, forcing her to answer questions of our devising. We are told, with Bacon, to torture nature in order to become, with Descartes, her masters and possessors. Where sensation becomes servile subjectivity, abstractive understanding becomes militant subjectivity. Their philosophical idolatries are parallel but reversed. For sensation, external things are infinite in their outward wealth, and the mind is finite; it is, as empiricists say, but a pale copy, as it were, a mental spook, of the thing. For abstractive understanding, the external thing is finite, and subjectivity, because independent in mind, is infinite, the unbounded spirit, the unfettered spook (the *Geist* in the machine, so to speak), capable of forcing its own form on things. One extreme resigns itself to absolute dependence on the given, the other declares its absolute independence. To negate its own formalistic emptiness, abstract understanding becomes a will to power. Philosophy fails to become the cultus of mindfulness and instead becomes logical magic, an organon to dominate otherness with abstractions.

Hegel has been denounced as a magician of such abstract thought, but in all fairness he does think that reason must free itself from these complementary idolatries. Likewise he has been accused of an idolatry of pure logical form, but here the issue is complicated by his claim that his logical category is itself an identity of thought and being. In any case, these different philosophical idols remain trapped in dualism and division: they stick to this estrangement, cleave to themselves as if absolute. Like the unhappy consciousness, they are pervaded by the sense of opposition. And as we saw with mastery and servitude, opposition means that to affirm one thing is to cancel another. Just so, the affirmation of sensation here is the denial of thoughtful inwardness, the affirmation of understanding is the denial of meaningful outwardness. We discern here a logic of exclusion, a logic of the "either/or." This is a sectarian logic, so to say. Sensation imputes infinity to externality but refuses it to selfness; understanding ascribes infinity to abstract selfness but withdraws it from externality. In both cases we find an infinitude mastering a finitude, now from the side of outwardness, now from the side of inwardness. We find logical war between finitude and infinitude.

Properly speaking, philosophical reason arises only at this juncture, that is, in relation to radical thought about the problematic middle between the other in its otherness and the self in its inwardness. The war of logical contradiction bespeaks the breakdown of the mediating power of abstract mind. But it also calls for a more radical activation of that mediating power, a breakthrough into a more ultimate realization of philosophical mindfulness. Since sensation truncates the self in its fullness, and since understanding contracts the concrete in its fullness, they need each other for the complementary plenitudes they differently deny. Of themselves, however, they do not recognize this need or its meaning. Philosophical mind properly emerges as simply the comprehension of this need, the self-consciousness of it. It seeks the self-consciousness of sensation—its need for articulating selfness; it seeks the self-understanding of understanding—its need for articulated concreteness. As a mode of mindfulness, philosophical reason thus is not extrinsic to either, nor imposed on them *ab extra*. They exhibit incompletely mediated mind, and reason is simply the fuller mediation of the promise of both as potential forms of mindfulness. Reason's purpose is not to negate them as such, but to negate their partiality and so to realize their import.

Thus, we are pointed to the need of a genuinely concrete reason. Philosophical thinking must fulfill the intention of sensation which is openness to concrete being as other to mind. It must also fulfill the intention of understanding which is to freely and actively articulate the meaningful thought of the given. Concrete being is not merely an aggregate of finite entities: while finite things are subject to the principle of limitation, they are manifested as concretions of the original power of being, which itself is more than any finite being. The original power of being, concretized in finite being but not exhausted by finitude, manifests infinitude. The manifested otherness of being is the concretion in the finite of infinitude.

Similarly, the thinking self is finite but not simply so, for to think is to recognize limits and thus to transcend them. As the power to surpass the limitations of prior thought, the finite self reveals a power of mind that is potentially infinite. And so on the sides of the self and the other, "subjectivity" and "objectivity," we are not confined to an "either/or" between finitude and infinity. We must consider a possible "both/and." We must pass beyond the exclusive logic of any sectarian epistemology: The true universal is the community of being as ontologically catholic.

For Hegel infinitude is manifested in both the finitudes of the concrete and the self. Philosophical reason, to be concrete and free, must seek to do justice to both infinitudes, to what he calls the subjective and objective infinites.[49] This is not to allow one side to dominate the other in dualistic opposition. It is to think through their coexistence, their mutuality, their togetherness, their reciprocity, with all its tensions and conflicts, with all the precariousness involved in preserving their balance, with all the possibility of unbalancing to one side, with the resulting tyranny of one and slavery of the other. Here we can make sense of Hegel's notion of reason, as well as asking if this notion reduces the double infinitude to a *singular* self-mediating infinitude.

Reason reveals in the self an infinite capacity, yet it also shows the self to be a capacity for the infinite. In that sense, reason for Hegel is spirit and hence at once can be both individual and universal. Reason reveals the concrete universality of spirit in that, while remaining concrete, it can limitlessly transcend the contracted concreteness of particularity. I, this individual, as reason, as spirit, am not confined to my particularity: I can rise above particularity: I can extend to the whole of otherness: as reason my individuality is openness to the universal. This need not negate individuality; rather in this openness individuality may receive its fullest expansion, its concrete flowering. I will come back to the question of the place of particularity as particularity in Hegelian reason. Does Hegelian reason demand a sacrifice of particularity to generality, a sacrifice that does not consecrate but violates particularity as recalcitrant to dialectical comprehension? Is Hegelian reason always a piety of the universal for which every recalcitrant particularity is impious, indeed evil (see chapter 4)?

Remember that reason emerges in the *Phenomenology* just subsequent to the unhappy consciousness. It comes to explicit awareness as, in Hegel's phrase, the conscious certainty of being all reality.[50] Reason is the certainty of its sameness with reality, such that the dividedness racking the unhappy consciousness proves to be *reason's own self-dividedness* which, on now being understood, is seen through and overcome. At this point Hegel strongly asserts the truth of idealism: reason as the conscious certainty of being all reality. The remainder of the *Phenomenology* simply works out the manifestation of this claimed certainty of identity between reason and reality, in its full concreteness as *Geist*.

In sum: Reason brings to articulation the latent infinity of finite selfness; but the unfolding of this infinity is also the self becoming unblocked to the infinity in being as other and actual. Trying to be true to the subjective and objective infinites, the thrust of reason is beyond finite thought. Philosophy is a thrust towards absolute thinking, a thinking itself absolute, a thinking true to what is absolute in the actual. For Hegel this absolute thinking tries to grasp the dialectical *synthesis*, the togetherness of the subjective and the objective. It seeks to articulately affirm this synthesis, bring this dialectical togetherness to explicitness. This synthesis is neither the formal, empty one of abstract understanding nor is it the external aggregation or juxtaposition that sensation supplies. It might be called the immanent reciprocity of the self and ultimacy. Hegel determines such reciprocity in terms of a dialectical synthesis. What this means for Hegel is rational self-consciousness of the truth that the other is not other to the self, so as to constitute an ineradicable basis of its self-estrangement. The other is the self in *its own* otherness, which in being recognized as such returns the self to itself, with the more complete self-knowledge of its own being, as a self-completing process of dialectical self-mediation.

The Double in Philosophy: Against Making an Idol of Self-thinking Thought

Against Hegel I would speak here of a metaxological togetherness which preserves difference as the articulated space of a mutuality or a bond. Philosophical reason, as itself *both* dialectical and metaxological, tries conceptually to body forth this reciprocity. This involves the coming together (in Hegel's terms) of the "subjective" and "objective" infinites.[51] Hence, its exigence is always internally complex, indeed double. It requires self-knowledge wherein the self seeks to become at home with itself: yet this self-knowledge must be radically attentive to the infinitude of the other. Philosophical reason is openness to the closeness of self and other, but this closeness is not to be closed up.

Can we then take seriously claims such as: reason is the conscious certainty of being all reality? Well may one ask. Certainly Hegel's idealism here is not subjective but is always a realism; as a realism, moreover, it is never naive. It is beyond the subjective idealism of analytical understanding and the naive realism of sensation, trying to balance the positive truth of both in a position beyond the dualism of realism and idealism. It claims itself to be the dialectical reconciliation of thinking and being. But consider: Hegelian reason recognizes that it *itself* is the unity of the two sides that are dualistic alienated for the unhappy consciousness; the double is not a double, but mistakenly taken as a dualism of self and other; the double reveals itself to Hegelian reason as two sides of the same unity which reason recognizes as simply *itself*. Hegelian reason is the self-knowledge of the unhappy consciousness; it is the completed self-mediation of the process of which the unhappy consciousness is an incomplete and self-alienated stage. In terms of the two infinitudes of self and other, these are not now two, but dialectical moments of an absolute unity that embraces both sides and with which Hegelian reason claims to know its own identity. The circle closes.

I do not think this is faithful to the middle. Recall that we are bound to truth yet distanced from it; as so bound to an other, truth is not the philosopher's possession; the philosopher is intermediate, in between. We now see Hegel saying: this between is mistaken by the unhappy consciousness for a middle whose extremes are opposed; in truth, the extremes are two aspects of the middle; the middle is but the process of the dialectical self-mediation of thought; Hegelian reason *is* just that middle, just that process of dialectical self-mediation; hence it does not matter whether you approach the middle from the side of the self or the other, for both of these are the same, as two moments of the middle as a singular, total process of dialectical self-mediation.

One cannot underestimate the importance of the point for Hegel. It recurs again and again throughout the system. I need only cite here the triple syllogism of *Geist* in the *Encyclopedia* (§§ 575–577) where the absoluteness of Hegelian philosophy is determined in its most ultimate form. The Idea of philosophy is self-knowing reason, and this is a middle that divides itself into nature and spirit; but each extreme is also a middle, and every reunification of extremes is the reunification of the self-dividing middle. In the third syllogism (§ 577), nature and spirit are manifestations of the Idea self-dividing into two appearances; the two manifestations are dynamically united in the self-knowing reason as the absolutely universal middle. The eternal work of the eternal Idea is the dynamic unity of the double in the self-reunification of this self-doubling. This is the total process of self-mediation. Hegel's reiteration of Aristotle's *noēsis noēseōs* crowns this triple syllogism, concludes and completes the circle of the system.

I agree that the middle is open to dialectical self-mediation, and the unhappy consciousness wrongly confines otherness to dualistic opposition. I disagree in respect of the mediation of otherness beyond dualistic opposition. We need not reduce otherness, identified with dualistic opposition, to this singular process of dialectical self-mediation. I repeat: the thinking self knows itself to be in the middle between its intimacy with truth and its distance from it. Philosophical perplexity, as known by the philosopher, is not a mere blank ignorance; it is an intermediate, deeply stressed by the desire, hence anticipated presence, of what it knows it currently lacks; the fuller unfolding of philosophical thought is simply the mindful articulation of this double intermediate. Intermediate being need not yield the unhappy consciousness; nor is the mindful articulation of the middle solely a matter of dialectical self-mediation. If it were Hegel would be right and there would be no radical otherness. But it is always a matter of both dialectical self-mediation *and* metaxological intermediation with otherness.

In the middle philosophy experiences the exigence of a double mediation: self-mediation and intermediation. The first stresses thought thinking itself; the second, thought thinking its other. Hegel privileges self-mediation, and hence thought thinking its other is dialectically incorporated into thought thinking itself. His radical claim here is that the double exigency of philosophical thought is incorporated into a singular process of total self-mediation. The Hegelian philosopher claims to totally overcome the unhappy consciousness within himself. This cannot be right if the doubleness within the philosopher is not identical with unhappy consciousness (though this may be a side of the doubleness), nor reducible to a total process of self-mediation. The god of the philosopher cannot be just thought thinking itself; otherwise we lose the agapeic origin that grants the other its otherness as other; the "whole" collapses into an absorbing god.[52]

I can put the point in terms of the double desideratum presented by sensation and understanding. Hegel says, in effect, that reason is the dialectical self-comprehension of sensation and understanding: the implicit sense of being and thought that each implies, reason brings to explicit self-knowledge, self-mediation. I think this is correct up to a point. The difficulty, however, is that both the sides of self and other become moments in the process of singular self-mediation of philosophical reason, and inevitably the sense of the other becomes subordinate. I take as true some sense of the togetherness of the self and the other, and indeed the claim that there is a certain infinitude to both. But just because of that infinitude I say that the doubleness, while not a dualism (after all, it is a mutuality or togetherness) is not reducible to a singular process of dialectical self-mediation, nor to one overarching infinitude that sublates all otherness and finitude within its own self-mediation. Certainly the dialectical self-mediation of the infinite, which sublates the finite, is superior to a dualistic opposition of finitude and infinitude, but it is not adequate to the inexhaustibility of agapeic infinitude, that is, its otherness to finitude, as articulated by the intermediation of the metaxological double, which also is beyond dualistic opposition.

My claim again is this: The intermediation of two dialectically
self-mediating wholes cannot again be solely dialectical self-mediation.
If it were, the double would always be reduced to a unity: one more
complete dialectical whole which sublates the other. If we say, and
Hegel would say, that such wholes are infinitudes, the mediation
between them cannot be such as to reduce the infinitude of one to
the encompassing wholeness of the other. The resistance of such an
infinitude, on both sides, to the totally comprehensive embrace of any
whole, must be respected. Each such a whole as infinitude has its own
inward otherness that would resist the complete determination, either
by the other or even by itself, of its own self-mediation. Such wholes
would be infinitely open, ineradicably open, hence perhaps not best
described as "wholes" at all. The being of such overflowing, hence
overwhole "wholes" is grounded in being itself as agapeic. An
infinitely open "whole" is an agapeic origin. A community of such
agapeic originals must remain metaxologically open.

The inward otherness of every whole shows it to be double: both
self-mediating and yet grounded in an otherness that makes self-
mediation possible, yet resists complete self-mediation. If every whole
is thus double, how much more recalcitrant to complete self-mediation
must the intermediation of a plurality of such doubles? How fitting
at all is the language of holism to such "wholes?" For every concept
of a "whole" is haunted by a certain metaphorics of circularity in
which the beginning embraces the end to form a totality, enclosed
in itself, hence set against what is outside the circle. The primacy
of thought thinking itself in the philosophical tradition is the conceptual counterpart to such a metaphorics of circularity. Both conceptual
and metaphoric circularity deeply imbue the spirit of Hegelian philosophizing. The ghost of such metaphysical metaphorics has to be
exorcised to think the double differently and to respect transcendence.

For Hegel every double carries the taint of dualism and hence the
potential estrangement of the unhappy consciousness, and so must
be transcended. Yes, we cannot wallow in wretchedness. But there is
a double of metaxological community which is always, already the
promise of being beyond wretchedness. The double of metaxological
intermediation will grant the community of self and other, their
fundamental mutuality, but philosophical reason, as I see it, need not
be the thought that circles around that community and encloses it
in a total thought that then simply thinks itself, albeit in and through
the otherness. No: philosophical reason will be the mindfulness
emergent in the middle itself between the self and the other, and in
that middle it will again have to meet the double desideratum:
thought thinking itself, thought thinking its other.

In a very impoverished way, sensation answers to the second, analytical understanding to the first. I say impoverished because otherness is not exhausted by sensuous externality, and the self-mediation of the knowing self is not identical with the mediation of abstract intellect. Hegel may agree but in the process he will risk a *third impoverishment* in his dialectical response to these two impoverishments. The double mediation in the middle is reduced to a singular process of dialectical self-mediation wherein the pluralized redoubling of being is enclosed. We avoid the dialectical impoverishment by seeing that philosophical reason is to be articulated as the pluralized intermediation of metaxological mind, radically open to the given plenitude of being as an agapeic redoubling of originals. The metaxological double is a being-at-home with the extremes, not the wretched self-dividedness of unhappy consciousness, a being mindful, a being-at-home that can even be at home in not being-at-home. This is a being mindful in the between which mediates the extremes, and hence is more than dualistic opposition, but which does not reduce to one or either side, or flit to and fro between them, bouncing restlessly from one to the other in endless vacillation, or like Hegel, reduce plurality to an encompassing unity that dialectically mediates only with itself in mediating the extremes.

Is Hegelian God-service an Absolution?
On Speculative Abandon and Release

We cannot remain absorbed in the concept, so let us return one last time to Hegel's strange saying: Philosophy, too, is *Gottesdienst*. We can now reiterate, more radically than we did at the outset, that this service escapes instrumentalization. Philosophy is not servile service: it is one of the *artes liberales*, free arts, not one of the *artes serviles*, functional skills. Philosophical knowing is not a tool or instrument which interferes with the object.[53] Its purpose is not control of the "object" but openness to its essence and its otherness, mindful openness to what is at work and at play in the middle. The will to power with its instrumentalities relates externally to every matter at issue. In willing to master the matter as an alien, it is unwilling to become properly coimplicated with it. Will to power actually confines philosophy to the finiteness of merely functional work, the fruit of the Fall, where we are estranged from the givenness of being as other and sweat to impose our stamp on it. When speculative mind is thus instrumentalized, it falls to being an *ancilla* to a fallen world.

Without denying work's necessity, the speculative Hegel, with Aristotle, looks to the end of toil in the highest activity, an activity not itself instrumental work but leisure. Philosophy looks to leisure, is itself leisure, *skolē*, an activity enjoyed as an end in itself, a goal whole within itself, yet open, making the human being at home with being's otherness. As Aristotle piously puts it: A man living in philosophical leisure lives not as a mere man but as having the divine dwelling with him.[54] Speculative thinking then is not simply the production of human will. Hegel himself says: It "demands abandonment to the very life of the object."[55] This abandonment is reason's release to what is more ultimate than the obstinacies of closed self-will, its willing openness to the hierophany of the manifested otherness of what is absolute in the concrete.

What is this abandonment? This is my question. Hegel immediately qualifies this abandon, by seeing it as less ultimate than the *return of the knower to itself*. I will comment on this below as suggesting a failure to fully understand the agapeic nature of release. Nevertheless, abandon need not be a vacuous receptivity, nor a mere passivity; it can be an achieved openness, a mediated result. At the outset we are cramped within a narrow finitude, closed upon ourselves. We need to pass through the trial of negation of dualism, doubt and opposition. These are real, but philosophy is not servile to them. Its abandonment is the end of a process of transformation. Hegel calls his *Phenomenology* a "highway of despair" (*Weg der Verzweiflung*: we note again the reference to the double, *Zwei*), recording the purgatorial passage through the valley of illusion.

Philosophy, like cultus, must be more than a merely immediate relation to the ultimate, but calls for a mediated elevation of mind beyond the workaday world of dualism. For Hegel we exist in immediate relation to the absolute: *Das Absolute ist schon bei uns*, he says.[56] Philosophy does more than exist in this relation: it reflectively mediates it, thinks through its significance. Moving towards this mediated articulation, it does not exclude the immediate. This may now be grasped as a mediated immediacy: at once a form of being and an explicit signification. The "ordinary" is not "ordinary" but manifests the "extraordinary" and is known to manifest it. Again here Hegel's thought is not linear but circular. And while I reject the closure of the circle of dialectical self-mediation, the circular metaphor might be seen to open itself affirmatively in this sense: the end in question is not a dead end but a new beginning, a renewal of the beginning. To the dualistic and instrumentalist mind, the Sabbath is just the end of the workaday week, a mere dead day. For the speculative philosopher, the Sabbath can seep into the everyday for the self, beginning anew the festive Monday of the second week.

This demands a repudiation of Wittgenstein's view of philosophy as a kind of sickness that arises when language "goes on holiday." Wittgensteinian philosophy quarantines itself within the everyday, within common, "ordinary" language. But the holiday celebrates the hierophany of the divine. Being as festive agapē ruptures this quarantine of commonsense. The everyday is absurd if not open to the holiday as the festival of agapeic being. Without the holiday of philosophy, common sense becomes common nonsense, mere endless toil. Philosophy is the festive thinking of agapeic mind. By contrast, Wittgenstein is the unhappy consciousness (the fly in the fly bottle—buzzing) who seeks a cure in a direction counter to speculative philosophers like Hegel, turning from the absolute towards the relativities of fragmented multiplicity. Hegel treats his sickness differently. We are led to wonder if the contemporary distaste for speculative philosophy reveals an obsession with finite toil, an envy of speculative ease; does contemporary skepticism mask a dogmatic finitude?

The health of philosophical mind is not will to power; it is beyond the dichotomy of power and impotence. But impotence, like will to power, is not without metaphysical significance. Impotence reveals the *apatheia* of the energy of being: it is a *mē-energeia*. Just that negativity, that "counting for nothing," erupts not only in the unhappy consciousness, but in the philosopher, indeed in Hegel himself. Our response to that "nothingness" allows a plurality of rejoinders. Aristotle says being is said in many ways; one can also say "It is nothing" in many ways: *to mē on legetai pollachōs*. "It is nothing" can be the gesture of nihilistic disgust and dismissal that Nietzsche detects in most religious cultus, the Greek pagan excepted. Such a gesture is neither an erotic nor agapeic abandon: it is the nihilistic abandonment of being as a rejection, a repudiation, a betrayal of being.

Can we say "It is nothing" otherwise? Yes. "It is nothing," can be the gesture of a release, of an absolving, an absolution. I think such a gesture can be totally other to Nietzsche's claim that God is the deification of the will to nothingness.[57] In respect of the metaphysical meaning of powerlessness and this release, consider here Hegel's well-known letter wherein he tells of a state of total depression between his twenty fifth and thirtieth year, tells of his suffering from a "hypochondria" so severe as to paralyze all his powers. Eventually, he says, he cured his sickness by accepting the necessary abandonment of individuality, which absolute knowing required, going on in later years to build monumental philosophy.[58]

What is this philosophical abandon? Is it the sacrifice of the philosopher? Must one *die* to become a philosopher? What must die in the human being for one to become a philosopher? Must one *kill* to be a philosopher? What must one kill? One's humanity in order to become a god? One's finite particularity to become universal? God commanded the faithful Abraham to kill, sacrifice his son Isaac. But who commands the philosopher to kill, to sacrifice? Are these questions themselves too violent for the philosopher? Is philosophical abandon our flight from the existential self that Kierkegaard excoriated in the objective thinker? A flight to the anonymous system from the idiocy of such selfhood? Is philosophical abandon the self-forgetfulness of concrete individuality or the transformation of individuality in the light of a certain mindfulness of the more embracing community of being? Is philosophical abandon just Stoic resignation to the cosmic logos, or Spinoza's *acquiescentia animi* or Nietzsche's *amor fati?*

And what of the death of God? What kind of philosophical God-service acquiesces in such a monstrous death? Can this service really be divine, or is it service at all, demonic service, betrayal, like Judas' abandonment of his Master? Service has to offer itself to the other; it must not pass through the other as the means, the medium of its own self-possession. If God-service is simply a religious metaphor for the logic of closed self-mediation, is not God the sacrificial victim of speculative logic? The violence of the sacred would be the violence of the philosophical concept. The philosopher would lift himself, sublate himself to self-sanctification through the subordination of the divine other. Philosophy would then be blasphemy, the philosopher a criminal, a murderer. Is Nietzsche here more honest than Hegel? If God is sacrificed in the name of Reason, who is the consecrating priest, who the sacrificial victim—the philosopher or God? Would the slaughterbench (*Schlachtbank*) of world-history be the altar of time on which Hegelian reason sacrifices God?

This is a cascade of violent questions. I think an honest philosopher cannot evade asking them, even if it is not at all easy to answer them. Ambiguities in Hegel's whole enterprise force them on us again and again. But let me offer an interpretation of philosophical abandon, where the ambiguity does not entirely disappear but assumes a less violent form.

We cannot be too literal in our interpretation. Negatively, abandon recalls the unhappy consciousness, its forsakenness, its aloneness. Positively, however, abandonment can mean a freeing, a release. Hegel, as we saw, suffered a paralysis of his powers, but to abandon oneself need not be to efface or betray one's powers. To be abandoned might be to be unloosed. *Before* Hegel is shrunk into himself; *after* he is graced with a release. One forsakes the constraint of self-enclosure, and finds the freeing, the unfreezing of disabled power. Abandon is then a prevailing over a refusal. It frees power, power to be mindful, in the form of openness to what is more ultimate than oneself, not power in the form of wilfully forcing this ultimate to submit to one. We are reminded of the Biblical wisdom: the grain which falls to the ground grows only where it dies, otherwise it remains barren, hardened and alone. We are also brought into the neighborhood of Heideggerian *Gelassenheit*.[59]

Can this abandon, this unloosing, this gracing, this rebirth be explained dialectically? Is it not the other way around: the power of dialectic is grounded on it; dialectic's power is grounded on a releasing that is other to dialectic? The philosopher's abandon does exhibit certain dialectical features in being both negative and positive. Negatively, being abandoned is being deserted, being confronted with absurdity and the absence of intelligibility. Positively, it issues into a commitment, not a betrayal, a dedication, a celebration, even a praise: to abandon oneself is to *trust* that, despite absurdity, being is not unintelligible. The pietas of philosophical reason is this trust: trust in the power of reason itself, trust in the ultimate reasonableness of the real. If the negative side is symbolized, as we saw, by the feeling of the unhappy consciousness that God is dead, the other side might be seen in the fact that, after his agony, Christ gives up his spirit, commends himself into the hands of *another*.[60] But especially here, does not the face of an unmastered other stand before dialectical logic? Will such logic only say about this other: "It is nothing?" Must we not say "It is nothing" differently to the way dialectic says it?

Hegel was first sick with "hypochondria," a sickness that is no sickness, a sickness in spirit. He found philosophical abandon to be healing, recuperative, unblocking the self to the other, liberating the power of spirit in the self, offering it some wholeness. He found that openness to the universal allows individuality to come into its own. He found that if we assert a disjunction between individuality and universality, and bind ourselves to individuality with a sterile stubbornness, we but more deeply entrench disjunction, and cutting off individuality, undermine it. Openness to the universal becomes the opening out of individuality.

But what is this universal? How deeply does it allow us to say "It is nothing." Are there negativities beyond dialectical recuperation? In Hegel's notion of the concrete universal, it is the whole which mediates its abstract universality through its externalized particularity and which returns to itself in the universal individual that is the complete process of singular self-mediation. Hegel will say that the unfolding of the particular self toward the universal means for the self to be found again, to find oneself again in relation to what initially seems foreign. The point is not to project oneself narcissistically into the other: this is but a ruse that on the surface looks like self-transcendence. Nevertheless, with Hegelian abandon, we are given *ourselves* back again in the other: openness to the other releases us to ourselves. The other is not a dualistic opposite, and it is so, not because we *make* it in our image but because in this openness we *find* ourselves in the other.

What if the universal is not the dialectically self-mediating whole, but the metaxological community of being? Then Hegel's formulation is seen to be questionably ambiguous. For it might imply that the other, even in abandonment, serves always as a means for the self, as the mediating detour by which it comes to itself. Dialectical abandonment ultimately would then be a passage to self-recovery, which would always covertly serve to justify the abandon. But is there a metaxological abandonment in which there is an even more radical giving up of justification in terms of such self-recovery? Is there a going towards the other such that the secret thought of return to self may be radically sacrificed?

I think there is. In fact Hegel's own use of the representation of Christ's sacrifice is indicative of this giving up, against Hegel's dialectical appropriation of this representation. To my mind this giving up to an other is not a dialectical *means* by which the spirit can return to itself at some putatively higher level of *self*-appropriation. The abandonment to the other radically gives one into the hands of the other as other, not into the other as simply one's own other, one's own self in otherness. There may be acts of abandon whose point is precisely a giving to the other, or going towards the other, in which what is lacking is precisely any certainty for a justification in reconstituted dialectical self-mediation. And yet one must give oneself up.

There is an erotic abandon and there is an agapeic abandon, corresponding to the two senses of eternity, invoked previously. Recall again that the erotic absolute entails the process of dialectical self-mediation, which becomes and returns to itself in the progressive movement of constituting the whole. Recall that when Hegel mentions abandonment (see note 55 above), he explicitly underscores the return of true knowledge back into itself, having taken the fullness of the content back into itself.

By contrast, the agapeic absolute is already full in itself and hence does not constitute *itself* via the detour of the other as a moment of its own dialectical self-mediation; rather from this overwholeness, which as self-mediating is infinite, it gives itself to the other, which in this is given to be other, in a sense irreducible to the agapeic giver:

the other is loosed as a free other. Expressed in terms of the cultus of these different absolutes, erotic abandon would be Hegelian *progressus*, which recuperates itself by dialectical self-recovery in the other; agapeic abandon would be a metaxological intermediation with the other, a gratuitous othering of self towards the other. In the latter (applied here to the *human* giver) there *may* be a self-return (in that the other *may* give back, return its own irreducible giving). *But such a return would not be the essential point.* For the original giving would be for the other as other, and not for the other as the mirror in which the self will finally recognize itself.

In both the dialectical and metaxological abandonment, the other is not an alienating, dualistic other. In both, philosophical mind rejects any idolatrous divinization of isolated subjectivity. Anything thus isolated, in fact, cannot manifest the divine at all: any isolation of subjectivity rather robs it of the divine. Philosophical mind must transcend both the despotism and the debility of such subjectivity. Even when the self seems utterly derelict, the call of community is inherent in its being. Philosophical mindfulness would free this community, this togetherness of the self and the other, free it for mediated articulation.

Philosophical mind negates our ascription of absoluteness to the relative yet it is on speculative watch for the appearances of the absolute in the relative. It detaches and distances the self, but in the distance it may involve mind deeper with the other. Its speculative watch is vigilant towards the togetherness of the self and the ultimate other. The speculative watch is the openness of mind to this togetherness.

In this sense, and with suitable qualifications for a thinker deeply modern, Hegel inherits and carries forward the Greek notion of philosophy as *theōria*. I mention this because once again we discern the connection of philosophical mind with festive cultus. The *theōroi* originally were delegates, messengers, representatives sent by the Greek cities to the religious ceremonies and public games. They were observers, watchers. But to observe a religious festival is always double: It transcends any exclusive dualism of the spectatorial and the participant; it is not to assume a spectatorial stance that is apathetically external. *Theōria* is speculative reason, and the speculator is indeed a watcher; but his watching is an *involvement*, hence participation in what is ultimate. *Theōria* is a performative enactment of the doubleness of speculative mind as participant in, yet, as participant, other than the *energeia* of the being of the ultimate.

Speculative watchfulness that is attentive to otherness is a metaxological mindfulness that would not interfere through abstract categories with being as other. The theorist does not give himself over to a neutral universe, an indifferent cosmos. He gives himself to a divine cosmos in play. *Theōria* is not disinterested in the sense of being devoid of interest: it is the highest interest, an attentive wonder to what is of absolute interest. It stands not in a sterile world where dead facts are dualistically juxtaposed with subjective values. Being itself is most worthy of contemplation, worthy in the highest degree.[61] As spectatorial, the *theōros* is receptive: but as freely participating in the festival around him, he is active. His is a free openness, a receptivity that is highest activity, an intermediated balance of identity and difference. Being is an *agapē*. Speculative mind, as vigilance of being's otherness, is agapeic mind.

In that sense the philosopher must genuinely be a *philos*: a friend of truth, not a *turranos*, not a slave. If we recall Aristotle's distinction in the *Ethics* between three types of friendship, we must say that philosophy is not the friendship of sensual pleasure (subjectivity), nor yet is it the friendship of utility (the worker or the master). It must be the third friendship of virtue—where virtue here is power ordered by justice, that is, by proportion between the human and divine. This proportion, even in their essential disproportion, would ultimately be their metaxological community. This friendship helps heal the self of its servility and hubris. As with the cultic observance, there is here both an opening and a fulfillment. A cultic observance is again not a spectatorial inactivity but a religious doing of the sacred truth. Philosophical mind is observance in that sense, the doing or performative enactment of truth, the being at work, the *energeia* of truthfulness. The philosophical unfolding of mind toward what is ultimate is the being at work of truthfulness; as *energeia* it is also mind's enjoyment of ultimacy.

Is not something like this implied by one of Hegel's famous religious metaphors, metaphors the panlogist Hegel found impossible to avoid, dialectical metaphors that, in fact, point towards what is beyond dialectical logic: Truth, he says, is the bacchanalian revel where not a one is sober, a revel which nonetheless is nothing but a state of transparent unbroken calm?[62] This metaphor is dialectical because it articulates a *coincidentia oppositorum*. But it also points us to what is other to dialectical logic in that its enigmatic, ambiguous power springs from a *persisting doubleness* that resists reduction to univocity, even a "higher" mediated univocity. This religious metaphor images the cult of philosophy as beyond logicist impiousness and as turned towards what is other to philosophy.

The metaphor cultivates this other thought: In the middle the opposites meet, the extremes cross: self and other intertwine and separate in an orgiastic gesture of welcome and excess, when a community of being dances. The dance, the bacchanalian revel performatively enacts the agapeic excess of the original power of being. The revel, the dance, offers an occasion of the manifested otherness of this ultimate power. But the agapeic excess of the original power of being *as other* grounds the middle as the metaxological community of being. Philosophy, its cult, the religious cult, dialectical thinking, too, are grounded in this excess which, in the beginning and in the end, always exceeds them, always is beyond them. And surely we do not need to wait the permission of Nietzsche's *imprimatur* to ponder the meaning—Hegelian yet other than Hegelian—of this metaphysical metaphor?

Chapter 3

Speculation and Representation:
The Masks of Philosophy and
Its Religious Double

Speculation and Representation

The theme of speculation and representation offers an important variation on the relation of philosophy and religion. What is sometimes called "representational thinking" is denounced by thinkers like Heidegger, Levinas, Derrida, Foucault, Deleuze. What exactly "representation" means is not always univocally clear, but it certainly draws forth a hostile criticism of speculative philosophy. Speculative mind is criticized as a domineering rationality that reduces all otherness to its own "representations" and hence does violence to whatever resists encapsulation in "representation." Such "representational" thinking seems characteristic of post-Cartesian philosophy and especially in its idealistic forms: knowability is reduced to representability which arises from the active knower—whether seen as the *cogito*, or the transcendental ego, or perhaps Hegelian *Geist*—as it brings the other as "object" before its imperious survey. The concepts of this knowing subject do not ultimately represent that other as other, but rather serve as representations for the subject, hence as "self-representations."

The critique of representational thought then seeks to break the enclosure of subjectivistic immanence, and restore ontological weight to the other as other, beyond all representation, beyond the power of self-representation. In this critique Hegelian idealism is as much at stake as is Husserlian transcendentalism, indeed as is *all* speculative metaphysics that wants to reduce being and knowability to being made present to, being representable to the surveying subject. One sees immediately the connection of representation thus conceived with the critique of speculative metaphysics as "metaphysics of presence." The ideality of pure absolute presence is identified with speculative mind, and both together are rejected in favor of different forms of "non-representational" thinking, beyond the reduction of the other to "objectivity," or of the self to "subjectivity."

I am sympathetic to this critique relative to some of its intentions. I put it thus: The tradition of speculative philosophy has always had a predilection to privilege *absolutely self-mediating thought*, with the philosopher trying to become identical with this ideal. In the ancient world we see it in Aristotle's God: *noēsis noēseōs*. Were it open to him as a mortal, the speculative philosopher would be such a God. Stoic self-sufficiency illustrates a version of the ideal of absolute self-mediation in inwardness, in thought, in ethical inwardness too. The Cartesian *cogito*, the thinking of the idealistic tradition or the tradition of transcendental philosophy, Hegel's self-thinking Idea, all offer modern versions of the ideal, where the constitutive power of "subjectivity" receives more sophisticated articulation than in ancient and medieval metaphysics. *This* strain of the speculative tradition was not always sufficiently free of the "metaphysics of presence." I have criticized the absolutizing of self-mediating thinking when it closes thought to what may be radically other to our thought. I believe Hegel courted this closure. Nevertheless, I find philosophical thought to be always double: thought thinking itself *and* thought thinking its others. Metaxological philosophizing requires both these mediations of mind. The second mediation, intermediation with the other, breaks open, breaks through every enclosure of self-thinking thought, including Hegel's dialectically self-mediating speculation.

In this chapter, I continue the defense of this metaxological double with reference to Hegel's view of speculation and representation. Hegel also criticizes representation but for reasons very different to the above post-Heideggerian critique: Hegelian speculation claims to *complete* the project of *self-mediation* more absolutely than does representation. Contra these contemporary critics, Hegel seeks this completion by going beyond representation, because the latter is not absolutely self-mediating but is always limited by a relation to *an other*. I want to say: I agree with Hegel—representation has a necessary relation to an other; but I defend this necessity as essentially positive. Against the absolutizing of self-mediating thought, I defend the double in representation as itself the promise of an *openness to the unrepresentable*.

The post-Heideggerian critique of "representation" aims to preserve this openness, rightly so, against imperialistic subjectivity and the "metaphysics of presence." But I see something other in representation, namely, an imagistic concretion of the double mediation of metaxological mindfulness. Hence I agree and disagree with Hegel. Agree: representation necessitates relativity to an other. Disagree: we do not have to see this necessity as an incomplete form of absolute self-mediation. I agree and disagree with contemporary critics of "representation." Agree: we must break with imperialistic idealism and respect the thought of the other beyond thought. Disagree: representation, differently understood, especially religious representation, already contains the promise of this break, and this thought of the other beyond thought.

Representation and Religious Doubleness

The issue of religious representation has these other ramifications. Questions about the nature of religious language have been a central concern of contemporary philosophy of religion. This is consonant with a widespread emphasis upon the exploration of language itself. The defense of religious language, generally within the context of a pervasive scientific culture, and particularly against positivistically minded attacks, is an important strand in this emphasis. Yet this contemporary concern restates a perennial problem: the precise status of religious representation, especially vis-à-vis the norms of rational reflection.

The representational and imagistic dimension of religious language has often been noted as one of its chief characteristics. Yet religious representation and rational reflection seem to tussle on the same terrain and enforce different demands. Religious representation invites us to participate in a sacred universe with its rituals of worship and reverent invocations of divinity. Rational reflection, by contrast, seems to introduce a critical pause in this participation, demanding a detachment from naive commitments, asking the thinker to consider crucial ambiguities that may mark religious representation.

Reason and representation appear to be a double in tension, the tension between critical detachment and reverent participation. The critical bent of reason, taken to the extreme, seems corrosive of religious reverence. This double in tension has repeatedly surfaced throughout history. In the ancient era we come across it in the tension of *logos* and *muthos*, revealed clearly, say, in Plato's *Euthyphro*, in the respective approaches of Socrates and Euthyphro to the definition of piety. In the Middle Ages we come across it in relation to faith and reason. In the modern era, the attack of the *Aufklärung* on superstition and fanaticism expresses one aspect of the problem. In our time, scientific reason, particularly in its positivistic interpretation, raises continuing questions about the role of religious language. The drive for "demythologization" marks a related desire within religion itself, namely, to acknowledge and come to terms with the rights of rational norms.

A crucial aspect of the problem is that religious representation is essentially ambiguous. No religious representation is entirely univocal. Representation itself seems double, indeed potentially plurivocal. It does not carry, as it were, its own immediate interpretation; nor is it always self-interpreting. Different responses to this ambiguity are possible. We might react negatively, and in positivistic fashion, dismiss such ambiguity as a sign of the inherent untenability of religious representation. The positivist in essence decries such ambiguity for its failure to live up to his ideal of scientific and logical clarity, namely, the ideal of univocity: that a term have one determinate literal meaning. The positivist dismisses religious representation as merely equivocal, that is, mere duplicitous confusion from the standpoint of scientistic or logicist univocity.

We might react less reductively, as does the hermeneutical philosopher. This response implies: the modern scientific person has difficulties in understanding the representations of another, non-scientific culture; yet with proper discernment, the meaningful interpretation of such representations is possible. The ambiguity of representation is not a mere logical equivocation, either to be reduced to univocal literalness, or dismissed as logically dissident for failing to meet the standard of univocity. The ambiguity must be interpreted, thought through, in a mode of mindfulness that is not scientistically reductive. Hermeneutical thought thus embodies a certain critical respect for the religious representation as a significant *other* to scientific discourse, an other that, in being interpreted, is to be respected in its otherness.

Hegel's dialectical-speculative response offers another possibility. As I understand dialectical thought, it refuses the ideal of simple univocity, since every unity is inherently complex and self-mediating. It also refuses to be arrested by equivocity, since it holds that differences need not be bifurcated into dualistic opposites but can be mediated in a more complex self-mediating unity which embraces differences within itself. Hegel cannot be characterized in terms of the two alternatives just mentioned, though he exhibits features of both: with the hermeneuticist he holds that the representation must be interpreted; and while dialectical thought rejects any merely scientistic reduction to univocity, the question remains whether Hegel's own speculative appropriation of religion is itself a rational, albeit dialectical, reduction of its rich ambiguity, or something else again.

This dialectical response calls for thought for other reasons. For one, Hegel's philosophy of religion, as Fackenheim indicates, is not concerned with "object" theology, but with "relational" theology.[1] Religious representation is not just an "object" for external investigation, but a "relation" for reflection: representation does not just pin down a fixed "object" and classify this as "God"; rather it gives concrete articulacy to living relations between the human and divine. True, Hegel denounces his own contemporaries who would speak of religion without speaking of God. My point is simply: in Hegelian thought the nature of God, and the relativity of the human and divine, are themselves intimately related. In addition, the relation of representation and reason, of *Vorstellung* and *Begriff*, and more generally between religion and philosophy, is controversial in Hegel himself and continues to be controversial among his commentators. This is partly conditioned by the predominance of Left Hegelians after Hegel's death, and the anthropological reduction of theology by thinkers like Feuerbach and Marx. This controversy continues because this reduction squares uneasily with the subtleties of Hegel's own somewhat elusive teachings.[2]

Most importantly, the issue remains controversial because Hegel did claim, whether successfully or not remains to be examined, to do rational justice to the ambiguity of representation. He did so in a manner that inevitably appears unsatisfactory to those completely critical of religion and those who would brook no criticism at all. He tries to avoid these alternatives. On the one hand, we must not dodge the issue by separating religion and reason, defusing the difficulty by claiming that they have nothing essential to do with one another, as is a temptation in Wittgensteinian "fideism."[3] There is a genuine tension between the two, such that philosophy and religion may clash. On the other hand, this clash need not generate the corrosive criticism of the *Aufklärung*, nor the reductive criticism of post-Hegelian humanisms, nor yet again the destructive criticisms of scientism or positivism. The real tension of religion and philosophy also reveals a relation, a bond.

Consequently, philosophy must assume a complex stance: at once open to what representation may reveal, and yet capable of critically reflecting on its claim to absolute truth. That philosophical reason can be double, that is, both affirmative and critical reflects, as we shall see, something of the rich ambiguity of representation: that representation may reveal a highest attainment of spirit, yet even in this, be marked by a limit, or rather mark a limit, to the beyond of which it also gestures. The issue with Hegel is not just historical, but philosophic and systematic. Focusing on the ambiguity of representation, his account is not itself always free from ambiguity. This, coupled with the recurrent nature of the problem, makes a rethinking of the issue necessary.

What will emerge is a further ramification of the theme of dialectic and the double mediation. By representation I will mean what in *Philosophy and its Others* (chapter 3) I called the "double image of the sacred." Such a double image would articulate a world of signification unto itself, hence be self-mediating, hence offer us some self-knowledge; but it would also be marked by reference to an other, hence be *inter*mediating with what is beyond; moreover this openness to the beyond might itself be double as allowing *both* an erotic openness on our part to the other, *and* an agapeic irruption of the other into the circle of our self-mediation, an irruption of the other as appearing, as self-disclosive to us. Both these latter mediations are not reducible to dialectical self-mediation.

Overall the ambiguity of religious representation articulates a doubleness that at best, I claim, relates nonreductively to the otherness of the divine: the relation of man and God is metaxological, hence susceptible to a double mediation which preserves difference from the two sides, without the difference having to be conceived as a dualistic opposition, nor rearticulated as but two moments of a complete, singular process of total dialectical self-mediation. This is not to deny that dualistic opposition may emerge precisely to the extent that the doubleness is interpreted in negative terms. My major question overall will be whether Hegel's speculative appropriation of religion reduces that double mediation to a singular process of total, dialectical self-mediation of which Hegel's logical system of thought thinking itself is the absolute and complete expression. This latter is not the more common scientistic or logicist reduction to univocity, but it is a reduction nevertheless, albeit dialectically conceived.

Of course, Hegel ranges widely over the many sides of religions and the religious.[4] For present purposes I concentrate on these essential points: First, I speak in more general terms about the tension and bond between philosophy and religion. Second, I offer some remarks on Kierkegaard and Hegel: there is a doubleness in philosophy itself as sometimes a mode of masked thinking. Third, I outline Hegel's characterization of religious representation. Fourth, I look at the ambiguity or doubleness in this account which allows it, despite its positive account of representation, to be exploited for negative purposes by a Left Hegelian reading. Fifth, I return to the issue of the double mediation by raising the question whether religion itself through its own resources can deal with its own ambiguous representations, or whether ultimately only the movement to philosophical reason, conceived dialectically, can do so, as Hegel suggests. Or does speculative reason demand a metaxological mindfulness that does not reduce the double mediation and that is differently open to the otherness of the religious? This will bring us at the end to the thought of the unrepresentable.

Religion and Philosophy:
A Double in Discordant Mutuality?

Religion and philosophy have always coexisted in uneasy tension. Religion claims to orient us to what is ultimate, to reveal the mystery of being, to situate us as participants in a divine drama, to heal the divisions that rack our being. It claims absoluteness in addressing the whole being of the self in its relatedness to ultimate otherness. Its prayers and observances, offerings and silences would mediate our relation to the divine. It often claims to so mediate *via* a tradition of divine wisdom. One must place oneself in this tradition, accept the wisdom it propagates, have faith in the power of its truth. This is very evident with revealed religion: one is given over to a truth that is transhuman, other in this sense. One assents to a wisdom that is not of one's own generation, though one's belief entails one's assent.

Philosophy claims to rely on the unaided powers of rational mind. Instead of reception of truth from the other, it essays to think through the truth for itself. Here arises philosophy's predilection for mind as *completely self-mediating*, a predilection reduplicated in its God— thought thinking itself, as we see clearly with Aristotle and Hegel. I am not now talking about metaxological philosophy, which qualifies this predilection, but of a dominant traditional ideal. This ideal of mind's own self-reliance itself emerges in relation to the tradition of religious wisdom. Such a tradition may not be homogeneous or self-consistent; it may display a heterogeneity or otherness, dissident to complete logical self-mediation. Philosophers have been recurrently wary of any such logically dissident otherness. As Plato indicates in the *Republic* and the *Euthyphro*: the gods themselves may not be self-consistent; that they fight among themselves is the mythological sign of the possibility of logical contradiction nesting in the divine pantheon itself.

How are we to think of such internal discord of the divine? The moment he asks this question, the philosopher finds himself potentially at odds with religion. To question is, if only provisionally, to suspend belief, and thereby to introduce a distance, however small, between oneself and belief. It is to be critical, and so to risk being a destroyer of tradition. It was no accident that Socrates was accused of impiety, accused of the seemingly contradictory charge of being both an atheist and an inventor of new gods. To question philosophically is potentially impious because it implicitly risks hubris: to insist that our mind can rely totally on itself, and if need be, in opposition to the divine as mediated through a tradition of religious wisdom. Philosophical mind seems to will to be totally self-mediating, either appropriating the otherness of the divine or refusing it, closing itself off from it. The hubris of rational mind is that thought thinking itself wills to be its own god. Aristophanes clearly saw through this possible hubris of Socrates.

Subordinating the reception of truth from the other, philosophy sets a goal *for itself*. When Socrates famously said that the unexamined life was not worth living, the point was to live mindfully, that is, to live philosophically. Philosophy becomes the rationale of being, philosophy *is* the significance of human being. Philosophy is a way of life that tries to become *the* way of truth, in so far as the human being is privileged with thought. Socrates did not say: I am the way, the truth and the light. But he did imply that I, not as Socrates the particular bodied being, but the I as rational thinking, I as the thought of the universal, I as ideal representative of the Idea, as such an I, yes, I am the way to the truth and light. Again we must add, as Hegel does: from the standpoint of the nonphilosophical traditionalist, Socrates was guilty as charged. He was impious. Though Socrates might claim to pursue the truth of the religious tradition, by its very nature this pursuit risks the dissolution of this tradition. Hegel actually agreed with Aristophanes on this point.

There is a Socratic face, then, that to the nonphilosopher appears double, perhaps duplicitous. Despite its protestation of reverent service of the god, philosophical thought is the perennial possibility of atheism. To think questioningly implies an unwillingness to foreclose an answer, and again this is to put the truth of religion in suspense. A sigh of relief might greet the mildness of this benign agnosticism. The relief is premature. For philosophy will make its own claim to absoluteness. In essaying to comprehend the whole, it would criticize everything partial that mistakes itself for the whole. This puts it in a position of potential hostility to the implicit pretentiousness of all other forms of mind or being, including the religious.

Philosophy sets itself a goal in accord with what it claims is the intrinsic exigence of rational thought, whose reach cannot be arrested by anything partial but extends to comprehension of the whole, if not in actual attainment, then unavoidably in desire. This desire, this desideratum of the comprehensive thought of the whole, seems to be the new god philosophy invents, the new god of reason to which alone it will finally submit. Again the new god of reason seems to be itself reason, the philosopher's reason. What the philosopher seems to adore is the ideal of thought as completely self-consistent, mind as absolutely self-mediating.

The very otherness, even grandeur of religious claims invites reflective scrutiny. Sometimes religion itself will welcome such scrutiny. It becomes bitten by the serpent of philosophical distrust. It cannot tolerate the thought that its own grandeur must be entrusted to the embarrassment of the seemingly capricious. It does not want God to be an other that is dissident to reason. Were God a dissident other, far from redeeming absurdity, God would seem to immerse us more deeply in absurdity. We would be reconciled with truth and untruth alike by the expedient of putting out our eyes. Even Kierkegaard, who glories in religion's dissidence, will think twice here. If religion has truth, it can stand up. One might be given stones as well as bread. How do we discriminate the difference? Mindfulness will seek to discriminate the true and the untrue. Inevitably, philosophical thought intrudes again.

Thought is here critical in the sense of its Greek root *krinein*: "to judge," "discriminate." The goddess reveals the truth to Parmenides, but then we are enjoined *Krinai de logoi*: judge with logos. If Parmenides is to be the logical judge, must he not then put the goddess herself under the judgment of logos? But then the logical judge seems to stand superior to every matter being judged, divine or human. Nor can the arrival at judgment be a matter of complexifying the ruse by which we safely arrive back at our first secure truth. Philosophy, the logical judge, refuses to be merely the *handmaid*, the ancilla of religion. To the nonphilosophical believer this logical judge of all of being is unutterably pretentious and arrogant. Again witness

Aristophanes' mockery of Socrates. Did Socrates realize he gave the game away when he said in the *Philebus* (28c): All the wise (*sophoi*) agree, whereby they really exalt themselves, that mind (*nous*) is king of heaven and earth?

Of course, there are different kinds of kings, and not every king is a despot or tyrant. With the king who is friend (*philos*) of wisdom (*sophos*), there is the promise of something affirmative, beyond *nous turranos*, as we might put it. This promise invokes the very *justice of logos* itself. In this sense, philosophy would release mind into its own speculative freedom. But there is still risk here. To inquire about the truth of religion is not merely to rationalize one's belief, concoct the camouflage that pretends to question but which has the answer ready to hand anyway. This is *not* to open philosophical mind to the ultimate seriousness of religion as other. It is to play an inconsequential game of ratiocination, where since nothing is risked, nothing is gained. The tension between religion and philosophy is real, sometimes radical. We cannot be said to have done justice to either without standing in the struggle between them, without enduring the stress engendered by the coexistence of their differences.

A Hegelian way of putting the point would be: the feeling of absolute *certainty* possessed by religious faith may not in fact coincide with *truth*. The feeling of certainty does not immediately guarantee truth. Hegel considers this possibility, not only with respect to religion, but with respect to many other modes of mind and spirit in the *Phenomenology*, including philosophy itself. To ask about the truth of religion is to suspend the immediate certainty of faith. We have to dwell in, perhaps pass through the middle ground of this suspension to a mediated truth. But this suspension is *ambiguous* from the outset: it is not *per se* destructive or constructive, though it may be either. To dwell mindfully in the middle ground of this suspension is philosophically to come to terms with religion. We might refuse this step, for by it we step out of the security of immediate certainty. Thought, however, cannot avoid this step into this doubleness of ambiguity; philosophically it is a necessity. This necessity may not turn out to be only negative: it may be a step into a new speculative openness to the truth of religious faith. This would be a religiously benign way to read the Hegelian *Aufhebung*. I will return to this.

Of course, the middle ground can split into a dualism of opposites and become a site of strife. Philosophy will claim that religion is unthoughtful and fails to provide for itself any rational foundation. Religion will counterclaim that philosophy is superficial, impotent to penetrate the heart of the matter. Both will again make claim to absoluteness, but pursue the claim antagonistically, each sundering itself from its hostile other. The philosopher's God will be in the image of reason itself, variously characterized as Pure Being, or the Absolute Mind, or the One, or cosmic Nous, or some such. The God of religion will claim to be the living God human beings adore. Pascal will remind us of the God of Abraham and Isaac, the God we tremble before, not the God we think, the God that impassions and gives joy, not the desiccated God of dry reason. Religion will see the philosopher's absolute as an abstract, dead god.

Even Nietzsche, the pious pagan, will ask: Is not this God really a God of death, the deification of nothingness? Who can live or die for Pure Being, the last emptiness of evaporating reality, the exhalation of stale gas of the *Être Suprême*, as Hegel himself puts it? Who can give up, abandon his whole self to such a One? What healing transfiguration of being is effected by the thought of cosmic Nous? Philosophy, making a Moloch of its own self-mediating mind, strips the real God of the urgency of ultimacy, of the passion of living transcendence. It neuters the mystery of the ultimate, and robs us of reverence. The pietas of the atheist Nietzsche is here not unlike the reverence of the Christian mathematician, Pascal. Pascal would destroy the mathematical Baal of Descartes. Nietzsche's piety would destroy the Gods of philosophy and monotheism together, and resurrect the polytheism of paganism under the sign of Dionysus. But in a sense Nietzsche, with Pascal, is closer to St. Paul, when he derided as folly the wisdom of the Greek philosophers. Nietzsche rejects Christian redemption and chooses the sacred yes of tragic wisdom. But both this redemption and this yes see themselves as essentially other to the logical wisdom of the philosopher.

It takes two for such strife, and religion can also exacerbate the difference between itself and philosophy. It can absolutize the dualism by rejecting reason, calling for a sacrifice of the intellect. Resorting to the direct, living feeling of divine presence, it can claim immediate communion with ultimacy. Reason, ridiculous reason, reduces the cold rational self to a dead voyeur of being, ensnares us within the sterile circle of self-consciousness. Religion leaps, dances beyond reason. Whether in Kierkegaard's leaping Christianity or Nietzsche's dancing paganism, religion can be a proud, boastful, provocative celebration of what seems irrational. Philosophy can again mirror religion here by itself making an idol of *rational* opposition. It will scornfully dismiss superstition, take apart religious passion as nothing but nebulous confusion, congratulate itself for its coldness before the seductions of enigma. Analysis will anatomize being, make less wanton the religious urgency of ultimacy. The philosopher will not leap before he looks, and when he looks at the other of reason he may refuse to leap at all. Idolatrous children are in the grip of the father-figure, but when we become philosophical adults, all the opaque charms of innocence vanish. Lucid logic liberates from subservience. Very well. But the mocking question still rings out: Can mind still dance, can thinking sing?

Philosophy and Religion: The Convergence of the Double?

One significant version of this agonistic oscillation in the middle is evident in the hostility, yet collusion of pietistic faith and Enlightenment in Hegel's time. Hegel himself saw through the hostility to the collusion in terms of his own dialectical conception, a conception precisely tailored to see through all such dualistic oppositions. Similar considerations mark the differences between Kierkegaard and Hegel. Kierkegaard strongly emphasizes the difference between religion and philosophy, and to the point of coming close to a dualistic opposition, in his vehement rejection of Hegel's dialectical conception of their togetherness. In the next section I speak of Kierkegaard but for the moment I ask: Where does Hegel stand?

Not unexpectedly, Hegel refuses to acquiesce in the dualism. Doubleness must be dialectically, not dualistically conceived. The dualism can be stultifying for both religion and philosophy. It can be stultifying for religion, for should religion give itself up to the irrational, it diminishes its own stature. It congratulates itself in a thoughtless self-assurance, and so is unfaithful to the full metaphysical disquiet of human existence as thinking being. The dualism can be equally sterilizing for philosophy. A religion itself contracted invites the reaction of a rationalism, itself poverty stricken. Religious irrationalism and sterile rationalism prove to be two manifestations of a fundamentally similar predicament. They are made for each other, like the hand and the glove. Their mutually antagonistic and proud self-assertions are, in fact, bound to each other by their complementary emptinesses. Their complementary power is their complementary impotence. Sterile reason feeds on a rejection of irrational faith, but its rejection does not suspect the possibility that irrational faith might be itself a contraction. It does not get beyond being a reaction to a diminishment, hence the risk of its own impotence. Instead of mirroring each other merely in hostility, I suggest that for Hegel the religious and philosophical mediations of being mirror each other in a positive manner which shows them to dialectically converge in the middle. Let me try to explain.

Systematically in Hegel's *Phenomenology* religion is the last form of *Geist* prior to philosophy, but as last it is *prior*, in the sense of being spiritually superior, to everything else. In the *Encyclopedia* it is the penultimate mode of absolute spirit, necessary for philosophy, yet ultimate in its own mode: philosophy presupposes religion, but religion does not presuppose philosophy. The importance of religion is historical as well as systematic. An historical actuality itself, religion is the representation of the eternal Idea in time. Hegel notes that the emergence of philosophy itself in Greece presupposes religion. Again there is ambiguity to be interpreted. I suggest that Hegel sees the coimplication of religion and philosophy this way: Philosophy needs religion while surpassing it; religion calls for thought to complete its own mindfulness; each needs the other to be fully itself; but to be fully themselves, both need *thought*; Hegel will interpret this last need in terms of thought thinking itself; dialectical self-mediation will triumph once again.

First, philosophy needs religion. If we consider Socrates once more, it is significant that he claims to begin his philosophical quest, not with pure thought, detached in a vacuum, but when confronted with the enigma of the religious oracle at Delphi. Is he lying when he says that from the outset he does not want to negate the oracle? Is he lying when he says that he accepts the oracle, and rather attempts to interpret its puzzling opaqueness. If he is not lying—and one cannot be certain with the sly, ironical Socrates—religion provides the concrete occasion on which the philosophical question emerges. Let us believe Socrates, if only for the moment, for this allows us to say: Philosophy is a perplexed reflection upon the enigma of the religious occasion. Philosophy, even in its difference, retains its link with the religious occasion of its own origin, even should it turn against this origin and try to negate it dialectically.

This openness of philosophy has consequences also for religion. The doubleness of the middle opens up the possibility of a *two-way mediation*. This brings out the second need: Religion cannot ignore the exigencies of thought, for within its faith germinate the seeds of thought. Hegel will repeatedly exploit this virtuality. Religion need not be blind, for at its heart is the call of knowing. To answer this call it may become a *fides quaerens intellectum*. But then faith and reason are no longer simple antitheses. Faith may be lived but it may also seek its own articulation in reflective terms, mediating what is immediate, thinking through what first is lived. How thorough can this thinking through be? This will be a question for Hegel. If faith sees things through a glass darkly, is there any absolute bar on seeing things face to face? Hegel will say: religion *promises* just that full seeing, but only philosophy properly redeems this promise. To think through what is seen in the glass is to surpass the religious glass speculatively. In that sense, philosophy is *necessary* to religion, if the latter would be true to this exigence of thought, that is, be true to itself.

Suppose the believer says: the truth of faith is guaranteed because revealed by the divine other. The certainty of faith is directly identified with the word of God. As one with this word, faith is absolute and thus is its own certification. The difficulty again is the hermeneutical problem of equivocity. God's word often displays a perplexing plurivocity. Moreover, that word is not spoken to a nobody but to those who listen or can listen. To listen is to have ears. To have ears is to interpret the significance of what is spoken. God, if he speaks, does not speak a univocal language. His logos, even if appearing to finite humans, is manifestly enigmatic. It requires mindful mediation.

Heraclitus said it all (Fr. D107): "Eyes and ears are bad witnesses (*martures*) for persons with barbarian souls (*psuchas*)" Because its ambiguity requires interpretation, thought springs up as a necessity. It becomes incumbent on us to discriminate true from untrue mediation, adequate from inadequate interpretation. Thus, the plurivocity of the sacred word throws us back on the powers of our own mind. A God who, in exacting faith, would welcome thoughtlessness, would himself prove to be a God of mindlessness. If the sacred word is never unambiguous, to remain true to its meaning must demand that we try to think its perplexing opacity. If the divine word makes sense, it makes sense to ponder its meaning. And this is to think.

I have put the matter in words that are not Hegel's, but they are not inconsistent with his view. There is a difference between philosophy and religion, but this is underpinned by a deeper mutuality. He will even claim an "identity" between them. The standard way he expresses this is: they are identical in content, but they elaborate this content in different forms. Religion reveals the absolute in the form of representational thought (*Vorstellung*). Philosophy attempts to rise up to the non-pictorial thought of the speculative concept (*Begriff*). The intent is not simply to negate representational thought (in a glass darkly), but to articulate the same content, present in representation, but not conceptually expressed. Speculative thought looks into the glass but also beyond it.

This claimed identity does not reduce to a univocal sameness. Nor are we stuck with an equivocal difference. Thought mediates the ambiguity of religion, saves it from equivocity. For Hegel this mediation yields an identity that is dialectical. This is not a static unity, but Hegel's understanding of their mutuality. A dialectical identity is an active process of mediation binding together realities normally considered as opposites. Hegel sees the relation of religion and philosophy as dialectical because of the convergence in the middle of their respective mediations of being: the one relating to philosophy's openness to the religious occasion of its own origin; the second relating to the thrust towards thought that is immanent in religion itself.

So the two are bound together; bound together, they are in tension; but their respective mediations mirror each other and converge in the middle. Hegel's dialectical identity tries to name this tense bond. On the side of philosophy, it reminds us of the discipline of mind that develops reason from the level of finitude and opens it to what is absolute. Here religion offers the greatest challenge to philosophy. To be true to itself and this challenge, philosophy must be capable of entering into the religious view and doing justice to its truth. Otherwise it cannot justifiably make any claim to be comprehensive. On the side of religion, this tense bond is worked out in so far as faith seeks to explicate what is inherent in itself. Religion has a bond with philosophy because inherent in it is the thought of the absolute. Religion is not true to itself, if it lets this thought remain dormant. To be true to belief, one must think about what belief means and this is to philosophize. This may risk the loss of faith; it may also be to confirm its solidarity with thought.

Hegel claims to have the courage of this risk, and the confidence in this confirmation. For Hegel dualistic opposition suggests a blind religion or an impoverished philosophy. But when both are fully true to themselves, this opposition is not absolute. We do not leap into bland reconciliation, a peace of indifference. We must *think through* their opposition. True reconciliation is not the collapse of distinction but that convergence in the middle we call mutual life. There the bond of coexistence does not negate the tension of difference. Does Hegel preserve the full difference? Does he do justice to such mutuality and the full complexity of convergence? This is the hard question.

The answer I suggest, and this will be worked out more fully, is: In the mirroring of the religious and philosophical mediations, it is crucially important that Hegel stresses that *thought* is at work in both. Thought is the mediating power that promotes convergence and mutuality. The convergence of the two in the middle will make Hegel say that the discord of their doubleness is the dialectical prelude to their speculative harmony in and through thought itself. But then the double is always dialectically penultimate; *the thought at work in the two must complete itself as the thought that completely thinks itself.* Ultimately the double must yield to the synoptic thought that completely thinks itself, that is, to *Hegel's idea of philosophy.* But

if so, where is the ground of genuine mutuality, since then there is
no ultimate otherness?

The issue will be whether the true ultimate finally does attenuate
the doubleness, whether philosophy becomes the one that more
ultimately embraces the double, whether the final speculative
harmony through thought thinking itself tilts the privilege of
ultimacy towards a certain kind of philosophy, such that the complete
self-mediation of that philosophy takes the place of the double
mediation between philosophy, otherwise conceived, and religion. The
question will be whether the Hegelian way of thinking the matter
through, in terms of the dialectical self-mediation of the speculative
concept, preserves a strong enough sense of difference and otherness,
necessary to preserve the otherness of religion and the religious sense
of divine otherness.

We must continue to question the privileging of mind as thought
thinking itself. Self-mediating mind is not rejected, but its claim to
appropriate all otherness, hence its claim to self-closure is suspended.
Self-mediating philosophy must be opened beyond thought thinking
itself. Beyond merely reactive debunking, beyond the negative dialectics that equivocates between suspicion and openness to otherness,
beyond Hegelian dialectic that sublates everything other into thought
thinking itself, a different philosophical mindfulness must cultivate
a reasonable openness to all the ways of being, even in their otherness
to reason. If reason is to be at all reasonable, it presupposes this
openness.

This philosophical openness must embody metaxological mindfulness: a relating of self-mediating thought to the ultimate others of
thought, a relating that does not close the circle of self-mediation,
nor reduce the other to itself in its own radical self-transcendence,
a relating that may break all possessive claims on the others of
thought, since it asks thought to be with its others in a non-violating
intimacy. Such mindfulness must especially be open to those ways of
being that make claim to ultimacy. Philosophical reason becomes less
than philosophical, becomes contracted, if it does not embody this
openness to religion and its representational relativity to otherness.
This metaxological openness means that we must preserve the
doubleness of religion and philosophy, the tension of their otherness
and relatedness. This tension prevents both from resting with less
than their full promise. In their quarrel both vie for the welcome of
the ultimate in a rivalry that respects the other. Philosophy needs
an other preserving thinking, a vigilant readiness for transcendence,
beyond the dialectical *Aufhebung*.

Why Could Kierkegaard not Forgive Hegel?
Discordant Mutuality and the Masks of Philosophy

The Hegel above painted is the blood brother of a speculative theologian like Scotus Eriugena when he said: True religion is true philosophy; both seek wisdom, both seek divine reason. He is the brother of Aristotle when he identifies *prōtē philosophia* with theology. He is the kin of Anselm when he himself says that philosophy of religion is true theology. He stands in the same tradition of speculative metaphysics as Plato, Plotinus, Eriugena, Bruno, Cusanus. Commentators mesmerized by the problems of post-Kantian transcendental philosophy excise this Hegel. The "God" that is repeatedly on his lips, even most especially in his *Logic*, becomes the metaphorical placeholder of a rhetorical concession to *hoi polloi*.

There is no God-service if philosophy is exhausted by transcendental epistemology, but there is more in Hegel. We cannot even suspect this "more" without an awareness of the long and profound tradition of speculative philosophy that reaches far back behind Hegel. Heideggerians may dismiss this tradition as ontotheology. There is an atheistic, or perhaps atheological dismissal of speculative philosophy that is indistinguishable from a fideistic dismissal. As we saw, Hegel perceived something like a collusion of atheism, atheology and fideism with respect to Enlightenment and faith. Enlightenment reason dismissed religion as superstition from the past; Heideggerian thinkers and those in thrall to its rhetoric claim to dismiss Enlightenment reason; but they have a complementary dismissive attitude to the past, seen as the metaphysically superstitious tradition of ontotheology.

Turning again to the agonistic oscillation in the middle between faith and reason, Kierkegaard is an important religious antagonist to Hegel. But first I reinvoke Pascal—religious antagonist of Enlightenment reason, famous for the choice he enforces between the God of Abraham, Isaac and Jacob, and the God of the philosophers. I will not pretend that there may be here a difference that resists complete mediation. I will say that the philosopher's "godlessness" can be more intricate than exoteric appearances suggest. Great philosophers are plurivocal thinkers, often masked and hidden, despite even an exoteric commitment to aggressive univocity. To every system there is an underground; its explicit concepts are often grounded on something hidden, esoteric to the surface demands of univocal clarity. Hegel himself uses the distinction of the exoteric and esoteric in discussing the relation of religion and philosophy (*Encyclopedia*, § 573). Who can deny that philosophers have slandered religion? Who can deny that

religions have returned the slander with interest? Philosophers will
even mime this religious slander and themselves become philosophers
who slander philosophy. But with a dialectical thinker like Hegel,
God-service and godlessness strangely mingle. We have to think
beyond the masks and the slanders.

Pascal saw beyond the metaphysical mask of Descartes' mathe-
matics, and its talk of God, and said: "I cannot forgive Descartes: in
his whole philosophy he would like to do without God; but he could
not help allowing him a flick of the fingers to set the world in motion;
after that he had no more use for God."[5] There is a sense in which
Pascal is undoubtedly right. On the surface Descartes seems to
acquiesce in Augustine's passion of knowing: *Deum et animam scire
cupio. Nihilne plus? Nihil omnino* (God and the soul I wish to know.
Nothing more? Nothing at all). Augustine will say "nothing more,"
not because he has clear and distinct transparency with respect to
God, but because God is the "more" that ever resists encapsulation
in clear and distinct ideas. Yet this "more" always calls for further
unremitting thought, mindfulness before the mystery of the ultimate
other.

Suppose we ask Descartes: *Nihilne plus?* Nothing more? Descartes
will very clearly reply: Now that I know of God and the soul, and now
that these can be epistemologically trusted as foundations of scientific
reason, I can go on to something more, namely, constructing my real
heart's desire—the new science of mathematicized nature. God and
the soul, the easiest of things to know for Descartes, are put in their
place. Their perplexing otherness is subjected to a clarity and
distinctness that robs them of all enigma. Their alleged clarity and
distinctness serve as epistemological means to the end of mathematicized science. Yes, one sees how the great mathematician, Pascal,
saw through the mathematical mask of his blood brother Descartes.
But the "more," the "*plus*" that Pascal saw was a *ne plus ultra* beyond
all mathematicizing. Pascal was interested in "nothing more" than
God, but this "nothing more" is *always* "more" than our clear and
distinct ideas, an otherness eternally in excess of our most masterly
concepts.

What is there "more" in Hegel's vision? He suggests: The *ne plus
ultra (die letzte Spitze)* of inwardness is thought.[6] Nor is it in doubt
that he often identifies rational thinking with the divine. I suggest:
As Pascal was to Descartes, Kierkegaard was to Hegel. I imagine
Kierkegaard saying something similar about Hegel: I cannot forgive
Hegel. Why so? In the end his philosophy amounts to the dispensation
of God, even if this dispensing is couched in the rhetoric of speculative
God-service. Hegel's God may not give Descartes' fillip to the world,

but it is simply the universe, or the universe of thought, as a rational totality. Kierkegaard will say: Hegel masks his involvement with God right up to the end, but the end reverses everything, and the philosophical universal of post-religious reason finally reveals Hegel's speculative atheism. All speculative enigma vanishes in the pure self-transparency of the speculative concept. The speculative virtues of Hegel are only splendid vices, the *splendida vitia* of pagan philosophy dressed up as Christian thought.

Why could Kierkegaard not forgive Hegel? Kierkegaard, Hegel's dialectical blood brother, claims to see through the speculative mask. On reading Kierkegaard one can come away with the impression that Hegel is both a subtle and a violent dissimulator with respect to religion. Kierkegaard himself assumes the persona of the truly righteous defender of religion in its truth. The issue between these two is connected with the very enterprise of philosophy itself, with philosophy as a speculative venture. I take Kierkegaard as wanting to say: the sin of philosophy is its rational pretension, a sin sometimes secret, sometimes overt. This sin of reason is nowhere more audacious, more shameless than in the Hegelian system. Moreover, the sin is at work here in a dangerously insidious way. The appearance tells us that Hegel is close to Christianity, but this very exoteric closeness masks an unbridgeable distance between Christianity and Hegelianism.

The rational Hegel does claim to comprehend the truth of Christianity in his speculative system. This seems to be a gesture of respect on Hegel's part. For even to desire to comprehend is to name the other comprehended as *worthy* of systematic and speculative thought. Kierkegaard sees here a spurious respect and will have none of this. His response is: What rational foolishness! The speculative wisdom of the philosopher is folly, and not divine folly either. Kierkegaard's repeated satires attack the philosophical pretension of "going beyond" Christianity, as if Christianity were something that one might "go beyond," as if already one was on a par with it, indeed more than on a par.

Let us put to Hegel Augustine's question about God: *Nihilne plus?* Nothing more? Hegel will clearly say: yes, "more" indeed; "more" than God as representation, there is the speculative concept of the Idea. The Idea is "more" than the Christian representational God; the Idea is the speculative *ne plus ultra*, beyond which there is nothing more, beyond which there is no beyond. Kierkegaard will now ask again: How could one go beyond Christianity? Is not this speculative "more" really a religious "less"? He will say: One might go beyond what is a caricature of Christianity masquerading as true Christianity. Far from being a rational comprehension of the truth of Christianity, any such claim to "go beyond" speculatively is a dangerous falsification, a conceptual counterfeiting of the true reality. To "go beyond" thus is to destroy every "beyond."

Hegel's sin is precisely the claim made on behalf of speculative philosophy as comprehensive, as comprehending what is essentially other to its systematic categories. To Kierkegaard this audacity is intolerable. With difficulty he restrains himself when the word "speculation" comes to be uttered. He barely conceals his holy rage. Speculative reason is *the* hubris with respect to religion. The Kierkegaardian wrath does not itself escape flirting with a kind of fideistic insolence to reason.

In fact, quite a number of strands of post-Hegelian philosophy are deeply Kierkegaardian in this sense. Again and again Hegel is accused of being the abstract thinker. Once this mask can be made to stick, it quickly follows that there is no great difficulty in rejecting him. Marx, otherwise an antipode to Kierkegaard, repeatedly brands Hegel as an abstract thinker. But the disposal of Hegel is more complex. This is so, not simply because Hegel makes claims to a speculative concreteness; such claims might be persuasively rejected. It is so because the attacks often are effective because they assault one shadow of Hegel, tearing off but one mask of Hegel, let us say, an abstract of Hegel.

With Kierkegaard the whole task of philosophy itself is in question. He asserts his undying respect for Socrates; but the fact is that he believed that within the particular context of *Christianity*, any effort to think of the whole philosophically was implicitly an idolatrous hubris of reason. Kierkegaard wants to tear off the mask of the idolatrous thinker. Kierkegaard himself is willy nilly a philosopher, but as such he is not always free of a certain animus against the entire enterprise of philosophy. Philosophy is essentially pagan, tolerable within that context. In a Christian context, the situation gets knotted: Christendom as a simulacrum of Christianity aids and abets Hegelian philosophy in presenting a counterfeit identity as a Christian philosophy. The mask of Christian philosophy worn by Hegelian thought dissimulates the pagan face that Kierkegaard detects behind the Christian mask. It is the confusion of identity between paganism and Christianity, between philosophy and religion, that Kierkegaard excoriates, execrates.

Hence Kierkegaard is a religious thinker at what he sees as the end of philosophy. Hegel believed that the end of religion offers the beginning of philosophy. But for Kierkegaard, Hegel brings a certain type of pagan philosophy to its limit, and at this limit reveals the

religious stupidity, the religious coarseness of reason. At this limit
the only thing that makes sense for Kierkegaard is religious, that
is, Christian faith. The end of philosophy is the beginning of religion.
When philosophy claims to transcend faith, what is risible is the
dialectical inversion, not to say perversion of the true state of affairs:
The speculative transcendence is really a reversion to a position of
spirit below Christianity rather than beyond it.

Kierkegaard tries to drive home this point about the end of
philosophy: When we reach the limit of philosophy, we must bow before
faith; any effort to go further is to be blind to just that inescapable
limit. In his distinctive way he agrees with Kant's famous saying: I
deny knowledge to make room for faith. Kierkegaard viewed his own
era as infected with this blindness about philosophy's limit. Worse
still, his era was conveniently presented with a rational justification
for this blindness in the guise of Hegelian reason. The age was falling
religiously asleep under the spell of Hegelian reason. This reason
presented itself as the wakefulness of religion, but this wakefulness
was the deep slumber of faith.

In the dialogue of philosophy and religion, I think we need a wider
perspective—beyond the equivocal oscillation between them, beyond
their dualistic antagonism, beyond the dialectical reduction of their
doubleness. Suppose we consider here a contrast of *Aquinas* and
Kierkegaard, one entirely relevant to the issue of the end of speculative metaphysics. Aquinas tried to reconcile Athens and Jerusalem,
Aristotle and Augustine, philosophy and revealed religion. Moreover,
Aquinas stood in the same tradition of speculative metaphysics as
Hegel. Nor should his God-service, both philosophical and religious,
be in doubt, even to a professing Christian. But what happened to
Aquinas at the end of speculative philosophy? What happened was
a certain enigmatic silence. There came a day when Aquinas told his
secretary he could not go on; indeed his sister and relatives wondered
if he was perhaps mad. Was this idiot wisdom? A trauma, an upheaval,
a rupture happened, after which he could not go on as before. Aquinas
saw "something more" and said about all his previous thought: It
seems to me as so much straw, *videtur mihi ut palea.* Having seen
"something more," he would write "nothing more."

This transrational silence before the "more," the "something more
beyond which there is nothing more," is at the limit of philosophical
thought, at the end of metaphysics. Compare this silence before the
"more" to what at times is a certain fideistic shrillness in
Kierkegaard. What explains the difference between this silence and
shrillness? Perhaps I am wrong, but they seem to me to come from
different worlds. Has Aquinas' bond with the tradition of speculative

metaphysics something to do with the character of his silence? I do not find in Aquinas the sometimes excessive sense of war between religion and philosophy that I suspect in Kierkegaard. I do not find in Aquinas' "It is as straw," a gesture of triumphal dismissal of thought. I interpret it to suggest: I have done my best, I have thought to the utmost, the limit, and yet there is "More," the "More" that was, is and always will be "More." Compared to the excess of its transcendence, my saying of it is as nothing. Even my saying that "My saying is as nothing" says all the more that this excessive transcendence is always and ever "More."

There is a silence of thought that is a metaphysical gesture of deep consent. Such silence is the "So be it," the "*Ita est*," of thought. It is the amen of thinking at the limit and highest point of metaphysics. It is metaphysical thought itself at its richest extremity or end. And Kierkegaard's shrillness? Does Kierkegaard show signs of also being secretly infected with the godlessness he excoriates around him in modernity? Hence his need to protest? Must we say: Kierkegaard doth protest too much? Was the spectre of godlessness too much his own, and his protest on behalf of faith as much his own self-exorcism of faithlessness as an effort to retrieve faith? Aquinas falls silent. Is there more of unfathomable God-service in this eloquent silence than in all of Kierkegaard's fideistic protestations? More indeed than in Hegel's complete dialectical speech of systematic logic?

But Kierkegaard could not forgive Hegel for his doctrine of absolute spirit in this sense. This doctrine, as one recalls, places art, philosophy and religion at the highest level of spiritual achievement, at the unconditional level. Kierkegaard conveniently forgets that Hegel does after all think of religion as an articulation of the unconditional: it is absolute. He is silent on the fact that Hegel repeatedly states religion's absoluteness. What Kierkegaard cannot forget and what rouses his ire is Hegel's belief that philosophical thought is also absolute. This is unforgivable, the philosopher's sin against the spirit. This seems doubly unforgivable in that Hegel then has the insolence to imply that the absoluteness of philosophy is dialectically, speculatively, more ultimate than the absoluteness of religion. This is too much, a speculative excess that cannot be tolerated.

I notice that in articulating the stages of life's way Kierkegaard deals with the aesthetic, the ethical and the religious. But why is the philosophic not singled out as a sphere of existence, as a way of being? This is strange, especially given Kierkegaard's stated reverence for Socrates. Socrates was not interested in a speculative system but in the philosophical life. This is why Plato offers us the philosophical memorial or testament of Socrates' *Apology*. An apology tells the story of a singular "this"; it does not offer a neutral *eidos*; it tells the *philosophic story* of a particular self and does not simply argue a general systematic case. There is something irreducibly singular about an apology, even a philosophical one: it is other than system, the story of a unique "I," a mindful "this," that may be in search of the universal but is not itself a logical universal. There is no universal apology, for apology is other to, irreducible to system. The piety of the philosopher takes shape in this gap *between* system and apology, the in-between where the "I" of the philosopher lives philosophy as a distinctive way of being mindful of being. Why does Kierkegaard not play up the fact that philosophy might also be such a way of being, with its own mindful respect for ultimacy, and not just a conceptual system? Is he too obsessively intent on attacking Hegelianism for making philosophy into the latter?

Consider another very singular philosopher—Spinoza: Spinoza who was singular in his philosophical desire to efface singularity in the rational universal. Even here one cannot say that Spinoza was simply a speculative thinker in Kierkegaard's sense. I say this despite the fact that his philosophy is exoterically "geometrical," and his God identical with Nature. Yet there is much that is masked about Spinoza. His passion for ultimacy is the spiritual underground of the geometrical system, an underground that always exceeds the univocity of geometrical concepts. True, at time one suspects that with such geometrical univocity Spinoza tried to straitjacket or stifle this very passion for ultimacy. But there is no "geometry" of this philosophical passion, contrary to some of Spinoza's own exoteric statements that he merely treats of human emotions in the way one might treat of planes, angles, and triangles. The philosophical passion for ultimacy, even when articulated in a geometrical system, is not itself explained "geometrically." The eros that produces the system is itself other to the system, preceding and exceeding its determinate, "geometrical" concepts.

Spinoza's philosophical eros for rational truth, his passion for ultimacy, was an ethical as well as "speculative" quest. His great work, after all, is called *Ethics*. Thus, he lets the mask briefly drop, for those who can catch a quick glimpse. More generally my point is: There are nuances within the philosophical venture to which Kierkegaard seems ill attuned. Perhaps this is not quite right. Better to say that Kierkegaard masks his own awareness of such nuance: the pseudonymous religious thinker also masked Kierkegaard as himself an *esoteric philosopher*. In my view Kierkegaard is selective, strategically so no doubt, in stressing those aspects of philosophy that he wishes to criticize. What infuriates him is that philosophy, no matter what its form, should make any claim to absoluteness.

Kierkegaard does not give enough weight to the possibility that philosophy has its own peculiar piety. Philosophy as speculative reveals a continuity with the entire metaphysical tradition; its thought may be the*ōria*, but *theōria* is also a religious category, as we saw before. One cannot explain Socrates' *death* if one sticks exclusively to the Pascalian opposition of the Gods of philosophy and religion. Nor can you explain Giordano Bruno's death, nor Spinoza for that matter, whose geometrical metaphysics exposed him to attempted assassination. One does not put one's life on the line simply for a definition or mathematical idea; there is always "more" at stake, often a hidden or disguised "more."

Thus, there is a Socrates who is other than the "official" Socrates whose identity is to love intellectually the lifeless eternity of the unchanging Ideas. Socrates' life and thought as *other* were masked in the official identity of his search for the logical definition of the Ideas. One does not sacrifice oneself, die for a lifeless Idea. One might die for the living, eternal Good. Socrates' very death has a rebound effect on our sense of his *philosophical life* in forcing us to question the official Socratic identity and to ponder an other, much more enigmatic Socrates. What God does this other Socrates serve? This question was to obsess his son Plato, the masked philosopher par excellence. His dialogues should be read as dramatically presenting the plurivocal agon of sometimes open, sometimes masked philosophical thought.

The masks of philosophers and the enigma of an other piety is forgotten by those post-Hegelian critics who excoriate this tradition of speculative metaphysics, not least because Hegel is thought to have completed and exhausted it. Kierkegaard, more radically than Schelling, emphasizes the particularity of the thinker, the subjective thinker, as he puts it. Speculative philosophy, it is said, is a thinking that wants to liberate thought from the confines of particularity and surrender to a universality that encompasses the whole. In its will to system, speculative philosophy forgets the speculative philosopher himself as a particular. In Kierkegaard's criticism, forgetting this concrete particularity and surrendering to the rational universal, also means forgetting the otherness of God. Hence the self-forgetting is the falsification of ultimate being.

I agree that these are entirely legitimate questions to put to Hegel. I agree with Kierkegaard that Hegel cannot be acquitted without severe reprimand. I will take the point up later in this chapter, and again in my discussion of evil and dialectic. I especially agree that speculative philosophy runs the risk of excising the speculative philosopher himself in its rush to complete thought in an impersonal universal system. This is to reduce the plurivocity of the philosophical task to one dominating, systematic "voice." In fact such a philosophical "voice" does not want to be a "voice" at all; it wants to be the nameless articulation of an anonymous universal. Hegel himself wanted to deny that there is such a thing as *my* philosophy.

This reduction of philosophical plurivocity may go so far as to pretend to excise all voices in their ineluctable particularity; and the system is said to be the "voice" of itself, of faceless thought thinking itself, the faceless voice of an anonymous everyone which is a universal no-one. The philosopher will want to excise his own ineluctable particularity in the anonymous universality of the system. But this is to forget that the system as universal is the child of a philosopher as a profoundly mindful *this*—a this that is ineradicably a *someone* thinking, this *someone* thinking, a Socrates, a Plato, an Aquinas, a Kierkegaard, a Hegel. These are "thises" of which there is only one. Every such "this" is outside, beyond, "more" than any system that the thinking "this" itself creates. The follower—the Platonist, the Hegelian, the Thomist, the Kierkegaardian—may duplicate the system but never the "more" of the "this" of its founder.

Kierkegaard is absolutely right to refuse to allow the philosopher to forget himself. He also helps us question the speculative domestication of otherness. Nevertheless, I resist fastening on one point in a fashion that truncates Hegel's manysidedness. Likewise, I refuse to slander philosophy. Such slander itself reduces philosophical plurivocity to a polemical univocity. Today a truncated Hegel and a bowdlerized tradition are too easily available for ideological drubbing. We repeat with comfortable facility the kinds of criticisms first patented by a Kierkegaard. But Hegel as an *other* is polemically reduced. So is the tradition of speculative metaphysics. It is remarkable that quasi-Kierkegaardian criticisms have been formulated by thinkers who are deeply hostile to the religious alternative Kierkegaard recommends. Again I think of the pervasive Nietzschean hostility, not only to speculative metaphysics but to the Christian religion. There is an irony here in Hegel's sympathy for speculative metaphysics, and antipathy to merely hostile debunkings of religion. Relative to the post-Nietzschean execration of religion, Kierkegaard's religious piety is closer to Hegel's philosophical piety than Kierkegaard might find comfortable.

After all both pay homage to Luther. True, Hegel will silently lay aside Luther's insolence towards thought and, in filial piety to Aristotle, Aquinas' philosophical father, refuse to tear out the eyes of the whore, as Luther calls natural reason. But we do not need to gouge out reason's eyes. The face of reason is not the mask of a strumpet. Reason as whore is reason as *ancilla*, reason as instrumentalized into handmaiden mind, available for use when the ideological price is right. Philosophical reason is not an instrumental drab, but a *philos* of agapeic mind, a friend capable of love of the other for the sake of the other. The whore gives herself to many with a fake, instrumental love; the whore does not really give herself to anybody at all; there is no speculative abandon or release. The *philos*, the friend can give himself over to the other, love more than one in the community of others, and without reducing that community to a monistic one.

The need of the philosopher as a *philos* of truth is for a plurivocal thinking that struggles to see with many more eyes than the Cyclops eye of univocal reason. Plurivocal philosophy tries to see with the eyes of many, with the eyes of many others and not the voyeur eye of the reductive one. The latter is not the watching or vigilance of speculative thought. And if philosophy always had its masks, it was always implicitly such plurivocal thinking, since the thinker always had a multiplied identity, and not just the exoteric official one of univocal logic. Beyond the official Plato, the offical Aristotle, the official Aquinas, the official Spinoza or Hegel or Kierkegaard, there is always an other Plato, or Aristotle, or Aquinas, an other Spinoza or Hegel or Kierkegaard. The features of such an other are suggested more richly in some of these thinkers than in others. Heraclitus' statement, previously applied to the hermeneutical mindfulness required of religion, must also be applied to philosophers: eyes and ears are bad witnesses to those with barbarian souls. Plurivocal philosophy must cultivate eyes and ears that are not barbaric, the eyes and ears that are for those others, the eyes and ears of agapeic mind. And who can read, who dares read the mask of this mind?

Hegel and the Double Mediation of Representation

I now rehearse some chief features of Hegel's account of representation. The intricacies of his view, spread over many of his writings, need not detain us,[7] but the following points are necessary. *Vorstellung* is essential to the articulation of the religious consciousness. *Vorstellung* is not purely rational thought, for it is always marked by some sensuous or imagistic dimension. At the same time, it is not a sensuousness devoid of significance. *Vorstellung* is something intermediate between purely rational thought and thoughtless sensuousness. *Vorstellung* indeed is a form of thinking, though a thinking not fully free from the need of a sensuous image. As such it must needs entail a process of mediation. In its religious representations the human spirit mediates with itself in terms of its own sense of religious significance, and also mediates between the human spirit as finite and God conceived of as infinite Spirit or *Geist*. In this sense, its mediation is a double mediation. The question returns: Can this double mediation be speculatively reduced to a more encompassing dialectical process of singular self-mediation?

As a form of mediation bound up with a sensuous and imagistic medium, religious representation always has an essential root in the finite world, even though the meaning it aims to convey cannot be exhausted by the sheerly finite, taken separately. Religious representations are inevitably *particular* representations, though *what* they represent can never be confined to the level of any merely objectified particularity. Invariably, then, representation exhibits a tension between the sensuous and the supersensible, between man's own self-mediation and his mediation with more ultimate powers, perhaps even the mediation of the ultimate other from its own otherness. This latter is a point Hegel does not deny since his idea of God is self-disclosive. Hence a genuine representation of the divine is not just a human self-mediation but involves some self-revelation of the divine to the human. Again we see the shape of the double mediation emerging. Properly speaking, we should call this double mediation an intermediation, where the emphasis is on the "*inter*," the between. This between points towards a non-reductive togetherness, that is to say, a metaxological togetherness between the human and divine. Thus conceived, religious representation is a *community* of spirit between the human and divine. This, too, is Hegel's view, but the question turns on whether we conceive community in terms of dialectical self-mediation or metaxological intermediation.

In the emergence of the double mediation we find this further tension: between finiteness in the *mode* of representing the divine and the infinitude of the *content* thought to be represented. Religious representation purports to be a disclosure, in and through a finite reality, of a "reality" that is not itself just finite. Here the Thomist doctrine of analogy, for instance, might be seen as responding to this tension between the finite and the infinite. Analogy serves the role of mediator, since it brings to articulation a certain complex conjunction of finite and infinite. Analogy, too, tries to articulate a non-reductive community of being between the human and divine.

By contrast, more positivistic views preclude such community since the totality of being is nominalistically reduced to an aggregate of finite entities. This view starts from the finite, but also just stays there, since any mediation with something further or "more" is excluded by its principles of meaningfulness, and its determination of the whole of being as an aggregate of finite entities. The positivist view is, of course, an extreme. But any empirically minded philosophy must face this difficulty of mediation, as the doctrine of analogy tries to do. Likewise Hegel—contrary to the view of him as the abstract thinker par excellence—insists strongly on contact with the concrete, and attempts to meet the problem of mediation in his own terms.

Hegel focuses on this aspect of religious representation by speaking of its *form* and *content*. He is quite willing to grant religion its involvement with a "reality" that carries ultimate significance, being other than, "more" than finite entities. Religion's involvement with and articulation of the ultimate, constitutes the content of religious representation. Religion reaches this attainment in its own right and on its own terms. It does not have to wait upon philosophy for a certification of genuineness. Within religion itself a "lifting up," an "elevation" (*Erhebung*) of the finite to the infinite is *already* in the process of being accomplished.[8] The dynamic and dialectical process of being, as always effecting this *Erhebung*, is itself a community of the human and the divine already at work, already *wirklich*, prior to any philosophical mediation or reflection.

We meet again Hegel's doctrine of absolute spirit. Religion is one of the three highest modes of spiritual significance, with art and philosophy. It is marked by an absolute dimension, which comes most to the fore when we discern that the content of its representations is God. It does not get this content from philosophy, nor need it wait upon philosophy for it. I stress that Hegel can be read to say that absolute spirit *is not* univocally identical with philosophy. Absolute spirit *manifests itself* in threefold form—in artistic, religious, and philosophical form. Though this its content may confer on it its absoluteness, the religious mode of representing the absolute is not correspondingly absolute. The form of religious representation always takes shape in the finite as disclosing the infinite, and so this form never completely shakes itself free from finitude.

Put differently, the sensuous, imagistic side of *Vorstellung* does not have its purpose completely in itself but rather in its purported manifestation and articulation of a significance that is spiritual (*geistig*). By its very nature representation is defined by reference to an other. This is where we come across the ambiguity inherent in representation. The sensuous form itself tends to function in a double way. (Recall the point, in chapter 2, about the doubleness of bread and wine within the sacred cult.) On the one hand, we need to pass through and beyond its mere sensuousness, in order to apprehend its non-sensuous, spiritual content. On the other hand, since we have to pass through the sensuous form to attain contact with the spiritual content, invariably the sensuous form seems to separate us from the content. As a mediator, the sensuous form of representation both unites us with the content and separates us from it. The sensuous form of representation reveals itself as relative to the finite and the conditioned, while the content it claims to reveal is said to be infinite and unconditioned. If you like, it seems to be both a gateway giving us access, and yet a gate that bars our path.

This double way of apprehending the religious representation is reflected in a certain "doubleness" in Hegel's own evaluation of representation. The representation as gateway is cause of rejoicing for most philosophers, since it promises to be a way of knowing; correspondingly, the gate that bars the path seems to be a cause of cognitive dismay. The case is, in fact, more complex, since the second characteristic—the recalcitrance of representation to complete conceptualization—may prove to be absolutely essential to the truth of religious representation as inherently guarding the mystery and otherness of what is manifested. Manifestation may not be total. Or rather, what may be manifested is that the mystery of the divine withdraws from complete human determination, even in its manifestation to the human. Hegel does not draw this conclusion from the doubleness. Rather he emphasizes the limit of manifestation as an incompletion that is to be turned into complete manifestation. By its nature *Vorstellung* cannot effect this completion. The speculative *Begriff* will have to bring the process of manifestation to its full explicitness.

Let me provisionally grant that the present sense of doubleness can carry traces of *equivocity*. Let me grant that it may not yet be the affirmative doubleness of the metaxological. I think it helpful to say that Hegel's dialectical response to religious representation finds in the doubleness a certain equivocation. His response is at once critical and affirmative. It is affirmative in that representation can disclose a genuine, indeed absolute content. It is critical in that, while the content disclosed may be absolute, the form or mode of its disclosure may not be itself absolute. For Hegelian dialectic there is an incommensurability between the form and the content which produces ambiguity, here meaning equivocity, at the heart of the religious representation. This result generates a certain internal instability in representation which Hegel believes forces us to consider a further form of disclosure of the absolute content, namely, the philosophical concept, or *Begriff.*

The *Begriff* dialectically appropriates the putative equivocity of the representation and claims to free it from its duplicity. This duplicity implies the reduction of the relation of human and divine to a dualistic opposition or perhaps to a vacillation between these two as poles radically antithetical to each other. So for Hegel, the sensuous form of representation sets the content at a *distance before* the mind (the *vor*—of *Vorstellung*). This distance persists, even granting a certain inwardizing of the content effected in *Vorstellung*: the inwardizing is not dialectically complete. This *vor* of *Vorstellung*, and the gap between the content and the self, tempt us to continue to think of the absolute content in the form of finite things.

There is for Hegel the additional difficulty that this setting of the content at a distance imparts to it an inappropriate otherness. On the one hand, the *Vorstellung* intends to manifest or make present the content, and indeed to do so in religious inwardness. On the other hand, its form tends to fix this content as a *Jenseits*, a beyond. The content is re-presented; it is not fully presented, made present in the fullest form. In a word, the form of *Vorstellung* makes the content to be both present and "elsewhere." The absolute content is doubled between the here and the beyond, with the resultant possibility that religious consciousness always risks the double, divided being of the unhappy consciousness. This doubleness always skirts sheer equivocation, that is to say, unmediated difference between the human and the divine, and the endless shuttling to and fro between these extremes without genuine dialectical self-mediation.

As should be clear from previous discussions, if the doubleness is reduced to equivocity, Hegel has an important point with which I agree. The chief difficulty with such equivocity is, I think, that if we inappropriately accentuate this "elsewhere," then the "doubleness" of representation begins to turn into a dualism between man and God, with the result that their mediation, in and through the representation, collapses into their *opposition*. Hegel, I suggest, is not saying that this *inevitably* happens. Rather this is a perennial danger, given the ambiguous character of representation. The real affirmative intention of representation is to mediate the opposition of finite and infinite, the human being and God, and thus to transcend the separation that may alienate the two. The form in which it effects this mediation, however, may be liable to reinstate the estranging separation it purports to transcend. For this reason the form of representation may not itself be completely adequate to *its own religious* task. Seen in this light, religious representation might be said to point *internally* to the limitations of its own necessarily ambiguous form. I return to the significance of this crucial point below, for it will allow us to think of the doubleness in other than equivocal terms.

I conclude this precis of Hegel on representation with the following observations. The richest of religious representations all point towards the annulling of the alienation of man and God. Not surprisingly, for Hegel, Christianity appears as the absolute or consummate religion, or the religion in which this annulling is most completely effected. Indeed, the central representation here inevitably becomes the Incarnation: the Logos made flesh, the spiritual and the sensuous wed together in intimate union. The Incarnation is *the* representation which mediates finite and infinite, and annuls their alienation. The difficulty for Hegel is that even this representation, given that it can be interpreted to portray an historically contingent happening, is liable to misrepresentation. Its significance may be set at a distance in time and place, and it may be thought that the reconciliation it reveals just happened in that time and place. We neutralize its significance in an historical event that just happened then, and that is already gone by. We consign it to an event we regard externally as historical spectators, not properly grasping it speculatively, as a significance that spans time and is the interior meaning of all history. We misrepresent the meaning of the representation and fail to bring out its full rationale. Whether Hegel's view is true to the particular as particular is a question already asked in various ways, and that will be asked again.

For Hegel it is the coming of spirit, the appearance of *Geist* in *its own form*, that annuls the sensuous externality of the form of *Vorstellung*. *Geist* is the meaning of *Vorstellung*, its true content, even though its sensuous form may sometimes mislead us on this point. Hence *Geist* must be grasped in its indwelling, but the mode of its indwelling can never be fully grasped in the form of sensuous externality. The indwelling of spirit is in the community of spirit. The limits of representation become evident but again from sources *immanent* within religion itself. It is, as it were, that *Geist* itself dismantled the claims to absoluteness of every form of religious representation, since no representation, given its form of sensuous externality, can be completely commensurate with *Geist* in its non-sensuous absoluteness. Here also becomes evident the sense in which Hegel thinks that the truth of representation is a community—with the advent of spirit, the truth of religion is just the indwelling of spirit in the community of worshippers. Cultus is the sacred drama of that community of spirit.

The Left-Hegelian Reduction of the Religious Double

Hegel holds it necessary to move to another level to meet these difficulties of representation with the form of sensuous externality. The philosophical *Begriff* is said to effect this movement: it provides us with a form of thought where form and content are commensurate; the *Begriff* reveals *Geist* as dealing with itself, and in the form of *Geist* itself.[9] Conceptual thought is alone capable of complete self-mediation, alone capable of being the speculative thought that thinks itself. The *Begriff* is the truer cultus of *Geist* than is the *Vorstellung*. Philosophy then is *Gottesdienst*, but in the purity of rational thought, the sensuous and imagistic side of *Vorstellung* is laid aside, or at least its limitation suspended.

How do concept and representation relate? In accord with the doubleness, Hegel's interpretation, once again, is both affirmative and critical. If we grant the affirmative side, Hegel cannot be said to reduce the significance of religious representation simplistically to rational concepts. His purpose is rather to understand the significance *already inherent* in representation, to bring it to a further explicitness. Religious representation, in Hegelian language, is meaningful in-itself (*an sich*), but not always for-itself (*für-sich*). The movement to the second state is towards a condition of rational self-consciousness. It is Hegel's version of *fides quaerens intellectum*.

One must acknowledge that this movement has a preserving aim. Even if rational self-consciousness transcends representation, Hegel intends the significance of the latter to be sublated, *aufgehoben*: what we transcend we may negate in one form, but we may also affirm and conserve it in another form, within another more inclusive context. It is the form of representation that is negated but its content is affirmed, reaffirmed and conserved in another form. Hegel is often said to cancel or replace representations with concepts, or even to "swallow up" religion in philosophy.[10] Such language can produce a flattening of the sublating side of Hegel's philosophy. To "transcend" representation here means to "release" it from the restriction of sensuous externality, and so to reaffirm its content, now more fully freed into its absolute dimension. Hegel's philosophy, certainly in its intention, wants to be the conservative of religion.

That said, the second side of Hegel's evaluation, the critical, is not to be denied. Historically this has been more influential, especially as turned to their own purposes by the Left-Hegelians.[11] We need to approach the ambiguity of religious representation critically, not only on philosophical grounds, but, as we saw, on religious grounds. If the double" reading is correct, this necessary criticism need not be intended destructively. It might be intended purgatively; or in contemporary idiom, it might aim to "demythologise" a too literal reading of the representation.

Criticism now serves to mediate a more discerning, discriminating mindfulness, particularly against the circumscribed understanding that interprets religious representation in too literalist, too fundamentalist a fashion. The literalist loses touch with the complexity of the content because of his narrow fixation with the form.[12] Criticism might serve a freeing of the content from its fixation in any frozen finite form. When Hegel speaks of philosophy as absolute, this might be seen, not as dissolving religion's content, but as absolving us, in this sense of releasing us from that fixation with merely finite form.

Of course, this freeing can be mistaken for an evaporation of content, a making of the content into almost nothing. If we cannot fix the content, the absolute content, the idea of God, into finite form, the suspicion may arise that this idea has no content: that God is nothing. This difficulty, coupled with the doubleness of representation, confers sufficient ambiguity on Hegel's overall position to allow it to be exploited by Left-Hegelians for purposes at odds with Hegel's. The Left-Hegelians simplified Hegel's critical stance, cutting rather than untying this Gordian knot.

Criticism then becomes a matter of "reducing" the representation, not a matter of bringing to explicit mindfulness its genuine, religious meaning. Put otherwise: representation is understood to be an image, but an image of "nothing," except perhaps a projection of human need or power. So the Left-Hegelians affirm the human being as the true content of religious representation, not the conjunction of the human being and God, as in Hegel. Or rather, for Hegel religious representation mediates the movement toward conjunction of the divine and the human; philosophical criticism must release into the light of reason the true content revealed in this conjunction. For the Left-Hegelians, religious representation portrays only the movement of human power, being alienated into an opposing principle; philosophical criticism does not reveal a movement toward conjunction of the divine and the human, but a movement of reduction of the divine to the human.

Hegel criticizes the form of religious representation, but not the content; the Left-Hegelian criticizes both the form and the content, and moreover reduces both to human power. Hegel is cognizant that the ambiguous form of representation always runs the risk of *anthropomorphism*, or the mistaking of the infinite for the finite: criticism must free the infinite content from the finite form. In his discussion of the Incarnation, Hegel makes clear that there is a certain anthropomorphism he would defend. The superiority of the Christian to the Greek conception of divinity is that the former is more acceptably anthropomorphic: the suffering, torture, the infinite grief of the human is not excluded; the Christian conception embraces the negative in all its devastation, and hence is truer to being. The point at issue in this "anthropomorphism" is a deeper and more embracing concept of divinity, not any anthropomorphic reduction in the more usual and superficial sense.

Relative to the same ambiguity of representation, the Left-Hegelian discovers *nothing but* anthropomorphism in religion, anthropomorphism in the more usual sense. Criticism must free finite humanity—now said to be the true content—from entanglement in an alienating infinite, and henceforth release in humanity, species-man, its own infinite promise. Hegel would have us guard against reductive anthropomorphism in religion, not just for humanistic but also for religious and philosophical reasons. The Left-Hegelians, by contrast, would disengage anthropomorphism from its falsifying form in religion, but in other domains of life they would elevate anthropomorphism into the principle of a new humanism. This is very clear in Marx's will to humanize the initial otherness of nature through labor. We see the elements of the view in Hegelian sources, but we also see how the exploitation of these elements diverges from these sources.[13]

Can Religion Deal with Its Own Double?

Hegel speculatively acknowledges the representational doubleness which, as ambiguous, allows the anti-speculative reduction by Left-Hegelians. I now consider a crucial point, previously noted but not developed: namely, that the limits of representation can be acknowledged from *within* the religious realm itself. Hegel is cognizant of this fact but thinks that difficulties on one level are to be resolved at another, purportedly more comprehensive level, transcending the first. This is at the core of any dialectical approach, applicable to all experience and not only to its religious form. Hegel intends to preserve in the higher form what is transcended in the lower. Yet, given the two sides of his view, its affirmative and critical sides, one sees how with less penetrating minds the transcending of the limits of representation easily loses the preserving moment of *Aufhebung*, and becomes just a simple supersession of representation.

Why emphasize the way the limits of representation are granted from within the religious realm itself? Its importance lies in the manner that the religious way of being initiates a *questioning of itself*, initiates its own self-questioning.[14] This reopens the possible continuity of representation and speculation in terms of the non-reductive community of religion and philosophy, as each a distinctive mode of being metaxologically mindful. Representation displays resources of its own for dealing with the difficulty Hegel presses, namely, the putative disparity of form and content.

First, we reiterate that the religious requires some representation for the articulation and conservation of its own significance. An image, a name, a depiction of the divinity is essential to mediate the gap between the seen and the unseen, the sensuous and the spiritual. Without some image or representation, the divine becomes the Nameless, and the Nameless has a tendency to dissolve into the merely nebulous. In naming and representing God, of course, we always run the risk of anthropomorphism. Our discourse about the divine imbues the divine with sometimes incongruous human attributes. This follows from the necessary reliance of representation on some form of sensuous image.

Here the important point is that anthropomorphism can be approached from two opposite directions. On the one hand, it can be exploited by those hostile to the Holy, like Marx, who use the charge of anthropomorphism as a device to explode religious representation: the images of the gods are, religiously speaking, really images of nothing, except perhaps of man's own lack and need; positively, they are projections of human power and ought to be reappropriated as such. On the other hand, the problem can be approached in a contrary manner. Anthropomorphism is an issue for *both* the sympathizer with and the antagonist of religion. Those sympathetic to the sacred may grant this difficulty of anthropomorphism, but having done this, instead set out to purge the representation of any falsifying anthropomorphism. Thus, Xenophanes' criticism of anthropomorphic gods was in the service of a truer, non-anthropomorphic conception of divinity. Similarity with Plato's criticism in the *Republic*: the representations of the gods ought to be images of proper perfection, but turn out to be depictions, reduplications of human imperfections; but criticism must free divinity from such distortions, not destroy divinity as such.

Anthropomorphism expresses but another aspect of the risk of reducing an infinite content to merely finite form. In Hegelian terms, because *Vorstellung* implies reference to an other which is a *Jenseits*, it risks the "reification" of its own content; it risks the "objectification" of the infinite *Geist*, the turning of it into a merely finite "object" (*Gegenstand*). Since some such danger is always possible with every religious representation, Hegel is correct if we understand him to insist that the mindful self cannot avoid some critical stance toward representation. Hegel's protest against the "positivity" of some forms of religion, particularly in his earlier writings, can be understood here: "positive" religions treat the content of the religious consciousness as a mere thing or object "out there," and consequently insist on their own truth in the manner of a sheerly external authority. The truth in its inwardness has not been appropriated, the genuine truth where the form corresponds to the content, that is, where both form and content are known as spirit, as *Geist*.

Hegel is not straightforward enough about, nor does he insist strongly enough on, nor draw the full implications of, the fact that the religious itself tries to deal with these inherent difficulties it recognizes with its own form of representation.[15] The dangers of "anthropomorphism," of "reification," of "objectification," are fully acknowledged by the mature religious self. Religious maturity precisely tries to rectify, to counterbalance these dangers inherent in its own form of representation. Religious maturity is religiously suspicious of itself, vigilant about its own unnamed idolatry. One mark of the truly mindful religious self is: it possesses an essential *self-consciousness* about the form of its own mode of representation.[16] It refrains from investing the form of representation with a false absoluteness.

Representation is not misunderstood as the simple "objectification" of a divine content; it is seen to entail some element of "self-objectification," "self-mediation." As entailing some "self-mediation," representation involves the revelation or disclosure of spirit, which now comes to recognize something of itself as articulated in the otherness of representation. Spirit recognizes spirit in the representation, a recognition central to Hegel's view. This recognition is, however, a two-edged sword. There is the danger of a dialectical idolatry in which the otherness of the divine is not properly safeguarded. The form of religious representation becomes an insurmountable obstacle only when the religious self is excessively literal-minded. But to be thus excessively literal-minded is *not* to understand something essential about the form of representation, namely, that it is just that, a representation.

The mindful religious self can be vigilant of this already, prior to the point where developed philosophical reason might supervene. It is not deceived. It may well be on its guard against all representations, precisely because it is inwardly attuned to their ambiguous complexity, their enigmatic richness. It may be quite willing to admit that there is no absolute sensuous representation of God completely free of this ambiguity or enigma. The genuine content of the representation is not to be treated as a mere thing "out there," an objectified *Jenseits* existing in immobile separateness. Religious mindfulness can "interiorize" the divine content in and through the form of representation. The very form itself ceases to be a mere external trapping and becomes itself progressively "interiorized." A merely external relation to God proves to be impossible. Hegel himself was aware of the innering movement of mind in representation when he connected *Vorstellung* with *Erinnerung* (*Encyclopedia*, § 451).

Hegelian innering dialectically subordinates exteriority and otherness. As I understand it, the representational innering or interiorization of the sense of God need *not* compromise transcendence. Religious inwardness, dwelling mindfully in the representation, opens in itself to otherness. The mindful movement of religious interiorization is not simply a dialectical appropriation, hence surmounting of the excess of transcendence. Religious interiorization brings to light in inwardness the metaxological community between the human and divine, and hence the double mediation again. There is no reduction to a singular mediation, whether that of a humanistically appropriating self or an absorbing god that would include self and other in a totality. Consider for example Augustine's description of his own journey as a *double* movement: *ab exterioribus ad interiora, ab inferioribus ad superiora*; from the exterior to the interior, from the inferior to the superior. The advent of the superior within the interior, its advent in its inward excess to interiority itself, breaks open any pretension on the part of interiority to be the measure of the superior. Interiority itself cannot be completely self-mediating, for into its most profound self-mediation an other otherness, even beyond its own inward otherness, breaks through.

Even Augustine's economical statement of this double movement is incomplete. As stated, it omits to add that the second movement between inferior and superior itself admits of a double mediation. Augustine is well aware of the point. That is, there is a possible erotic movement from the inferior to the superior, from human lack to divine plenitude. This movement, in part, answers to what I am calling self-mediation. But there is also an agapeic movement from the superior to the inferior that is the mediation, metaxological intermediation of the other out of the excess of its own transcendence. This is the overflow of the surplus of transcendence toward the finite being and for the finite being as other. This second movement is an agapeic advent, an advent in interiority that comes to the self from the other, and hence is radically resistant to description purely in terms of dialectical self-mediation. It is the agapeic rupture of all self-mediation that claims self-sufficiency or completeness.

The point is not a knockdown argument against Hegel, who is one of the most searching critics of merely external relations between the human and divine. I am trying to clarify an ambiguous complexity intrinsic to representation that shows the continuity of religious and philosophical mindfulness in a manner both consonant and discordant with Hegel's view. I also want to suggest the internal resources of religion itself that preserve it against the onslaughts of an exclusively negative, "critical" rationality. As the above interiorization of representation develops, the religious consciousness increasingly ceases to be rigidly literalist. While recognizing its own need for representation, it increasingly becomes alert to the temptation of mistaking the image of God for the original itself.

The Hebrews insisted that no representation could completely encapsulate the divine content. But in recognizing the problem of representation, the response was to counter it on religious grounds and in religious terms. It was not simply to conceptualize the representation in a new unambiguous rational form, but to purify the religious self of its own proclivity to idolatry. The connection of representation and idolatry is suggested by the Greek word for image: *eidōlon*. When representation becomes an idol, it is not due to any special character intrinsic to the representation itself. It is because we take the representation with a literalness, with an undiscriminating mindfulness, without the proper interiorization of its truth. One might say, we take the representation mindlessly. We do not take its truth to heart. When we take the representation thus, we really misunderstand its very form; for in idolatry we worship the image *for itself*, and not for what it represents—as a mindful appropriation of its form would require. Idolatry testifies to the lack of discerning mindfulness with respect to *both* form and content.

No religious representation is ever absolutely free from the possibility of misappropriation, and so every representation might be used, abused rather, to serve the purposes of idolatry. When the representation is mistaken for the absolute original itself, we become shackled to it, in bondage to it. Instead of the elevation of a finite reality into a revelation of the divine, the infinity of the divine is diminished to the level of a finite fetish. In being attentive to the difficulty of anthropomorphism and the possibility of idolatry, mature religious mindfulness already appreciates the form of representation in its essential doubleness—that it may both reveal and conceal the divine. It also knows that in the double mediation, the second mediation, beyond self-mediation, unshakably testifies to the irreducibility of the other. The double mediation implies skepticism regarding the possibility of complete self-mediation, religious skepticism regarding the absolutization of any self-mediation. This religious skepticism is founded in a sense of the reserve of the sacred other, its mystery beyond all conceptual encapsulation.

This response is not just to negate representation, but to call for the appropriate orientation to the representation, a qualitative mindfulness informed by the character of *both* the form and the content. A different light, other than that generated by the literalistic, idolatrous mind, is to be thrown on the representation. This light does not so much replace representation as transform it, transfigure it. Religious mindfulness does not just deal with its own form by retranslating its own content into conceptual form; though it may do this too. It transforms the ambiguous form by differently dwelling within the representations, with something like the doubled interiority implied above. It does not review their content from an external vantage point; it transforms them from within by progressively penetrating to their true spiritual content. For Hegel, of course, it is the Christian consciousness which attains the acme of this transformation. But we can see the possibility of this transformation present in all religious representation. We move beyond the ambiguity of representation to the enigma of divine excess.

Religious *Vorstellung*, as Hegel grants, incorporates its own form of thinking or *Denken* and the more sophisticated the representation becomes, the more it frees itself from whatever is extraneous to its own inherent content. This sophistication of religious mindfulness, at once reverent and skeptical, accentuates its kinship with philosophical mindfulness. Both insist on proper self-knowledge—one which may know the self's own inward otherness, one which implies no closure to otherness beyond all self-mediation. Philosophical mindfulness need not replace religious mindfulness. This view, as imputed to Hegel, is dialectically equivocal. The imputation is understandable if religion has only the absolute content but not the absolute form, while philosophy has both absolute form and absolute content. The danger with this characterization, Hegel's own, is that it misleads us into thinking of philosophy as supplying something positively, which religious representation of itself lacks, the form of spirit.

This characterization *does* follow if philosophy yields the *Aufhebung* of religion. But if philosophy and religion both evidence the double mediation, we need a different characterization in which both are different metaxological ways of being mindful. This latter characterization is not entirely incompatible with a re-reading of Hegel's position, a re-reading of dialectic from a metaxological standpoint. Mindful religion tries to appropriate its own form; it knows that what makes representation genuinely religious at all is that it is *informed* by spirit, without which it would be lifeless and dull. It might even be claimed that the mystical dimension of religion, properly understood, constitutes a certain acme of indwelling, informing spirit, in that it repeatedly calls attention to the limits of representation, and insists upon us avoiding the pitfall of mistaking the image for the original. In this sense mysticism might be seen as religion in the process of purifying its own sacred representations. And it is not incidental that Hegel himself couples his own notion of speculative reason (*Vernunft*) with the mystical.[17] This relation of reason and the mystical is a further story. I will offer just a few remarks in conclusion.

Representation and the Thought of the Unrepresentable

Hegel's comparison of speculative reason and the mystical seems to point us to the thought of the unrepresentable, beyond all representation. Does Hegel then bow before the ultimate enigma of God at the end? Or is there a dialectical twist to Hegel's tale which seems to promise this outcome, only then to give us, in the end, religious stones that are said to be speculative bread?

Hegel's absolute is the mystical in the sense that it passes the understanding, *Verstand*. *Verstand* gets bogged down in the thought of a double, the human and divine, that endlessly reduplicates itself as dualistic opposition. The mystical negates this double as dualistic opposition and assents to the *unio* of the human and divine. The negation of this double seems to correspond exactly to the movement of dialectical thinking which breaks down the fixed antitheses of the understanding by simply thinking through their opposition more deeply. Dialectical negation, like mystical *askesis*, is beyond the fixity of *Verstand*, is the very dynamic movement of mind beyond such fixation. Speculative reason is for Hegel the affirmative union of the opposites that are thus dialectically released from their fixity and opposition. Speculative reason is the mystical beyond understanding. Note that the mystical so comprehended is not a mystery for speculative reason; it is a mystery for *Verstand*, but for Hegelian reason it is the only thing that makes sense. Hegel's admission of the correspondence of the mystical and the rational is suggestive, but we must not forget that for him the ultimate mystery is an open secret, a comprehended mystery, and hence in another sense, no final mystery at all.

Can we subscribe to such an *Aufhebung* of representation into the concept, even in this disingenuous sense, perhaps we should say *gnostic* sense, of the mystical?[18] There are deeper difficulties, signaling deeper differences that recall us to Kierkegaard and the discordant mutuality of philosophy and religion. Here are some final thoughts about the positive significance of the doubleness of representation.

Consider again the issue of "representational thinking," spoken of at the beginning. As we recall, the contemporary critique of "representation" is intended to release a non-representational thinking that is open to the other. One immediately divines a hidden connection with the mystical. For that matter, the post-Heideggerian critique of the human subject, its willful interfering knowing, strikes me as a secular counterpart to the metaphysical and religious critique of anthropomorphism. The major religious criticisms against anthropomorphism vis-à-vis God reappear in this so-called post-philosophical deconstruction of human subjectivity, reappear in a form that is embarrassed to acknowledge any bond with the religious. Does not the deconstruction of subjectivity, the so-called "death of man" point equivocally, disingenuously towards an a/theological mysticism?

Hegel's criticism of representation is different from the post-Heideggerian critique: his speculation claims to complete the project of self-mediating thought more absolutely than does representation, because the latter is always defined by a relation to *an other*. Against Hegel, I defend this latter necessity as essentially positive. Against the post-Heideggerian critique, the double in representation in itself is the promise of an openness to the unrepresentable and the thought of the other beyond thought. Nor does the bond between philosophy and religion embarrass me.

Mysticism can be seen as religion purifying its own religious representations. Mysticism is the form of religious skepticism par excellence, religious skepticism about all the forms of religious representation.[19] In this religious skepticism, no name is the name, no representation is the representation, no image is the image. For every name, representation, image is *unequal* to the absolute original beyond all representation. Mysticism, if you will, involves the religious deconstruction of all fixed representations and the hubris about the divine they foster. But it deconstructs representation, not simply to negate, but to release a freer mindfulness of the absolute original, beyond all representation. This release towards the beyond of all representation is articulated in a passage in and through religious representation itself.

I suggest that, from this other viewpoint, the putative limitation of representation is paradoxically double, and its limitation is one of

its affirmative resources. What Hegel sees as a limitation can be seen
as preserving the promise of religious release towards the absolute
original, beyond all representation. As always the carrier of a reference
to an other, representation necessitates a relatedness to an other that
the representation itself does not absolutely encapsulate. I see this
representational relativity as a standing for an other, a standing
before the other, a standing up for the other as other. It stands for
the affirmative irreducibility of a certain heteronomy. Hegel tries to
determine negatively the inherent *disjunction* that informs representation, whether between form and content, whether between the
human and the divine; by thus negatively determining disjunction,
he wills to surmount all disjunction dialectically. I see the promise
of disjunction in another light: it is a sign of the positive promise of
the essential reference to an irreducible other that must not be
conceptually subordinated or dialectically domesticated. In its
seeming poverty, the inherence of disjunction in representation is its
very power, its paradoxical richness.

So the doubleness of representation itself images a difference or
otherness between the human and the divine that is always to be kept
open. This openness would hold sway even in the mystical, understood
as a community of the human and the divine, a community very
different from the kind implied by Hegel's speculative union. For there
the ultimate enigma of the divine would not be rationally dispelled,
but deepened beyond all human measure. The limitation of representation, which the mystical more than any other form of religious mind
takes most to heart,[20] is just its enactment of a religious reverence
at the limits of human power. This gap for Hegel is not the place of
reverence but of a new dialectical restlessness that wills to overcome
the gap and make what is hidden conceptually manifest. The limit
is understood as something to be negated and *aufgehoben*, rather than
an essential delimitation of finiteness that is to be celebrated. Hegel
wills to incorporate dialectically the double mediation of representation within a total process of dialectical self-mediation.

I must restate the double mediation. It is double on both the side
of the human and of God. On the one hand, human self-mediation
and its mediation with God as other; on the other hand, the mediation
of the divine itself, its self-mediation, but also its mediation with finite
creation as an other. Now what Hegel implies is that the first human
self-mediation is also its elevation to mediated unity with God, the
Erhebung mentioned earlier; as self-mediating, the human being
necessarily is caught up in a process of becoming one with God.
Likewise, the second self-mediation of the divine is its necessary
intermediation with finite creation, which creation for Hegel is really

only the divine *itself* as other—hence these two mediations are one, and God necessarily moves towards becoming man. The self-becoming of God, in Hegel's view, is the process by which God "creates" the finite world as its dialectical other; in the finite world as other, God moves to become and recognize Himself in the human being; hence God's "creation" of man as other is the self-othering of God, and man is the dialectical middle in which God recognizes Himself.

In summary: For Hegel the overall mediation from one side, the side of "immanence," is the necessary dialectic by which the human being moves towards self-consciousness, and in this becoming at one with God. The overall mediation from the other side, the side of "transcendence," is the necessary self-mediation of God by which God wakes up to Himself as human self-consciousness.

While the directionality of the two mediations seems to be opposite, that is, from the human being to God, and from God to the human being, Hegel will say that the forms of the two mediations are essentially the same. Difference of directionality will not count dialectically, since the two directions are different articulations of the one process of total self-mediation. Hence they cannot be sustained as dualistic opposites, indeed cannot be sustained in any sense as other to each other, but must be dialectically seen as two moments of the one process of total divine-human mediation, self-mediation. And so the double mediation collapses into this total and single self-mediation. I am stating what I see is the essential core of the Hegelian position: what the religious representation sees as two mediations are from a more encompassing point of view merely one mediation and the difference between the two gives way to their unity. It is only Hegelian philosophy that properly comprehends this speculative unity.

I think this is wrong. The double mediation is irreducible. Why so? Recall again the difference between the erotic and the agapeic absolute. An erotic absolute is initially marked by a certain lack or indeterminacy; to complete itself concretely, to overcome its lack, it must articulate itself in time; finite being is hence the necessary process of articulate self-development by which the erotic absolute mediates with itself and brings itself to completion. "Creation" is understood as dialectical self-mediation. By contrast, an agapeic absolute in itself is absolute: in itself it is not lacking indeterminacy, but a plenitude that is *more* than any determinate entity, a plenitude that is overdetermined and infinite. Its relation to finite being is not that of a necessary determination that will fill up its own lack. In itself it exhibits the affirmative indeterminacy of inexhaustibility, the overdetermination, more than determinacy, of plenitude in itself. An agapeic absolute allows the absolute to be absolute in itself, hence

other to finitude; but it also allows finitude to be other in itself.
Agapeic creation is the giving of being to the other that lets that other-
being be as other. To be *itself,* agapeic eternity does not have to recover
finite being; hence finite being can be let be as irreducibly other. This
double otherness does not preclude intermediation, but the *inter* can
never be entirely mediated in terms of any singular self-mediation,
whether of the human or the divine. Agapeic creation cannot be
reduced to God's own dialectical self-mediation, but gives an ontological freedom that escapes the dialectical claims of a singular,
totalized self-mediation.

The agapeic absolute is the "more," the *ne plus ultra* of thought.
It is the Unequal Itself in being unequalizable by any finite
determinate counterpart or substitute. As the Unequal Itself it has
no dialectical equivalent with which it could be speculatively inter-
changed. The *directionality* of its giving of being out of excess or
plenitude is all important. No directionality of *our* giving out of
finitude would be its proper equal or dialectical equivalent. There is
a divine *disproportion* here beyond all equalization, undertaken from
the side of, or for the sake of immanence. Any "equalization," out of
transcendence, can only be an agapeic gift of the Unequal Itself, not
a necessity of dialectical logic. What I called agapeic abandon (see
chapter 2) is a faltering effort to name this gift.

To undercut dialectically, as Hegel does, the differences in
directionalities in relation to the double mediation of representation
is, in effect, to collapse the difference between the erotic and the
agapeic absolute. Indeed it is the collapse of the second into the first,
such that the radical creation of the finite other as irreducibly other
becomes unthinkable. What also become unthinkable is a more
profound sense of a mediation which goes from the self to the other,
but for the other, or a mediation that goes from the other to the self
but not for the other as self, as itself. Hegel's absolute is erotic, and
in the end every other is the other in which the self-constitution of
Hegel's absolute, its self-recognition and self-appropriation, is effected.
That is, there is no absolute other, in the end.

I take the doubleness of the representation to be an imaginative
enactment of a stronger and justified sense of otherness than is
acceptable to Hegel. The limit is the limit of an ontological acknowledgment that the being of the divine other always exceeds our
comprehension. It also is the ontological acknowledgment that the
finite creation is other than God in a manner other than and irreducible to God's own *self-creation.* The representation imagistically
enacts this double salutation of excess, of transcendence. It redoubles
the double by a certain yes to it, a yes that is not thought within any

"it is good"

concept that dialectically reduces an opposition to an underlying unity or elevates it to an overarching totality.

The limit of the representation, enacted in its doubleness, is precisely its very power and greatness, namely, the naming of a certain powerlessness on the part of the human being in the face of the ultimate excess, the Unequal Itself. This naming is not the abject impotence of the unhappy consciousness. It is the grateful acknowledgment that all being and power is given from the other, the agapeic absolute. It is a mode of metaphysical praise and thanks for the other and what is given from the other. The double is no dualistic opposition. Far from being infected with dualistic opposition, the doubleness of the representation may itself be an agapeic acknowledgment of the absolute original as the uncircumscribable, unreserved excess of agapeic being.

Suppose we think of Jesus here as a testimonial representation: scandalous witness of what is beyond representation, yet the manifestation and mediator of this beyond. The mediation is double, a community of the "I am nothing" and the agapē of absolute being. This is not just a dialectical coincidence of opposites. This representation is a self that is infinitely deep, deep beyond words in its suffering, as also in its relativity to all others, including the maligned other. In this double middle as self, there is an inward otherness whose enigma escapes us, as does its relativity to the absolute other. This is the enigmatic double of this middle: A world unto himself, an original, yet imaging the absolute original; an absolute singularity, yet the individual concretion of community between the human and divine; other than world-history, yet transforming world-history; an idiotic this, yet with universal significance. There is no dialectical concept of this idiot wisdom, sign of a double abyss: abyss of self, abyss of God.

What Kierkegaard could not forgive about Hegel is precisely his reduction of the double mediation with the divine other to a singular process of absolute self-mediation in which the human being and God turn out to be two complementary moments. What is unforgivable is the historicist equalization of the eternal Unequal. Historicist hubris matches speculative idolatry. Kierkegaard sometimes risks defending the double in too dualistic terms, but this is a risk worth running, if we bear in mind the absolutely essential reaffirmation of divine transcendence.

The result, of course, can risk turning the doubleness of relation between philosophy and religion into a dualism of opposites. Their mutuality is suppressed by their discord. I think that a proper understanding of the double now makes us ask whether a plurivocal philosophy, truly open to the other as other, must not acknowledge, more radically than Hegel's speculative concept, its *debt* to representation. Must the concepts of philosophy more profoundly acknowledge their own corresponding doubleness? The way I have been putting this is that philosophy must be *both* thought thinking itself, and thought thinking its others—others irreducible to the complete self-mediation of philosophy itself. This opens up a more genuine two-way interplay between philosophy and religion. This would be a metaxological philosophy, one which would genuinely open up the dialectic to the other in a dialogue between philosophy and its others, a dialogue that in the end could not come down to the self-mediation of thought thinking itself.

Against Hegel, metaxological philosophy denies that there is *one* comprehensive dialectic that subsumes all the others. Such philosophy does not dialectically sublate the otherness of art and religion into its own self-thinking thought, as we find in the final totalizing move of Hegel's absolute spirit. I understand Kierkegaard's insistence on the otherness of religion as a rejection of any totalizing *Aufhebung*. His insistence on religion's otherness is not sufficiently guarded against a new dualistic opposition with philosophy, as if philosophy were exhausted by a Hegelianism, identified with a panlogist thought thinking itself. If metaxological philosophy is open to the thinking of otherness, it is also open to religion's otherness, and hence this dualistic opposition is untenable.

Hegel stresses philosophy's own self-mediation in its dialectical relation to what is other; Kierkegaard, in the counter movement of faith, stresses religion's otherness as resistant to philosophy's complete self-mediation. Metaxological philosophy is a plurivocal thinking that seeks to avoid dualistic opposition in regard to Kierkegaard's emphasis, and dialectical subsumption in regard to Hegel's. But plurivocal thought can find a place for both emphases, suitably qualified: on the one hand, philosophy's self-mediation must become newly open to the other, even those others that occasion the *breakdown* of self-mediating thought; on the other hand, any fideistic hostility of religion to mind must be converted to a new reciprocity with thought.

Right up to the end Hegel offers the face of strong sympathy with religion, only then to reverse this face into the mask of the speculative concept with a seemingly atheistic visage. I now suggest this: In thinking through the doubleness of representation, Hegel goes all the way to the limit. At the limit, what opens is no ordinary gap; what opens is an abyss, for no human mediation will ever cross this gap completely through itself, nor can any human mediation command that the Unequal other cross over to us. Can the gap, the abyss of the middle then be mediated at all? For in this abyss arises the majestic yet horrifying thought of divine incomprehensibility. This is the ultimate otherness, this is the otherness that robs all human pretension, religious and philosophical, of its security, of every self-secured foundation.

And did not this gap, this abyss horrify Hegel? How else could he have entered with such existential rapport into a figure like the unhappy consciousness, or named so passionately the negative hierophany of the death of God? But the abyss nevertheless was an abyss, and the doubleness would not budge, all dialectical exorcisms to the contrary. Hegel would go further, and there is nothing wrong with this per se. This is the absolute unrest of the human spirit in its restless search for the ultimate; this is human self-transcendence that makes the human being the extreme metaphysical animal. This is the metaphysical insomnia of mind that puts the philosopher in the space between the human and the divine, in the space between time and eternity. This is the transcendence of Platonic eros as energized in the being of the philosopher.

Hegel knew this, Hegel lived this, Hegel tried to think this through. Hegel was between, his dialectical thought was between. But what happens to the between? Is it preserved as the abyssal space between the human being and God, between time and eternity? Is it preserved as the metaphysical space of a deep double that has a profound truth of its own and that is not reducible to the unity of the extremes that bound it? Hegel will not simply reduce it to the extremes, but as standing in the between, he would go further by speculatively reformulating the middle as the ultimate medium wherein is effected the absolute dialectical self-mediation of the whole. The abyssal middle becomes the dialectical medium for the speculative conquest of the majesty and horror of God's mystery. The between is understood in terms of a necessary dialectical self-mediation instead of a free metaxological intermediation.

In the end Hegel could not tolerate the pathos of doubleness, could not accept any otherness that finally resisted appropriation, could not accept that the other might freely, gratuitously give itself across the between. The gratuity of this giving is abysmal for dialectic; yet it stuns thought to think the absolute original as agapeic. Hegel will dodge this thought, miss it, by saying that it is too "representational." Instead, by a *necessity of logic* Hegel would determine God to come across the gap of the abyss. Hegel's God, as an erotic absolute, will be logically necessitated to come across, for outside of the coming across such an erotic absolute is nothing in itself, hence no absolute.

Hegelian logic is blind to the excess of transcendence of the agapeic absolute, and can make no sense of the gratuity of agapeic creation. There will be no gratuity in God's coming across, for the logical concept dictates, under Hegel's dictation, that there will be no final, irreducible gratuity.

Then for Hegel God and the human being become the limiting others of the dialectical middle itself; but these two, as such others, are not really others but the means, the media by which the middle necessarily produces and effects its own complete self-mediation. This is an extraordinary move, and an extraordinarily complex one, extremely difficult to formulate adequately, much less formulate in such a manner as allows us to see, not only what Hegel is doing, but also what is questionable about what he is doing. There is nothing to be gained from putting questions to Hegel at a level below the complexity of his views. Yet in the end we find something very elemental: Hegel could not philosophically stand, philosophically stand in, the abyss of this doubleness. He had to build a web of dialectical mediations putatively to bridge the abyss; in fact all he does is cover it over with speculative concepts. But beneath the grand logical web, the gap of this sacred abyss still persists, and its very "nothingness" always threatens the self-secured foundations of the logical web.

Beneath the logical web, or above the logical web—for it does not matter whether we say "above" or "below" about this excess; this sacred abyss is neither up nor down, for it is high in the Latin sense of *"altum,"* which can mean either high or deep, or both high and deep—beneath and above the logical web, there is a high/deep other which eludes every dialectical appropriation of otherness. Hegel's circular system might seem closed to this otherness, but in truth there is no ultimate philosophical protection from it, and its very otherness may erupt at any unexpected moment or place, like Plato's *"exaiphnēs,"* to mock every pretension of self-sufficient closure. The pure self-transparent light of self-sufficient speculation is englobed and penetrated and invaded by this abysmal sacred darkness.

Dialectical thought will try to build its logical shelter, but once the thought of this abyss breaks through, speculative philosophy can never henceforth be entirely at home or at ease in this shelter. The consoling peace of logic is broken forever. Thought becomes unhoused before this other, stripped of its self-certainty, naked before the limit of the illimitable. Hegel is right in one regard: there is no limit for thought, and every limit as drawn, as thought, is already transcended. But there are no limits here, because we come across a limit/unlimit, at whose edge there is no conceptual protection from the ultimate other. In truth we do not come across it, it crosses us. Thought does not erase such an unlimit/limit through its own infinite self-transcendence. Rather the self is transcended by the limit of an unlimited otherness that erases or cuts across every circle of self-sufficiency, erected by thought for its own secure self-mediation. When philosophy is suspended in the abyss of this between, it knows a breakdown of dialectical self-mediation. It may also acknowledge the breakthrough of an other to thought, beyond all dialectical self-mediation, an other to which thought is unequal.

If the absolute original is agapeic, and if we metaxologically comprehend what this implies, Hegel would have to say about his own salvation in logical necessity: It is as nothing, it is as straw. And *this* "It is nothing," he could not bring himself to say.

Chapter 4

Dialectic and Evil:
On the Idiocy of the Monstrous

Speculation and Evil

Speculative mind opens us to the otherness of being in metaphysical astonishment before the being there of what is. Is there a negative correlative to metaphysical astonishment? Suppose there is and we call it metaphysical horror? Suppose we undergo the horror of this "negative" in what we call evil. How will speculative metaphysics respond? Is it capable of thinking the monstrous? If it can, how can it? When we encounter evil, speculative mind seems to run against a wall it cannot scale, can never scale. Will we offer a logical reason for the monstrous? Must not metaphysical mindfulness ask for more? What more can speculative philosophy say? Must we fall mute before the monstrous? Can we rest satisfied with a dialectical logic of evil?

Evil rouses a storm of spirit wherein logic finds it hard to maintain its shelter. Can dialectics explain evil? Certainly Kierkegaard will say no.[1] What about Hegel? It seems to me that evil is both an extremely important issue with respect to Hegel and also a supreme test of claims he makes on behalf of speculative dialectic. Below I look at his most extensive discussion of evil, namely, in the *Lectures on the Philosophy of Religion*. But first I underline the importance of the issue. The frequent dismissal of Hegel is related to this. His dialectical holism is subliminally identified with something like the rational optimism parodied in Voltaire's Dr. Pangloss. Hegel is Dr. Panlogos, who will always see or anticipate a silver lining in the dark clouds of every world historical turbulence. Reason rules the world. When this is uttered by Hegel a reactive howl of disbelief goes up. Why? A brief reflection brings us back to the horror of history and its unrelenting blood and evil. Hegel is seen as covering up the recalcitrant

189

reality of evil by dialectical sorcery. But—the claim is—this sorcery loses the magic of its spell once we advance from the circle of pure concepts and confront face to face the concrete horror of real evil.

Is this a caricature of Hegel? Or, if it is a caricature, is there enough of truth in it to make us uneasy? We must ponder both the truth of the "caricature" and the persuasiveness, perhaps seductiveness of Hegel's interpretion. We must ask, more generally, about the strengths and limits of conceiving evil according to speculative dialectic. This raises the crucial question: Is there something about evil that repeatedly resists all our rationalizing, even that of dialectical reason, something that testifies to a recalcitrant other that puts before all philosophy a limit or boundary to its own discursive rationalizing?

I must dwell on this last point. Hegel rejects the view that philosophy should prescribe how reality ought to be. This repudiation of prescription can be read in a number of ways. It might be read as a canonization of the status quo—social and political, as well as ontological. It might also be read as articulating a philosophical contempt for thinkers dissatisfied with reality as it is. To be dissatisfied with the real is to see being as an evil, and to will it to be *other* than it is. By contrast, not to prescribe appears to make one complacent with the *same*, to manifest a refusal to face otherness. All is well as it is—implying a mystifying quietism that prevents us from working for the betterment of what now is. This line of interpretation recognizably informs the Marxist critique: Hegel's ontological reconciliation (we must consent to being as it is, for being is rational) blinds us to the evils of social and economic exploitation.

Clearly evil is bound up with claims concerning the rationality or irrationality of the real. If the real is the rational, evil seems to have been blinked. Hence, we must grant the implicitly *ethical* dimensions of almost all protests against Hegel—whether justified or not. These protests persist, and while couched as epistemological or ontological objections, are almost never reducible to purely epistemological or metaphysical terms. Shadowing these terms is the imputation of ethical blindness, not to say callousness.

Hegel sees philosophy as offering a comprehensive and systematic rational account of what is. Can one offer a systematic rational account of evil? Hegel's comprehensive claims makes us expect that his dialectical-speculative thinking will offer such an account. My question again is: Is there something about evil, is evil a certain other to reason, that subverts every thought claiming to comprehend it conceptually? Is there something about evil that always remains radically perplexing, radically enigmatic for human minds?

A philosopher significantly reveals or betrays himself in how he responds. A philosopher who is blind to the potentially enigmatic character of evil strikes one as driven by such a logicist hubris that he may be incapable of even acknowledging that there is a deep question here. Such a logicist might say: What is can be rationalized; evil as part of the process of being can also be rationalized; if it cannot, it may be of interest to the psychologist or the pastor but it is of no interest to the philosopher as a reasoning mind. This response fobs off the conceptually recalcitrant and is, alas, common enough.

Consider the way logical positivism would immediately refer one, and not without complacent condescension, to the priest or psychoanalyst. The logical positivist merely reveals in more open fashion (due to naivete in philosophical self-consciousness) what is a perennial temptation for all philosophers—running away from matters that take us to the edge of the logical, if not beyond. Yet as a philosopher one must also ask: Does not such a logicist quarantine on evil amount to humbug? If philosophy cannot think about the hardest cases, the cases that may even defeat it, is the game worth the candle? But philosophy can and sometimes does think about such cases. In my view Hegel deserves some respect here. He is not without ambiguity. His view that evil can be rationalized raises suspicions of a dialectical domestication of evil. Nevertheless, he does not run away from evil, but tries to incorporate its negative otherness within the dialectical life of reason itself. There can be an honesty and seriousness to this. Whether it risks neutralization of the horror is less clear—I think there is this risk.

There is also the following problem specific to the Hegelian system. Without exaggeration one can say that evil is crucial in the definition of Hegelian philosophy, indeed wisdom. Consider how in the *Phenomenology* Hegel is in search of the standpoint of philosophical science: thought thinking itself in its other and in complete self-transparency to itself. This is the end the philosopher is to reach on attaining absolute knowing. How do we get to this end which is, in fact, the real beginning of Hegelian *Wissenschaft*—for only at this end can there commence truly philosophical thought? To get to this end/beginning we have to cross the terrain of evil. Evil names a fundamental alienation, an active antithesis, a hostile opposition between the self and itself, the self and the other, the self and the whole of being. Absolute knowing must surmount such estrangements.

I suggest that as the malign genius is to Descartes' quest for certainty, the dialectic of evil is to Hegelian system. Descartes must overcome the malign genius if philosophy and the new mathematical science of nature are to be logically and ontologically credible. The malign genius is the radical other to the *lumen naturale*, the natural light, the inversion of every rational certitude. It epitomizes *the cunning of unreason*. Were the nightmare of this supposition not quelled, instead of absolute mind, we could not escape the terrifying thought of a monstrous malice nesting in the mind itself, a malice that mind on its own, or thought thinking itself, could not apprehend. This is why this thought charges mind with being radically apprehensive.

Relative to Hegelian science, a crucial turning point in the *Phenomenology* occurs in Hegel's discussion of evil and forgiveness. I find this discussion equivocal for the following reasons. The central issue of the one and the double, and the metaphysical determination of irreducible plurality, appears again. In Hegel's account, one is not always sure whether it is the *same one* Spirit that is *both* the evil consciousness and the moral consciousness; or whether there is a real *duality* of consciousnesses here, the one irreducible to the other, such that the forgiveness of one is irreducibly the forgiveness of an *irreducible other*. In the first possibility, evil would be the evil that Spirit as a *one*, as a dialectically self-mediating unity, inflicts on *itself*, and hence all forgiveness is self-forgiveness, *Geist's own self-forgiveness*. In the second possibility, evil might be inflicted on an other as genuinely other, and not on just the self in its own otherness; hence forgiveness would also be a radical gesture of acceptance of the other as radically irreducible to the self. Hegel's discussion equivocates between these two: Is it the one Spirit that is divided into two extremes at war with each other; or two spirits in extreme war with each other?

Before the end of Hegel's discussion, the second seems the plausible interpretation in that we appear to have a genuine duality of "I's." But at the point of forgiveness and in Hegel's subsequent discussion, Hegel's dealing with a putatively irreducible plurality of spirits alters. Instead the stress is singularly on Spirit as an "I" that has *expanded itself into a duality* and now in the act of reconciliation has brought back to itself its own alienated extremes.[2] The difference between these two possibilities has serious implications. As we shall see later more fully, Hegel understands evil and its forgiveness in terms of the *dialectical self-mediation* of Spirit, *Geist*; hence also undercutting the radical duality of the second possibility. My own thought with respect to evil moves in the direction of a radical doubleness, which is not forgiven by a dialectical self-mediation of spirit, but by a certain metaxological intermediation between two irreducibly other selves. This intermediation implies the breakdown of every effort to close the circle of dialectical self-mediation and a breakthrough into a form of mindfulness beyond the dialectical. Something of this will also become evident.

Whichever of these two we accept, and even if Hegel wavers between the two options sketched above, though coming down on the side of the unity of Spirit reconciled with itself, Hegel does take seriously the condition of radical opposition, an ethical war of extremes. At a certain point these two extremes break through their opposition, break beyond their war, break down their antagonism. Hegel speaks of the breaking out of a chorus of yea, yea. This is the shape of Spirit he calls forgiveness, a shape that really makes possible the actuality of Spirit as at home with itself in its other. Such forgiveness presupposes the acknowledgment of evil, as well as its being somehow laid aside in a reconciliation of the previously hostile extremes.

Here the putatively *evil* consciousness is the first to renounce willingly its extreme one-sidedness and to appeal for forgiveness. The other judging consciousness, putatively the *most moral*, preens itself with the rhetoric of duty for duty's sake—this consciousness proves itself to be the *more deeply evil*. Though claiming to be the universal consciousness, it really refuses to set aside its own stubborn individuality. Hegelian dialectic sees through this refusal—it is the mask of hypocritical self-righteousness. The moral consciousness is the unforgiving consciousness and hence the more evil. Hegel is dialectically insightful here in a way that anticipates Nietzsche's critique of morality as the mask of high-mindedness that camouflages a secret rancor and self-serving egotism.

The important issue is the interpretation we give to the breakthrough that occurs with forgiveness. I mentioned above, relative to metaxological intermediation, a breakthrough into a mindfulness beyond the dialectical. This is the way of being mindful that in *Philosophy and its Others* I call "thought singing its other."[3] This is *not* Hegel's absolute knowing, though both have a relation to what I am calling "breakthrough." Thought singing its other is not Hegel's thought thinking *itself* in its other; rather it entails a thinking of the other that is for the other; it does not ask the return of the other to the self but lets the other as other be as other. Hegel sees the breakthrough of forgiveness culminating in the return to the one, the unified self. I think that letting the other be as other, singing the other, is more ultimate. Forgiveness is always before the other and in some sense from the other. There is no absolute self-forgiveness; we forgive ourselves because we have been forgiven by the other. Forgiveness implies agapeic mind and the generosity of being as already pure giving. Breakthrough must be interpreted metaxologically, not just dialectically.

For Hegel this breakthrough really signals the dialectical emergence of Spirit as Spirit. In the *Phenomenology* this breakthrough is a turning point, a turning around in the whole development of consciousness towards absolute knowing. Only subsequently to this breakthrough does Hegel advance to absolute knowing. Only on condition of the forgiveness of evil can we be released for final philosophical knowing. Hence, philosophical science is itself impossible without passing through radical evil and its overcoming. If this is the case, and if we cannot make sense of evil and its overcoming, we cannot make complete sense of philosophical mind, as Hegel conceived of it. The old adage says: To understand all is to forgive all. We have to reverse this and say: To forgive all is to understand all. Only having forgiven evil, or having been forgiven, is philosophy as absolute knowing possible. Or as thought singing its other.

The question intrudes once again: Can dialectical thought understand evil and such reconciliation? In the Hegelian scheme is there room, not only for radical evil, but for a recalcitrantly evil other? Such possibilities raise questions about the power of speculative dialectic to acknowledge and deal with radical otherness itself. We are close to the vulnerable heart of Hegelian philosophy, where dialectical thought, as it were, shakes the foundations of being and mind. But does not dialectical thought itself begin to shake, too? Some of Hegel's most daring claims, indeed of any philosophy worth the name, stand or fall here.

My question is not simply the traditional question about evil as posed, say, in relation to a variety of theodicies. Elsewhere I have discussed the theodicies and especially aesthetic theodicy in Hegel and Nietzsche, relative to what I call "the transfiguration of the ugly." My question now is rather the implication of evil for philosophy itself. Is evil an other for which dialectical philosophy can honestly claim to have genuinely accounted? If not, then are there limits to dialectical thought? Limits that do not ask a renunciation of thought, but perhaps point to non-dialectical ways, perhaps a metaxological way, of acknowledging the recalcitrance of evil? Is philosophical forgiveness only a song of self, or a song of the other, a song for the other?

Hegel did not want there to be any radical other that reason fails to comprehend. If Hegel refuses any radical other, and if evil is a radical other, albeit a negative otherness, has he failed to deal with evil properly? Or if evil is said not to be a radical other and hence essentially comprehensible, has Hegel from the outset framed evil within a certain conceptual space that serves to neutralize its awful challenge? And if Hegel has dialectically neutralized evil, has he not also failed really to think through the meaning of radical forgiveness?

Did he realize that what is required of speculative metaphysics is that it be a mode of agapeic mind?

Three Strains of Evil:
Existential, Logicist, World-Historicist

In this and the next three sections, I will examine what Hegel says about evil in his *Lectures on the Philosophy of Religion*. This offers Hegel's most extensive discussion, though scattered throughout the large systematic works one finds repeated reference to the issue and particularly the use of the story of the Fall as an illustrative *Vorstellung* for the dialectically developing process of spirit.

This will be my major point: We do not find a simple Hegel, but a plural and, in the end, ambiguous Hegel. We will see a strongly *existential* side to his treatment of evil. At times one shakes one's head at the Kierkegaardian echoes reverberating in his discussion. Then one remembers Luther and the ancestry of both Hegel and Kierkegaard in Lutheran Christianity—the echoes become less startling. But this "existential" side coexists with a strongly *"logicist"* strain. Over the long run, the latter shows Hegel articulating evil in terms of the same rhythm of *dialectical self-mediation* that pulses throughout the system as a whole. From this logicist point of view, evil becomes one moment in the dialectical self-mediation of the concept.

These two strains, the existential and logicist, do not coalesce in a seamless harmony. Perhaps they cannot, and hence their tension is not any cheap point against Hegel. It would be a point against Hegel if he were concerned to gloss over the tension. I think the drift of his thought is less to gloss over this tension as to want dialectically to pass through it. Teleologically understood, the tension becomes subordinated as a moment of otherness that is dialectically sublated in the final reconstitution of harmonious accord. Can one so dialectically insist on such a reconciling telos as to diminish the recalcitrant horror of evil?

This question comes home to roost in a third strain in Hegel's account, namely, a vision of evil in *world-historicist* terms. Hegel's vision is teleological. This vision articulates the final reconciling harmony that is produced by dialectical development and hence commits Hegel to an understanding of evil in strongly historical terms. As Hegelian *Geist* deepens its own self-knowledge through its own historical unfolding, it also deepens its sense of evil as a logical necessary constituent of its own dialectically self-mediating concept. This means that the world-historicist strain, in situating evil relative to the panorama of world-history, displaces our philosophical concerns from the existential side, with its inevitable emphasis on the particularity of the existing individual, towards the logicist side, with its more insistent emphasis on universality and logical wholes more encompassing than any particularity. The world-historicist strain points to the historical concretion or embodiment of what the logicist strain stresses in its universality. This third strain, then, emerges from the tension of the other two. I will argue that in tilting us predominantly towards the logicist understanding, it finally underplays the existential side, especially in its recalcitrance to dialectical incorporation in the concept.

Keeping in mind these provisional remarks about the three fundamental strains, I now discuss some major points Hegel makes in the *Lectures on the Philosophy of Religion.* There are three different and consecutive sections where evil is the major theme, and I will comment on these in turn. As I proceed I will offer comparative comments on thinkers as diverse as Augustine and Nietzsche. Overall I will underscore Hegel's insistence on the necessity of evil, an insistence that follows an understanding of evil in terms of the logical life of the concept and the dialectical rhythm of its constituent moments. In answer to my question whether dialectic can comprehend evil, Hegel answers: Dialectic does not first comprehend evil; rather evil itself embodies the logic of the concept that dialectical thinking itself comprehends; hence dialectic comprehends evil only because evil itself is to be seen as first a concretization of what is necessitated by the dynamically self-unfolding structure of the logical concept.

Evil and Onto-Logical Necessity

Hegel first takes up the issue in a discussion of finitude and in relation to the natural goodness of humanity. His account follows a discussion of the second moment of the divine life, understood in Trinitarian terms. This second moment of the divine life is its manifestation in finite nature and its articulation as the Son. This is the necessary moment of the absolute as appearance, as determinacy. In this second moment, God is seen as other to God in Himself in the finitude of the created world which, in turn, is seen as the self-othering of the divine life. Hegel's treatment of evil is wedded to a focus on the necessity of the finite as such. Evil is bound up with finitude as such.

While there is a logical necessity for finitude as an expression of the divine life, this necessity is marked by a certain freedom. The finite world, as it were, is let go as independent by the Idea in its own self-particularization. Hegel's discussion here of the divine life stresses the moment of particularization and self-alienation. He speaks of the finite world as the *heteron*, the other.[4] Otherness is essentially connected with the definition of evil. More generally, human evil is to be situated in the more encompassing context of a larger process which itself conforms to the logically necessary moments of the concept. This second moment of self-externalization, finite determination, estranged particularization and the freedom marking it, is logically necessary to the full unfolding of the absolute process, whether we name this the divine life, or the Idea, or the concept.

This emphasis on the necessity of evil, a necessity both logical and ontological, continues when Hegel remarks on the human being and evil. In treating of the goodness of natural humanity, he says that in a certain sense the human subject exists in a state of untruth. Those who say the human being is good by nature are correct at one level, but it is a subordinate level. There is a deeper level of consideration. Such an affirmation of the goodness of the natural man does not attain the deeper conception of the human being as spirit. For Hegel the human being as human is spirit, and so is given over to difference and otherness. The human being as spirit is *necessarily* given over to estrangement from the immediacy of natural being. Properly speaking, by nature the human being is neither good nor evil. It is simply innocent. Good and evil refer to categories of spirit, and not of nature.

And yet the human being as *spirit* is evil by nature, that is, by a necessary requirement of its being. Hegel puts the point by saying that *cleavage* is within the subject. The human subject is cleavage and to that extent its being is simply contradiction. The point to note is that what is specific to the human being, namely its nature as spirit, is necessarily evil, in so far as evil is to be identified with a cleavage within the being of the finite self, seen in the particularity of its otherness to the universal. There is a necessary disjunction between the being of the self as particular and its concept. By necessity the human being does not initially live up to its concept, and hence lives in evil. This again implies that the inherence of evil in the particular self cannot be understood without reference to the concept.

It would be a wrong impression that Hegel wanted to denigrate the human being by underscoring the dark side of its necessary evil. This is not so. The evil, which is logically necessary, is simply an ontological structure inherent in the being of the human self, namely, that a sense of internal difference or rupture necessarily defines that being. Internal disjunction defines the logic of that being. Moreover,

this internal cleavage is not a *static* ontological structure but ingredient in a dynamic process of differentiation and development. What
Hegel is calling evil is logically necessary to the unfolding of this
dynamic structure, without which the human being would not be an
ethical being at all.

It is here that the affirmative side of the negative begins to make
its appearance. One is not immediately born an ethical being. One
becomes an ethical being. The internal cleavage, as the logically
necessary differentiation which defines evil, puts us into the sphere
of spirit and hence of the ethical. But the latter in its fullness means
that implicitly the human being as spirit is good, that is to say, the
human being may become good in the proper unfolding of its own self-
becoming. "Proper" for Hegel means that the self must attain
coincidence with its own concept as spirit, that it must live out of and
up to the full promise of what it means to be ethical *Geist*. Since evil
is necessary for the proper unfolding of this self-becoming, one can
say that evil is also a dialectically implicit good. Once again the latter
is not natural innocence; rather the self-cleavage of the human opens
the space of the higher freedom of spirit, and only in this space is
goodness in the genuinely ethical sense possible.

So for Hegel nature is bound up with both innocence and evil. The
necessary cleavage of the human being is tied to the particularization
of the self when it asserts its particularity in opposition to all of being,
and especially in opposition to its own deeper self, namely its concept,
its being as fully explicit spirit. The cleavage is necessary for the self
to step out of its immediate unity with nature. Hence, evil as cleavage
is necessary for the self-development of the human. Our involvement
with evil is a necessary presupposition of our becoming ethically good.
Natural innocence is a given that in the case of the human being is
already implicitly self-transcending. But in so far as the human being
by its nature tears itself loose from its immediate grounding in nature
and insists on itself as difference, it is evil. This is already implicit
in the natural state itself. The natural state turns against its own
innocent immediacy. Hegel goes so far as to contend that a recognition
of man's natural evil is a higher spiritual state than those who would
insist simply on his natural innocence, goodness.[5]

Suppose we recall here thinkers like Rousseau or that figure for
whose empty purity Hegel had unbounded contempt—the beautiful
soul (*die schöne Seele*). Hegel's contempt involves the judgment that
such purity masquerades as good only by refusing to adventure in
otherness. Hence, the beautiful soul is not ethically good at all. There
is a dialectical inversion here reminiscent of the inversion mentioned
at the outset with forgiveness and the putatively moral consciousness

in the *Phenomenology*. Just as the unforgiving moral consciousness is more deeply the evil consciousness, so the beautiful soul, in its disgust with otherness and the external world of acting, is deeply suspicious of all being as other and so is really an *ugly soul*. Its own claim to ethical purity is paid for by infecting everything else with the taint of evil and ethical impurity. In its pure innerness, everything else is disgusting otherness—the beautiful soul performs an anesthetization of evil, which turns otherness into the ugly. Once again, as I hinted before, these inversions of the unforgiving moral consciousness and the disgusted beautiful soul remind us of similar inversions pointed out later by Nietzsche in relation to the *ressentiment* of slave morality.

Consider here that Nietzsche also situates good and evil relative to a rupture, in this case a rupture in the human being's own animal nature and between nature and culture. For Nietzsche the distinction of good and evil emerges in man's violent break with his animal past: the moral self emerges in the violent repression of animal energies and the turning back of their force against the animal man himself. The rupture, or cleavage comes with the decisive enclosure of the animal man within civilization. Nietzsche's view is a modern *naturalized* version of the transition from a guiltless animal placement in nature (this is a secularized Eden) to civilization and history that are the humanly created contexts of values. These contexts themselves issue from Nietzsche secular surrogate of the Fall, namely, the human being's will to power, as violently turned back by the animal man onto the animal man. Man is the sick animal, Nietzsche said. Living in the rupture of evil and good infects the human animal with this sickness, the sickness of the bad conscience.

I think that Nietzsche does not give a convincing account of this rupture. It just happens. Why it happens is not clear. Moreover, the consequences of its happening seem entirely disproportionate to the initial break with nature. Perhaps one cannot give any final answer as to the origin of evil. Perhaps all one can do is name it. Yet there are different modes of naming. The myth of the Fall is such a naming, a mythic naming with deep significance, as we shall see. Some modes of naming evil flatten its complexity, or betray its existential challenge, or neutralize its horror, whether by ideological special pleading or religious complacency or simply by human superficiality or spiritual cowardice.

As a *naturalistic* account Nietzsche's mode of naming is unconvincing in the following respect. For Nietzsche, as for Hegel, nature is innocence. Recall Nietzsche's assertion of the innocence of becoming and his rejection of any moral order as an ontological constitutive realm. Morality is a human creation. But every creation of the human animal as a being of nature must itself share in the innocence of becoming or nature. So the violence of the human animal on itself is itself quite natural and hence a violent continuation of the same innocence. If becoming is the totality of which we are part, then becoming as this context of contexts is marked by a radical innocence, as finally are its constituent parts, the human being included. If Nietzsche is right, killing the other, murder, lies, rape, and pillage must be offered the exoneration of what we might call "the theodicy of innocent nature." This theodicy in the end says: such things just happen. Again perhaps there is a point when, in the end, all one can say about evil is "It happens." But there are different ways of saying or naming this "It happens." Does Nietzsche's naturalistic naming do justice to the happening? I cannot see that it does. Must one not say: Despite many things that he says, there cannot be a radical rupture in nature for Nietzsche, for every rupture within a naturalized explanation is a *continuation* of the same will to power that marks all being, hence not a radical rupture at all.

When Schopenhauer said that to be is to be guilty, he has a more profound sense of the rupture than has Nietzsche's in his sometimes flat naturalistic moods. (Heidegger occasionally gives expression to contempt for Schopenhauer but the contempt is cheap: Heidegger's *Dasein* is also in guilt by an ontological necessity of its being; no amount of terminological camouflaging will hide the fact that this fallenness is "original sin" for the fundamental ontologist.) Nietzsche wanted to escape the implication in Schopenhauer, as in other philosophical and religious systems, that nature was not innocent, that all being was somehow guilty. This is a view we find as early as the so-called first fragment in philosophy, the Anaximander fragment. Anaximander implies that *to be as determinate* was the primal ontological sin by which limited things tear themselves free from the unlimited, *to apeiron*. By simply being, and by continuing to be as free particulars, things incur the original ontological guilt, and with it the destructiveness and death that the nemesis of time will bring. Instead of the innocence of becoming, in this view, time is the original punishment or nemesis for the primal ontological guilt.

Nietzsche shared something of this view in his first work, *The Birth of Tragedy*, where the source of all suffering and guilt is simply *individuation*. The suffering of tragedy dissolves this individuation and returns the separated and divided being to Dionysian rapture with the whole. Tragic suffering is, as it were, the ecstatic expiation of the primal ontological guilt of separated particularity. Subsequently Nietzsche wanted to stop what he saw as the Schopenhauerian slandering of being, and what he claimed was the entire tradition of religious and philosophical nihilism that lay behind it. Here we might say that Hegel, as much as Schopenhauer and the early Nietzsche, is an offspring of Anaximander. In this respect, Schopenhauer is closer to Hegel than to Nietzsche with regard to evil. This is evident if we recall what we saw above: when Hegel situates evil relative to the second moment of the Idea, he is a clear descendant of Anaximander; that is, evil emerges with otherness, particularity, differentiation, finitude, with alienation from the pure, eternal in-itself of the Idea. The claim about evil is ontological; the alienation is ontologically necessary.

When Nietzsche says that evil originates in the human animal's redirection of will to power against itself, does he take us very far, beyond naturalistically renaming an enigmatic rupture, indeed reversal? Can we make intelligible sense of this reversal on Nietzsche's own terms? Does not this account finally amount to a naturalistic "theodicy" of the terrible, an "aesthetic theodicy," as he himself calls it? Is this not simply an acquiescence in the monstrous, amoralized by the innocence of becoming? In the end does not Nietzsche neutralize, amoralize evil, given the innocence of nature? Once again, if man is a natural being, he, too, is innocent; even as the sick animal, even as the violently sick animal, that is as the sickeningly violent animal, he, too, is innocent, an amoral spawn of the innocence of becoming. Everything he does, simply everything, including killing, lying, pillaging, every value, disvalue are finally amoralized in the valueless becoming of the process of the whole. It is not incidental that Nietzsche chooses Zarathustra as the singer of this reversal. Nietzsche's Zarathustra is to reverse what an earlier Zarathustra had wrought, namely, the first cleavage of Zoroastrianism, cosmically conceived as a dualistic conflict of good and evil. Nietzsche's Zarathustra wills to wipe out this cleavage in the renewed innocence of becoming. Nietzsche's Zarathustra provides a link with Hegel's views of the Parsee religion, as well as Augustine's struggle with Manicheanism, on which I remark below.

Though Schopenhauer hated Hegel, in some ways he is more profound than Nietzsche and closer to the Hegel who says: cleavage, hence evil is in our being. There is a rupturing difference to the human being that resists explication in terms of the flattening continuities of any simple naturalism. If naturalism is to be at all preserved, it will have to become more ontologically complex to do justice to the ontological complexity of human nature. As ontologically constitutive, the rupture has to be seen as going all the way down in being. By contrast, though the innocence of becoming seems to allows us to sing dithyrambs to fate, it also allows us to squint at the horror. Nietzsche sang but squinted; Schopenhauer did not squint, nor did he sing, though he sometimes wished he could.

Another similarity with Nietzsche is that Hegel underscores *the will* in understanding evil, more specifically the will in its self-insistent particularity. Admittedly, Hegel's view of the will in its particularity is very un-Nietzschean in the end. To be naturally innocent is to be only an animal, without a will. But without the will one cannot be good in an ethical sense. The result would be a kind of indifferent insipidity to this natural innocence.[6] For Hegel it is the *singularity* of the individual will as a natural being that is just its evil. This singularity is the selfishness of the will, its privacy; it is the will's unwillingness to be subject to universal law and principles. By contrast, the will that is good in an ethical sense is one that has been rationally cultivated into universality.

Hegel and Nietzsche agree on some of the hypocrisies of the moral consciousness, hypocrisies both try to expose to dialectical reversal. But the dialectical reversal for Nietzsche issues in a refusal to escape into the universal; rather the self must cultivate its particular will-to-power less hypocritically. For Hegel the universal is not necessarily a ruse of moral hypocrisy; the genuine universal is just the opposite in fact. Hence, the dialectical exposure of hypocrisy is a merely negative breakdown of a false ethical universality. The particular will must be educated into the true ethical universal. This cultivation to universality has yet to come.

It is worth repeating (regardless of the difference from Nietzsche) that for Hegel a certain understanding of singular "thisness" is intimately bound up with the condition of evil.[7] Hegel is again a late heir of Anaximander who implied: as detaching themselves from the ultimate source of all being, *to apeiron*, particular things as particular violate the integrity of the original whole, incur the wrath of its justice, *dikē*, and the punishment of particularity will be death and destruction. Differentiation per se is the ontological sin, the cutting, the wounding, Hegel would say the *Ur-teil* of the original whole. (Nietzsche, as an heir of Anaximander in the *Birth of Tragedy*, is actually a Dionysian Hegelian: the primal sin of individuation is the separation of the determinate thing from the *Ureine* of the Dionysian source or original of all.) For Hegel, to insist on being a *this* is to be shut in on the singular self in a manner divorced from universal rationality. This is also to be divorced from one's own concept. Hence to insist on being a this is to be in contradiction to oneself as an ethical being; for to be an ethical being is to exhibit a universal will. To be a universal will is to be an individual in conformity with its own concept, and so reconciled with itself at the highest level of spirit.

In sum: throughout Hegel's account a dialectical logic is at work. Hegel puts it thus: "The condition of evil directly presupposes the relation of actuality to the concept; this simply posits the contradiction between implicit being or the concept and singularity, the contrast between good and evil...."[8] The concept is identified with good and *singularity as singularity* is identified with evil. This contrast reveals a necessary antithesis. So it is wrong to pose the problem in terms of a non-dialectical either/or: either man is only good by nature or only evil. Implicitly, according to its concept the human being is good, but this implicitness is only one-sided. And this one-sidedness consists in the fact that the actual subject is a "this," but only as a natural will.[9] In one sense good and evil are essentially in contradiction, but just this contradiction is essential to the ontological structure of the human being as self-differentiating, beyond its own natural immediacy. This ontological structure of existential contradiction is the cleavage without which could not take place the dynamic development of the human being into an ethical self. Good and evil, even in their essential contradiction, are dialectically bound to each other in their very opposition.

Representation and the Fall

Let me now comment on Hegel's next section.[10] Following the first more "conceptual" account of evil, Hegel turns to the religious representation of the origin of evil in terms of the paradigmatic *Vorstellung* of the Fall. Hegel refers to the Fall in many places of his corpus (see most notably the *Encyclopedia Logic*, § 24, *Zusatz*), using it to illustrate the logical and ontological necessity of differentiation. The main points I want to note are the following.

Hegel strongly rejects any interpretation of this representation as historically literal. Further he insistently emphasizes the importance of *knowledge* in interpreting the story. Evil is intimately connected with knowing. The stress falls on the importance of the knowledge of evil in the self-development of humanity. Hegel explicitly connects this with consciousness: cognition itself proves to be the source of cleavage, the source of evil. Animals lack the self-relation, the free being-for-self in the face of objectivity that marks the knowing being of the human self. Hence, animals have no sense of ethical evil and good. The knowing sense of cleavage is the evil, which contains the two sides, the good and the evil. So Hegel claims to universalize

the implicit meaning of the Fall by freeing its representation of the
original humans from the particularity that is necessarily associated
with any *Vorstellung*. The point is not these original, particular
human beings; it is original humanity itself that is at issue. What
is to be understood is implicit humanity *according to its concept*, not
some historical or individual Adam or Eve.

In this regard Hegel tries to make sense of the notion of inherited
sin. He grants the truth of the notion, not in terms of some quasi-
biological inheritance, but in terms of the implicit concept of
humanity. What binds humanity together across a span of temporal
becoming is that every human exhibits the ontological structure of
"cleavage." To be articulated in the cleavage of knowing good and evil
is simply the being of human becoming. It is in terms of this structure
that the notion of the inheritance of sin and evil is interpreted. As
we have already seen, all human beings according to their implicit
concept are evil. As Hegel says: All humanity as humanity enters into
this cleavage.[11] Let us not forget Hegel's intention here. This is not
at all to dualize the human being, but to think good and evil
dialectically. The cleavage is not a dualistic opposition that fixates
two poles in rigid antithesis. This would be a kind of Manicheanism.
In the measure that this cleavage is the source of evil, it is also the
midpoint of the conversion that consciousness contains within itself,
whereby this cleavage is sublated.[12]

The emphasis on knowing and necessity is linked to a *dialectical
elevation* of the human being through evil. Hegel delights in pointing
out that the story of the Fall states that human beings will become
like God in eating of the tree of knowledge, in their knowledge of the
cleavage. He is at pains to say that this outcome is not contradicted
by God. Indeed God says: look, they have become like us. It is *knowing*
that makes us gods, and especially the knowing of good and evil.
Hence, knowing evil is dialectically necessary to the self-elevation of
humanity.

For us to become as gods entails a necessary transgression. Does
not the dialectical character of all this attenuate the taint of transgression? The transgression, precisely as necessary, and as dialectically interpreted, is not one that might not have been, but is an
absolute necessity that had to be, if the human being were to become
the spirit it implicitly is. This dialectical conception amounts to a
radical rational justification of the necessity of evil. This necessity
is not simply the unavoidability of evil acts. It is its *rational, logical
necessity* with respect to the being of the human, with respect to its
self-becoming as an ethical being. What or who rules the world or
world-history that, in essence, is initiated with the rupture of evil with

innocent nature? Is it *Vernunft?* Is it *Geist?* Is it God? Or is it the Prince of Darkness, the serpent that Hegel seems to vindicate dialectically?

After all, for Hegel the Prince of Darkness is Lucifer, the first born Son of Light.[13] This explains why Hegel's stress on knowledge is equally evident in his hermeneutic of the tree of *life*. Emphasizing again the childlike nature of the *Vorstellung*, his point about the tree of life is that the natural being must die in order for the spiritual being to come into its own. Here is revealed the significance of death and suffering; also the significance of labor, which occupied Hegel in other places (e.g., the *Phenomenology*; the *System of Ethical Life*)—we must work to make ourselves what we implicitly are as spirit—work spiritualizes humanity. I note that *individual* immortality disappears as Hegel restates the issue of immortality in terms of cognition. He says: "Cognition and thought are the root of human life, of human immortality as a totality within itself."[14] Only in the act of thinking and in cognition is humanity immortal.

This is a conceptual transposition of the representation for which the religious person might not be grateful. In itself this transposition might be defensible. But it is not a restatement in conceptual terms of what the religious consciousness thinks in relation to immortality, in so far as this is conceived in personal terms. Hegelian immortality is the immortality of knowing, and not the knowing of any individual human being but of humanity as a spiritual totality. Hegel's translation violates the representation while it claims to comprehend it conceptually. If he openly said that personal immortality is childish fantasy, we would have to consider his correctness. Hegel is not entirely open in this way. What he means by immortality, namely, the immortality of knowing, cunningly replaces such personal immortality. There is a dialectical switch of horses in mid-race, and the Hegelian horse of universal knowing comes home as the winner, but wearing the number of the religious horse of personal immortality.

As I say, Hegel could make the claim that as religion represents the issue, immortality is childish. And then the truth of his dialectically substituted claim might be argued. But when he presents an intimate continuity between his concept and religious representation, any claims he makes to properly respect the latter are surely disingenuous. The divergence between the religious consciousness, as lived from within, and its putative Hegelian conceptualization is evident. When Hegel implies continuity between the representation and his own concept, he not only may be downplaying something essential in the former; but also he may be fudging a potential choice, indeed conflict between the two, a conflict that might put not only religion, but also philosophy itself, to the test.

In more general terms, we see here the tension between the existential and logicist stresses. The existential strain emphasizes the particularity of the will and its living internal cleavage; the logicist strain stresses the dimension of universal structure that is tied up with a cognitivist interpretation of evil. I find a tension between these two in Hegel's account. Thus, the claim of universal cognitive immortality is consistent with a noticeable displacement throughout Hegel's discussion in the notion of the will. There is a displacement from will as individual to cognition as implicitly universal; and from immortality as personal perpetuation to the abstract, general immortality of humanity as such. This means that in both cases the *this as this*, the singularity somehow at the source of evil, is really only a subordinate moment of the dialectical story, or rather dialectical logos as a whole. Evil and immortality are essentially transposed into a dialectic of logical cognition. Even the existential cleavage and anguish are clearly tied to the development of humanity, not the individual human being, but humanity as species-being marked by knowing and self-thinking spirit. This displacement from the this as this towards the universal or humanity as an historical totality is a crucial point to which I will return.

Evil, Inwardness, and World-Historical Teleology

Turning to Hegel's next section on knowledge, estrangement and evil, we have what is, in some ways, the most interesting discussion. We see the tension between existential and logicist strains, but now this tension is energized more dynamically. We must qualify any impression that Hegel only reduces evil to a merely abstract cognitive condition. Or: though he does emphasize cognition, what he means by a condition of mind or knowing is necessarily at the same time a condition of being—an ontological condition, not just an abstractly logical one. This should not be unexpected, given the logical for Hegel contains its own necessary reference to being: the Hegelian concept is onto-logical.

So when I say that there is a logicist strain in Hegel's discussion, there is no intent to reduce his concept to a merely abstract generality. This is to misunderstand what Hegel means by the concept and by logos. The logical concept is ontological and hence, Hegel claims, concrete. Without denying that this is Hegel's intended meaning, still the dynamism of Hegel's onto-logical concept is such as to make particularity as particularity into one dialectical moment of a more encompassing universal process. As we have seen, in the Hegelian scheme particularity as sheerly insisting on its own self-particularity is simply evil. One might object that the Hegelian concept serves to sublate the difference between the existential and the logicist, and hence to undermine their tension by transcending it. The essential difficulty, as will more fully emerge, is whether something about this tension is not open to such dialectical *Aufhebung*, whether this tension can ever be completely overcome dialectically. Granting the sense of concreteness that Hegel wants to ascribe to his concept, the question is: Is there is a non-dialectical sense of concreteness? Does evil confront us with such a non-dialectical otherness?

First there are additional complexities in Hegel's account. What we find in this third section is: While Hegel does speak of the contradiction and cleavage in terms of their *being known*, nevertheless being known immediately implicates a reference to developed *inwardness*. The logical as ontological has a necessary existential reference, as is unmistakably evident if inwardness must be taken into account. The result joins Hegel to Kierkegaard, in that Hegel shows himself attentive to the anguish we experience in knowing evil. When we become aware of the living cleavage of contradiction there is produced the condition of anguish. "Anguish is present only where there is opposition to what ought to be, to an affirmative."[15] The German is *Schmerz*, not *Angst*. Nevertheless, *Schmerz* brings before us the pain, ache, grief, sorrow. There is the element of affliction and distress. Something *schmerzvoll* is sorrowful, agonizing with the element of pathos in the sense of suffering undergone. Evil is in our being and known as such, and the result is affliction. Being as inwardness is burdened with sorrow.

I now underline that once again a dialectical displacement begins to occur in Hegel's discussion. We discover the emergence of the *third strain*. Hegel does not *dwell with* the inwardness of anguish as an inwardness. Out of the tension of the existential particularity and logicist universality, he dialectically displaces the interest to the stage of *world-history*. This is the *world-historicist* strain in Hegel's scheme. Its emergence is absolutely necessary for Hegel if he is to redeem the promise of his own *teleology* of evil in concrete history. Were he to have only the existential strain, there would remain something about evil that as pure particularity resists dialectical comprehension, and hence resist dialectical teleology. Were he to have only the logicist strain, Hegel might not be capable of completely shaking the suspicion that evil as concrete is betrayed in terms of a merely abstract structure. The world-historicist strain intends to rescue his dialectical account from the imputation of abstract logicism, while at the same time claiming to meet the requirement of concreteness on which the existential strain insists.

Now Hegel speaks of different ways in which the anguish of knowing evil is registered. But he substantiates this claim in terms of a series of historical gradations of inwardization, starting with the Parsee religion that keeps the cleavage external in terms of a clash of good and evil principles. The character of this turn to history is entirely consistent with Hegel's other series of lectures on art and world-history itself. I detailed something of this in chapter 1. In all cases, the Oriental world does not initially have adequate differentiation. Only with Persia do we get clear disjunction and hence an arising above the immediate unity of immersion in nature. This is also consistent with Hegel's view of the logical concept as progressing from immediate unity to articulated disjunction and thence to articulated unity. Only after the break with Oriental immersion in immediate unity with nature does cleavage come on the world-historical scene. An interesting question hence arises: Does this not mean that there is no world-historical evil or good in the Oriental world? If Hegel were right, the Oriental world would be one of dreaming immediacy, natural innocence. Would it not be paradise? Would it not then be outside of the ethical in Hegelian terms, properly speaking?

Thus, while the emphasis on the experiential inwardness of evil might seem to align Hegel with the existentialist stress on the singular as singular, the case is less clear-cut. Certainly anyone who speaks as does Hegel must speak from intimacy with the thing itself, from inward exposure to the affliction in question. There is nothing abstractly objective in Hegel's account. It is unfair to treat his discourse as if it were delivered in tones of univocal neutrality and disinterestedness. Hegel is engaged with the pain of evil from within the pain of evil.

That said, one cannot blink the fact that there is a turning away at the level of *content* from particularity as particularity in Hegel's decisive turn to *history*. Let us say that though the tone is "subjective," the content now becomes "objective" as Hegel turns away from the particular as particular. Of course, this is consonant with the way dialectical thought drifts towards the world-historical. The result is a discourse wherein we detect significant tension between the inwardness of evil as experienced in its concrete intimacy and the more public arena of world-history, where forces always more universal than the individual play out their dialectic. The individual himself becomes seen in the light of the way different *epochs* understood the antagonism and cleavage and affliction. This emphasis on evil in the light of world-history as exhibiting a certain dialectical development is not Kierkegaardian.

Hegel's reference to Persia calls to mind an earlier "Kierkegaard," namely, Augustine, a religious thinker obsessed with the question of evil, and significantly in relation to Manichaeanism. I remarked on the Persian connection relative to Nietzsche and Zarathustra. There is here also some subterranean affinity between Hegel and Augustine, though in the end I think the two differ significantly. Some comparative remarks will be helpful.

Manichaeanism was the form of this Parsee dualism that dominated the thought of the younger Augustine. Augustine's turn to Christianity was also a turn to an understanding of evil in terms of inwardness and will. This turn to the inwardness of willing (Kierkegaard is very Augustinian on this score) is a rejection of the Zoroastrian/Manichaean fixation of evil in terms of an external dualistic opposition of cosmic powers. Augustine rejects Manichaeanism because this external dualism finally betrays the ontological and existential intimacy of good and evil in the human being.

I recall that in Augustine's turn to the inwardness of the will, he discovers a radical cleavage of the will itself: the same will is at odds with itself, the one will is double, as we find in his famous account of the two wills. This is self-divided inwardness that cannot do the good it wills because the same will that wills the good also wills the evil. It should be noted that the word that Hegel uses for the rupture or cleavage is *Entzweiung*, not *Entfremdung*,[16] Hegel's more customary word for "alienation." *Entzweiung*, with the word *Zwei*, two, a double, gives us the sense of a process of doubling, dualizing. The word "endoubling" might be an attempted English equivalent, in that the "en" recalls us to "in" (*vide* the inwardizing of the doubling) or to the one (Greek *hen*), while the "ing" calls to mind the ongoing processual nature of the doubling. It is the oneness of inwardness that finds itself dynamically doubled in the process of emerging from immediacy into the condition of being an ethical will.

This Hegelian "endoubling" echoes the process of the doubling of the ethical will in Augustine: in this doubling of the will in inwardness the anguished struggle between good and evil is fought. If the reader recalls my claim at the outset that evil has significance for philosophy itself and its mode of thinking the other, let the reader also remember that the word Hegel used in his first philosophical publication, the *Differenzschrift*, to describe the condition out of which philosophy itself arises is none other than *Entzweiung*![17] Philosophy itself arises in the middle from an "endoubling," from an inwardizing, an *Erinnerung* of a doubling.

While Hegel, like Augustine, acknowledges the inward intimacy
of the ethical will and its inner doubling, he effects a more radical
displacement of this intimacy onto the public stage of world-history,
more radical than in Augustine's historical theodicy. In the
Augustinian sense of Providence, world-history is not at all the
ultimate ethical tribunal. *Weltgeschichte* is not *Weltgericht*. Augustine
did not deny Providence in history. But in world-history the City of
God and the City of Man intermingle in a manner human beings
cannot entirely comprehend, and certainly not in any way that yields
its final secret to the importunate knocking of dialectical logic. This
temporal intermingling of the Cities of God and Man is, as it were,
the historical endoubling. But in history itself this endoubling will
never be reduced to the final sway of a singular realm. There is an
intimacy of being, whether in being evil or being good, which in
relation to the City of God is *other* to world-history and which remains
always other to the City of Man.

Hegel's historical teleology of evil sees world-history as bringing
together in a dialectical unity the City of God and the City of Man.
Augustine rejects such a final unity in *world-history* itself; there
remains an otherness to the divine. Likewise the struggle of the Cities
of God and Man *within* the *inner* doubling of the ethical self will
always have a constitutive dimension of irreducible inwardness that
will not necessarily appear on the public stage of world-history or be
commensurate with what happens there. Kierkegaard's later
emphasis on the irreducible constitutive inwardness of the religious
relation simply repeats Augustine. With respect to the place of history
for both Kierkegaard and Augustine, we find some version of the
double vision in which eternity is irreducible to time, the transcendent
to the immanent (see chapter 1). Augustine here, again like
Kierkegaard, is a Christian son of pagan Plato in the final conviction
that the orders of time and eternity retain an otherness to each other,
which prevents the reduction of their doubleness to a monistic unity,
even one as complexly qualified as Hegel's dialectical holism. In
Augustine one may also find some version of the doubleness built into
religious representation, which keeps this otherness open as an
otherness (see chapter 3) and perhaps also the doubleness that Hegel
consigns to the unhappy consciousness (see chapter 2).

There is a similarity between Hegel and Augustine in that the
latter sees the original sin as a *felix culpa*: a transgression which
in itself was disastrous but which still made possible a subsequent
good greater than the first condition, through the overcoming of the
loss of that first condition. This is reminiscent of Hegel's teleological justification of the primordial transgression. Nevertheless, in

Augustine evil is not a necessary logical moment in a dialectically unfolding process from immediate unity through differentiation to restored, mediated unity. Hegel's sense of the logical necessity of evil is other to Augustine's sense of the human freedom at the origin of evil.

I think Augustine would say to Hegel: By making evil dialectically necessary to the logic of the divine life, this divine life is itself inculpated and hence its absolute goodness is compromised. Augustine's emphasis on free will is intended to preserve the divine life entirely unstained from such an imputation. God is good; His creation, though finite, is intrinsically good; indeed all being, whether finite or infinite, is simply good. This intention to preserve the radical goodness of God and the created goodness of finite being is consistent with Augustine's effort to think of evil as a negation, a defection from being, a nihilation of being as good, a nihilation produced by the evil will. This nihilating defection from being is other to being itself as good. It is what I would call a negative otherness. That negative otherness resists complete logical articulation and so remains ultimately an enigma.

For Hegel, by contrast, every otherness, even as negative, is said to be incorporated into the dialectical process of articulation and hence is said to be logical. Religiously put, this means that evil finally is no radical enigma, but must be a necessary moment of the divine life itself. Augustine would see this account as betraying the absoluteness of God, God's absolute goodness. One might reply: Does not Augustine's God take evil upon itself in the redemption effected by Christ's death, a redemption that makes Augustine think of the primordial fault as a *felix culpa*? True. But there is a difference between taking evil on oneself thus and the claim that evil is an essential and necessary moment of the divine life. Indeed it is hard to see how one "takes on" evil in the second case, given that in any case evil is a dialectical necessity. In Augustine there is a certain *gratuitousness*, both about the beginning of evil and the redeeming act that overcomes, forgives it. From the standpoint of Hegelian logic, there is nothing essential that is finally gratuitous, since finally everything finds its necessary place within the absolute process as dialectically self-mediating.

Hegel would say that any such gratuitousness, whether conceived in an Augustinian way or otherwise, is due to a fixation with the element of contingency in every religious representation, and the failure to take, as he sees it, the final philosophical step: the *Aufhebung* of the representation into the concept. This final step does away with the element of contingency in religion as penultimate, and hence also of any putative gratuitousness. But, of course, this is just the issue at stake. Does philosophy, must philosophy sublate religious representation thus? Must philosophical thought overcome every gratuity? If there are radical gratuities, would not this overcoming blind philosophy to what is there: Philosophical thought dictating to thought itself not to think what resists transformation into logical necessity? But this would be metaphysical whistling in the dark, even if the tune is dialectical. If there is a gratuitousness in evil, let us say a sickening gratuitousness, does it not resist a dialectical *Aufhebung* in Hegel's sense? Must philosophy then think of this negative otherness in other than dialectical terms?

I referred above to the unhappy consciousness in connection with Augustine. In that there remains a gratuitousness in Augustine's scheme of things, Hegel would find the basis for continuing unhappiness, since for Augustine the human mind has failed to make complete rational sense of evil. It is entirely appropriate to remind ourselves here of the unhappy consciousness, since in the *Phenomenology* this figure is the very epitomization of cleavage as a fixed dualistic opposition between the temporal and the eternal, the immanent and the transcendent, the human and the divine, indeed the human being and it own very self. This brings us directly back to the *Lectures on the Philosophy of Religion*.

As we recall, Hegel details certain historical gradations of the inwardization of evil, first referring to the Parsee religion that keeps external the cleavage, clash of good and evil principles. In coming to know the cleavage in their being, human beings become the unhappy consciousness. In the measure that Augustine wants to keep evil radically other to God as good, Hegel would accuse him of a not-yet-overcome dualism, residue of his involvement with Manichaeanism, and hence accuse him of being caught in the stage of the unhappy consciousness. I think we can interpret Augustine otherwise. There might be doubles, dyads that are not merely dualistic oppositions to be dialectically *aufgehoben*: dyads that recall us to senses of otherness (like the affirmative transcendence of God) that resist complete conceptual comprehension by us, without consigning the mindful self to the wretched alienation of the unhappy consciousness.

The doubling of the will might be seen as the upsurge of the exigence of the double mediation required by the metaxological sense of being: both self-mediation and intermediation with the other. What happens in the doubled will is the struggle to overcome the temptation to reduce this twofold mediation to a shut-in process of singular self-mediation. In mediating with itself, the genuine will opens up to the appeal of the other; and thus it may live the double mediation in an ethically affirmative sense; the good will may instantiate respect both for itself and for the community of others. By contrast, the will at war with itself fights the closure of its own self-mediation completely in itself; for this closure is also a closing down of the second intermediation with the other. Such self-closure is a refusal of the metaxological community of being and the open intermediation with the other which it requires. From the metaxological point of view, the evil will expresses the absolutization of a closed self-mediation that sets itself in hostile opposition to all otherness. But inevitably, the exigence and appeal of the double mediation will make itself felt even in this closure of self-mediation and hostile opposition. Hence the ambiguous doubling of the will testifies to the free possibility of our refusal of metaxological community and yet also to the final impossibility of such a refusal, since every such refusal is ultimately grounded in the metaxological community of being itself. The evil refusal of the community of being is let be by the community of being as ultimately agapeic. The refusal is the living of the shut will in darkness.

My present purpose is not to offer a full metaxological rethinking of evil. This could be done, and I have offered some suggestions elsewhere.[18] I am simply suggesting that the double will of, say, the Augustinian account could be reinterpreted in terms of metaxological community. It need not be seen simply in terms of the unhappy consciousness, though even if it was, this, too, could be seen in the more complex light I suggested in chapter 2. The one and the double might be interpreted monistically or dualistically; they can be interpreted dialectically; they can also be interpreted metaxologically.

In Hegel's own account of what is at play in the alienation of the doubled will, two forms of the cleavage are noted: one in relation to God; the other in relation to the world. The first is the absolute cleavage, the most radical of all. It is the one with the greatest depth. It can generate not just a particular or finite anguish; it can generate infinite anguish concerning oneself. Hegel powerfully puts its: "Anguish is precisely the element of negativity in the affirmative, meaning that within itself the affirmative is self-contradictory and wounded."[19]

This wound of self-contradiction must be known in inwardness for the anguish to be infinite. It is essential that the disjunction be known as such. For such anguish to take effect, the consciousness of the good and its infinite demand must be present in the inmost being of the human subject. This is also linked with the consciousness of the one God as a pure spiritual God. Hegel seems to imply that the way anguish is absorbed in inwardness also signals the absorption of inwardness into itself and thence into God, understood as spirit. Nor should we think of Hegel as some bland Polyanna. He points to the infinite nature of the task of living up to what one is in concept, the demand of corresponding to what one ought to be. There is no escape from this demand, nor from the evil which goes with the consciousness of knowing that one is not what one ought to be. "And thus the contradiction remains, no matter how one twists oneself about. . . my lack of correspondence to my essence and to the absolute remains; and from one side or the other I know myself always as what ought not to be."[20]

When Hegel takes up the second opposition of evil, namely, our antithesis to the world, he explicitly makes reference to the unhappiness of this separation. It is not incidental that the word he uses, *Unglück*, is the same word for the unhappy consciousness, *das unglückliche Bewusstsein*. Here the human subject undergoes the dissatisfaction of spirit and the inability of the world to satisfy its longing. This unhappiness is again dialectical for Hegel in that its sense of opposition has the effect of pressing the self back into *itself*. Within itself it finds the demand that the world be rational, a demand that the world in its externality does not satisfy. Hegel invokes the Jewish people and their sense of good and evil. Such a sense is as much ontological as it is ethical and religious: ontological in that the entire being of nature and the being of the human self is metaphysically marked by a certain pervasive understanding of good and evil. With the Jewish people, we have a developed sense of the one God and hence a sense of spirit as other to nature. As a people driven by this restlessness and dissatisfaction of spirit, we also find a decisive turning way from natural being.

Relative to this second antithesis of the self and world, Hegel then turns to the universal unhappiness of the world in the Roman period. Again evil is interpreted in terms of the epochs of Hegelian world-history. The Roman period contributes world-historically as a crucial epochal expression of the antithesis and cleavage in which the self is driven back into itself. The formal inwardness that we find here is related to Stoicism and Skepticism (it is also reminiscent of Legal Status in the *Phenomenology*).[21] Hegel connects these with the sense of humiliation, and the absorption of self in itself. In the Stoic and Skeptic sage the self is supposed to find itself at home with itself. In fact "here antithesis is at its height, and both sides embrace the antithesis in its most complete universality—in the universal itself—and in its innermost essence, its greatest depth."[22] Hegel thus brings to attention a sequence of historical instantiations of the sense of cleavage, doubleness, which are dialectically related to each other, and which ostensibly play out in the epochs of history the plurality of possible relations between the self and what is other.

The point is to bring the dynamical cleavage to its most radical expression. This is implied by Stoicism and Skepticism, but a reader even cursorily familiar with the *Phenomenology* will detect a markedly similar unfolding in the lectures on religion. A crucial turning point occurs just here in the *Phenomenology* in consciousness' efforts to be at home with itself in its other: antithesis is developed to its most radical antagonism. The violent antithesis of master and slave is internalized in the divided consciousness of the Stoic and Skeptic and reaches its most extreme form in the Unhappy Consciousness. Though in the *Lectures on the Philosophy of Religion* Hegel does not explicitly mention the Unhappy Consciousness, everything he says fits this figure, as is borne out by the word *"Unglück."* What is at stake in the cleavage is not concentrated in *one particular figure*, as in the *Phenomenology*, but distributed more *universally* in a manner having application to a diversity of interpretations of evil in different historical epochs.

Certainly Hegel insists that now we come across the center of evil and anguish, of self-absorption and alienation, of the sense of humiliated finitude and agonized longing for salvation in a beyond.[23] Relevantly, at this point in the *Phenomenology* the theme of the death of God appears with reference to the Unhappy Consciousness. In the *Lectures on the Philosophy of Religion*, just subsequently to this development of the cleavage to its absolute extremes, the same issue emerges in connection with Jesus Christ and the overcoming of evil in the reconciliation of the human being and God. Again the dialectical rhythm of the concept is Hegel's primary organizing focus in his presentation of the world-historical panorama of evil.

Relative to this rhythm, the thought of absolute opposition, while a moment of anguish in itself, is a moment in transition, for it is also the deepest moment of dialectical *reversal*. When we think the absolute opposition through to its extreme, the opposition itself turns around into its opposite, absolute reconciliation. The dialectical reversal begins to effect the turnabout of evil into the good. On the stage of world-history, evil, even when developed to the extreme of radical rupture, proves to be the penultimate moment of the good, dialectically conceived as the achieved coincidence of opposites. So at this point, when the antithesis has been developed to its most universal, its most inward and its most extreme, Hegel brings in the concept of *reconciliation*. This is the beginning of the dialectical reversal in the death of God.

I will not now say anything extensive about reconciliation beyond noting the following. Hegel speaks of reconciliation in terms of the Christian figuration of good and evil, first in terms of Jesus Christ, and finally in terms of the community of spirit. Reconciliation is ultimately inclusive of evil in a total process of dialectical self-mediation. We are reminded of how, as we saw in chapter 3, the two movements of man to God and God to man become two moments of one total dialectically self-mediating whole movement. In the reconciliation of this dialectically self-mediating whole, God no longer seems to be the Unequal who is the agapeic other, and evil seems no longer to be a malign otherness to which we are unequal.

I note also this tension between particularity and universality. On the one hand, Jesus is acknowledged as a unique I. On the other hand, Jesus serves as representative of the universality of the unique I which all humans are. The historical Jesus as a unique I is also an individual embodiment of the divine process which is eternal, universal, hence more than merely particular. Inevitably with respect to this second side of the Hegelian standpoint, the first side, namely, Jesus as a unique I, stands in need of being *aufgehoben* by the philosophical *Begriff*. And so we find the same tension (between existential particularity and logical and world-historical universality) in Hegel's account of reconciliation, as we discovered in his discussion of the Fall.

The same question must be put to the former as previously was put to the latter. Is Hegel guilty of having it both ways, in first insisting on the unique I but then undercutting that stress, by even more strongly insisting on the necessity of its philosophical universalization? Is this Hegel's duplicity or is it an ineradicable *doubleness* that inevitably comes to appear when we think about the matter at stake? Can we ever do away with the tension between existential particularity and the logicist and world-historicist universal? But perhaps Hegel primarily wants to get to the death of God as the death of death, and hence as the deepest religious *Vorstellung* of the dialectical reversal. The true reconciliation, Hegel will say, shows the power of spirit to set the evil at nought. The way Hegel puts this in the *Zusatz* (to § 24) on the Fall in the *Encyclopedia Logic* is: The hand that inflicts the wound is also the hand that heals the wound; spirit can undo what spirit itself has done; the negative can negate itself and so be affirmative. Thus Hegel essays to think about forgiveness dialectically.

Notice that Hegel here also says that *thought and only thought* is the principle of restoration. What kind of thought is meant, and hence what kind of forgiveness? Is it again thought simply thinking *itself*; or is there a thought of the *other* that is not reducible to thought just thinking itself? What role does the other beyond self-thinking thought play in genuine forgiveness and restoration? Does the other play only a dialectically subordinate role, such that all forgiveness is only self-forgiveness—a possibility I previously suggested with respect to forgiveness in the *Phenomenology*? If we give an unHegelian modulation to the other that we must think beyond self-thinking thought, do we not have to reject the implication that all forgiveness is dialectical self-forgiveness? If there is an affirmative double not reducible to a dialectical one, might there not be a metaxological forgiveness of the other, or forgiveness of the self by the agapeic other?

To say that the hand that wounds is also the hand that heals, does this explain anything? Does it not really rename the happening of forgiveness, albeit mapped on a dialectical geography of concepts? Is not the latter essentially a certain naming, an *acknowledgment* of the fact? Does not the dialectical naming of forgiveness, in the light of self-thinking thought, make us squint at the irreducible generosity of the other? If the happening of forgiveness is agapeic, is there not a sense in which it is more proper to acknowledge it metaxologically rather than questionably to claim to have comprehended it dialectically? Does not the enigma of forgiveness remain an enigma? To say that spirit undoes itself is to describe, as if it were a dialectical explanation, what is profoundly recalcitrant to such a determinate account. What is this undoing? If there is an otherness beyond dialectical thought, is not the "affirmative" undoing of forgiveness as enigmatic as the "negative" undoing of the evil itself?

I also find Hegel's doubleness in his striking ambivalence with respect to the putative radical singularity of Jesus. On the one hand, Jesus is said to be irreducibly singular; his singularity is not a singularity in general. Yet this singularity is identified with sensuous immediacy, for Hegel a necessary moment in the appearance of the absolute. Some human beings have come in history to believe that irreducible singularity is ingredient in the divine life, as in the Christian stress on the uniqueness of Jesus Christ. In effect Hegel converts this religious belief into a historical mode of recognition by the *Weltgeist*, wherein sensuous immediacy is at last grasped as a dialectically necessary moment of the appearance of the absolute, or the self-particularization of the concept. On the other hand, despite this ambiguous emphasis on singularity, Hegel later will more explicitly bring out what is here veiled. And so in Hegel's third moment of the Holy Spirit/community, the singularity of Jesus as an historical *this* is done away with, and the universal holds undisputed sway again.

Let me try to summarize. Hegel offers an extremely complex discussion. I have not exhausted its potential by any means. Overall his account of evil essentially follows the logic of the concept. In the

Encyclopedia Logic this correspondence with the logic of the concept is most explicit: The myth of the Fall is used there to exhibit representationally the logical structure of the concept. But the same logic of the concept is deeply at work in the *Lectures on the Philosophy of Religion*, albeit sometimes less directly. There the dialectical account follows the logic of the concept as a kind of existential unfolding from the innocent unity of immediacy through the cleavage of consciousness and self-consciousness, through the mediation of this cleavage in consciousness itself up to the most radical antithesis, to the third moment of the dialectic when the absolute radical extremes turn towards each other and become reconciled in a dialectical *coincidentia oppositorum.*

This account inevitably leads to a displacement of philosophical mindfulness from existential concerns to logicist and world-historicist perspectives. The tension that concerns us is whether the "reality" of evil in its singularity can be subordinated to a larger universal structure or process, whether it be the logical or world-historical universal. Perhaps the best resume of Hegel's view might be: His dialectical account of evil stands between the intimacy of existential pathos and the objectivizing neutralism of world-historical necessity, though the logical necessity of the concept to supersede singularity finally wins out.

The hand that wounds is the hand that heals, Hegel says of *Geist*. We now ask: Is the Hegelian hand that gives irreducible singularity also the Hegelian hand that takes it away? Which of these two Hegelian hands is the one that heals and the one that wounds? Which hand offends and which hand reconciles? Are they always the same hand? What hand does the other play in all this? Must we come to terms with, live with *both* hands? If so, is there a doubleness in Hegel, and is it essential to dialectical thought? What then is the status of such a doubleness that seems ineradicable? Can dialectical thinking remain solely dialectical when it thinks through its own nature? In that ineradicable doubleness does some other otherness, an other than dialectical otherness, always stay open, in an openness that will always resists dialectical comprehension? And does that opening of ineradicable resistant otherness lie in wait for thought at the heart of dialectic, patiently ready to confound its claims to complete comprehension? Can dialectic comprehend one of the hands: the this as this of evil in the existential intimacy of its inwardness; the idiocy of evil, the idiocy of the monstrous, in the Greek sense of *idios*, its otherness to the public universal? Can Hegel's saving dialectic, through itself alone, through thought alone, restore to vigor a hand withered to a stump by its own deforming iniquity?

World-History and the Idiocy of Evil

I return to my opening question: Is there significant incommensurability between dialectical thought and evil? I restate some major points. Dialectical thinking seeks to articulate rupture and opposition; the sleeping innocent unity of immediacy must necessarily be ruptured; the necessity of rupture is inescapably ingredient in the process of differentiation. But the rupture is itself overcome and an ethical, as opposed to innocent unity reinstated; this is the mediated unity rather than an immediate one; the rupture serves the reconstitution of this mediated ethical unity. The process of differentiation is teleologically bound to a unity that includes opposition and otherness within itself. Evil is the necessary prelude to a good more complex and differentiated than the first immediacy of innocence.

From the outset, the teleology of dialectic looks forward to the overcoming of all otherness. Dialectic thinks opposition, not to be torn apart by the rupture, but to embrace both sides of the antithesis in a richer *coincidentia oppositorum*. If we shortcircuit this final reconstitution, at best we have a merely negative dialectic, held back from fulfilling the affirmative intent of thought in positive speculative reason. From the endpoint of this affirmative telos, every evil is inherently commensurable with dialectical comprehension. Relative to the fullest unfolding of the dialectic, evil itself is othered and reversed into its opposite. It becomes a transitional episode on the longer way of progress to the Hegelian good, and in a sense there is no radical, or absolute evil. Retrospectively everything can be justified as finally for the best. Evil is evil but also dialectically good.

This is related to what has been called the "aesthetic theodicy."[24] From the standpoint of the whole all rupturing otherness turns out to be a contribution to the good, like the spots of shadow in a beautiful painting whose very darkness provides an essential contribution to the rightness of the whole. As has often been pointed out, there can be something offensive, even sinister about any justification of present evils from the standpoint of a future perfection. As we know, in our century this justification has been used to sanction murder on a world-historical scale, both by revolutionary leaders of the Left and the grim politicians of race.[25] The shadow of the world-historical universal darkens the present: history's to-be-realized future telos serves to exculpate present evils, said to be instrumentally necessary to realize that telos. We fertilize the future with the blood of the present. To say the world-historical universal "darkens" our time is to use a word not dark enough. The red blood of numberless, murdered innocents blackens our century. Worse still: this malevolent blackness justified itself with a logic of world-historical perfection.

Both Stalin and Hitler were guilty of this vile fertilization, shielding itself behind the rationalization of a future world-historical perfection. The logic of Communist murder was a certain logic of historical perfection: the world-historical perfection of the coming Communist paradise justifies making an instrumental hell of the present. A similar logic of world-historical perfection informed Nazi murder: the future perfect Aryan race will arise, a Phoenix of death, from the purging of the alien element, especially the Jew—a purging worse that purgatory, producing a hell worse than hell. There is a clear logical line leading from the projected paradise of the world-historical future to the chill hell of the Gulag and to the burning Inferno of Auschwitz. When the City of Man claims to be identical with the City of God it fails to be even Plato's City of Pigs; it becomes the City of Executioners, the Necropolis of Enlightenment Logic.

One cannot accuse Hegel of this, though certainly his left-Hegelian heirs have made use of the logic of the dialectic and the universal of world-history as an ideological rationale. The Left-Hegelians instrumentalize the dialectic, an instrumentalization dressed up in the high sounding rhetoric of revolution. Hegel's Marxist successors especially instrumentalized present evils in an ethically blithe way, a way that would have made Hegel himself recoil, as is clear from his disgusted shock at the Terror of the French Revolution.

If it is unfair to tar Hegel with the brush of the Left-Hegelian instrumentalization of the dialectic, still the question will not go away: Is there something about evil that is never redeemed dialectically? Is there a "negative" that is never taken up as a moment of self-developing *Geist?* What rational basis has Hegel for asserting that every negative is so taken up? The Marxist, emboldened by the dialectical necessity of evil in the Hegelian scheme of history, might reply: well a few crimes here and there—what do they matter to the march of the world-historical universal? This is an escape, not only false but sinister: in advance one washes from one's hands the blood whose present shedding logic will shortly serve to justify, in light of the revolution's future. Need I add that the Nazi washed his hands in a similar historical solvent, a similar historical absolvent?

Against this historicist dissolving of the horror of evil, I suggest that there may be a quality of absoluteness to evil that has nothing to do with any quantity of influence, conceived in world-historical terms, whether Hegelian or Marxist, or National Socialist, or Capitalist. Evil might be a negative absolute, as it were: not Hegel's "bad infinite," but a different "bad infinite," an "evil infinite" which resists every Hegelian mediation and dialectical transformation into the "good infinite." I can envisage an evil act, a qualitatively evil act, which may have absolutely no influence in world-historical terms and yet it has this quality of being absolutely evil. It is "outside" history. It is other to the world-historical universal. It cannot be recovered in terms of the march of world-history. Its significance may lie in an entirely different dimension. It may be an offense or desecration or rejection or monstrous malice which at a certain level is, as it were, completely invisible to dialectics. And yet the reality of such offenses might be absolutely significant in the spiritual destiny of a human being, perhaps also of a community. Will Hegelian dialectics leave us in the lurch at a certain point?

Suppose we first put the question whether there is something about evil that exceeds dialectical comprehension in terms of Hegel's speculative appropriation of the myth of the Fall. We need to keep in mind that the myth of the Fall is not itself an explanation, nor does it explain evil. It presupposes its existence. This is not to say that it is meaningless. Not at all. It is to say that it strategically names this "reality" and situates it within a context of imaginative meaning, with religious, ethical, metaphysical implications. It focusses our attention, names and highlights certain fundamental perplexities and enigmas. This mythic naming sometimes can seem to exorcise the enigma, but this is not a necessary outcome. Does the Hegelian *Begriff* serve to raise mythic enigma to conceptual transparency? Hegel presents his own dialectical concept as the true mode of rational accounting that overcomes the externality and contingency of religious representation. But does the dialectical account, in fact, give an account of evil that is thus free of these putative limitations of representation?

I think it does not. The dialectical account does not really explain anything. It reiterates within a complex context of conceptual determinations that evil is a necessity; that the emergence of evil correlates with moments of the concept; that evil's necessity is the necessity of the concept; that it is the moment of division, necessary to overcome the sleeping innocence of immediate unity, necessary for the further reconstitution of self-knowing unity or reconciliation after the cleavage of being. The dialectical rhythm of the concept is articulated in this rhythm of natural unity, cleavage and the birth of spirit, self-knowing identity of spirit. . . . We are now only too familiar with this. But suppose that the very contingency of the representation deeply mirrored something about the "evil" being depicted: namely, its final resistance to being transformed into conceptual universality? Would not the Hegelian conceptual transformation then already work against the grain of the representation, whose essential content it claims to respect and better articulate?

Surely it is important that such strong language of rupture or radical discontinuity is built into the story of the Fall. Yet Hegel's conceptual transformation of this *Vorstellung* finally undercuts the dimension of discontinuity in its insistent mediation of the radical gap that the *Vorstellung* itself insists on bringing to our attention. After all, the Fall mythically names a *fall*. For Hegel this fall is a necessary moment of a process of differentiated mediation; the discontinuity is merely the dialectical presupposition to reconstituted continuity. Radical discontinuity, dialectically conceived, proves not to be radically discontinuous. Dialectically speaking, this might seem to be Hegel's reformulation of Augustine's *felix culpa*. But if from the very *beginning* and by a dialectical *necessity* the *culpa* is *felix*, if the fault is happy, the radical rupture is already, and from the outset, not radical, perhaps not even a real rupture at all. Can we avoid the result then that in seeming to think through the rupture we are really only thinking it away? Does dialectic then exhibit the magical power of conceptual exorcism?

You might object on Hegel's behalf and say that this congruence of the rhythm of the dialectical concept and the unfolding of innocence and evil is itself the rational account to be given of the matter. If we are to account rationally for evil it can only be in such terms. There is a certain persuasiveness to this, but only up to a certain point. If we accept this as the last word I suspect that we can come to share in the blindness to which some philosophers are prone: namely, believing that when something has been mapped on a certain conceptual geography that then we have fully accounted for the reality. In Hegel's case we do not have a reduction of evil to a category in the more ordinary sense of an abstract universal. But we do have a reduction to a category in the distinctively Hegelian sense: the concept is the category; and in so far as evil is placed within the dialectical rhythm of the concept/category, then it, too, has been assimilated to the category. To be sure for Hegel, the category is a dynamic structure and this is the power of his view, but evil is nevertheless reduced to rational necessity, mirroring the dialectical becoming of division, alienation and reconciliation.

Why is this not enough? I said before there are different ways of naming, acknowledging the happening of evil. Systematic concepts may articulate the context of a way of naming, but such a web of concepts does not constitute the central acknowledgment itself. I now add more explicitly that there is a *gap* between the reality of evil as lived and the concept of evil as thought. There is a *disproportion*

between evil as either suffered or done and evil as said to illustrate
the structure of rational necessity. Being and thought are *not the same*
here—despite what father Parmenides said about the sameness of
noein and *esti*, despite its reiteration by Plotinus and others, including
Hegel. There is a non-dialectical difference between being and under-
going evil and the thought of evil. As God would be the agapeic
Unequal other of human thought, evil would be the baneful unequal
of thought. So I reject the confusion of being logical with being ethical,
such as happens when innocence is identified with the logical category
of immediacy, and evil with the category of otherness. I am not
objecting to the use of those categories. The issue is the discontinuity
of the category and being evil, whether in that discontinuity
something basic escapes the category. The category mediates our
understanding of being evil, but the mediation becomes a conceptual
blindness when it becomes oblivious to what in evil cannot be
mediated, when it forgets what is other to conceptual mediation.

Consider. When I commit an evil act, I can be told, or can tell
myself, that what has happened, or what I have done, reflects the
universal structure of being. This may be true. But it bypasses what
I call the *inward thisness or inward otherness* of the evil act as mine.
I did the evil act. Neither being nor the concept did the evil act in
pursuit of their own inherent rationality. I did the act. I may refuse
to own up to this fact; but the refusal is my refusal. I may agonize
in remorse about the act as mine and seek forgiveness; but it is I who
agonize and am sick at heart for having done an irrevocable evil. I
may even use Hegelian philosophy to rationalize my act, but the
equivocation, even duplicity of this strategy is already borne by the
word "rationalize." There is no consolation in any genuine sense in
the claim that evil conforms to the rhythm of rational, dialectical
necessity, for since the evil act is mine, I cannot escape myself into
any more universal structure. To escape so is to diminish this
irreducible otherness of the evil act as a this, between which and all
universal structures there is a gap.

The I that confesses "I did that" does not speak as an instance
or representative of a universal humanity (this is not at all to deny
that the I may share in a universal, communal humanity, or that in
some respects I may even be representative of humanity). About such
a confessing I there is an absoluteness in singularity or a singularity
that is absolute. Singularity is absolute in a sense of being *a solo*:
from itself alone. The I that confesses must speak for itself alone. This
is the burden and grandeur of such an I. It does not confess as the
representative of something other; one cannot confess for another, nor
another for one (perhaps one might apologize for another, but that

is a different matter). This confessing on one's own behalf is, as we say, literally "to own up to the deed"—no one but the I as singular can own up in this sense. This is what ultimate ethical responsibility means. There is a myness that is irreducible—in the sense of not simply being an instance of a more universal structure or condition.

This is not to deny that the I, in the full range of its being is also implicated in a whole host of mediating relations which articulate and concretize its involvement with others. This is entirely consonant with a metaxological sense of community. The singularity of the responsible I as confessing and the essential relatedness to others of the self are not antithetical. Indeed without the absolute responsibility of the I as singularity, I cannot see how the relation to the other can be realized as a properly ethical relation.

Again I do not deny that often one only becomes a singularly responsible I with the help of the ethical support of the others, that is, because the ethical other has welcomed the articulation of the ethical promise of self-being. But I cannot see that we have to choose between this responsibility of the singular individual and acknowledgment of the bonds that tie the individual to others. In radically owning up to one's deeds, one may do this before oneself, one may do it before the other. The singularity of the confessing I is not an inarticulate monad but is internally complex: acknowledging the rupture in itself, the rupture between itself and being that is other, willing to renew its bond with the deeper ethical energies of its own being and the other. It is metaxologically double in the sense suggested before. A double mediation is at work in the confessing I: its own dialectical self-mediation, and its metaxological intermediation with what is other to itself. Thus, too, the absoluteness of the confessing I is evident in considering the word "absolute" from another aspect: the absolute singularity of owning up can be experienced as absolving, as freeing, as releasing. Let us say that now one owns up in absolute singular responsibility, not only to accept the deed as mine, but to ask for release from its evil, to be absolved, to be forgiven.

From the standpoint of this forgiving absolution, the absolvent of any world-historical rationalization is exposed as an ethical evasion. Here arises the suspicion that, to the extent that dialectical thought privileges the dimension of universal process or structure, it allows such a world-historical escapism from this irreducible ethical singularity. If the reality of evil is to be located at the level of the concept of the whole, then the ineluctable participation of the individual becomes merely an instance of this more universal structure and hence secondary or derivative. One could then say: it is not I who has committed the evil; it is the concept that necessarily is the evil. The same point applies to the good: indeed some Hegelians seem to have identified themselves with God on this score. Of course, Marxists and Nietzscheans have performed analogous identifications. Nietzsche gives this game away when he exclaims: If God existed, how could I endure it not to be God. There is a logically self-exculpating evil in the identification of the negative with the concept, just as there is a self-dissolving mysticism that slides toward our self-forgetful identification with the so-called good. The singularity of the I in its difference is wrongly sacrificed.

While Hegel does not deny the agony of such sacrifices, as when he speaks of the spectacle of history as a *Schlachtbank*, I would prefer to find in his *logic* sufficient protection against any turning of such a "slaughterbench" into an altar of "reason" on which the death of innocents is offered to the devouring Moloch of history. Hegel speaks of the cunning of reason (*List der Vernunft*) using certain individuals as puppets, or agents of its own intentions: the individual thinks it pursues its own passion, but it is really an instrument serving the purpose of the world-spirit. This is a world-historicist secularization of the theological doctrine of Providence. But after Hegel we now know bitterly that the God-service of history has too often sacrificed to abomination. Dialectical logic does not offer us sufficient reason to cry out in intransigent horror. Logic stifles horror. But this stifling of horror is the logical horror.

Dialectical escape into the world-historical universal is fundamentally false in relation to what a mindful human being experiences and does as evil. There is a gap between the universal structure of evil, which is essentially anonymous, and the individual as evil and its evil act as *singularly owned*. This gap is such that the evil act as lived from within eludes dialectic in so far as the latter articulates a structure, albeit a dynamic process of structuration. For Hegel such owned singularity becomes just the logical moment of particularity, a necessary part of that dialectical structuring of the concept. But evil is not a structure or process of structuring; the evil act is not a structure; the evil will is not a structure; these are perhaps better called "destructurings," in the sense both of being a negation of structure and as being other to all structure. They are, as it were, negative indeterminacies that can never be entirely objectified into any determinate structure: negative indeterminacies that remain negative and indeterminate, even while shadowing all historical processes of structuration and determination.

This has to do with the radical intimacy of the spirit that is always the accompaniment of dialectical development and thought, but that dialectical development and thought can never completely objectify and hence can never completely comprehend. I would go so far as to say that there is something *idiotic* about evil, again in the Greek sense of *idios*: a certain intimacy that falls outside the public system of rationalized behavior. This idiocy of evil is an irreducible other to the universal of world-history.

Radical Evil

Suppose we ask about what falls outside in terms of the question: Is there such a thing as *radical evil?* Hitler and Stalin come to mind, of course. These are clearly "public" figures, not at all idiotic in the above sense, and moreover, public figures who exemplified versions of the rationalization of the world-historical universal. But for just those reasons, one cannot dismiss the issue of what remains other to the world-historical universal. Why are we fascinated, sometimes morbidly, sometimes otherwise, with speculations about the *inner* being or motivation of such individuals? Why do we continue to try to peer into that idiotic murk, and not with much success, even when we have masses of objective historical information about their times and actions? Is it not because we know, perhaps very inarticulately, that there is an intimacy of spirit to every human being as singular, an idiocy that even the powerful players of world-history cannot finally evade or deny? Do we remain fascinated because we see that this intimacy and idiocy still remain beyond our comprehension, and may always so remain? In asking about "radical evil" one is asking about the *radix*, the root or source of the evil, and its susceptibility to determinate explanation. Is not our recurrent perplexity here due to the sense that this root still remains hidden, even after all the determinate explanations are given?

Hannah Arendt might question the existence of radical evil with her controversial idea of the "banality of evil," put forward in relation to Eichmann. This will not touch the point I make about the idiocy of evil. The putative "banality" of evil presupposes, in fact, just that very intimate inwardness, which in its monstrous indifference, is an ethical possibility for every single individual. I, too, you too, might be that singular one. The singular I in its idiocy and intimacy, of course, can be easily and wrongly confounded with the anonymous "one." This confounding is the basis of the "banality" of evil, but it is a confounding nevertheless. The bureaucratic "banalization" of evil is *already* an attempted confusion and evasion of the intimacy of spirit of the singular I.

Indeed, the most monstrous indifference is often the indifference that evades its own ethical darkness with an ethical rationalization. Eichmann claimed to be a good Kantian, having never done anything that he felt transgressed the categorical imperative. The stock images of demonic malevolence may have nothing to do with radical evil precisely because of this idiocy and intimacy. The wolfman does not have to howl for blood under a malign moon; the wolfman may be just that sleek executive who, even with all the panache of world-historical culture, is an efficient "desk murderer." Every image, stock or not, as every concept, dialectical or otherwise, may be always insufficient to the idiocy of evil. The "banality" of evil is itself another image, a profoundly shocking image, of its monstrousness. It is the paradoxical appearance of a deformed intimacy of spirit that does not itself appear, or want to appear. Perhaps it could only appear before a God, and then because it could no longer hide. The monstrousness of the banal would be laid bare.[26]

In relation to radical evil, suppose we think of Shakespeare's Iago. Many reasons can and have been cited for Iago's cold and calculating incitement of Othello to jealousy of Desdemona, to his loss of trust in her and her consequent murder. But despite the many possible reasons, something remains elusive and enigmatic. No explanation completely satisfies. Hence the sense of Iago's "motiveless malignity," as Coleridge called it. Spontaneously we look for a rational explanation; it is our nature to do so; yet though we have made any number of explanatory efforts, the nagging doubt persists that something was missing, or somehow missed. Moreover, we are made very uneasy with the lack of satisfying explanation, for rational explanation helps us place an event or occurrence. It allows us to sleep soundly again. Iago's evil resists being completely placed; it remains "nowhere," and makes fitful the sleep of rational mind.

Suppose we do grant a radical evil that eludes complete explanation. But even to do this already makes uneasy the "Hegelian" in every philosopher. Even the anti-Hegelian philosopher is much more Hegelian in this respect than he knows or cares to acknowledge: the thought of what is other to reason induces epistemological anxiety. How does dialectical reason, a sophisticated articulation of the power of reason, shed light on the this as this of Iago? Iago is Iago, evil Iago, unique, irrepeatable, even granting that other individuals might also incarnate radical evil, indeed that every individual harbors it as a possibility. How will dialectic deal with this lightless this?

Or think of Milton's Lucifer: one who makes a virtue of refusal, who says "evil be thou my good," one who pursues the negative freedom of pure, absolute refusal. Here we find an absolute willfulness in its negating power, a kind of perverse mimicry of divine will. Remember: Lucifer, the first born of light, embodied in the serpent that Hegel's dialectical account of evil exonerates. Remember too: Milton's Lucifer, like Shakespeare's Iago, was *cold*, with a coldness tangential to both the "banalization" of evil and its stock demonization, a coldness of spirit. Is not the absolutely willful I, in its sheer refusal, recalcitrant to inclusion in any system? Is it not other than all system, willfully placing itself in its perverse particularity outside all universals? Reason would like to situate everything in an essentially public system of intelligibility. But there is here a recalcitrant idiocy or intimacy to the willful I. This refusing will is a wild, lawless otherness. Might we not speak of the wholly other, *das ganz Andere*, but in malign, perverse form? Do not all mediations come against a limit here, come across an impasse where mediation is arrested, mocked, brought to grief, broken down?[27]

A standard Hegelian ploy at this point to preserve a mediating universal would be to remind one of the dialectic of sense-certainty in the *Phenomenology*. There, it is claimed, Hegel shows how every effort to say "this" immediately implicates a whole tissue of universals; hence the saying of the this as this always fails. This failure dialectically turns us, returns us to the universal. I cannot enter into the intricacies of sense-certainty here, beyond saying that significant non-Hegelian lessons might also be taken from it. For instance, the sheer "that it is" of the being there of the particular being might arouse ontological astonishment, rather than the will to systematic, universal science. Such ontological astonishment would have to be said differently and not in terms of a dialectical logic.

But even suppose that we grant something of Hegel's point relative to sense-certainty, seen as a move in the philosophical game of transcendental epistemology. Will not the same dialectical drift towards universality with respect to evil in its particularity occasion a different kind of resistance? For the issue is not simply a question of logic. One need not deny universal structures or the search for them; this is ingredient in all philosophy. But phenomenologically the "reality" of the evil act is in its essence particular: it is a this, a *mine* in a way that is falsified if we think that something like the dialectic of sense-certainty captures its particularity.

Nor will it do to say that all immediacy is mediated and, presto, we are off again to the dialectical races. There are particulars that, as it were, stick like a hook in one's throat, and struggle as one may, one cannot pull this hook out. The thought of evil sticks in the throat of dialectical saying like such a hook and rasps the smoothness of its voice. In the interplay of immediacy and mediation, there is something which is at the edge of dialectical mediation. Simply to play the game of dialectical self-mediation is to be obtuse to this edge. This edge is existentially sharp and cuts into one's being, making a wound that will never be entirely healed.

You might retort that a kind of repentance will effect the healing. But again, where is the dialectic? One might plausibly show the articulation of my repentance within a mediated process which exhibits dialectical features. I do not deny this. But the core act of repentance as mine has no dialectical structure. It is a breaking down and a breaking through, a cutting and an opening of being that is placed within a process that may unfold with certain dialectical features but which itself is not simply dialectical, and especially not so in virtue of such breakdowns and breakthroughs, cuts and openings. Repentance brings with it an inversion, and a reversal and a leap. In fact, Hegel will make use of all this language, and necessarily so to the extent that he remains true to what is at stake, but as we shall see there is an essential non-dialectical side to such language.

The Idiocy of the Monstrous

I have been insisting that there is something idiotic about evil, in the Greek sense of *idios*: an intimacy of being falling outside the public system of rationalized behaviour. I am reminded of Augustine's description of God: *intimior intimo meo*, more intimate to me than I am to myself. Does the idiocy of evil indicate an analogous intimacy, only it would be the intimacy of spiritual malice rather than that of generosity of spirit? I think here that Kierkegaard's almost obsessive insistence on inwardness has to be taken with great seriousness. In terms of any form of objective thinking there may be instances of evil that cannot be identified and recognized. They may be idiotic to objective thinking. I am not agreeing with Kierkegaard that Hegel is an objective thinker: he is a dialectical thinker, which is something more complex. But the very moment of inwardness that Hegel himself knows is central to dialectical thinking has a dimension of intimacy, idiocy that resists total self-mediation. To the extent that Hegel thinks that this intimacy of being can be totally mediated, that is, brought out into the domain of public, conceptual discursivity, he is a kind of objective thinker and hence always in danger of understressing that qualitative inwardness of evil of which Kierkegaard reminds us.

One might recall that Hegel hated, hence also feared, the beautiful soul. The beautiful soul is, as it were, the epitome of vapid inwardness. I agree with Hegel about the vapidity of this form of inwardness, but

Hegel's contempt for this beautiful soul at times shows alarm, not just at the vapidity but at the claim made by the beautiful soul (a claim that need not be peculiar to the beautiful soul): that the inwardness as such, vapid or no, resists complete determinate articulation in some public exteriorization. Such vapid inwardness is not what I mean by the intimacy of being, the inward thisness of the particular will as good or evil. This inward thisness is also an inward otherness because it is always at the limit of a dialectical structure, because it is not a structure. I immediately add, again to avoid the suspicion of vapidity: inwardness that resists dialectical encapsulation need not be empty inwardness, nor need one deny the public nature of some evil. The intimate and the communal, the *idios* and the community are not dualistic opposites. Kierkegaard himself did not always avoid speaking as if they were.

Let me try to indicate further what I mean by this intimacy and idiocy. Many of us will be familiar with the great outcry of Dostoevski, in the mouth of Ivan Karamazov, against the suffering of innocent children, and this outcry too in the context of a struggle for faith in God. I suggest that the source of this outcry comes from the depths of our being that elude dialectical encapsulation. The Psalm has it: *De profundis ad te Domine clamavi.* What are those depths? In all honesty can one rest satisfied with the Hegelian implication that these depths are just the initial natural unity that subsequently will be reconciled with itself, having dialectically passed through the cleavage of evil? Surely there is more?

When Hegel speaks of grief/anguish (*Schmerz*), he chooses the apt word. The human spirit is in agony before evil. But there is no dialectical structure to agony. Agony voices itself in a cry from the heart. But what is a cry from the heart? A systematic science of such cries? Surely this is nonsense. What is the heart? Is the heart that mechanical pump whose structure Descartes so lovingly described in the *Discourse*? Is there a mechanics of the evil heart, the agonized heart? Or is the heart, as it is for Pascal, the metaphysical metaphor for what we are in the deepest intimacy of our spirit and being? Hegel is no Descartes of the heart, but neither is he a Pascal of its deepest intimacy. Like Spinozistic geometry, Hegelian system tries not to weep. The concept tries to console, beyond agony. But a cry from the heart, such an outcry—this is something elemental. Is not the heart a deep, an unfathomed abyss?

Hegel is not entirely heedless of the heart. Yet he wills to find articulated reasons of reason for the immediate reasons of the heart. The heart has reasons, not of which reason knows nothing, but of which Hegelian reason will want to know everything. An intimacy of being that will always be essentially intimate bothers reason, makes it uneasy. Reason blushes before the intimacy of being, and then puts on a stony face of universality. In principle there will be no intimacy of being remaining other to the complete self-mediation of the public concept. But the heart as elemental is an immediacy of ultimacy, an abyssal "immediacy" that is not to be completely mediated by the dialectically self-mediating concept.[28]

Consider this: I read in the newspaper about a child so badly battered by his father that the coroner said that the injuries were more severe than could be sustained were the child run over by a motorcar. The death of this child has no effect on world-history. I read further that the father had left his three-year-old son to die for three weeks just before Christmas, after first inflicting the injuries. The boy actually starved to death in his broken body. When I read this report, all I could do was put down my head on the table. A crushing weight descends upon me, like a night of the spirit in which I swoon or black out or go blank. I shudder as if a dark abyss had opened up and swallowed all sense and my sense. My being and mind undergo a liquefaction in which all determinate sense seem to be reclaimed by a malign formlessness. I think that this is the natural response to the enigma of evil. This is the agony of evil.

I can give many psychological, sociological explanations and so forth, for the behavior of the father. He had a deprived childhood, lived in intolerable social circumstances and so forth. These "explanations" help us situate the evil in a more or less determinate context, and to that extent certainly aid us in making it intelligible in some measure. The necessity of our seeking as comprehensive as possible an understanding of such a determinative type is not to be denied. We must try to understand to the utmost possible. But such "explanations" become obscene, if they take away from the particularity of the evil suffered as suffered. That is its idiocy as lived from within the intimacy of this horror. True understanding ought to bring us to the limit of this intimacy, not talk its way around it or away from it.

This intimacy of horror is something at the limit of sense or meaning, and our response to it is itself at the limit of sense and meaning. We ought not to fake our metaphysical helplessness with the bustle of pseudo-explanatory discourse. That is why all I can do is put down my head, crushed under the burden of something that in the end it would be obscene to try to rationalize. The evil suffered by this child is an obscene surd, and no rationalization will ever do away with that obscenity. The weight that descends is the night in which the light of the spirit is extinguished; this very night of emptiness and horror is the very sinisterness of evil itself. The response is to be crushed. But being crushed: there is no logic to being crushed; there is no dialectical structure; it is other to logos, other to structure. It is a destructuring indeterminacy, a negative otherness that resists total recuperation in the logic of dialectical concepts.

Do not simply say about evil and being crushed: Where is the argument? Ask: What is it that we must *acknowledge* about this recalcitrant yet revealing happening? Is there not something elemental in a properly mindful response? Being crushed exhibits a lack of dialectical structure because it is a collapse or retraction of the energy of being, a metaphysical oppression that resists being reduced to any mediated account. As the collapse of the energy of being into an inarticulate void, there is no dialectical logos of being crushed.

The same point might be made from the side of forgiveness. Here there is a leap into trust, but there is no dialectical logos of this leap, if by such a logos we mean a completely mediated articulation. The directionality of the energy of one's being is reversed from being crushed, but is there a dialectical logos of this reversal of directionality? The first is a negative otherness on the edge of dialectical structure; the second is a positive, indeed agapeic otherness which, as leaping, is likewise at the edge of dialectical structure. It is never a dialectical structure that forgives; it is the generous energy of the being of a particular human being, or a God. Dialectic may structurally *flank* these others but it can never be identified with them. In the end both being crushed and leaping into trust cannot be completely expressed in a discursive way. They are done, not said; they happen. There is no exhaustive logical account or explanation of either.

I said before in relation to Nietzsche that perhaps all one can say is "It happens." The crucial provisio was that "It happens" can be said differently, *legetai pollachōs*, as Aristotle would say. It all depends on the complex mode of naming in which it is embedded, or the web of thoughts or concepts which help to situate the saying and give it some articulate significance. I do not object to dialectical thinking if it is seen as articulating such a web of concepts that serve the purpose of drawing mindful attention to a "happening" that is to be acknowledged, but acknowledged as not known completely, nor totally comprehended by the web of dialectical concepts. A dialectic that acknowledges its own harboring of such non-dialectical otherness, such a dialectic must be preserved for philosophical thought. The problem is when the dialectical web of concepts claims to mediate completely this other, and hence claims to dissolve or absorb it in such concepts. This second response is untrue to the truth of the "It happens." We need something other and more than dialectical system.

A web of concepts that is metaxologically articulated is more true t the otherness of this "It happens."

I call to mind Wittgenstein's claim that philosophy consists in assembling certain reminders, with a particular purpose in view. I agree: the mode of mindfulness of philosophical thought has to be a fundamental reminding, Plato would call it an *"anamnesis,"* Hegel an *"Erinnerung."* The open dialectic I suggest above is a metaxological mindfulness which, in one of its modes, seeks to say such an assemblage of reminders. But the relevant assemblage is with the purpose of acknowledging what cannot be reduced to the assemblage of concepts. Philosophical thought, in thinking through its own concepts or thought-determinations, reminds itself, is reminded by the *Sache selbst*, that thought must also think what is other to thought, precisely as other. Its thought determinations are also determinations by thought that it be open to the other, which, in turn, and from its otherness, solicits thought that is to be *more* than self-determining. Philosophical mindfulness is not just the singular dialectical self-mediation of thought thinking itself. It is the double intermediation in which thought both thinks itself and also thinks its others, thinks what is other to thought as thought thinking itself. This double intermediation is philosophical thought as metaxological mindfulness. The greatness of philosophical thought is when it brings itself thus to its own limit, and submits its thinking to the *anankē* of its unmastered other or others. The metaxological acknowledgment of evil occurs on this limit.

On reflection I must acknowledge that the story above, a true story, is like the theological story of the divine father and son, but in reverse. The reversal is a perverse form of the natural bond of love between father and son: a malign father kills a son in senseless suffering, an innocent child, victim of a senseless death, alas too a murder more prolonged than the Golgotha of Jesus, three weeks, not three hours, and no resurrection whatever. The intimacy of its thisness comes out in this shaking fact also: the irreversibility of the evil act, its irrevocability, the irrecoverability of the fragile being of a self; the life of the son was a this, an absolute "once," but now a never again, and for all we know, an absolutely never again.

The fact that I have to tell a story to make a philosophical point is relevant to the metaxological mode of naming the happening of evil. As philosophers, we cannot escape from the truth of the story in its representational particularity into the impersonal universal. The story keeps us mindful of the intimate truth of particularity that the philosophical concept is tempted to subordinate or supersede or forget. Metaxological naming must be both imagistic and conceptual to do justice to the mindfulness required by the matter at issue. And there is no speculative *Aufhebung* of the story into the concept. Rather the naming of the philosopher must be plurivocal. Our very concepts must themselves try to maintain in themselves the memory of the truth that the story tells. The concept must bear in itself the traces of its own origin in its other, the originating story.

The story told is a true story of a father and son, in which the son is destroyed by the father, with no saving recuperation. There is no sacred violence of the sacrifice here. Why emphasize that no concept will replace the story? This: Hegelians and others will talk about the death of the son, the death of Jesus as representational and then dialectically sublate the representation into the concept. We displace mindfulness away from the particularity of a brutal violence on a self. Are we so familiar with death to be thus at ease before it? Is the death of Jesus so familiarly named that it can be so easily used as a "mere" representation? Why do we squirm at the death of a boy, and yet with dialectical smoothness pass from the "representation" of Jesus to the universal concept or the reconciling community? Does not mind really recoil at the idiocy of both horrors: the death of the sheer particular as an irreplaceable I. This I was once, unique, unrepeatable. This I is not a mere substitutable "representation" of a universal concept. It is not that this "onceness," unrepeatability, irreplaceability is antagonistic to the universal. But ingredient in its universal significance is the paradoxical universality of the idiocy of being.[29]

I think now of the agony in the outcry of another father at the death of an irreplaceable child—Lear at the death of Cordelia: "And my poor fool is hanged! No, no, no, life? / Why should a dog, a horse, a rat, have life, / And thou no breath at all? Thou'lt come no more, / Never, never, never, never, never." (*King Lear*, V, iii, 307–310). This Never is an absolutely crushing word. Perhaps never has it been uttered as crushingly as by Lear. Can dialectics take us beyond this Never? Can the universal of logic or world-history ever unharden the irrevocability of Lear's savage, reiterated Never? What can Hegelian dialectics ever tell Lear, what consolation could it give him in his elemental grief? When Lear carries the dead body of his child onto the stage, his logos is no dialectical logos, but a word of horror at the edge of all words: Howl, howl, howl, howl! Where is the concept of this Howl? Can the concept accommodate this Howl? Does not the Howl blast to pieces any logicist pretension to complete intelligible lucidity on the part of any philosophical concept, Hegelian or non-Hegelian?[30]

One must bear in mind that Lear was once a kind of Hegelian himself: while still king, he thought that being was exhausted by the public stage of the kingdom, essential actor for the universal of

Hegelian world-history. Exiled from this stage, having passed through madness, Lear discovered the intimacy of being, the wisdom of its idiocy. And did he not reject, in effect, Hegelian dialectic when he says to the still living Cordelia that they would take upon themselves "the mystery of things, / As if we were God's spies; and we'll wear out, / In a walled prison, packs and sects of great ones / That ebb and flow by th' moon." (V, iii, 17–20).

What mysteries could there be for the dialectical concept? Could Hegel be called "God's spy" in his comparison of his *Science of Logic* to God's thoughts before the creation of nature and finite spirit? Or does that logic remain silent about what Lear sees? Does Hegel's God, as the world-spirit of world-history, dialectically ebb and flow by the moon, borne in devouring time by the packs and sects of great ones, or as Hegel would say, the world-historical nations and individuals? Does the dialectical theodicy of Hegel fail for all Lears? Is not the complete speech of his logic finally mute before the elemental grief of fathers and mothers, mute before murdered children, the Golgotha of the intimacy of particularity? Despite any rational comfort we may glean from dialectics, does the mystery of iniquity still remain a mystery?

And what does death become in Hegelian thought? Death becomes a metaphor for determinate negation, a representation of the dialectical structure of thinking. How apply this to the death of the child, or the death of Jesus? Hegel might hector us not to get fixated on the particularity of Jesus and to let ourselves be released into the universal. We must pass over the death of the particular to the "resurrection" of the universal. How easy it is then to overcome death? How compliant death is with our concepts—as if this "resurrection" were always happening. Once would be marvel enough, I would say. It would shock us, shock us more deeply than Lear's Never, Never, Never, Never, Never. But this Never makes it all but impossible to think such a Once again.

It is facile to turn "resurrection" into a metaphor for a necessary moment of the self-developing concept. Think again of the idiocy of Jesus's death: he dies radically alone, in an outcry of abandonment: "My God, my God why hast thou forsaken me?" This is the idiocy of Jesus' Never. And here, too, we find the intimacy of the Never more. The shock will be softened for the believer by saying: Jesus will come again, rise again. Hegel will go further and soften the shock to reason by saying: Here we have the logically necessary moment of reconsti- tution. But if there is any truth to resurrection, is it that of dialectical necessity? Rather: Against the Never, here we are asked to think the marvel of a Once again. If this is a marvel, it should be allowed to shock philosophy, even if it is madness to reason. Let reason recoil from it as a madness, if necessary.

Let us not fudge. An astonishing claim is made. Let us not dim the astonishment. "Resurrection": an absolutely strange thought, absolutely other; an absolutely astonishing claim. It is unbelievable. The marvel of being from nothing in agapeic creation; the marvel of being from nothing again; creation from the Never into the Once again, as a pure agapeic gift. If "resurrection" is this marvel, let us neither gild death, nor rationalistically soften this shockingness. Dialectical reason seems to say yes, but in fact gives us a version robbed of its strangeness, its otherness domesticated. Its idiocy, if true, is folly. I am not giving a philosophical argument for "resurrection." I do not think one can. I am only asking for honesty. Philosophy can be honest about its strangeness, ponder its otherness. I do not think Hegel is honest enough, his thought parasitical on an otherness it tames in seeming to affirm.

I do not want to be unfair to Hegel. He often is in between. He does clearly show mindfulness of the lived recalcitrance of evil. The sense of horror comes across at the beginning of his philosophy of history: history is a *Schlachtbank*; the innocent are trampled, and honest contemplation allows no escape, no consolation. Of course, by the end of the lectures on history that horror has been mitigated in the fulfilled secular present of Hegel's own time. His philosophy of history is explicitly presented as a theodicy of reason. But there is more to him than the dry panlogist who sucks the life out of reality to encase the dead results in categorial form.

In his aesthetics we find his liking for a statue of a Silenus figure holding the infant Bacchus, handling the child "with laughter and infinite sweetness and grace."[31] He considers the Madonna's love for the Christ-child as "the most beautiful subject to which Christian art in general, and especially painting in its religious sphere, has risen."[32] He acknowledges the grief at her son's death that breaks the heart of Mary, yet her "living beauty of *soul*" shines through the suffering.[33] I suspect that what Hegel says is more applicable, for instance, to the early *Pieta* of Michelangelo in St. Peter's which has the superb and finished polish of aesthetic perfection. There is a different weight of grief in the later "unfinished" *Pietas* of Michelangelo. There is the all but unbearable *Pieta* (sculpted for his own tomb) in which the hooded Nicodemus, with the face of Michelangelo himself, strains to support the weight of the dead Jesus, whose heavy limpness crushes the unpolished, disfigured face of Mary. The endeavour to support the dead Jesus is doomed, as the weight of death inexorably presses living and dead down to the earth.

This *Pieta* is a work that images the truth of being crushed. The stone speaks the spiritual truth of being crushed at the limit of all saying: the Never enacted without flinching, but not without compassion; the Never between which and the Once again lies an absolute gulf or abyss, impossible to bridge by any human act. It is an artwork of great philosophical honesty, spiritual honesty.

This image shames our evasion of truth through concepts; it demands the revitalization of concepts with elemental honesty. Hegel did know the grief of the death of children, but to realize this we must consult his *Letters*. There we meet the private Hegel who is *between* the intimacy of the existential and the public world of contemporary social history and philosophical logic. In his letters there is no dialectical consolation when dealing with the death of children.[34] He was deeply moved, indeed I suspect was at a loss for what to think regarding his own sister's breakdown. His response to the death of children, the children of friends and one of his own, is revealing. We find sympathy without easy consolation. We do not find any facile reasonableness. We find hints of a noble pessimism before some of life's inevitabilities.

His being at a loss before his sister's breakdown makes one wonder about Hegel's *silence* about Hölderlin after his breakdown? Was the more intimate Hegel here at a loss too, before the existential breakdown of a beloved this, a breakdown that was not merely dialectical? Was the howl of the disordered mind, and especially the madness of an intimate, a friend, something he could not accommodate in his logic? Is Hegel's silence revealing about the intimacy of being in Hegel himself, Hegel's own idiocy of spirit as a unique this? In general the letters reveal the idiotic Hegel, the Hegel of existential intimacy, not the magister of the logical *Begriff* as he is in the *Wissenschaft der Logik*. My sense is that the idiotic Hegel exhibits a different wisdom in the intimacy of being than is exhibited by the Hegel of public works. The idiocy of evil is allowed some place, one without dialectical encasement. Hegel does not logically fake his metaphysical helplessness. The idiocy of being strikes home to reveal elemental home truths that cannot be discursively articulated in the *Wissenschaft der Logik*.

Nor will it do to say: Hegel the private citizen is concerned with evil; but this is not really relevant to Hegel the philosophical writer of the *Logik*: here evil is just another category. This is to evade the issue, which to Hegel's own credit, he does not. His logos is not a formal logic; dialectical logic incorporates otherness in the concrete universal; we cannot escape by the sleight of hand of a private/public dualism; we must come to terms with evil and in its idiocy. We must respect Kierkegaard's reminder about the privacy of the individual philosopher. Obsession with world-history can produce forgetfulness of the idiocy of the philosopher's life. World-history and philosophy as science may give us surveys of macromovements in time and philosophical positions, which are exoteric and available to public categories. But the idiocy of the philosopher is that of the living individual trying to think. There is always something *esoteric* about the living philosopher as a thinking reed, hidden to world-history. Hegel's system tries to play mum about the idiocy, but this playing mum too is a form of philosophical idiocy, once we have ears to hear the significant silence.

Dialectical thinking tries to stay true to the dynamic unfolding of a process of development. Yet despite Hegel's desire for fidelity to concreteness, the dialectical explanation of evil in terms of the logical and world-historical universals risks neutralization of what must be named in all its non-neutrality. We find then an objectification of what cannot be objectified. Fidelity to the dynamic process is shortchanged in favour of the determinate structures that emerge in the process itself. The concrete "dynamism" in its otherness to thinking has a dimension of idiocy, intimacy of the individual will as individual, that cannot be reduced to any structure, even when it does instantiate universal structures. The consolation of a logic of evil then offers itself in place of the irredeemable ambiguity of good and evil as lived from within. If dialectical thought stays true to the dynamic process, there comes a point when, in respect of this process, it must acknowledge that something is beyond its power: an other it has not, cannot subordinate to itself. The honest dialectical thinker then must say: I cannot make sense of this, try as I may. . .

You will say: What about the acknowledgment of forgiveness in Hegel? Hegel is to be commended for not being silent on this. But my point could be reiterated. I have already hinted that forgiveness, too, if it is genuine, always exceeds complete dialectical structuring. There is never any rational necessity that one person forgive another; there is a *radical gratuitousness* about the act of forgiveness. This, too, is a kind of surd, but not the obscene surd of evil. It is, as it were, the benign or agapeic surd. What I am saying is quite well-known in its elemental intimacy, though perhaps for just that reason it is not always properly made the theme of philosophical reflection. If one attends to forgiveness, one will have little difficulty discovering this gratuitousness.

Consider: Another has offended, hurt me; my whole being has been insulted by this offense; but the other is sorry and asks for forgiveness. We all have the memory, in response to such an appeal, of being able to provide a host of reasons why forgiveness is not reasonable. One says: I will teach him a lesson; this insult is too much and there can be nothing between us anymore; my refusal to forgive will be justice for the first slight and so on. Reason can become extremely busy thinking up reasons why forgiveness makes no sense. The matter can be approached from the other side too. One might marshal all the reasons why one ought to forgive, and yet one may be incapable of forgiving. For forgiving is a willing, between which and reason there is a gap. It is a willingness rooted in the intimacy of being. It is in this gap, in this intermediate zone, between reasoning and willing that the gratuitousness of forgiving makes itself apparent.

To the self in this between there is a respect in which forgiveness makes no sense. To the rationalizing mind the deeper willingness of forgiving, as rooted in the intimacy of being, may appear idiotic, and in the worst sense. The between creates a kind of ethical epochē. I cannot find an absolutely necessary reason to forgive, an absolutely necessary reason not to forgive. A host of reasons, formal, informal, dialectical, transcendental, might be adduced on either side. But then, perhaps in a sudden moment of softening, I cease to be obdurate and yield: I forgive. Phenomenologically speaking, I believe there is no smooth dialectical transition to forgiveness. It is a leap in the middle, and across a gap that from the standpoint of one side makes no sense, but once having being made, makes absolute sense.

So it is not that forgiveness is senseless—Hegel is right in that regard—but something central to its mode of making sense does not have a dialectical structure. Invariably we have to resort to *metaphors* like "I softened, I gave way, I warmed to the other. . . ." These point to a leap of trust, of renewed trust in the offensive other. This leap of trust, bringing the energy of willingness to mind from a source of being beyond self-mediating mind, is an act of opening to the other that springs out of the intimacy of my being. Again here, the I as the willing I, like the I as the willful I, lives its own being with an inward thisness that is something idiotic; it cannot be included in a system. It precedes any system and exceeds all system. Like the cry from the heart, there cannot be a systematic science of forgiveness, for forgiveness is an act of assent whose most important concrete reality is its thisness as a this.

That we have to resort inevitably to metaphorical language means that the effort to think forgiveness dialectically in terms of the pure concept shows an unavoidable drift back to just that representational language Hegel claims to have overcome in pure philosophical discourse. Willy nilly, the Hegelian concept reveals itself as *continuing* to be in tension with the representational language it claims to sublate. The necessity of the representional language persists. You will say that Hegel takes care of this in that his dialectical *Aufhebung* is said always to have a moment of *preservation*. I know this, but this is not my point, not the kind of persistence I am talking about. This persistence is not just a moment of a dialectical *Aufhebung*, for it shows us the continued need of philosophy for its others, indeed the need of the dialectical concept itself for what is other than the concept, and in the concept itself.

This means that the philosophical concept can never be purely thought thinking itself in pure possession of the absolute content and in self-possession of the absolutely pure, that is for Hegel, nonrepresentational form. The other of the dialectical concept is within the concept itself, but not as an other that has been completely *aufgehoben*, hence completely comprehended, but as an otherness than always threatens to explode the pretension to such complete comprehension, should we simply *continue to think* about this always persistent otherness. The putative sublation of the other carries into its own putative self-transparency a Trojan horse that threatens the viability of all claims to absolute self-sufficiency that pure thinking makes on its own behalf. The other of thought is within the thought that tries to think itself, not as the completely appropriated other, but as a recalcitrant inward otherness that shakes dialectic from within, an inward otherness that produces from within the liquefaction of every claim made by dialectical thinking to absolutely self-sufficient self-mediation.

Thus in forgiveness, Hegel is dealing with a happening at the edge of dialectical thought. If he still wants to say that this is what dialectic thought is, namely, as I put it above, that leap across a gap that makes no sense from one side but *mirabile dictu* does make sense from the other, very well. But then we have to acknowledge clearly gratuities, surds, discontinuities within dialectic itself, and so abolish the general exclusion or overcoming or attenuation of these by the Hegelian system as a whole. I am not averse to a kind of *open* dialectical thinking that is the akin other of forgiveness. But then dialectic will have to shed some of the identifying marks that the panlogist Hegel ascribes to it. Dialectic would be other to dialectic, or be the power to open thought to its own other. But then it would not be dialectic in the sense that Hegel wants to retain.

It is not that Hegelian dialectic is not open to thought's other. It is. It is that it is open to thought's other in order to appropriate this other within a more encompassing process, within a totality of thought thinking itself. Thought thinks the other. Result: the other is thought. Ergo? Thought thinking the other is thought thinking the thought of the other. Ergo? Thought thinking the other is thought thinking itself. Result: Hegel will say we have *the* result; I will say we have barely begun. The logic is impeccable, but then the question is: Does logic leave us in the lurch at a certain point when thought is thinking the other? The answer is a very complex yes; but it is one that does not give up on logic either. The open dialectic I am suggesting could never be finally identified with thought thinking itself; for the other to which it is open, in the present instance, evil, is precisely a *breaking otherness* that breaches and irredeemably wounds the self-sufficient closure of thought thinking itself. To do justice to this sense of otherness, Hegel's dialectical self-mediation would have to be impelled beyond itself and become metaxological intermediation.

This means that one has to take very seriously the possibility that there are internal strains in Hegel's thought about which he may not have been self-conscious. Perhaps he might have shunned their implications had they been evident to him. For their full spelling means a rethinking of the nature of dialectical thinking as more radically open to the others of dialectic, others that cannot be simply thought on the paradigm of thought thinking itself. I think, in fact, that the power of Hegel's own thought comes not only from the formal structure of dialectic, but also from an ambiguous mixture of elements that are in strong tension with dialectic itself. Within the conceptual pacification the strife of being, the ontological strife lives on.

Meontological Perplexity and Evil:
A Negative Other than Negativity

Am I proposing the end or cessation of philosophical thinking? Does the matter so stun and paralyse philosophy that no further thought is possible? Not at all. Though evil and forgiveness are others to dialectical thought that philosophy can never entirely encapsulate, the deepest point is this: about such recalcitrant others philosophy, in fact, *can never stop thinking*. The point is not to give up on the thinking of these others, but dialectic will only take us so far. Dialectical philosophy comes to a limit that exceeds its thought. And yet we cannot but try to think that excess and that limit. A perplexity of thought arises that makes mind sleepless.

We cannot do away with philosophical thought. Hegel claims to think evil. I also say: Let us think it. But if what I say has any truth, the dialectical claim to comprehend evil turns out to be a lack of comprehension. The tension is between elemental philosophical honesty and systematic completeness. Philosophy needs to think honestly. It must not swindle thought with pretension to a comprehensiveness it cannot sustain. Here again many non-Hegelian, even anti-Hegelian philosophers are often more Hegelian than they realize. They want to sleep in the necessity of reason. The paradox is that there is a certain logical necessity that produces a slumber of spirit, a stopping of thought. The thought of evil produces a speculative insomnia that is the refusal to stop thinking. One cannot stop thinking about evil; it *makes* us think. Philosophical honesty says: here is an essential enigma to which thought must return again and again, without end.

Let me put it this way. Evil and forgiveness and related happenings are certainly susceptible to determinate accounts. Within certain limits one can speak of them discursively and at great length and with great illumination. Such determinate accounts are *ontic* articulations. But evil is most deeply an *ontological* enigma. I am not using these terms in any specifically Heideggerian sense, though Heidegger's distinction is not irrelevant. By an ontic articulation I mean one that explicates what is determinate in the matter at issue and that relative to philosophical comprehension is oriented to a certain determinate knowing of a determinate something. This is deeply related to the traditional requirement for intelligible discourse: that the philosophical saying or logos regard a determinate somewhat, in Aristotle's terms a *tode ti*, and that the saying itself be a determinate articulation. An ontological concern, by contrast, refers us to the grounds of the ontic with respect to its being or perhaps nonbeing, and hence takes us to the very edge of all determinacy. For the ontological ground of the determinate is not another determinate thing. Nor is the ground of ontic saying simply another determinate, ontic proposition. Thus, to speak intelligibly of all determinate things implies a necessary indeterminacy that grounds intelligibility, but that is not intelligible in the same determinate way.

What I am calling the ontological dimension with respect to evil emerges in relation to what I have called the intimacy of being. It also emerges in relation to an indeterminacy preceding and exceeding every determination, the negative otherness that resists complete determinate saying. If evil raises an ontological perplexity, there is no determinate ontic proposition that will univocally answer or resolve this perplexity. There is no ontic answer. If there is a resolution or absolution it will be elsewhere, if anywhere at all. In another sense the "resolution" will be "nowhere," and perhaps we might better speak here of a *meontological* dimension, in that the matter at issue refers us, not to the being of being, but to the "apparition" of a non-being (*mē on*), a nothingness in being and as an irreducible other to determinate being.

I am not talking about a determinate negation in the Hegelian scheme where, following Spinoza, determination is negation. I am talking about a negative indeterminacy other than determinate negativity. I am talking about a more radically resistant otherness, even the logically impossible "happening" or "apparition" of the "altogether not" (*to mēdemōs on*). This may seem impossible for logic, as Parmenides was the first to point out; but the logically impossible nevertheless happens, and hence this impossibility is not impossible, not existentially, not ontologically impossible. Indeed Parmenides logically tries to quarantine this thought of nothing which, as the thought of nothing, is not a determinate thought at all, and hence a non-thought. But this effort at quarantine, indeed exorcism, implicitly , testifies to the continued "happening" of this thought/nonthought, testifies to its persistent dissident threat to the respectable discourse of determinate logic. Are not Spinoza's determinate negation and Hegel's dialectical negation only more sophisticated reformulations of Parmenides' logical doctoring of the thought/nonthought of evil as such a nothing, a negative indeterminacy? Are not their senses of determinate negation shadowed by a "negative" that precedes and exceeds their systematic articulations?

If the thought/nonthought of evil reveals this ontological/meonto-logical negative indeterminacy, or never-to-be-fully-determined nega-tivity (as other to every determinate negation), if evil is such an enigma, then it does not pose a question or problem with respect to our ontic ignorance. In a significant sense there is no *problem* of evil; for every problem is determinate and hence implicitly presupposes its correlatively determinate solution. There is no determinate problem of evil; there is no determinate solution to evil. For evil as ontological precipitates an essential perplexity, always other to determinate knowing, always in excess of determinate accounts, a perplexity that in its meontological recalcitrance gives us, you might say, a kind of metaphysical migraine. Moreover, even when we have made the effort to say everything determinate that is possible, we still find ourselves wrapped in this metaphysical perplexity. To this perplexity the philosopher is forced to recur again and again. One of the supreme nobilities of speculative metaphysics is its willingness to mindfully return again and again to such ineradicable yet essential perplexities.

At times Hegel's dialectical account functions chiefly as an ontic account; at other times, he touches on the ontological dimension of the perplexity, only to draw back again to the ontic level. He is sometimes between these two sides in a thought-provoking way; sometimes he wavers between them only to flee the metaphysical migraine and lose sight of the ontological perplexity. It might even be the case that Hegel lays out many of the potentially relevant ontological dimensions: cleavage, anguish, reconciliation, and so forth. But his particular way of putting these together is finally to diminish the ontological dimension of the matter, which as meontological is not really properly described as a "dimension" at all. This diminishment would be consistent with the entire thrust of Hegelian dialectics that insistently travels from indeterminacy to complete determination. But it is just such a complete determination that evil as meontological always resists, I think.

At times one suspects, indeed detects in Hegel's thinking a wavering between negativity understood as determinate negation and a more radical indeterminate negativity. But Hegel always draws away from this wavering by saying that the more radical indeterminate negativity *determines itself through its own dialectical self-mediation*, and hence all negation is finally determination, in fact, the dialectical self-determination of the absolute process. So, as we have seen, evil becomes one moment of this total dialectical self-determination. And hence the radical indeterminate negativity is said to be finally overcome in the dialectically self-mediating whole. The presupposition of Hegel's audacious claim to comprehensive *Wissenschaft* is the inclusion of the negative within the absolute. This inclusion is related to what I termed an erotic absolute: the erotic absolute must determine its own absoluteness by comprehensively negating its own lack of initial, empty indeterminacy. But what if evil reveals an indeterminate negativity always other than determinate negation? What if it reveals, not an erotic negative indeterminacy, but the perverse other of the agapeic overdetermination of being as good in itself? Then it cannot be included in a system and the Hegelian system is not finally completable. This is why Hegel's claim to systematic completeness stands or falls on how we understand evil. That is why the very nature of the philosophical enterprise is at stake here.

Hegel's belief that all indeterminate negativity is included in the dialectically self-mediating whole is consistent with his acquiescence in the Cartesian substitution of doubt for wonder as the beginning of philosophy. The issue of evil as a negative otherness other than determinate negativity thus bring us back to the question of the beginning of philosophy, a very Hegelian theme. Wonder (*thaumazein*) is the pathos of the philosopher, Socrates and Plato say, and also its archē, as Aristotle reiterates. But if all otherness, negative or affirmative, were to be domesticated by dialectic in a complete determinate account, this originating wonder would vanish, for then there would be no enigma, no hiddenness any more.

Since Descartes, doubt, not wonder, has been the beginning of philosophy. Doubt can be seen as wonder's negative counterpart, and their difference mirrors philosophically two senses of transcendence or excess. Doubt treats negativity as essentially determinable, hence treats every ontological perplexity as an excess that thought will transmute into a problem susceptible of a completely determinate account. Wonder, by contrast, is a mode of astonishment or marveling. Most fundamentally it is a mindful marveling, metaphysical astonishment at the "that it is" of the sheer being there of beings and of being *simpliciter*. Wonder is also astonished at negativities that seem to open like abysses. Hence, it treats ontological perplexity as an excess that thought can never exhaustively determine as an ontic problem, a perplexity that can be deepened but never completely dispelled, an excess that cannot be mastered, though it might be mindfully acknowledged in profound metaphysical reflection.

Horror too is a kind of wonder, but a negative wonder that does not marvel before being but recoils before a deforming nihilation of being. The word "monstrous" itself indicates its own bond with wonder and the marvellous. "*Monstrare*" means to show, as in "demonstrate," one of the loves of the philosopher. *Monstrum* is also related to "*monere*"—itself connected to *mens*, mind; *Monēta* was the name of the mother of the Muses, Greek *Mnēmosunē*; *monere*—to point out, to remind, to admonish, warn. The monstrous implies a spectacle of the excessive, the "too much"—and we can be exceeded by dark abysses as by high mysteries. For instance, in Catholic sacramental practise the "Monstrance" is the sacred , glass-faced shrine by way of which the body of God is shown. In both horror and wonder we find the paradox of an excess that is shown and that yet cannot be shown, demonstrated by any logic of determinate concepts. The horror of the monstrous shadows all showing. We are reminded of what Milton calls "darkness visible." Our fascinated horror with "darkness visible" hints at the meontological perplexity that is the shadow of wonder as ontological perplexity. Metaphysical mind must admit this horror and try to think it through, as best it can.

Hegel's search for a completely determinate account is evidenced in his hubristic claim in the *Phenomenology* to have transformed the philosophical love of wisdom into actual knowing. Hegel wanted to overcome doubt through doubt itself, as the negative that negates itself and hence determines itself completely. So the *Phenomenology* evidences what Hegel calls a self-accomplishing skepticism (*sich vollbringende Skeptizismus*).[35] This is to share, indeed to claim to complete Descartes' quest for certainty in purely autonomous self-thinking thought. The Hegelian Idea as the thought that thinks itself is a more complex reformulation of Descartes' *cogito me cogitare*, implying as it does the recovery of Aristotle's *noēsis noēseōs*, but in the post-Cartesian light of Kant's transcendental unity of apperception. Let us grant that in Hegel's corpus we can find places when dissident forms of otherness seem to stray outside the circle of completely self-determining thought. Nevertheless, whichever way we parse it, Hegel's claim about absolute knowing as thought thinking *itself* always implies a dialectical subordination of otherness. Thus, again with reference to the *Phenomenology*, Hegel seeks the dialectical identity of truth and *self*-certainty. Hence his controversial claim that philosophy as love of wisdom (where ontological wonder is never put to rest, only deepened) at last becomes wisdom as science (*Wissenschaft*), where the negatively transcending power of doubt is affirmatively transformed into completely determinate systematic knowledge.

Can our agonized ontological perplexity before evil be fully translated into an ontic "doubt," a negative that will negate itself, and so become amenable to being completely thought as self-determining? Or does this other negative flee before our every effort to determine it completely in such a determinate ontic way? A negative other than determinate negativity that defeats our epistemological curiosity—even in its very provocation of our metaphysical perplexity? We must ask once again, out of the metaphysical migraine of ontological perplexity: Does not evil as a recalcitrant, negative otherness chasten, if not irremediably chagrin, the self-assurance of this claim of Hegel? Does it not shame this claim?

Does this question not transmute into ashen grey the green certainty of the younger Hegel of the *Phenomenology*? Did the older Hegel not secretly know this and secretly communicate it when saying: philosophy paints its grey on grey; the Owl of Minerva takes flight at dusk? What is the meaning of metaphysical grey? An old Hegel with secrets? But from the standpoint of the system, there are supposed to be no secrets. If Hegel had his secrets, does not this confirm my point: that there is an intimacy of thisness, of inward otherness that philosophy itself must address. Is not this intimacy of inward thisness that of the philosopher himself? Is this not the inward idiocy of the philosopher himself, and precisely as a *philosophical thinker*? Would not this be an idiocy out of which the system is spoken but which the system itself cannot determinately explain or overtly acknowledge? Does not the system that renounces, denounces all secrets paradoxically hide its own ultimate source, continue to keep its final secret—Hegel's own thinking mind in its inward otherness?

One recalls the story that Hegel said only one person had understood him, and even the understanding of that one was not certain. Was not Hegel talking about himself? Would not such an admission make a mockery of any pretension of the system to logical completeness? An other Hegel will claim to explain everything, including the thoughts of God, but can he completely explain what is deeply intimate to his own thought, namely, Hegel himself, the inward idiocy of the philosopher himself? The Owl may take flight at dusk, but at uncertain hours between dark and dawn the ghost of ontological perplexity begins again to flicker and to haunt the philosopher's mind. The metaphysical migraine returns.

You object that Hegel knew this. He might say: I recognize the limits of what can be philosophically said. But there are certain things that are not appropriate for philosophical saying. He might say that his dialectical categories hold "generally," "for the most part." He need not deny contingencies that lie outside complete categorial incorporation. He might even claim, as he does, that only his logic finds a place for contingency as a necessary category. But there are certain contingencies, he will say, that are not finally of philosophical interest. Will this rejoinder give us philosophical peace? Or will categorial peace still leave us with a different philosophical insomnia? As I said before, we might be willing to let this contingency by in cases like sense-certainty, even Krug's pen, but evil is a particularity that can hook into the philosopher's craw and not let go, even despite all this categorial coaxing. Talk of categorial "for the most part" will not philosophically wash with this devastating contingency, will not wash philosophy free of its contamination, perhaps devastation by this otherness.

I suspect that Hegel had a touch of bad conscience even about Krug's pen, as if it were an irritant or categorial gadfly he could not systematically swat. And the above categorial modesty might be generally acceptable, but Hegel himself is not so humble. In one sense, Hegel's philosophical greatness is that there is nothing for him that might not be made the theme of philosophical articulation. He will not resort to the escape tactic of simply separating philosophy from its others. This would be to dig a categorial bolthole for philosophy into which it might run every time a difficult perplexity arose. Philosophy lives in a dialectical and metaxological interplay with these others. Hence, it is challenged in its saying to be profoundly open and attentive to these others in their phenomenological richness. I agree with Hegel—my disquiet is not that philosophy should think these others, but whether the dialectical way of doing so blinds us to certain things which *philosophically* might have to be said *otherwise*.

I have no objection to the will to say such otherness philosophically. I question whether the reduction of philosophical saying to dialectic is itself at odds with philosophy's necessary openness to otherness. There may be forms of otherness, evil is one, on which dialectic breaks. To acknowledge this is not to reject dialectic *tout court*. It is philosophically to think through its nature. It is also to think through the nature of those recalcitrant others which rock philosophy back on the limits of its own special modes of mindfulness. Perhaps Hegel would agree with me on this double requirement of philosophy: to remain true to thought; to achieve thought truly open to otherness. My question is whether dialectical thought always remains true to this second requirement, even when it protests loudly that it does. I do not think so, and it is with the aim of respecting this second requirement that I have developed the notion of metaxological mindfulness.

Beyond the proprieties of categorial pigeonholing, the question of dialectic and evil is not only a matter of Hegel scholarship, but has a deep ethical and religious, as well as philosophical significance. It concerns an issue that perennially perplexes all thinking human beings and consequently has central importance for philosophy itself. I have suggested that the issue also concerns the ability of philosophical thought to face up honestly to questions that may finally resist its efforts to conceptually master them. This question of how philosophy is to relate to what is other to philosophy is one of the most debated issues in current discussion, since it touches on the very self-identity of the philosophical project, the limits of dialectic in relation to different forms of otherness, and also with the question of the limits of philosophy itself.

I think here of Theodor Adorno when he famously said that after Auschwitz one could no longer write poetry. He also implied there could be no speculative philosophy after Auschwitz, and this relative to his development of negative dialectics, in contradistinction to Hegel's affirmative dialectics. I sympathize with Adorno's efforts to raise the question of the non-identical, the other. I think, however, that Adorno does not do enough justice to the non-identical in Hegelian dialectics. He is too impatient to paint Hegel as a philosopher of identity. We have seen sufficient subtlety and richness in Hegel's view to reject the imputation of a mere philosophy of identity. Hard questions must be put to Hegel, but such questions have to be subtle, more subtle than subtle dialectic itself.

In implying the end of speculative philosophy after Auschwitz, Adorno states his sense of what philosophy ought to be in stating what philosophy ought not to be now, namely, speculative philosophy of identity. Is there possible a speculative philosophy of non-identity, a philosophical thinking that lives in an uncompromising acknowledgment of the irreducible others of self-thinking thought? I answer yes. I answer also that a thinking through of self-thinking thought leads us in this speculative direction. So the question of evil and dialectic concerns the very future of philosophy and what form its thought can take in the light of this negative otherness. I must side with Hegel against Adorno in rejecting the impossibility of speculative thought after Auschwitz, though I side with Adorno against Hegel in thinking that such speculation has to be the thinking of the other of thought. It seems to me that the thought of such otherness, in fact, implies the strongest rejection of any putative end of speculative philosophy.

To the extent that the thinking of evil has revealed aspects other to dialectical incorporation, to the extent that evil as an ontological perplexity brings back the old metaphysical insomnia, then speculative philosophy will never sleep easy and its future, as a thought that thinks not just itself but also its others, is not in doubt. Perhaps speculative philosophy conceived exclusively as dialectically self-mediating thought has reached a certain limit in Hegel, a limit that calls for a reassessment and rethinking of speculation. But at that limit, dialectical self-mediation may be opened by speculative thought, and not necessarily of a Hegelian sort, to the other in another way. And if I am right, philosophy did not have to wait until Auschwitz to be made sleepless by monstrous evil. The horror of Auschwitz magnifies into public visibility, if you like into world-historical visibility, that to which we are oblivious in the intimacy of being, the sleeping monstrousness in inwardness itself.

The philosopher does not have to wait for an Auschwitz to ask about the limits of dialectic. Indeed *after* Auschwitz we will soon want to sleep again. As we saw in the father's murder of the son, all that is needed to devastate the pretensions of mastering thought is *one* instance of evil as qualitatively unconditional. The category of quantity has secondary application here, if it has any application at all. One instance of evil as qualitatively unconditional provokes thought in relation to an enigmatic absolute singularity that is not a substitutable, replaceable variable and hence not an illustration of a general thesis.

Suppose such evil only appeared once and once only. Once is enough. There is a break and we are in a different world of thought. There is no going back behind this radical rupture and the sleeplessness of mind it will henceforth always call forth. Once is enough. Once is enough to change everything, certainly enough to force philosophy to ponder its enigma. In fact, it is our forgetfulness of this "Once" that contributes to the precipitation and repetition of the Auschwitzes of world-history. Speculative philosophy henceforth will have to think such enigmas, be on its mindful guard against the oblivion of this "Once." And yet here, in a lesson very other to the Hegelian lesson of sense-certainty, since it is an uncertain lesson in the senseless, our lack of mastery shows itself once more. Why? Because this "Once" is absolutely singular, we are always, almost at once, forgetting it once more. We cannot stand too long the thought of evil. Mind must sleep, else it breaks. And yet, break it must. Without this break there is no idiot wisdom.

Chapter 5

Comedy and the Failure of Logos: On Dialectic, Deconstruction, and the Mockery of Philosophy

Philosophy and the Mockery of Logos

The idiocy of evil shakes our confidence that dialectic offers the final word. A surd of negative otherness seems to mock its comprehensive claims. Should we fall to weeping at this humiliation of philosophy? Is this merely a humiliation? And is this then our only option, namely, a metaphysical lamentation before the meaningless? But is it really fair to say that philosophy's speculative venture has ever been a stranger to such extremities? Does not Hegel reveal his own ambiguous doubleness: at one and the same time, he grapples with what seems an utterly recalcitrant otherness, while always being tempted by the consolation of conceptualization, namely, the belief that the fully articulated concept will domesticate the otherness of evil? Have not philosophers—and Hegel is no exception—always existed uneasily in a middle space *between* the uncompromising desire to comprehend being in the fullest sense possible and a desire to acknowledge what may resist that first desire to comprehend? Have they not existed uneasily *between* the search for an articulate logos of being and the recalcitrant reality of different surds of otherness that chastise the conceptual ambitions of philosophical logos?

Hegel is a philosopher who *always answers back* such chastisements: he will not let the surd of otherness be an absurd other, will not take the chastising reminder as a final curb on speculative reason. That he always answers back is the basis of the impression that he *always has an answer,* that there is nothing that will ever stun him into silence. I recall again the way Aquinas was stunned into silence at the end of his life. I find it hard to think of Hegel saying with

Aquinas about his speculative work: it seems to me as straw, *videtur mihi ut palea*. This is the contrast: Aquinas is willing to say "It is as nothing," and say this *at the end*; Hegel is indeed willing to say, "It is as nothing," but not at the end; only on the way to the end will he say, "It seems like straw"; the "It is nothing" will be overturned at the end into its dialectical opposite and he will claim the triumph.

The last word for Hegel cannot be a word that subverts itself into silence. Hegelian speech would be a complete speech, a self-generating and self-authenticating logos. Always answering back, there will be no final other to stand opposed to it. The nothing of evil will be dialectically overturned into reconciliation. Hegel answers back on behalf of the world-spirit whose teleology in time, whose absolute reconciliation in history, Hegel answers for. If I am right, however, the idiocy of the monstrous talks back in a further sense: the complete self-authenticating speech is called into question; moreover, it is called into question by a logos that names the failure of logos to comprehend entirely or conceptually to master evil in a triumphal rationalization.

We can weep; we can be silent; we can continue to talk. But can we also laugh? Can philosophy laugh? How can philosophy laugh? Laughter is quite close to dialectic in that each in its own way tries to say "It is nothing." To say "It is nothing"—and yet to go on, to continue to be, perhaps differently. Are not both philosophy and comedy ways of dealing with the absurd: not simple denials of the absurd, but modes of saying "It is nothing," which are affirmative in revealing ways? Is laughter an other to philosophical logos that again exceeds dialectical mastery? Or are we not here significantly close to the heart of a crucial tension for the speculative philosopher, namely, that his speculative concepts look like madness, look crazy from the standpoint of sound healthy commonsense? Is not this another manifestation of the idiocy of philosophy? Can we now ask if this idiocy indicates more elusive, perhaps even a richer condition of being than even sound healthy commonsense offers?

After all, Hegel himself did say that philosophy seems to demand of commonsense that it walk on its head. We normally only think of acrobats or clowns as walking on their heads. Is this the crazy somersault that philosophy asks of mind? If so, is not philosophical logic mad? Is there not a kind of internal other, an inward otherness to philosophical logos in this turning around of mind, this rotation or *periagōgē* that Plato thought a necessary condition for enlightenment? How do we explain the speculative *peripeteia* of Plato's strange myth in the *Statesman* of the *reversed world*? Such inversions, rotations, reversals return us to the intermediate condition of the philosopher, his being between the soaring of speculative reason and the hard realities that brutally remind thought of an otherness its speculative surge has not exceeded, cannot exceed. The philosopher as intermediate is a mediator between these extremes. Dialectical thinking is just one mode of this mediation. Is it adequate to the extremes? Is it adequate to the comedy of thought that can sometimes be played out, leap in the between?

I am asking questions which will make the panlogist Hegelian shudder. The Hegelian who thinks of philosophy as essentially a logical doctrine will see these questions as renegade. They tell us nothing about the calm self-unfolding of the Idea. The logicist rebuke will be: there is no crazy mocking laughter in the pages of the *Wissenschaft der Logik.* But suppose the following. Suppose one were a Hegelian logicist, and suppose as one reads the pages of the *Logic,* an unexpected mocking laughter were suddenly to ring out? Ring out from where? From Hegel himself? From the Logos? From God? From Nothing? From the Silence? Let us say an agapeic laughter overflowing from an indeterminate/overdetermined Other. What logically would one do with that laughter?

One might say: "It is nothing," turn the page, and go on with the self-development of the Idea. Let us imagine Hegel as he was writing the *Logic.* Let us suppose he has gotten past the *category* of Nothing, and the entire dialectical unfolding of categories is well launched. And then suddenly a dissident voice whispers mischievously: "It is nothing," "It is as straw?" What would Hegel do? Would he be startled? Would the dialectical concept pause, look around and draw in its breath? Let us suppose Hegel, content on having put the category Nothing behind him, moves to another category, say *Measure.* As more dialectically developed than the category of Nothing, Measure would seem to have the logical measure of nothing. But would the startled Hegel have the measure of this "It is nothing, It is straw"?

One might imagine him saying: "Since I think the thoughts of God, how could it be nothing, how could it be straw?" And yet there is this persistent voice of logos that mocks logos and that will not be silenced. Suppose now there emerges a harsh edge to the mocking voice: "It is nothing; it is as straw." Hegel might perhaps retort with dialectical harshness, negate the negation, exorcise it with some secret incantation against misology, an incantation somehow passed on from Socrates and inherited through the secret life blood of the philosophical tradition. Perhaps this charm works and, yes, the voice grows more gentle under the incantation. But then, no, it whispers impertinently: "No, I am not the voice of misology; the voice that says "It is nothing," I, too, am one of the voices of logos; hear me!"

I would like to think that Hegel could not, would not silence this voice. For would not this voice give utterance to just that absolute unease that Hegel himself knew thought to be? The logicist Hegelian will impatiently ask: What then is the point of this ghostly voice? Something like this: suppose the ghostly voice was a dissident voice of *Geist*. Then the voice that startles us could not be dismissed as the voice of a misology that simply refuses to take seriously the power of philosophical logos. No: the voice of logos rather reveals itself as many-voiced, as plurivocal.

Let us say in an ancient metaphor, recently being refurbished, that philosophy is a conversation. A conversation must be many-voiced, plurivocal. Even monologue is only possible on the assumption of plurivocity; for in monologue, if the one voice is to converse, that same one voice has to *pluralize itself* into a diversity of different tongues. This plurivocity here means: the mocking voice that mocks the voice of logos is itself deeply intimate to that mocked voice. This means: the mockery of philosophy is itself a philosophical mockery that has heard the mockery of a non-philosophical other. The philosopher hears the voice of the other laughing at the madness of speculative thought. But the voice of the other, in turn, becomes his own voice, in an even more harsh form in the absolute unrest of thinking, which derides its own pretensions to absoluteness—just in its ineluctable search for absoluteness. Philosophy fails and cannot go on; philosophy must go and risk its failure once more.

Again: please do not reprove me and insist that mockery has nothing to do with philosophy; please do not scold and say that the logical concept is exempt from mockery. The logical concept may desire to exempt itself from mockery, but the philosopher himself as idiotic, as *idiōtēs*, is *between* the uncontaminated self-sufficiency of the concept and various happenings of rupturing otherness that interrupt just that putative self-sufficiency. Philosophers *mock themselves* by recounting the mockery of the others to philosophy. What is the necessary skepticism of philosophy but its willingness to let its own identity be marked by reason's cruel mockery, reason's own self-mockery?

Philosophical thought can be strange, a stranger even to itself. Consider here what Aristotle, grand philosophical pontiff of commonsense, says: the life of the philosopher is a *bios xenikos*: it is a strange life; it is the life of a stranger. I say: it is a life of thought that is willing to think of otherness, otherness undreamt of within the narrow confines of commonsense. This is speculative strangeness, the speculative otherness: *xenikos*, madness from the point of view of sound, healthy commonsense. The life of speculative thought is other, strange; and the irony is that it is Aristotle who tells us this—

Aristotle, the prince of all logicists who are at home in the temperate zones of middle being, normally called commonsense. The philosopher, who defends the commonsense middle, is driven to the extremities of middle being, and there becomes a stranger. Does his thought then become strange, not only to commonsense, but even to itself? Does it there exceed itself, find itself exceeded by what it cannot think and yet must try to think? Does it there not run the risk of not being master of its own conceptualizations? At the limit does it risk its own breaking, breaking of its own self-mastery, breaking on otherness that stuns it into silent astonishment, *thaumazein*? Was the silence of Aquinas this last silence of a *bios xenikos*? Is this strange excess of speculative thought its participation in the abandon of agapeic mind?

Remember that Hegel loved Aristotle, and closed the circle of his *Encyclopedia of the Philosophical Sciences* with an incantation that brings before the mind Aristotle's *noēsis noēseōs*. The closed circle of the speculative system gives us the apotheosis of thought thinking itself. (We are reminded also of Heidegger's reverent reinvocation of Parmenides' well-circled truth, *eukukleos Alētheia*.) There is a paradox here. This acme of speculative mind is described as thought being absolutely *at home with itself*. But what then of the *bios xenikos*? Is everything strange done away with in thought thinking itself? Or does mind's effort to be absolutely at home yield an opening to the absolutely strange? Does thought thinking itself open to the strange thought of the unthinkable, the thought of the ultimate other? Does the singular mediation of dialectical mind open to the double mediation of metaxological mind, and philosophy become, not just thought thinking itself but thought trying to think the ultimate other that exceeds thought? For there is this ineradicable difference between the philosopher and God. We philosophers find the thought of God the thought of the most strange; the most logical thought is also the most mad; and yet we try to be at home in this thought that makes thought utterly homeless.

The shadow of a fundamental strangeness, a fundamental unmastered otherness hovers over Aristotle's *noēsis noēseōs*, hovers over Hegel's pious invocation of its community with the Idea, an invocation that recalls a filial community of philosophers across the millennia. The sons of logos are shadowed by a strange paternal otherness, to which they, too, will become strangers if their will is to think only their *own* thoughts. It is out of this shadow, as though from nothing or from excess, that the voice saying "It is nothing" erupts. This is the voice of the agapeic other that withdraws from self-insistence in order to free philosophy to be the thought that thinks itself; the voice that, just in its withdrawal from self-insistence, cannot be completely

conceptualized in the philosophical thought that only thinks itself;
the voice that goads speculative philosophy to think the unthinkable
stranger or strangeness of being.

But we will not be allowed to lose ourselves in speculative
pretension, for the voice of strangeness will deflate us again. It will
return us to a more mundane mockery of philosophy. Consider the
classic story of this mockery. In the *Theaetetus* (174a ff.) Socrates
retells the tale of Thales and the Thracian maid. As we recall, the
story says that Thales was walking out one evening, so absorbed in
the heavens above as to be dead to the solid ground beneath and before
him. He fell into a ditch and a Thracian maid scornfully upbraided
this comic upturn and downfall. Sound commonsense will say:
philosophy will land on its head if it does not walk on its feet; in
soaring above the earth, philosophy tries to walk on its head but the
result is ridiculous. I do not know if Hegel was thinking of Thales
when asking commonsense to walk on its head, but there is no doubt
he was aware that speculative thought will appear ridiculous, risible
to healthy commonsense. But notice: it is not from the Thracian maid
that we know of this perhaps apocryphal tale of Thales. The Thracian
maid laughed and was silent, too busy to bother further with the folly;
the meaning of her laugh did not bother her, did not haunt her. But
that laugh, its possible meaning, did haunt, still haunts the philosopher. It haunted, always haunts the philosopher, for its stinging
meaning might be that philosophy is without meaning.

The radical unrest of the philosopher is his willingness to
entertain the possibility that the Thracian maid was right: philosophy
is a *bios xenikos*, that is, ridiculous, idiotic. The philosopher is willing
to think against himself, find against himself. He is willing to listen
to the voices of otherness, the laughter of the other, the Thracian maid,
from beyond his own thought. The Thracian maid laughed and passed
on, but Thales pondered this other. Socrates, Plato pondered this
laughter. Hence we only know of this laughter because *a philosopher
reminds us* of it. It is Socrates who renews the opportunity for all
Thracian maids to laugh once again at the folly of speculative
philosophy. It is *the philosopher* who lets ring across history the
mockery of the Thracian maid.

Logos cannot repress, does not want to repress that mockery.
Philosophers laugh at themselves; philosophers set themselves up for
a fall, *knowingly set themselves up for a fall.* Thus, it was inevitable
that a Hegel would generate a Marx in this sense: When Marx claimed
to turn Hegel upside down, what was this but the materialistic
mockery of speculative philosophy? The word of derision with this
materialistic mockery is: "mystification." Hegel is to Marx as Thales

is to the Thracian maid. In Marx the Thracian peasant has been reincarnated as a revolutionary proletariat, but what persists is the mockery of speculative philosophy and its rational dream of the absolute: the dream is derided as a wild goose chase after nothing.

It seems to me that the greater the philosopher, and the more he dreams of the ultimate, the more he is willing to let this voice ring out, the more he is mocked by the suspicion, even if only in brief interrupting moments of private thought, in the *peripeteia* of idiocy, that what he offers to us as absolute reason is as straw, is as nothing. The philosopher would prefer to be Hamlet rather than Fortinbras, prefer not "greatly to find quarrel in a straw." Hamlet: the princely stranger out of joint, timely and untimely; Fortinbras: warrior pretender to the domestic throne. Marx is one Fortinbras to Hegel's Hamlet—Hegel has had more than one Fortinbras. Is Hegel himself Hamlet enough? The greatness of philosophical thought is its willingness to break at the limits of thought, its readiness to turn its questioning on itself, and risk the thought that it too—genuinely great in its systematic grandeur—is as straw, as nothing. Philosophical thought, too, might be just the quintessence of dust.

Is not the greatness of philosophy its own suspicion of the misery of its greatness? Is not the daring of its eros its willingness to distrust its own eros? Will it not offer itself up as a sacrifice: the self-negation of closed thought by thought itself as self-transcending—thought that would give up all metaphysical conceit, willing to go under in its going beyond closed thought? What God-service, *Gottesdienst* asks these sacrifices? Is not the greatness of speculative mind its willingness to take all ground from under itself in its questing, its questioning of the absolute ground of all that is? Should not the philosopher himself be the first to ask: Is my systematic logic of the absolute but the dream of a thinking reed?

Deconstruction and the Mockery of Philosophy

I further pursue the matter in terms of the hostilities and affinities between deconstructive thinking and Hegelian dialectic. I will focus on these questions: What are the limits of philosophical logos, if any? Has philosophical logos been blind, or blinded itself to such limits? Has it masked the limits in pretence of their nonexistence, dismissing them with a hubristic "It is nothing"? Or has philosophical logos always exhibited its sense of the intimacy in logos itself of its own other? Has it displayed the speculative uneasiness of its own disquieting self-knowledge? Is there not a kind of philosophical laughter of the logos itself that delights in debunking itself, delights in the metaphysical comedy of exposing the failures of its own pretensions to absoluteness?

Deconstructive thought is a not very deeply veiled mockery of traditional philosophy, usually excoriated *en bloc* as "metaphysics of presence," or "ontotheology" or "phallogocentrism." A cue is taken from Nietzsche's mockery of philosophy as Platonism: the high-minded idealities of Platonic logos are debunkingly exposed as the ruses of secret, but lower realities, namely, the base energies of the body. The speculative gaze of Thales on the heavens above is brought down to earth again and the sometimes crass phallogocentric games of terrestrial will-to-power that thinkers play there with the woman, truth.

Let us say that the Thracian maid is revived in an unexpected place, and given a new life in deconstructive thought. True, the laughter is not any longer the elemental outburst of a peasant girl: it is the exotic textualist wit of a professor of *l'Ecole Normale Supérieure*, the philologically fastidious punning of a scholar who overtly presents himself as a daring member of the revolutionary avant-garde. The textual scholar replaces the peasant—though, since this form of marginal scholarship has ensconced itself as a new establishment, in fact it is the pseudo avant-garde pedant who has replaced the peasant woman. Whether we laugh at philosophy with a peasant outburst or a textual snigger, the fact remains that speculative thought is finally dismissed, sent on its way, as risible.

Deconstructionists like to laugh at a caricature of the philosophical other they purportedly debunk. At least Nietzsche was honest when he said in the posthumously published writings: *My Plato—a caricature!* One wishes that followers of Nietzsche took to heart the devastation this confession *ought* to wreak on the heavy-headed rhetorical strategies, used by these deconstructive followers to "overcome the tradition." Nietzsche's confession gives the game away. "Overcoming the Western tradition" simply amounts to laughing at Plato, mocking the metaphysician. I will not object to the mockery of philosophy. I will only repeat my point: It is not Nietzsche but Socrates, Plato's Socrates, who is the first philosopher who *mocks himself.* Are the deconstructionist spawn of Nietzsche capable of such wicked self-mockery?

The deconstructionist likes to *laugh at* the pieties of the others, the poor metaphysicians of pure presence, and their pathetic devotion to ideals like truth, goodness, wholeness. When these pieties do not invite mocking scorn, they precipitate a yawn. The derisive yawn says: after Nietzsche, after Heidegger, after Derrida, everyone now knows that we are finished with speculative thought, finished with philosophy. (Who is everyone?; when I hear the rhetoric of "After," I cannot suppress the thought of Schopenhauer's diatribe against the *After-philosoph*.) So please do not sigh with nostalgia for any absolute, but gird our tongues and texts in the brave new world of post-Rortian conversation. I will be silent. The deconstructionist likes to laugh at the other. I do not think he likes to be laughed at. I plead the excuse that I have learned the strategy from him. If the deconstructionist can laugh at philosophy, why cannot the philosopher laugh at the deconstructionist? This is supposed to be a *two-way* conversation, after all.

Or will the deconstructionist pull a fast one on the philosopher at this point and say: You have failed to understand me, you are misrepresenting me, please be clear and distinct. The scholastic whine of false representation (oops! I thought we were beyond representation) here means: I can debunk logocentrism, but when the philosopher tries to debunk deconstruction, then the deconstructionist issues his diktat to the philosopher from Mount Sinai: please be logical! There is a wickedly unwitting mockery in this plea to be taken seriously, but it is not the wicked self-mockery of the philosopher. A deconstructionist will say: there are no readings, only misreadings; but when the deconstructionist is misread, his irritation is palpable, as in Derrida's righteous rebuttal, let us call it "logocentric overkill," of Searle's logocentric critique of deconstruction. Too late we realize the hidden irony in the fact that the deconstructionist knows only too well how to play the logocentric game. But peasants and proletariats win my respect; they need no scholarly initiation here; this game is colloquially known to them as having your cake and eating it too.

Very well, philosophers have not always lived up to the truth of the old wisdom: what's sauce for the goose is sauce for the gander. I note in passing that this ancient wisdom escapes any charge of *phallogocentrism*, for it transcends the dualistic opposition of male and female. Let us call it the ancient basis for a new deconstructionist feminism. I am being frivolous, you say. But I have read many a deconstructionist text that makes a plodding virtue of frivolity and that might have been better served by a little respect for the domestic wisdom of commonsense. The fact is that the original Thracian maid did bother to laugh at Thales. Why? Because the speculative philosopher does manifest a genuine spiritual seriousness. I suspect that the woman would not even bother to laugh at the deconstructionist: textual scholars watching *themselves* for fear of falling into onto-theological ditches.

"What's sauce for the goose is sauce for the gander." This is wise because it is a commonsense platitude. Its great truth did not await the advent of deconstruction. Its implicit universality, let us say its charge that thought be open to all otherness, has always been ingredient in the task that philosophy has set for itself. The question between philosophy and deconstruction is: Who is the goose? Does the goose laugh at philosophy; or is philosophy the wild goose chase, the flight of mind on which the goose laughs at itself in its journey to the ultimate or on its migration to the world of otherness? And what of the other birds of philosophical thought? Why does Socrates, the swan of Apollo, have to sing on the eve of death? What can we make of the hoot of the Owl of Minerva at dusk? Is this hoot, too, a masked laugh? Kierkegaard offered a fine fable about a wild goose who became a domesticated barnyard bird, cackling on the ground but no longer flying. Is this goose a philosophical bird of paradise or a discontented denizen of deconstructive academe, busily lecturing from below the soaring birds of paradise above, as to why they should not be able to fly at all? And yet they soar beyond.

But who anyway is the goose? Or as Nietzsche teasingly suggests: Suppose truth were a woman? Was Nietzsche also slyly thinking of the Thracian maid and the laughter he could not put from mind? I think that an element of Nietzsche's greatness—a bird of paradise blown in before the storm, dazzling us with a brief beauty, but dropping, perishing in the exhaustion of the storm—an element of his greatness, his freedom of spirit, was his philosophical laughter.

If ontotheology and logocentrism are phallogocentrism, as Derrida says, a mischievous tease rises up: What would the overcoming (*Überwindung*) or destruction (*Destruktion*) of phallogocentrism mean? Who is being surmounted by the post-phallogocentric philosopher? What then is sauce for the goose and the gander? What then could be saucy at all? Would ontotheologians have to emulate Origen, become postmodern castrati but without the justification of making themselves eunuchs for the Lord? Are there any more Lords? Or Ladies? Must one renounce logical uprightness, erectness, correctness, *adaequatio* (postmodern translation: being up to it), and be no longer ontologically upstanding (*orthotēs*)? What will it mean to be with (*sunousia*) the truth? Must we cross out the copula, as Heidegger crosses out being?

But how can one be a lover of truth under erasure? Can one be a *philos* under erasure? What strange passion (*pathos*) would philosophical eros under erasure be? Eros under erasure: is this a joke? With the copula in *epochē*, how then are we to conceive philosophy? What conception at all would be possible? Schopenhauer said the genital organs were the metaphysical focus of the Will, but sought to transcend their *eros turannos*. Would post-phallogocentric philosophy be a new Schopenhauerianism, or a post-Heideggerian will-lessness whose injunction is: To enter the postmodern kingdom, pluck out the phallus or forever burn in ontotheological eternity, whose hell is the other? If this is frivolity, it is a joke, not an archeology of the frivolous. But philosophical eros, like sex, can be comic, as can other elementals such as eating and drinking, as swaggering Falstaff (a fat deconstructionist, no question) would uproariously tell us. The Thracian maid would say: Too true, thank God (a colloquialism outrageously, inexcusably "ontotheological"). A joke is neither Hegelian nor deconstructionist but elemental. Let Falstaff, let Heidegger, let Derrida drink to that and to the Thracian woman! And, if needs be, with the wine of Dionysus, a sometime Platonic *pharmakon* for tired or enfeebled eros.

Deconstruction and Laughing at Hegel's Failure

I will be serious; for the moment I put laughter from mind and in all scholarly sobriety I offer the following explication.

In the discourse of deconstruction Hegel occupies a central place. Derrida calls Hegel the last thinker of the book and the first thinker of irreducible difference. He says that in a certain sense all he does is read and reread Hegel, a process with no end.[2] Derrida displays an ambiguity towards Hegel, mixing criticism of the movement to closure with a certain marking in Hegel of difference, sometimes, it seems, against Hegel's own stated intentions. The situation is more complex in that Hegel epitomizes a way of thinking that arouses the deconstructionist's suspicion. There is the movement to closure which we find in the absolute's return to itself after its tortured peregrinations through the manifold forms of otherness, none of which adequately offers the mirror in which the absolute might completely, self-transparently, recognize itself. Here we are said to find a restricted economy of the same, culminating in a conceptual closure of complete self-appropriation.

In addition, Hegel is said to complete and exhaust the discourse of traditional metaphysics, "ontotheology" in Heidegger's term, the "logocentrism" that is "phallogocentrism" in Derrida's. Hegel's discourse is determined by all the binary oppositions of Platonic metaphysics, working out the interplay of these oppositions, claiming to sublate their oppositeness in an absolute totality wherein difference is subordinated to identity. While it would be wrong to call Hegel a dualist, a sense of metaphysical opposition does determine the unfolding and articulation of his system. Again, the claim is made that logic, logos reaches its apotheosis in Hegel: the absolute category in the *Logic* is the Absolute Idea; while in the philosophy of absolute spirit, the *Begriff* overcomes the last remnant of recalcitrant otherness that still persists in art and religion—the alogical richness of art, the resistant enigma of the holy are subsumed into the totalizing life of pure thought. Finally, Hegel's affirmative intent comes to fullest expression in his commitment to the idea of the process of history as itself the progressive manifestation and realization of the absolute.

The discourse of deconstruction rouses skepticism on all these fronts. It finds problematical, it renounces, all absolutes, be these theological or their philosophical surrogates, be they transcendental absolutes à la Kant or Husserl or humanizations of the absolute in the mode of Left Hegelianism. While it seems inhospitable to religious claims, it certainly finds in the aesthetic a recalcitrance to logical articulation that seems directly counter to Hegel. Something about art resists the pretension of philosophy to occupy the position of superior epistemological and ontological worth. Logos is never really the overcoming of *muthos* but involves a *poiesis* that dissembles its own metaphoric nature. The entire ontotheological discourse of Western metaphysics, with its preference for presence, must be subverted. The finality of the Absolute Idea, the implication of complete closure in its absolute self-mediation, must be contested.

In summary, the critique of deconstruction comes to the fact that Hegel did not place the proper emphasis on the Heideggerian project of thinking "difference qua difference." Difference is finally subordinated to identity, as in Hegel's famous description of the absolute as the identity of identity and difference. It is not that difference is rejected by Hegel, but there are forms of otherness on the outside or the margins of even difference, dialectically preserved. We need to think this other otherness. I am putting the issue in terms sufficiently broad to include critics who are not deconstructionists. William James' criticism of idealism as leading to a "block universe" might be included here.

Clearly I grant that Hegel's philosophy does raise questions in terms of the subordination of otherness to dialectical self-mediation. Nevertheless I read Hegel differently from his post-Heideggerian critics. I agree with Derrida that we will never be done with the reading and re-reading of Hegel. But we should be wary of reading him solely with a "hermeneutic of suspicion." We should be suspicious of any commentator whose hermeneutics is only one of suspicion. In the latter case, instead of listening to the other in its strengths, we will always in advance suspect the other of philosophical shame. Philosophical interpretation becomes hermeneutical aggression on the thought of the other—even when that aggression congratulates itself with the rhetoric of "openness to otherness."

I do not underestimate the Hegel of system and panlogism, but apropos our theme, I will offer some remarks on comedy and failure as significant for understanding the others of philosophy. A concern with these others of philosophy is important for the relation of deconstructionist thought to Hegel and the tradition of philosophy. I will say below that a certain relation to failure internally defines philosophy, and that a certain understanding of dialectic makes this evident. I detect significant affinities between dialectic and deconstruction with respect to failure and the spirit of comedy that germinates in that failure, affinities I will highlight later by dwelling on the significance of irony for philosophy.[3] I will say that both dialectic and deconstruction serve to articulate a sense of philosophical failure, name a certain comic breakdown in pretension to absoluteness. The comic is also relevant to the issue of being-at-home with being—a bone of contention between Hegel and many of his critics. The comedy of philosophical failure leads to an affirmation that stands beyond the absurdity it needs to debunk in order to be itself.

We get an initial sense of the issue if we briefly note some significant citations from Derrida regarding the risibility of the Hegelian system itself. I refer to Derrida's essay on Bataille. Here Derrida seems to side with Bataille who wants to "laugh at philosophy."[4] He argues that laughter will be the next moment in history to exceed Hegel's thought, signifying Bataille's "sovereignty" as opposed to Hegel's so-called mastery. This laughter will reveal "the limit of discourse and the beyond of absolute knowledge."[5] In Derrida's essay, the Hegelian *Aufhebung* is identified with lordship, or more generally a logic of domination within a restricted economy of the same. Speculative logic is a logic of the Lord. How does Derrida respond? He endorses what he calls a "[b]urst of laughter from Bataille," and goes on to say: "[H]enceforth everything covered by the name lordship collapses into comedy. The independence of self-consciousness becomes laughable at the moment when it liberates itself by enslaving itself, when it starts to *work*, that is, when it enters into dialectics. Laughter alone exceeds dialectics and the dialectician; it bursts out only on the basis of an absolute renunciation of meaning, an absolute risking of death, what Hegel calls abstract negativity."[6] He says ". . . laughter is absent from the Hegelian system . . . ," and again seems to endorse Bataille: "In the 'system' poetry, laughter, ecstasy are nothing. Hegel hastily gets rid of them. . ."[7] "To be indifferent to the comedy of the *Aufhebung*, as was Hegel, is to blind oneself to the experience of the sacred . . . ."[8]

Governing these statements is a sense of opposition between philosophy and the sacred, philosophy and the poetic, philosophy and comedy. Below I show that philosophy and the comic are not to be opposed. We have had occasion already to dwell on philosophy and the sacred: art and speculation are *Gottesdienst*. Is the above picture a bit of a travesty, born of reading Hegel through the dour, working, world-historical eyes of a Kojèvian, humanistic seriousness? Is Hegel void of the sacred, deficient in laughter, a stranger to imaginative discourse, devoid of poetic power?

On the Debunking of the Philosophical Tradition: Who Laughs Last?

I must remark on certain pervasive attitudes to the tradition of philosophy. The mockery of philosophy is sometimes embedded in the context of a totalized interpretation of that tradition, a hermeneutical suspicion towards it, and a will to "overcome" it. We find variations on Nietzsche's proclaimed overturning of Platonism and transvaluation of all values, or Heidegger's *Destruktion* of metaphysics or *Überwindung* of traditional thought. Since Hegel's death, "overcoming Hegel" has been a cottage industry among thinkers in the Continental tradition. One might think that he has been overcome so many times, by Kierkegaard, by Marx, by Schelling, by Nietzsche, by Heidegger, that his back by now is surely broken by the weight of those successors who have unceasingly climbed over it. It seems however that the Owl of Minerva is not a nocturnal bird, but a charmed cat with more than nine lives. Hegel mocks his descendants, all his overcomers, disappearing before those surmounters coming after, only to reappear around an unexpected corner. The surpassings of Hegel have sometimes been bypassings of Hegel *as the other*; this *philosopher* who is other is resurrected in thought once more.

One senses a will to be rid of Hegel. I say senses, because this will is often secret. But perhaps this thought is infected too much by the spirit of Nietzschean genealogy. So let that pass. Nevertheless for not a few, Hegel is *the* enemy. Through the fight with this enemy, a war is fought against the entire tradition of philosophical logos. Kierkegaard fights this war on behalf of Christian faith. Marx fights it on behalf of praxis and the socio-economic history traditionally put into second place by priestly, contemplative philosophers. Nietzsche fights it on behalf of tragic art. Heidegger fights the war on behalf of what in a pithy, nugatory category/noncategory he calls the

"Unthought." Derrida fights it on behalf of *différance*, which is also a "category" that is no category.

The Hegel attacked is clearly the panlogist Hegel, not the more hermeneutical Hegel who does display some respect for the others of philosophy, respect that sits uneasily with any logicist reduction of all forms of being to one totalizing conceptual logos. We ought to take seriously not only the internal complexity of Hegel but a certain doubleness in his dialectical strategies. If we emphasize only his panlogist side, our options for interpretation are unduly narrowed. While not denying this side, he does try to see the logos, the logic as actually unfolding in the realization of being, as already at work there in the concrete itself. This can be read to imply: Hegel must foster in his thought a respect for otherness as such, even despite the fact that his categories sometimes abbreviate what is there emerging in otherness, sometimes even deforming it. Derrida is right: we will never be done with the reading and re-reading of Hegel, but Hegel's equivocations do not simply have to be read in the suspicious spirit of deconstruction.

Hermeneutical generosity towards the tradition finds that the post-Heideggerian desire to think on the margins of philosophy is too nugatory. Why should we at all agree with Heidegger's desire to think *outside* philosophy? Has this desire not already straitjacketed philosophy? Philosophy is a little more elusive than "ontotheology" and "metaphysics of presence"—terms that now seem stock cliché.

It is said that all philosophy is only an imperialism of identity or the same. Levinas speaks of philosophy as allergic to otherness, an allergy that reaches its culmination in Hegel. This is surely not true of the philosophical tradition as a whole. This fact is revealed by the retraction that later follows for Levinas, when he points to a philosophical acknowledgment of the other, as in Plato's doctrine of the Good beyond being. The strategy seems to be: totalize the tradition as ontotheology, imperialism of the same...; thereby create the impression of being revolutionary, unprecedented in thinking the other; but then smuggle back ideas that in some form or other are to be found in the tradition; finally, acknowledge that there were instances of such ideas in the tradition.[9] Of course, most readers will have forgotten the first step by the time they get to the last, not seeing that the total claim made in the first step is now effectively done away with. My query is: Why not acknowledge the last step *at the start*? But if one wants to appear to be "overcoming the tradition," one cannot tolerate this, for it moderates all conceit to be unprecedented. Moreover, it is an impossible step to take if one is wedded to the hermeneutics of suspicion. For to make the last point first would require a hermeneutics of generosity and then also a different reading of the tradition.

I do not want to confound Levinas with Derrida and Heidegger. Levinas is very critical of Heidegger, and has always been marked by a deep spiritual seriousness that, if it marks Derrida at all, is so deeply masked as to be almost invisible. I suspect too that (given some remarks in *Totality and Infinity* on the wantonness of the feminine) Levinas would see Bataille's laughter as a lascivious laughing, full of erotic equivocation, all but indecent. Levinas himself mixes suspicion and generosity in the way he distinguishes between what he calls "ontology" and "metaphysics." Ontology marks a philosophy of being that always ends up reducing the other to the same. Hence ontology is a philosophy of the neuter that cannot do justice to the other, and the other most especially as ethical. Levinas criticizes Heidegger on this score, but also traditional philosophy. Ontology as first philosophy is a philosophy of power, where power involves violence and aggression towards the other as other. It is built upon the logic of a movement from the same to the other that is always for the same, and always returning to the same. This corresponds quite closely to my account of Hegel's logic of the concept as dialectical self-mediation, and its coherence with that strand of the tradition that privileges the movement of thought thinking *itself.*

By metaphysics Levinas implies a movement of thought that exceeds totality, most especially in the surplus to thought of the idea of infinity and the face-to-face relation of the ethical. Metaphysical thought might go from the same to the other, but not in order to return to the self. This corresponds to what I have outlined as the second movement of metaxological intermediation in which thought does not think itself, but tries to think its others, others on which its mediations may even break down. This second intermediation also corresponds to what I have called "agapeic mind." Throughout this work I have been criticizing Hegel's self-thinking Idea for being a dialectically erotic absolute that misses the more ultimate thought of the agapeic absolute, and that hence reduces the second intermediation of metaxological mind to a singular and total process of dialectical self-mediation. Thus, I am sympathetic to what Levinas' calls "metaphysics." I have developed the idea of the very surplus of infinitude in terms of an agapeic, overdetermined sense of infinity in *Desire, Dialectic, and Otherness.* My main point now is that the metaphysical movement of mind has always been a possibility in the philosophical tradition. Levinas cites Plato's Good beyond being in this regard. This is a case where we must not let Hegelian totality determine what we are to see in the metaphysical tradition and how we are to see it.[10]

Metaphysical philosophy as agapeic mindfulness demands a hermeneutics of generosity. Such a hermeneutics will try to give the dead other, the past philosopher, a posthumous life, resurrecting his thinking again. It will see the other philosopher as an *appeal* to us to rethink his philosophy in its fullest actuality, not bury it again in a grave of stereotype or caricature or packaged position. The promise of agapeic mindfulness asks for such a hermeneutics of generosity. It follows that the issues of the speculative tradition are the issues we need to think and rethink. It is not at all obvious that Hegel did exhaust the resources of that tradition. It will be obvious to a hermeneutics of generosity that Hegel's resources of thought are themselves extraordinarily rich. It always strikes one as no slight irony that a persistent criticism of Hegel is that he is a totalizing thinker. Yet I find in Heidegger and in Derrida (Adorno, too, for that matter) a plethora of totalizing characterizations of the philosophical tradition.

"Ontotheology" and "metaphysics of presence" are Heidegger's totalizations. But consider Derrida: "A noun is proper when it has but a single sense. Better, it is only in this case that it is properly a noun. Univocity is the essence, or better, the *telos* of language. No philosophy, as such, has ever renounced this Aristotelian ideal. This ideal is philosophy."[11] Philosophy here becomes philosophy *as such—* ironically, a very Aristotelian locution: a totalizing description allegedly to undo totalizing thinking. How can one respond to this description of philosophy as such? Dread of something like the Cretan Liar paradox grips, not philosophy as such, but the philosopher. If you deny the description, you will be accused of confirming it; if you do not deny it, the silence, too, will be taken for confirmation.

It is a reduction, travesty of the full tradition of Western thought to call it by such names as univocity, presence, ontotheology and so on. If this is so, one is not sure what precisely is the logocentric tradition that is being subverted. One must raise the question whether philosophical logos contains in itself the power to subvert supposed "logocentrism" and whether consequently talk about *the* logocentric tradition of metaphysics is a conceptual abstraction. Strangely, too, the subverters of this tradition charge that tradition with conceptual abstraction. This is an example of the anti-philosophical kettle calling the philosophical pot black. Let Plato again serve as a releasing example—the thinker on whom Nietzsche tries to pin the charge of "logocentrism." Plato was what I call a "plurivocal thinker," his thought spoken through many voices, and not just the univocal voice of logicism. Scotus Eriugena, Cusanus, Bruno, Schelling, Hegel himself are thinkers who resist classification as simple logocentric philosophers.

But Derrida is cautious, or should I say foxy? One is unsure where the stress of his interpretations falls. Sometimes he wants to find the other of philosophy also within philosophy. Yet he says (in a revealing interview with Richard Kearney): "I am not happy to be termed a philosopher." He then goes on to say something close to my concerns: "My central question is: from what site or non-site (*non-lieu*) can philosophy as such appear to itself as other than itself, so that it can interrogate and reflect upon itself in an original manner." I am not chagrined to admit: This is just the question I have been addressing. But immediately we part, for Derrida then says: "Such a non-site or alterity would be radically irreducible to philosophy. But the problem is that such a non-site cannot be defined or situated by means of philosophical language."[12] I am denying this, as in my interpretation of the *bios xenikos* of speculative metaphysics, where thought is most intimate with itself and yet most strange and other to itself. I am denying this in my sense of the laughter of the philosopher that is both inside and outside of thought at once. And it is not the neutral outsider laughing at philosophy *as such* (Derrida should really avoid those Aristotelian flourishes): it is the philosopher, in the agapeic energy of plurivocal mind, laughing at himself. I am not merely denying Derrida's view, I am enacting the truth of what Derrida denies. This is simply to laugh philosophically.

Sometimes Derrida *hovers* between celebration and indictment. Then one is unsure whether his point is to reaffirm the complexity of the "tradition" (say, in his discussion of "Violence and Metaphysics"), or to bring the stock post-Nietzschean accusations against the tradition. The focus shifts and slips. Sometimes we sense him to communicate: See how I show the internal intricacy in the textual treasury of great thinkers like Hegel. But then, very quickly, as quick as a Heraclitean river, the hermeneutical silhouette shifts from generosity to suspicion again, and the deconstructing thinker says: I have stripped you, washed away the mask of metaphysics, exposed to view the other you tried to cover over; your lies stand in full gaze.

Whichever of these two sides we take—and I think we have to take both sides, and indeed a kind of equivocal vacillation between them—it is ironical that with a slight dislocation of Derrida himself, his reading of some traditional thinkers might open up, and to a certain extent despite himself, that despised tradition in its overdetermined riches of discourse. Derrida is a kind of dialectical thinker who tries to use dialectic to confound dialectic. The results are, however, equivocal, as we see in this hermeneutical vacillation between generosity and suspicion. Deconstructive thinking is thus very close to Adorno's negative dialectic, but both Derrida's and Adorno's uses of dialectic to think against dialectic result in equivocal thinking. Derrida's equivocation is his vacillation between a Levinasian generosity and a Nietzschean suspicion.

Whether we elect to stay with Hegelian dialectic, or counterpose to speculative dialectic an equivocal dialectic parading grammatologically under the *nom de plume* of *différance*, or whether we develop the plurivocal thought of metaxological mindfulness, I want to resist the way charges like "logocentrism" freeze into polemical postures. When such polemical postures are applied to everything, they end up revealing almost nothing. The rhetoric contains dangerous equivocation against which a more generous hermeneutics is on guard. The tradition of philosophy cannot be reduced to the monolinear abstraction of logocentrism. Logocentrism is rejected because logos is identified with univocity and its reduction of plurality to manipulable sameness. But this rejection is equivocal because it harbors the reductive urge in its own antiphilosophical manner, namely, its already noted totalization of the tradition as "metaphysics of presence" under the dominance of the univocal ideal. Rather than equivocal dialectic we need plurivocal thought to do justice to the many possibilities of logos and their concretization in the tradition of philosophy.

Aristotle said that being is said in many ways; we must say that logos is said, or rather says itself, in many ways. There is a side to Aristotle that insistently seeks for univocity in philosophical speech, but this coexists with a strong respect for the plurivocity of metaphysical discourse, itself trying to be true to the plurivocity of being itself. Plurivocal thought demands that we give up the myth of univocity, not only vis-à-vis logicist reductionism, but also vis-à-vis hermeneutical reductionism. Philosophical logos is plurivocal, so one should not talk about *the* tradition of philosophy. What we find in Western thought is already pluralized in amazingly rich ways and in a manner resisting the totalizing pretension, whether of a Hegel, or of the post-Hegelians who, nominally anti-totalizers, in fact totalize the tradition with an eye to debunking it hermeneutically. The latter play the role, sometimes with a flabbergasting lack of philosophical self-consciousness, of hermeneutical reductionists and totalizers to Hegel's alleged logicist reduction and totalization.

The other or others of the logocentric tradition are not some aliens haunting the margins of the mainstream, but are potentially subversive and empowering participants within its plurivocal dialogue or philosophical conversation of mind. Let us return again to one of the fathers of the philosophical logos, Plato. Platonic thought might be said to be linked to a certain logocentric ideal in its respect for certain mathematical forms of thought. The motto above the entrance to the Academy is testament enough: Let no one who has not studied geometry enter here. But we also find the transgression of this logical regime; we are not confined to the sparse economy of an Aristotelian logic, and certainly not to any univocity of the concept. It is ridiculous to imply a hegemony of logocentrism in Plato, for the "mythical," "mystical," side of Platonism was indispensable, without any reneging on the commitment to reason. At times this other side verged on being even more important than this commitment. And this is to say nothing of Plato as a philosophical artist. Platonic thought does not reduce to univocity; nor is it merely equivocal. As a dialectical and dialogical thinker, Plato was a plurivocal philosopher, a metaxological thinker.

The fashionable mode of anti-philosophical denunciation will quickly post its label of indictment: Platonism is nihilism! I am not cowed by these decoy slogans of anti-metaphysical suspiciousness. One might agree with the criticism that Platonism is nihilism if, for example, eternity cannot be brought into relation to time (see chapter 1). Nevertheless, the quicksand of an exclusively hermeneutical approach is historicism, however sophisticated this approach may be. Deconstruction is a hermeneutics intoxicated with the virtuosity of its own textual and philological excess. Its debunking negativity will not finally help us here; indeed it will merely swallow itself up and be dissolved in the temporality it cannot transcend. In fact, time has already begun to devour deconstruction. That is to say, the blush of its first fashionableness is now fading fast, and the cannibalizing avant-garde spits it out as *passé*.

With a plurivocal philosopher like Plato, I suggest that within the form of logos itself we find the other of merely logical thought, just as the other of logic is itself tempered and given structured articulation by an ideal of reason. To detect this other in the logos, or at least haunting the logos, is part and parcel of the project of deconstruction. I have no quarrel with the desire to open the other for thought. The plurivocal thought of metaxological mindfulness must be more than univocal: it must be thought thinking itself, *and* thought thinking its others. It must be philosophy as self-mediating thinking; but it must also be thought thinking what is other, that is, philosophy as intermediating with otherness as possibly resisting its claims to complete conceptual mastery. To imply that the other or others were consigned to oblivion by philosophy, only to become an operative unconscious, an "unthought"—this implication is neither just nor true. What we find at the best is the coexistence in tension of different forms of thought, forms that make a kind of family of possible ways of mindfulness. Such a family will manifest the kinship of the different ways of being mindful, but no family is a seamless harmony or exempt from conflict. In fact, family quarrels are often the most bitter just because of the intimacy of the antagonists.

The tradition of philosophy is inherently ambiguous, unavoidably so. We can look at this in a non-accusatory way. This is required by the plurivocity of thought. No doubt, deconstruction reminds us of a tendency in Western philosophy to box thinking into an excessively narrow ideal of reason. But logos has not always been content to conform itself to this idealized narrowness, breaking the prohibition that its own narrowly constructed logic imposes. Logos is not always logical in this sense.

Hegel is not himself without equivocation. He shows little sympathy for Plato's "mythic" side, seeing this as a mere rhetorical convenience, which philosophy as systematic science has outgrown. The logicist Hegel accuses the Platonic myth of conceptual weakness. Yet on the other hand, at the highest level of absolute spirit, there is a certain dialectical porosity of art, philosophy, and religion. We might broadly speak of the logoi of religion and art, logoi not in the sense of rational accounts, but in the sense of significant articulations of ultimate meaning. Such religious and aesthetic logoi, which are not conformed to any univocal logic, infiltrate Hegel's philosophical logos. If taken in the narrow sense of the univocal ideal, the post-Hegelian protest against logocentrism has its point. But it loses most of its force if we grant a more embracing concept of logos to the tradition and to Hegel.

Dialectical logos itself may have been put in the shadow since Descartes and the rise of modern science to hegemony, and with this the hegemony of univocity. Scientific enlightenment can exhibit an imperialistic univocity that would dispel the supposed murk of equivocity in art, religion, ethics, philosophy itself. Hegel cannot be seamlessly fitted into this hegemony of univocity. Though he is a modern, he reaches back to retrieve possibilities of thought from the dawn of the philosophical tradition, possibilities both transcending and transforming the character of post-Cartesian philosophy. If there is no simple unitary logocentric tradition, not only is the rhetoric of logocentrism less helpful but also marginal otherness may turn out to be less marginal than it initially appeared. We may find in the tradition as much reverence for otherness as violence towards it.

I briefly illustrate in relation to Hegel's aesthetics. Hegel is not simply an a priori thinker who sees in the rich thereness of art only what his philosophical categories prepare him to see. I do not deny that Hegel does exhibit a strong desire to situate art within a systematic philosophy. But his practice here shows traces of a certain *double* mediation between philosophy and art. His thought is often genuinely open to the otherness of art. This openness ends in the claim that underlying the difference of art and philosophy is a kinship, a certain sameness. Must we see this as a philosophical imperialism of the same, a totalitarianism of the concept? A more sophisticated Hegel will ask us to call this sameness a dialectical identity in difference. But the idea of identity must not be falsely substantialized; we must break free of stereotypical concepts of univocal identity. Identity can be a pluralized concept, not just merely univocal.

When Hegel places art and philosophy along with religion in the realm of absolute spirit he is obviously saying that there is a sameness about them regardless of their difference. For Hegel this "sameness" is the fact that all of them are modes of articulation of the absolute content; their difference becomes a formal difference but in an essentially dynamic sense; each is a different formation of the same energy of the absolute. When most critics of Hegel hear the identity, sameness of art and philosophy, this is immediately understood as the reduction of art or religion to philosophy, reduction implying the sin of a certain conceptual totalitarianism. The issue in Hegel, rather the issue itself, is not so simple. Hegel is not speaking of a reductive univocity but of the dialectical togetherness of art and philosophy and religion in the shelter of absolute spirit. That sameness remains enigmatic, *xenikos*, precisely because the energy of the ultimate that art, religion, and philosophy articulate itself remains strange—and this despite Hegel's claims to have adequately articulated that absolute in conceptual terms.

This is not at all to deny that the idea of dialectical togetherness raises further, hard questions about the proper preservation of otherness as other. I have been pressing such questions throughout. The point at issue now is simply the charge against Hegel of reducing otherness to univocity. This charge itself risks being reductive. The question to Hegel should not be put at the level of an oscillation between univocity and equivocity. It should be put in full self-consciousness of the complexity of dialectical thinking and its transcendence of this oscillation. The question of otherness should be posed genuinely from beyond dialectic, not from below it.

In summary: I agree with the post-Hegelians—this question must be put; I disagree with the how and the whence of their putting the question. If not put properly, the question is liable to be absorbed by Hegel as a non-question. And *then* the other is dialectically absorbed in the same. Strange irony: without proper *philosophical* care, the anti-Hegelian anti-philosophers will then turn out, despite themselves, despite every deconstructive precaution or debunking, to be in dialectical collusion with Hegelian philosophy. Their mockery of Hegel will turn into Hegel's mockery of them. Who then will have the last laugh?

Logos and the Comedy of Failure

Returning to philosophy and comedy, indeed to the comedy of philosophy, I now ask about the failure of the logos relative to the deconstructionist charge that philosophy does not do justice to the other. I note the link of failure and laughter—both seem to be radical others to philosophical logos. Laughter seems to deal with the absurd, with what makes no sense. I think of Kant in the *Critique of Judgment* when he says that comedy arises when a strained expectation is suddenly brought to nothing, revealed to be absurd. There is a certain intimacy between the "It is nothing" and laughter. Likewise, failure shows what comes to nothing, what is recalcitrant to incorporation into a rational story wherein all the elements of the unfolding are recuperated.

Being brought to nothing in laughter, coming to nothing in failure—these seem entirely other to reason as ascribed to Hegel. Hegelian reason is said to be the imperial will to conquer all meaninglessness, all absurdity. Its mode of conquering is said to recuperate every element, initially resistant, into an embracing intelligible totality. It is as if Hegel said: Nothing ever really comes to nothing; every nothing is a coming to something (a non-logicist way to say: *determinatio est negatio*); indeed every nothing is a dialectical prelude to coming to the absolute. Given this, Hegelian reason would be radically other to laughter and failure. The previously cited remarks of Derrida/Bataille concerning laughter as in excess of the system would have their justification.

But this is not enough. Laughter, like thought and being, is plurivocal. One can laugh in many different ways, in many different voices. Some laughter is full of resentment or disgust or violence. Some laughter, even though coupled with the clearest consciousness of radical absurdity, is like a benign amen on being. Laughter, I think, has an intimate relation with the sense of doubleness that has variously occupied us. That is, laughter is grounded on a mindfulness, and not necessarily an explicitly self-conscious mindfulness, of the mixing in the middle of many voices of sense and nonsense. Laughter has roots in the excess of otherness within the metaxological community of being. It is grounded in a rich sense of ambiguity. If being were completely intelligible in a purely univocal way, laughter would not only be unintelligible, it would be impossible, nonexistent. Laughter is always a living refutation of any univocity issuing a totalizing claim: the claim refutes itself by its own risibility.

The plurivocity of the metaxological sense of being as multiply mediated can sometimes be seen as equivocal. The double meanings of equivocity are intimately tied up with the possibility of laughter. The equivocity can be the occasion of a debunking of univocity. But one has to guard against a debunking that itself is aggressively negating, and hence that is as implicitly imperialistic as the univocal mind. Equivocal laughter can be nihilistic. But the equivocal double can also point beyond the violent debunking of univocal mind to a richer, and more affirmative sense of ambiguity, and with this to a less nihilistic sense of laughter. I say that both the dialectical and the metaxological senses of doubleness and ambiguity point us in this more affirmative direction. An elemental joy in being breaks through the antagonistic equivocity of nihilism. The otherness of the energy of being as elemental breaks through. The breakthrough is more than just self-mediation. It may bring a moment of reversal, a moment of absolution, an abandon of joy in being as elemental. Laughter serves to release the festive celebration of the metaxological community of mind and being.[13]

In his *Aesthetics* Hegel himself distinguishes the merely laughable (*das Lächerliche*) and the comic (*das Komische*).[14] The comic deals with the self-destruction of the false in its contrast and contradiction with the genuinely true; yet in the self-destruction of the false, the self remains at home with itself. The mellowing presence of the latter being-at-home with self seems absent with the merely laughable. That is, the merely laughable may indicate a not being-at-home with being whose character is rooted in a certain rancor towards being. This laughter is a gesture of ontological aggression, not an elemental affirmative outburst. If we can find laughter in Hegel, it is not one nurtured by resentment or *disgust* at being. It is worth noting that Kant excludes disgust alone from the aesthetic presentation of the ugly. Kant would repudiate the aesthetic presentation of Sartrean nausea, metaphysical disgust at the valueless thereness of being. What kind of comedy could Sartrean nausea produce? And is there not much at stake when in the *Birth of Tragedy* Nietzsche speaks of the comic as a release from nausea before the absurd?[15]

Dialectic points to an affirmative sense of doubleness as the reconciled dualism beyond equivocity, the *coincidentia oppositorum* beyond the flat literalness of univocity. The metaxological sense of being also points to the affirmative sense of doubleness, but in a fuller sense: the plurivocal mind is capable of festive laughter in the middle of the community of being, itself pluralistically positive. "Home" is to be mindfully at home in this metaxological community of being, even in the ruptures of being that we have to undergo in the middle. The double is not reduced but the tension of otherness in it, that is not reducible to univocity, serves to release a certain festive energy of being. The affirmative sense of laughter, beyond merely debunking equivocity, is a metaphysical yes to home, a being-at-home in the overdetermined middle. It looses the agapeic energy of being in us as an affirmative excess, an agapeic mindfulness of the energy of being as itself an excess of agapeic otherness. A laughter beyond nihilism erupts in the joyful confluence of this redoubled excess, the agapeic excess of both the self and the other. This is festive laughter as metaxologically double.

This is not to forget failure.[16] Nor is it to be heedless of the absurd. Is Hegel heedless? No. The country of Hegelian discourse is a bourn of failure. I am not concerned now with the claim that Hegelian reason is itself a failure in its purported aim. I am saying that Hegel's thought can be read as a prolonged encounter with failure, failure ranging from minor breakdowns to the most radical negations. My main focus is on the failure of philosophical logos. I can state the point at issue in terms of Hegel's relation to some of his predecessors. I will look at Kant, Socrates, and ancient skepticism. All were concerned with the possible failure of the logos, with philosophy at an impasse. In Socrates' case we see this concern at the origin of philosophy itself. From its origin philosophy always was the calling into question of *itself*, acknowledging its need to come to terms with its own self-deconstruction.

Hegel developed his own thought, and continued to think, in the shadow of Kant. In my view, Kant can be interpreted as a philosopher of failure, and in a sense that is strongly post-Hegelian. Kant claims to show the failure, the necessary failure of traditional dogmatic metaphysics, transcendent metaphysics, that is, philosophy that was pretentious in an unwarranted way. Such traditional metaphysics was naive in that it did not first pass through the rational debunking of its own categorial assumptions. Kant implies that some of the desiderata of metaphysics were laudable but the implementations were rationally risible, ultimately a comedy of failed logic. Kant might be read to say: precritical metaphysics was doomed to deconstruct; traditional philosophy was destined to be a failure.

One of the most important examples of such failure is evident in Kant's discussion of the antinomies. This is the birthplace, certainly one of the seedbeds of Hegel's own dialectic. *Verstand* or the analytical understanding marches itself into a set of fundamental metaphysical oppositions, both sets of which are equally tenable, which is to say, equally untenable. The antinomies, in the terms I use, show a failure of univocity. On its own terms understanding cannot univocally decide for one or other of the opposites. On this score, its fixation with univocity breeds the logicist indignity of equivocity, sheer unmediated difference. We have the comedy of metaphysical undecidability, not unlike the laughable paralysis of Buridan's ass, though the ass now is the philosopher himself, frozen before antithetical abstractions. Deconstructionist thought tries to make hay with this metaphysical undecidability. But I find no joke in Derrida's response to Paul de Man's case as undecidable. I find an overkill of textualizing technique, itself equivocating between equivocity and univocity.[17]

Interestingly Hegel himself says that *der steife Verstand*, the stiff understanding, is least capable of being-at-home with itself, while being laughable in the extreme.[18] In my terms, *der steife Verstand* is univocal mind. The univocal mind, the stiff understanding is strait-laced, wooden, dead to the comedy of abstracted thought. It is paralyzed by lifeless categories. It chokes the energy of excess, the thinking transcendence of living mind. For Kant the outcome of the antinomies is a necessary failure; and Kant sets off to regain, by a different indirect route, some other way to success. Hegel, of course, sees more in this failure: it is the very nature of philosophical thought to fail, and especially so in the measure that it stiffens itself into the univocal mind and makes a fetish of its own abstractions; and it is of the essence of sophisticated philosophical thought to appropriate the meaning of this failure, to incorporate the principle of failure within its own way of thinking. In this respect, the Kantian antinomies were crucial in helping Hegel develop his notion of the dialectic. Part of the lesson of this failure is: we need a rethinking of the energy of thinking that is restlessly at work even in the univocal fixation of the antinomies. Mind must be unloosed from the paralysis of stiffened univocity.

Let me turn to Socrates as a predecessor more ancient than Kant. Again the comic and failure are relevant to philosophic dialectic. Much might be said, but the fact that Socratic dialectic is shot through with irony is a clear sign that our theme of reason's risibleness is being played out. What is at stake is not the risible nature of all reason, for that would yield misology, but the risibleness of almost all claims to reason. It is very significant that Socrates' remarks on misology in the *Phaedo* are offered as he tries to think the radical otherness of death; this is an extremity of failure when Socrates himself faces directly the possible coming to nothing of his own being. But even here in the failure of being and the logos that would affirm deathless being, Socrates retains trust in the logos. He is willing to continue his question and conversation even in the other world.

On *this* side of that failure or coming to nothing, the Socratic dialectic involves a conversation, interchange between a philosopher and an other. Nor does the other always play by the games of a rigid univocal logic. In turn Socrates himself is not always a practitioner of *der steife Verstand*, for he transgresses univocal logic, most notably in his presence/absence as an ironical thinker. Irony is a form of the comic, very dear to the heart of the philosopher because of its power to explode pretension. The ironical philosopher presents himself as nothing: Socrates says, I know nothing; *eirōneia* is a self-depreciation which suggests: I am as straw. So the ironical philosopher presents himself as *other* to what he is; for he is not simply nothing, and his thought is not simply straw. In a word, philosophical irony makes possible a plurivocal thought.

When Socrates speaks we inevitably ask: Who just spoke? Socrates? But which Socrates? Is there a one, univocal Socrates? Or is Socrates a nothing? A nothing that says: I know nothing? Or is Socrates not a possible plurality, perhaps a conversation of a number of philosophical voices? That we can ask such questions about the irony of the philosopher is tantamount to the admission that there is not just one voice for the dialectical philosopher, nor one simple univocal identity to his thought. That is why it is ridiculous to imply, as Derrida/Bataille do, that the comic is not acknowledged by philosophy as one of its most important others. Certainly for the Socratic ironist the comic is an other ingredient in the very definition of reason's intricate sense of itself.

Philosophical irony has the advantage of igniting the explosion of pretension from within the pretension itself. Philosophical irony contemplates turning things on their head, turning them upside down. It is not quite yet what I call idiot wisdom. But it does inhabit Hegel's *verkehrte Welt*, the world of thought that is topsy-turvy to the Thracian maid. But she is not alone in laughing at the upside-down reality. To parody Heraclitus by repeating him verbatim but in a different tone of voice: the way up is also the way down. Philosophical irony laughs at pretension because it moves in two opposed directions at one and the same time. This is something the *steife Verstand* can never do, since it will freeze those directions into a dualistic antithesis. Or should we say that philosophical irony sees the stiff understanding in fact moving in two directions at once and so always presenting the silly spectacle of thought tearing itself apart?

More positively, we should say: univocal mind cannot think beyond the equivocal double, to the metaxological community of the two directions in the affirmative double. For there is an entirely affirmative sense of moving in two directions at once. What is this? It is the double mediation in the middle: the erotic movement, upwards as it were, of the self towards the other; the agapeic movement, downwards as it were, of the other to the self. *Verstand* cannot understand this double movement at once; dialectic tries to understand, but emphasizes the erotic movement. The metaxological finds the middle that is the conjunction of the two, their community or communivocity, beyond univocity, equivocity, and erotic dialectic. And as the erotic movement is not the agapeic, as the dialectical is not the metaxological, so then the way up is *not* the way down. I contradict myself? I contain multitudes? Yes and No: I am all and I am nothing; I move between.

In the middle Socratic irony prises open a gap between pretension and actuality. The thinker does not see he is in that gap, that he actually *is* that gap, that he is a split or doubled reality. Irony widens the inner split, and in the laughable diremption, the pretentious self falls apart or should fall apart, if it is simply attentive to what is taking place, to what it is effecting on its very self. The self is brought by Socratic dialectic to an aporia by the ineluctable leading of its own logos. The aporia is an impasse of the dialectic itself, a failure of the logos in *dialegein*. That the explosion occurs from within, that the self is hoisted with its own petard is vital, because it means that only thus is the true meaning of the failure appropriated. Otherwise one is merely torn to pieces from outside and the wisdom of failure does not take root.

Again directly contrary to the cliché of philosophy as a metaphysics of presence wedded to the rigidities of a univocal logic, there is something significantly *dissimulating* in Socratic irony. With all due respect, Socrates was a liar. At times his talk verges on the equivocal, though to say he was a dialectical talker in an implicitly plurivocal sense would better express the point. It is difficult to believe Socrates entirely when he says he knew nothing. I think this is a lie, a noble lie of philosophical irony. Against the metaphysics of presence, Socrates is an essentially masked thinker who knows more than he is willing to say. He has to know more if he is to find the jugular, find the point of cleft that, if just touched deftly, results in the pretentious other falling to pieces like a flimsy house of cards. And yet there is another sense in which to say "I am as nothing," is to utter the naked truth.

Derrida's strategic mimicry of metaphysics, indeed at times his full-blown mimicry of Hegelian modes of thought, is full with a not dissimilar dissimulation. For example, his critique of Levinas in "Violence and Metaphysics," is saturated with the logical moves that

Hegel brilliantly uses in the section on Absolute Difference in the *Logic*. The mimicry of Hegel is so good that one is unsure if it is mimicry at all. The voice of the mimic, Derrida, is so like the voice of the original, Hegel, that all interpretation turns on the subtle tone of the voice.

Derrida will not thank me for talking about voice vis-à-vis his *written* text; nevertheless the necessity to consider the intonation of the text shows its proximity to Socratic irony and philosophical lying, let us call it, "white lying." The very same text might be read in a straightforward or in an ironical fashion. Indeed, contra Derrida's grammatological emphasis, the *spoken* voice in all the subtlety of its recalcitrant otherness can be an extraordinarily dense carrier of ironical rather than univocal presence. The voiced self rather than the written text is far more resistant to the univocity charged to the so-called metaphysics of presence.

There is a difference between Derridean mimicry and Socratic irony is that implicit in the latter is the insistent call of a standard of absoluteness that haunts even the most radical failure. This standard insinuates the hard question: Can your logos stand up under the debunking that is self-initiated, since it is the logos that calls itself into question? It is the logos that is nagged by the suspicion that its pretensions are laughable, its thought just so much straw. This relates to my claim that a certain appropriation of failure internally defines philosophical thought itself. The other of logos is internally related to logos itself, not necessarily in the sense of being assimilated to the logos, but in the sense that the disquiet it arouses is recognized within the intimacy of logos itself.

Hegel is not unaware of this, though the further question must be put: Is there a disquieting of the logos which, though intimate to the logos, communicates an otherness that will always mock any appropriating desire? This is a question for Hegel from those of us who are disquieted with his logos. Is there an otherness that exposes philosophical thought as so laughable that it is humbled, brought to a grief from which it will never recuperate? Kierkegaard certainly thought so, and called that other "God."

Hegel does see a disquiet intimate to logos itself, a point I will now consider by looking at another ancestor, namely, the ancient skeptic. The skeptic is Socrates' blood brother, though the debunking side of the dialectic is more unrestrainedly loose here. But notice: the site of ancient skepticism is also a territory mined with failure. I know that stoicism and skepticism are important in Hegel's *Phenomenology*. These deal with central failures and lead on to the turning point of failure there, namely, the unhappy consciousness. The unhappy consciousness is Hegel's name for the split self and for radical metaphysical failure. It prefigures Nietzsche's "God is dead" and his judgment on the putative failure of the religious and philosophical traditions stemming from Platonism and Christianity.

Below I return to the *Phenomenology* and the comedy of failure there, but Hegel is aware that one cannot be a philosopher without being a skeptic. Skepticism is a central philosophical way of appropriating failure. Thus, the problem of ancient skepticism with *equipollence*—that two opposite views seem to have equal rationality, and hence that the rational choice between them seems undecidable— deeply prefigures Kant's problematic of the antinomies. It is related to the problematic double of equivocity: between two opposites in equivocity there seems an unmediated difference that resists every effort at reduction to univocal unity. Sextus Empiricus says: "To every logos an equal logos can be counterposed (*panti logoi logos isos antikeitai*)." Not surprisingly, Hegel occupied himself as deeply with the ancient skeptical problem of equipollence, as with the Kantian antinomies. Hegel, in fact, describes the *Weg des Zweifels* (way of doubt) or the *Weg der Verzweiflung* (way of despair) of his *Phenomenology* as self-completing or self-accomplishing skepticism (*sich vollbringende Skeptizismus*). The split double of equivocity is manifest in doubt (*Zweifel*) and in despair (*Verzweiflung*). But as self-accomplishing skepticism, the *Phenomenology* passes towards the complete *self-mediation* of the equivocal double. The split of the equivocal double will be healed in the complete self-mediation of absolute knowing, when Hegelian philosophy will finally be at home with itself.[19]

One recalls that for Hegel the greatness of ancient skepticism resides in its showing that everything finite comes to nothing: the nothingness of the finite is its lesson. This nothingness is the laughableness of all finiteness; it is comic; it counts for nothing; it explodes itself; it brings itself to nought. With modern skepticism, by contrast, it is the finite that blocks the way to anything other and the skeptical impulse denies any such radical other. The ancients called this radical other, "eternity."

Ancient skepticism, Hegel says, is noble. One thinks of a self who can stand in the middle of destruction and in the very destruction still say its yes. This yes is noble, but to be honest it has to be won in the process of devastation, in the process in which everything comes to nothing. I am reminded of more recent absurdist pronouncements: everything comes to nothing, but we do not always find an ancient or Hegelian or Nietzschean nobility that would redeem it. Nor do we find it easy to hear the yes of agapeic mind.

The issue of noble skepticism has a double aspect. If the risible is what cannot stand and comes to nothing, for Hegel nothing is ever merely a void privation. As a determinate nothing, it is ingredient in the process of affirmation itself. Something explodes but something *is* in the exploding—the energy of spirit is what outlives its own debunkings. Hence, in the scoffing even of noble skepticism there is something that outlives negation; there has to be, despite the radical extremity to which negation has been pushed. Some such outliving is the only thing that makes sense. Hence, the comedy of failure itself is double: it is a breaking down but it is also a breaking through of something more ultimate than what counts for nothing. It is this breaking through that opens up, through failure, another affirmative possibility of being. I will return to this because Hegel's dialectic is more insistent on this breaking through than is the breaking down of deconstruction. This shapes his wariness concerning the merely laughable that empties everything of meaning.

Though Hegel grants the negating work of skepticism, it is a station on the way of despair, the *via dolorosa* of dialectic in quest of speculative reason, or *Vernunft* in its free release. This raises the possibility of a kind of philosophical success even in radical failure. Hegel points in this direction; indeed dialectic leads us in this direction; it articulates the shape of fundamental failure which is overturned, inverted into its opposite at the moment of extremity. The question is how is this overturning effected; for this is the axis on which is determined the possibility of breaking beyond the breakdown into the breakthrough. Hegel might be seen to claim that speculative reason is only a further radicalization of the breaking open process we find in the dialectic, but a radicalization that now fulfills itself by a breaking through into meaning. Is this breakthrough erotic or agapeic? Perhaps both.

The *Phenomenology* and the *Logic*:
Masks of Philosophical Comedy?

What light does this discussion throw on the *Phenomenology* and *Logic* as masks of philosophical comedy? The *Phenomenology* is the dialectical unfolding of a series of configurations of consciousness in which a quest for absoluteness unfolds. How does Hegel describe this absolute? His famous statement, the true is the whole, gives us sufficient direction here. What is absolute is what is truly whole and this obtains when, in other Hegelian terms, a reality is successful in coinciding with its concept. What Hegel shows is the pretension of each stage of consciousness to be such a whole, to be absolute.

Hegel calls the *Phenomenology* a "gallery of images," *eine Gallerie von Bildern*. I would say a "gallery of postures"—posturings of the absolute that are proven to be impostures. Every form of consciousness for itself or in relation to itself presents itself as absolute. What Hegel reveals is the repeated failure of this pretension, this self-presentation. Each *Gestalt* of consciousness take itself with the utmost seriousness, with absolute seriousness, takes itself as finally the home where consciousness can overcome its estrangement vis-à-vis otherness and rest in the peace of fulfilling self-identity. Every form poses as absolute; what the dialectic does is expose the imposture, shows the posturing for what it is, simply posturing. Its taking itself absolutely seriously proves to be a joke, to be laughable. It is exploded—it cannot be fixed, identified with its own self-understanding—on this score it is a laughable failure.

How is the failure revealed? Is the debunking negativity of dialectic just a form of philosophical *ressentiment* violently imposing the joke on these *Gestalten* of consciousness? Nietzsche implies this with regard to Socratic dialectic ("dialectic is rabble"), and Deleuze reiterates the charge by calling the dialectic "the ideology of *ressentiment*."[20] This again is too simple. Rather the joke unfurls *within* the form of consciousness itself. That it to say, since it is a form of consciousness, its own self inevitably comes home to it, and what comes home to it is the failure of its own pretension to absoluteness. As phenomenologist Hegel claims simply to watch the failure as it unfurls.

There is the fact, too, that each form of consciousness resists its own falling to pieces; it tries to hug its own pretension; in resisting its own breakdown, it hence tries to resist any breakthrough into a less pretentious form. Throughout the *Phenomenology* consciousness progressively is coming closer to itself, closing on its own reality, approximating more fully its identity with its own concept. The general point is: everything in the *Phenomenology* is a failure, only barring the final form of *Geist*. And one of the most intractable questions is: In what sense is the last form a success? Is it a success which excludes the comic? My claim is that philosophical success need not exclude the comic. It may be a form of being-at-home with itself and being, even in the absolute destruction of all absolute pretensions.

This is not to say that Hegel does full justice to the comic. It is to say that a virtuality of dialectical thinking points to its affinity with the comic. Hegel did not fully explore what this virtuality implies; he abbreviated a philosophical probe that would have brought to light in comic breakdown and breakthrough modes of otherness that are not simply moments of a process of dialectical self-mediation.

This also means that one should one be surprised or misled by the language of violent negativity in the *Phenomenology*, as in the life and death struggle of master and slave, and the discussion of freedom and terror. In relation to the breakdown, Hegel's view is that consciousness performs the violence on itself: thought is at war with itself, and the wounds it inflicts are self-inflicted. There can be a sharp edge of violence to laughter precisely because laughter responds to a kind of failure that is either exposed or rejected or even affirmed.

In relation to the comedy of failure, it is relevant that the language of the *Phenomenology* is woven of words like "reversal," "overturning," "self-opposition" (as, for instance, in *die verkehrte Welt*). This is the language of laughter which, while containing the possibility of violence, is not closed to affirmation. In the comic there is a process of coming to nothing and a renewed process of coming to be affirmatively. Hegelian dialectic is right to affirm both processes, rather than simply remaining fixated with a negative process which does not renew our affirmation of being—even though, I claim, there are manifestations of otherness in both processes that resist complete dialectical conceptualization.

Can one make similar points about logos and the comedy of failure relative to the *Logic*? Consider the general movement of categories there. The process of failure here is not that of forms of consciousness or *Geist* but of logical categories. We have a process in which a manifold of categories offer themselves as adequate to the thought of being. Each category offers itself as pretender to being the absolute category and hence the one that will make being to be absolutely intelligible. None is the absolute monarch of the Idea, all are pretenders to the throne, though some are royalty in waiting that will wait for ever. The *Logic* claims to show the failure of every category, short of the Absolute Idea, to deliver on its promise. Its pretension is revealed. Hegel claims not to be imposing a standard of absoluteness *ab extra* but to show how each category brings itself to grief, to the point of breakdown, in some cases of reversal, in all cases of breakthrough, if the process is to continue.

The comedy is not evident in the rhetoric of the *Logic* as it is the *Phenomenology* in which many of the turns of thought seems to be effected by metaphorical and ironical twists that give the lie to the thesis-antithesis-synthesis view of Hegel. I consider it important that some of his most memorable thoughts are not formal argumentations but condensed in tart, humorous images. One of the most famous philosophical sarcasms must be the description of the Schellingian *Indifferenzpunkt* as the night in which all cows are black. This is a joke and from the standpoint of logical argumentation it is itself laughable. But it is extraordinarily effective in taking the wind out of the sails of the Schellingian. It is a brilliant image that is so effective because it epitomizes philosophical mockery of what I am calling the comedy of failure.

Can we call upon this same power of the image to unsettle the culmination of the *Science of Logic* in the Absolute Idea that is totally at home with itself? Is there any laughter at this end, so seemingly secure from all failure of the logos, so secure in its sense of success at having surmounted all the previous logical failures? Suppose one were to say: Yes there is a night in which all cows look black, but maybe the philosopher has to venture into this night, after the dusk of Minerva's Owl has passed into pitch dark? Is there a knowledge of the night? Must not philosophy go into this night, go into the night with fear and trembling? In this night will we be like Aristotle's bats in sunlight: nocturnal creatures dazzled by an excess, pure light that is too much for us and hence is darkness to mind? Mind's blackout, mind's blinking in this excess—is this the *bios xenikos* of speculative metaphysics? Is this the strange thought of unmastered otherness to which agapeic mind says yes?

Or is this night only the sleep of mind, maybe even the death of philosophical thought? Would philosophy then be unmasked, its coming to nothing stripping it of pretense and posture, releasing it to be a thinking without masks? Would speculative mind become a kind of posthumous mind, a metaphysical mindfulness of being beyond death?[21] What *docta ignorantia*, what idiot wisdom might be possible for an ironical philosopher like Socrates, or a speculative philosopher like Cusanus? Or for Hegel himself? For is it not true that the Owl of Minerva still continues to fly by night? Or would we have to follow Nietzsche, give up on logic and sing a *Nachtlied*—the beautiful night-song of Zarathustra? What of the nightsong of Apollo's swan, Socrates, sung on the night before the day of death, the darkest night/day of all? Suppose in this night we do not meet the Schellingian *Indifferenzpunkt*, but hear—since now we are blind and cannot see—hear, I say, that gentle mocking laughter we imagined we heard before in thinking about the *Logic*: It is nothing, it is as straw?

Dialectic and Deconstruction as Masks of the Comic

What I am calling the comedy of failure in relation to philosophical logos is usually not so named. One of its philosophical masks is the enigmatic disguise: the dialectic. In some of its functions, dialectic articulates the logos of failure and the failure of logos. I will put the matter in terms of the critique of identity, a critique also central to deconstruction.

Dialectic is concerned with a being between extremes and the articulation of an interplay between the self and an other. This is clearly true of Socratic dialectic. However, in Hegel's case the other is never a radical beyond to the self, either as a *Gestalt* of consciousness or *Geist* or a logical category; the other is internally related to the self. Hegelian dialectic implies that the self can never be fixed to any univocal self-identity. This would be the empty formal tautology of A=A which Hegel criticizes on so many occasions, and whose pretension to absoluteness is as laughable as its absolute emptiness. We are in a world of becoming with Hegelian dialectic; hence it is impossible to fix a static self-identity; for the very nature of self is to other itself, to become other to fixed self-identity. Absolutely nothing can be or remain in a univocal self-identity; being is always a becoming other. Dialectic both explodes the pretension of univocal self-identity, and tries to mark the articulation of this process of self-othering.

Yet for Hegel, conceiving the logos as dialectical self-mediation, the other of self is again self. The critique of univocal identity need not produce a merely equivocal difference or an antithesis impossible to mediate. Thus in the *Phenomenology*, the other intended by the forms of consciousness is absolute selfhood. Each form sees itself as other, as absolute. The process of self-diremption issues from the self as it pretends to be the absolute as whole. The process of self-diremption is the self-subversion of merely univocal identity. What emerges then is a gap between what the self actually is and what it has othered itself to be. But that gap is within itself, it is the cleft within itself and its efforts to stabilize its self-identity as absolute. Dialectic can be said to articulate the energy of being that comes to expression in this cleft. This cleft, this difference, is the downfall of the claim to absolute self-identity. As it is properly articulated, the form of consciousness cannot maintain its own pretension; what it is, and what it is as other, prove not to coincide. The center cannot hold; there ceases to be a univocal center; the two sides of the between fall apart.

Dialectic brings the forms of consciousness to this point of breakdown. This is like a person with a foot on either side of a fault which as its widens threatens to split him in two. He may go down into the abyss that opens; or he may try to leap above this particular cleft. As Hegel uses it, dialectic seems to do both these things. It brings to breakdown; and if we stay simply at this point then we have failure simpliciter. But dialectic also seems to leap just at this point into another form of consciousness or category. This leap is the breakthrough of consciousness or logos into a new, more promising form. This new form, though reached by leaping beyond the gap of the previous form, nevertheless is still a dancing over the same abyss. It is better dancing because consciousness and thought have become more conscious of themselves just in the very process of their previous failure.

Failure may be thus one of the deepest occasions in which the self comes to self-knowledge in its interplay with otherness. It may liberate mindfulness of ultimate limitation and release in the middle. What Hegel seeks in that interplay is what he calls "pure self-recognition in absolute otherness" (*das* reine Selbsterkennen *im absoluten Anderssein*).[22] I demur about privileging *self*-recognition and want to give a different, non-Hegelian weight to absolute otherness. I think that such failure, dialectically revealed but metaxologically reinterpreted, is related to the wisdom of the ancients, the *pathei mathos*, the knowing of suffering. That said, dialectic does articulate the breakdown of univocal identity and the promise of an affirmative breakthrough emergent in and despite breakdown, a breakthrough beyond equivocal dualism.

I deliberately used the image of dancing over the abyss, because we are not dealing with a static ground or thing-like foundation. Dancing on the abyss may seem only the privilege of dithyrambic Nietzscheans or magicians. In fact Hegel does use the image of magic in the *Phenomenology: Geist* wins its truth only when it finds itself in utter dismemberment; its tarrying with the negative is the magic power which converts it into being.[23] And Hegel did invoke festive, dancing metaphors before Nietzsche, for it was he who compared truth to a Bacchanalian revel. I remarked on this at the end of chapter 2. I now ask: Can one have such a revel, such a celebration of festive being without much thunderous laughter?

I suggest: What we find *within* dialectic at times recalls the strategy of deconstruction in dealing with Hegel as *its* other. Thus, the concern of deconstruction with the failure of philosophical logos is intimately bound up with the question of difference. It takes seriously the Heideggerian view that there is an unthought in the thought of the Western tradition, and that in thinking this unthought the end of the Western tradition may be laid bare—laid bare in a double sense. Thus, in completing the tradition Hegel is said to show, despite himself, the unthought that exceeds the closure of absolute knowledge. In other words, the completion of the Hegelian closure is also testimony to the failure of the Western logos. If Western logos completes itself in an insuperable way in Hegel's logic, this absolute success reveals itself as failure from the standpoint of the unthought that nests in its very success.

Thus from a standpoint said to be *other than* Hegel's, we seem to discover in Hegel all the ingredients of the comedy of failure in relation to philosophical logos. We have pretension to absoluteness, and more, even a certain attaining of absoluteness in a sense (Derrida seems to grant Hegel this "success," as does Heidegger). With philosophical reason, as so often with other things, what is really laughable is never clearly evident in its embryonic state but is evident in its full unfolding. Thus, the highest moment of philosophical achievement becomes the moment of overturning, or reversal. Philosophical success reveals its radical other, namely, absolute failure. Absolute knowledge is exceeded by failure, and the way to "say" this failure is to laugh at, not just its pretension, but its actual success. It is as if the absolute intelligibility of Hegel's system, precisely in being successful, reveals its complete absurdity. This is the comedy of its success/failure. It is as if Hegelian logic, precisely in being absolutely logical, revealed its illogicality, its madness.

On the comic relation of the embryonic to the fully unfolded, I think of the bitter humor of Charlie Chaplin's *The Great Dictator*: the absurdity of absolute power in the hands of a nothing; but the absurd pretension of the nothing is only evident when its struts as the absolute master on the stage of world-history. This would be the comedy of totalitarianism did not its risibleness degenerate into a black night of blood. Chaplin's debunking of pretension is not un-Hegelian, but the black comedy of world-historical individuals is not Hegelian. For that matter why was it that Chaplin could laugh at the Führer, and Heidegger could not? The stiff-willed postures before world-historical destiny are deadly serious. Would the Thracian maid laugh at the "inner truth and greatness" of National Socialism? Is there not more truth of spirit, more ontological authenticity vis-à-vis the intimacy of being, in the rueful face of the sorrowing clown?

Deconstructionist strategies are subversive of any effort to fix self-identity, to fix a static unity. Though Hegel has been unfairly, not to say mindlessly criticized in this respect, deconstruction is right to question the notion of a fixed univocal unity, quite right to show that the effort to pin down such a unity absolutely falls apart, must inevitably come to grief and failure. Such a claim to unity, claimed, say, by a literary text, is shown, or shows itself, under closer scrutiny to be infected with inherent oppositions and strains that war against each other, that coexist in uneasy alliance, that reveal the cleft within the unity itself, making it precarious and less secure than the surface of univocity might suggest. I see the strategy of deconstruction as reminiscent of Socratic irony and Hegel's dialectic: it claims to take a text on its own terms, but just in those terms it exposes its possible pretension to seamless unity, reveals it to be other than it seemed, reveals this otherness within the text itself, reveals texts as themselves self-othering. For Derrida the texts of Hegel himself are "fissured" and so susceptible to a double reading. The pretension of unity is exploded from within.

I spoke of laughter as revealing an immanent breakdown. In a sense deconstruction as a strategy of analysis does just that: it claims to find the lines of fault within texts and by irritating those lines, causes them to redden into visible scars, worries them into wounds, and perhaps even to initiation of the self-breakdown of the text itself. (This is related to Adorno's notion of immanent dialectic.) If deconstruction is concerned with the failure of the logos, on occasion something like a breakthrough into something other is indicated. This breakthrough of otherness evokes a response reminiscent of a Nietzschean affirmation of the play of the world. But there is the extreme difficulty of *saying* this breakthrough philosophically, because such "saying" is itself caught within the economy of logos, and hence seems trapped within the so-called closure of metaphysics.

Derrida's writings often bring us to a moment of ominous expectation when a new, unprecedented thinking is "announced"—but then the promise is not redeemed. We read another of his essays, which returns us to the beginning, to bring us again to the fateful "announcement," only again to drop us back into cryptic silence. Is this philosophical eros under erasure, *eros interruptus*? One senses Derrida always holding back at the most climactic moment of possible breakthrough. This raises again the suspicion: That one is having one's philosophical cake and eating it too.[24]

Derrida sees the difficulty of saying but displaces it in "Violence and Metaphysics." He says that if you want to get close to the king to kill him you must feign his language; to subvert Greek philosophy and commit parricide on Parmenides, you must speak Greek. But he puts the real question, which, however, he does not answer: "And since it is a question of killing a speech, will we ever know who is the last victim of this stratagem? Can one feign speaking a language?"[25] It is perhaps easier to accuse Parmenides of univocity given his radical insistence on the unity of being. A more interesting question concerns the difficulty of murdering (putting under erasure, deconstructing) *Zeno* the Eleatic. Some of Parmenides' utterances signal a flight *beyond* commonsense to pure being and the logos in its well-rounded truth. Zeno is more dialectical in this sense: he is *in-between* commonsense *doxa* and logos/epistēmē. In the between we need dialectic to fight and to deflate false logoi. Such dialectic is between two worlds: doxa and epistēmē, the Cave and the Sun, healthy commonsense and speculative logic.

In his *Lectures on the History of Philosophy* Hegel agrees with Aristotle that Zeno is the originator of dialectic and discusses him more extensively than he does Parmenides. This is not surprising. In Zeno we find the elements of the *reductio ad absurdum*. And the *reductio ad absurdum* is perhaps *the* logicist way par excellence of laughing at the failure of a logos. The *reductio* is a philosophical tactic of rational deflation. In Zeno we also have what Aristotle (*Topics*, VII) calls *epicheirēma* (dialectical syllogism). But one might approach Zeno's *reductio* either as laughable from the standpoint of everyday opinion (*doxa*) and so revealing the comedy of logic—logic must be mad if it deconstructs motion and plurality; or we might see the *reductio* as logic itself showing the laughableness of everyday opinion and so revealing logic as comedy in quite a different sense. The second comedy is more difficult to murder as simple univocity. Zeno's mad/logical paradoxes remind us again of Plato's reversed world, or Aristotle's *bios xenikos*, or Hegel's suggestion that philosophy asks commonsense to walk on its head.

I ask again: Can the logicians laugh? Concerning the comedy of logic, the comic poet Epicrates indicates that the diaeretic method (descendent of Zeno' dialectic and antecedent of Aristotle's logic, but used sometimes comically in Plato's *Sophist*) was practiced in the Academy to the point of becoming a joke.[26] Thus, *within* philosophy there can be a comic play of logic, connected with dialectic, the *reductio*, and the interplay of univocity and equivocity. Far from being completely unknown to, or even repressed by philosophy, this play is to be found even in Eleatic thinking. The life of philosophy is even stranger than deconstruction suspects. This is true, too, of the restless debunking side of philosophy. We do not have to wait for Derrida to suggest the parricide of Parmenides. The suggestion is already made in Plato, in the *Sophist*. Are the repressive fathers of univocity so easily identifiable in the philosophical tradition?

The skeptical strain in deconstruction itself is worth noting. As we saw, skepticism is a philosophical way of naming nothingness in the form of the failure of the logos, the foundering of reason in trying to secure absolute certainty. Deconstructionist skepticism seems to me to be closer to Kant than to Hegel. This is not surprising in that one of the deconstructionist's more recent ancestors, namely, Heidegger, seems to be more Kantian than Hegelian, certainly with respect to the point at issue—the limits of reason. I detect in deconstructionist rhetoric a transposition of Kantian language of the "unknowable."

This is transposed in terms of a non-knowledge that exceeds knowledge; a non-knowledge which is not yet the "unknowable" considered as the dialectical opposite of the knowable and hence subsumable within the movement of dialectic. This issue permeates Derrida's essay on Bataille.

For a philosopher who, unlike Derrida, is proud, privileged to be called philosopher, all such talk arouses memory of the objection of Stillingfleet and Berkeley to Locke's "I know not what" or Hegel's criticism of the Kantian *Ding-an-sich*. On the face of it, it makes no sense. To say the unsayable is to say it, and hence not to say the unsayable. Deconstructive skepticism ends with an equivocation which we must think through even further. Perhaps we need another saying that is also an unsaying, a naming that confesses its failure to name, a representation of the unrepresentable that knows no representation will ever do. Or perhaps the rest should be silence. Better the silence of Aquinas' "It is as straw," to the tomes of anti-logocentric logos of deconstruction. True, the deconstructionist feigns to feel no embarrassment here, since he is quite willing to live with non-sense, non-meaning. It is as a *burst of nonsense* that the laughter of Bataille is celebrated. You may not be able to conceptualize what is supposed to exceed knowing but you may laugh at the failure of meaning or knowing that the excess occasions. This burst of nonsense is *not* what I mean by the agapeic festivity of metaxological thought.

There is also something "Kantian" in the deconstructionist refusal of the Hegelian breakthrough to the more affirmative side of the *Aufhebung*. *Aufhebung* recovers meaning on the other side of non-meaning; *Aufhebung* claims to redeem absurdity; *Aufhebung* is the joy of dialectically being-at-home with self after the joy of laughter has subsided, prepared by this breakdown and explosion itself. This Hegelian breakthrough is closer to what I mean by the agapeic festivity of metaxological thought. Granted, there is always the temptation to a being-at-home which is a neutralization of the negative. Let the reader recall my discussion of evil and dialectic, and this point needs no further remark. But the rhetoric of deconstruction sometimes seems to imply that all being-at-home is simply not decent. After Auschwitz, no speculative philosophy, no reconciliation, only the torment of thought. There is no home.

And so any desire to be at-home with being is said to disguise a will for security, reassurance, a desire for meaning sought by a spineless nostalgia. This kind of language reveals a kind of ideological dread of, even disgust with univocal unity. Deconstruction reveals a subversive thinking that overturns, explodes, breaks down, a thinking that reverses and perverts, that inverts, that laughs. This is the laughter of thought that *stiffly insists* on being homeless. This is an equivocity of thought that is too busy denouncing univocity to be silent long enough to listen for any possible gesture of reconcilement, any elusive hint of home.

Since the illusion of a unitary totality is the most laughable, for the deconstructionist Hegel turns out to be the most comic philosopher, unbeknownst to himself. I think such criticism of Hegel risks being compounded of caricatures. Admittedly, caricature can serve as a useful form of revelation, a conceptual mockery that serves philosophical truth. But in the present instance I say: in the rough strokes that draw the caricature, Hegel's unmistakable silhouette reemerges, but not as the face of the caricature, but as a master practitioner of just those strategies of self-subversion that the deconstructionist directs at Hegel himself. There are ironies within ironies here into whose laughter Hegel dissolves, not because he is being debunked but because he has already plumbed the abyss of self-debunking.

I am not hostile to some of the points against Hegel, nor to the effort to think of otherness in terms beyond dialectic. But there is more in Hegel, more to be learned from him. Until this is granted, all the talk about exceeding Hegel strikes me as laughable. It is not that the talk has no point but as talk beyond Hegel it really is talk beyond Hegel, but in the sense of bypassing rather than surpassing him. It may be beyond Kojève's Hegelianism with its excessive emphasis on the master/slave dialectic. Hegel cannot be boxed into this. Derrida's seeming approval of Bataille's laughing at Hegel as a strategy to exceed the closure of absolute knowledge and to assert Hegel's laughableness, makes one wonder if Derrida himself fails to listen for Hegel's own laughter. It makes one wonder if justice has been done to the poetic and the sacred in Hegel. His Kojèvian stress on the concept as *work* dulls Hegel's insights into the poetic, the comic and the cult.

I repeat Hegel from the *Differenzschrift*: art and speculation, too, are *Gottesdienst*. I reiterate from the *Phenomenology* that the deepest intimacy obtains between the sacrifice of Christ and speculative thought. The maligned other, the criminal undergoes a death that is meaningless and that yet makes sacred. In our time, speculative philosophy has frequently been judged an outlaw, been judged as outlaw thought. Is the death of such thought meaningless? Or must such thought not pass through the death of meaninglessness? For Hegel philosophical thinking must undergo its speculative Good Friday, its Golgotha. Maybe in our century Auschwitz is the Golgotha of speculative philosophy. But I see no reason for shame in a final unwillingness to acquiesce in death as meaningless, even while one looks on meaningless death. As I pointed out in relation to evil and dialectic, prior to the transition to this Golgotha, Hegel underscores the forgiveness of evil where the two sides of a hostile opposition break through to each other in a hosanna of yea yea. This points to what I called the breaking through, prepared for by the dialectic as breaking down. In his own dialectical way, Hegel philosophically wants to name this breakthrough.

As previous chapters make clear, I find difficulties in Hegel's articulation of the meaning of all of this in terms of dialectical self-mediation. There are forms of otherness that resist complete incorporation in such a dialectical self-mediation. Encountering such otherness, breakdown and breakthrough may occur. The language of dialectic gets at something of what is at stake in such breakdowns and breakthroughs, but not at all. Such breakdowns and break-throughs demand to be articulated in metaxological terms, in so far as these terms acknowledge that there are forms of otherness that are not conceptually mastered.

In the final breakthrough laughter is metaxological. Beyond univocity, equivocity and dialectic, it reveals an unmastered outburst of the energy of being as agapeic, nourishing in us the promise of idiot wisdom. I do not doubt that Hegel honestly addressed what to him was manifest of the *Sache selbst*. But since the Owl of Minerva only takes wing at dusk, the time of its thought is one when the crisp, determinate outline of things loses the garish evidence of the univocal day. The eyes of the Owl of Minerva, most of the time a philosopher's dead stare, are sometimes forced to squint. Sometimes they also wink and shine.

What Breaks Through [in] the Mask of Comedy?

In this last section, I return to the comic from this other side, namely, the recovery of meaning rather than the explosion of the pretension to meaning. I will say that laughter need not be mad, though there is a mad laughter; there is a generous laughing that is fundamentally affirmative in the dismemberment of negativity itself. Such generous laughter would overflow from the idiot wisdom of agapeic mindfulness. I will focus on two themes: the power of the comic in relation to being-at-home (not only in relation to the dialectical breakdown); the philosophical importance of irony, and the ambiguity of its deconstructive power in Hegel and his successors.

In relation to the first theme, we learn a lot by looking at Hegel's attitude to Greek comedy. Hegel says that comedy reveals the absolute negating power of subjectivity, and here again Socrates is important. Socrates represents the new world of subjective spirit coming to historical manifestation at the end of classical Greece. This is something new, and also, Hegel thinks, something justified. But what Socrates seems to oppose, namely, the accepted ethical world of tradition, with its mythic and tragic picture of the whole, has its rights, too. There is a tragic conflict between these two. Socrates was guilty as charged, but the Greek world was only executing itself, since the Socratic spirit had become part of its reality.

Now at play secretly in this tragedy is the spirit of the comic, and its sense of the inevitable failure of human pretension, a sense of human failure which is itself deeply humane. The Socratic spirit of irony is only possible for a self who has proceeded to a certain stage of inwardness, that is, found a distance, or difference opening up between itself and the given traditional world of myth and the tragic. This distance is essential to the possibility of laughter. Without the internal difference of a certain subjectivity, without a certain idiocy or intimacy of being, there can be no laughter; animals never laugh because they lack this internal difference of inwardness.

This distance, difference can take a skeptical form, a sophistic form, an ironical form, even a nihilistic form. It puts the self in a space of ambiguity beyond naive affirmation and negation. Moreover, since negation and affirmation now become self-conscious, we can succumb to nihilism here. And clearly Socrates knew what nihilism was; he certainly saw it in the debunking dialectic of the sophists. Irony is only possible where there exists a self-consciousness of affirmation and negation, an awareness of our ability to hover or be suspended between Yes and No. This is why Derrida's equivocating dialectic can hover, vacillate in the between. Hegel grants the necessity of all of the destructive power that resides in this new emergence. There is no going back to immediacy; the human spirit has to endure failure. This is also why Socratic selfhood prefigures Christian inwardness, which in fact fulfills the necessity of failure in even more radical form. God himself must fail, give Himself over to radical failure in dying; this is the Golgotha of being in the form of the death of God.

There is a death of god in the Greek world, too, which is linked to Socrates and the spirit of comedy. In Greek comedy there is a distancing of the persona (literally the mask) and the actor. In more archaic tragedy the actor *was* the mask; and since the persona might be the god, the god was there on the stage. With the emergence of self-consciousness, the separation of persona and actor signifies the eruption of the internal difference of inwardness; it is physically enacted in this separation. What happens is that the human actor

steps out from behind the divine mask; the divine mask is shown to
be just that, a mask. This divine mask is a game that we now cannot
play naively; thus this separation inevitably goes with a process of
debunking, of demythologization. Eventually the human actor stands
there without a mask, nakedly human and nothing more. And even
base humans, like slaves, can take the same stage that just before
was the privilege of the god. The gods are laughable because the divine
image cannot sustain the onslaught of self-consciousness. The naive
images break down, though it is really we who break down. Comedy
shows that our images of the divine, our masks of the sacred come
to nothing.

Does the divine itself become nothing? Is it the image or the
original that is straw? Is it we or the divine that is the straw dog?
Though the divine images cannot be taken with the previous naivete
any more, the question is whether something can still be preserved,
even in the act of debunking them. I think Hegel believes so. I agree
with Hegel on the breakthrough of affirmation, though not in exactly
the same sense. All images and masks must pass through a purgatory
of deeper metaphysical mindfulness. The ambiguity of the sacred mask
is not a mere equivocation that bears no mediation; the ambiguity
may generate equivocal laughter; it also points beyond equivocity.
Some of these ambiguities were faced in our discussion of representation and speculation. Elsewhere I speak of the matter in terms of
what I call a "releasing disillusionment."[27]

For Hegel the power of dialectical mediation is at work in this
entire process and so is already pushing us beyond equivocity. By
incorporating debunking into a comic order something is retained.
For this incorporation involves both negation and affirmation. It is
negation of naive consciousness, but it is a negation with a certain
joy of energy in which the self, new to its inwardness, is also at home
in itself in all of the debunking. To the extent that we are talking
about the breakdown of the traditional gods, we are dealing with the
figures who gave meaning to the communal whole of Greek life. The
debunking of the gods involves a comic demythologizing that reveals
a failure of the sacred masks. There is nothing trivial about this
failure; there is nothing trivial about the reconciliation that the
deepest laughter may effect. The failure of the sacred mask may be
the effect of the sacred itself as other to all masks. We laugh at the
gods, but the gods laugh back. They laugh at us through the cracks
of those masks that mark our pretension to master divine otherness.

What I have just said is both Hegelian and very non-Hegelian.
For Hegel will see the crumbling of these masks as the birth of our
self-mediating mastery. True, the full ripening of that mastery will

have to await our historical passage through the new and last mask of Hegelian *Geist*, namely, the Christian representation of God as incarnated in the human being. For Hegel the mask of the Christian God will also drop in time and the mystery of divine transcendence in its otherness will yield to the immanent historical unfolding of the logical Idea (see chapter 1). By contrast, in the crumbling of the masks I see the straw of every anthropocentric image that mistakenly identified itself with the absolute original. To laugh at the straw of the sacred masks arouses a divine "It is nothing," a forgiving "It is nothing," that generously opens once again the space of transcendence and the metaxological promise of the between. The mask deconstructs itself, and we can laugh at its falling apart, only because every image, every concept is ever exceeded by the agapeic being of the absolute original.

It is significant that Hegel's *Aesthetics* ends with the comic, with Hegel citing figures like Aristophanes and Shakespeare. What he emphasizes is the being-at-home with *self* that is there in certain comedy (not all obviously); the breakthrough to joy in being is there in laughing even in all breakdown of pretensions, hilarity in all the absurd craziness. Compared to Hegel's attitude to Socrates I sense an extremely warm, pleasurable approval of the comic spirit of Aristophanes. Part of that approval, I think, springs from the joy that permeates even the most extreme debunking in Aristophanes. It tells us something of the spirit of Hegel. I leave fuller discussion of this to the next chapter.

Let me turn to the second theme, namely, the philosophical importance of irony for Hegel and his successors. We see here the modern beginnings of the old age of inwardness. Hegel's orientation to being-at-home is often criticized, though I think one can find echoes of it in Bataille's laughing sovereignty. But crucial differences between Hegel and his deconstructive successors can be understood if we turn from Socratic irony and Greek comedy to Romantic irony. I think that the fashionableness of Romantic irony in Hegel's time is a sort of doppelgänger of the sense of selfhood emergent in Socrates' Greece. Just as in Socratic irony we find a certain return to self as thought, so in Romantic irony we find an emphasis on self, but now mediated by the transcendental turn of Kant's philosophy and by the furthering of that turn by Fichte's view of the ego.

In the first case, Socratic irony responds to the debunking of traditional morality by the sophistic insistence on the human self as the measure of being. In the second case, the transcendental ego, genuinely developed by Fichte, led to the vulgarized view of the ego as the measure of all being, as in Max Stirner's outburst: All things are as nothing to me! Notice how the power of the "It is nothing" has now passed over to subjectivity. Henceforth the self will claim for itself the power to originate and negate the being of the other, certainly the meaning of the other. Romantic irony arises in the wake of this shift to subjectivity of the "It is nothing."

Bear in mind that Hegel endorsed the shift to subjectivity as a truer account of his *Geist*, but actually criticizes this shift in the form of Romantic irony. Why? Because he held that Romantic irony perpetuates in the aesthetic sphere the fundamental defect of Fichte's ego, namely, that it is formal and empty. We must remember this when Hegel is accused of imperialistic subjectivism. The accusation is crude. In fact, Hegel accuses Romantic irony of just that imperialism of subjectivity, in this instance for inflating itself with the rhetoric of aesthetic genius. This is not to deny that Hegel will also privilege the self in the interplay of self and other by understanding their mediation as dialectical self-mediation. But he will claim that his self is not merely formal, precisely because it has faced and dialectically appropriated otherness.

Notice again how Romantic irony as a laughing is wed to the experience of failure. In this case it is the ego taking itself as the absolute that looks down on all otherness as unworthy, hence as open to debunking and negating. In Socratic irony we find a sense of the ideal as other or objective, and of the self as falling short of the ideal; in Romantic irony, we find a sense of the self as the ideal, and of otherness and objectivity as always falling short. Romantic irony laughs at what it always takes to be the failure of the other to live up to the pure standards of its own proclaimed aesthetic superiority. By comparison with the self, all otherness is as straw.

The Romantic ironical self is a radicalization of the Beautiful Soul in this sense: The latter retreats into a pure, unstained inwardness that shuns contact with disgusting, unclean otherness. But just this retreat eventually finds emptiness in the inner Holy of Holies. It finds nothing. This is the nemesis of its own unbridled power to say "It is nothing." It says to the other, "You are as straw," but itself ends up as nothing. The chicken comes home to roost. Henceforth the Beautiful Soul becomes disillusioned with *itself* and turns back on itself its previously outwardly directed disgust. That is to say, it comes to know, or rather produce, the double failure of unworthy otherness and vacuous inwardness.

Imperialistic aesthetic subjectivity thus produces a totalitarianism of ontological suspiciousness. Everything now is unclean, to be sniffed by an all-embracing "hermeneutics of suspicion." This is spiritual death, the complete loss of the philosophical generosity of agapeic mind. It is the inversion of a lacking, erotic mind as it tries to supplant the generous excess of agapeic mind. It is the complete imposture of agapeic mind in believing itself to be *above, superior* to all otherness. In its condescension it cannot really condescend at all, in the classic sense of being agapeically released or abandoned to the other as other.

In a last ditch action of retreat from otherness, the suspicious Beautiful Soul may try to maintain its own posture of superiority by hovering in the ambiguity of irony, between yes and no. For being ironical, and ironical about being ironical, seems to allow it to be at once both beautiful in its own eyes and unrelentingly suspicious of otherness. In fact, eaten away by its unbounded suspicion and its deepdown failure to face the other, the Beautiful Soul has already begun to metamorphose into the Ugly Soul.

Here we may find a seed of the self of modern *ressentiment*, harbinger of Nietzsche's self of rancor and indeed the decadent artist. In the long run, the stratagems of this ironical self cannot be upheld, for the power of dissolving must eventually boomerang on itself and become the debunking of itself. At this extreme the strategy of survival for this self will be for it to *parody itself* as Beautiful Soul or as genius or as pure inwardness, and then to *parody this parody* ad indefinitum. One is moving in the territory of failure but in this case we have a laughable effort to avoid having to face this fact. In trying to preserve itself from breakdown, this aesthetic subjectivity only succeeds in getting its knickers in a twist, and the more it struggles to escape, the more tangled this twist becomes.

Parody can push irony over into sterile frivolity. Such parody is the eunuch of irony: it can generate nothing of itself, except perhaps its "It is nothing," and even this its debunking is always parasitical on the creativity of an *other*. Resentful of this parasitical dependence, parody turns to self-parody, to parody of self-parody. . . .We now have an aesthetic "bad infinite," a hall of mirrors, an infinitude of images without any original. Rather every image of nothing calls itself the absolute original, but there is no real originality, only an endlessly disseminated mimicry.

One begins to see the silhouette of postmodern comedy taking shape. For instance, in the dark comedy of failure of Samuel Beckett's writing (the word or logos always fails here), the postmodern self/nonself reminds us of an aesthetic unhappy consciousness that, in knowing the failure of the Beautiful Soul, becomes a black Cartesian ghost vanishing into voiceless absence. Beckett is as artist seeking a "fidelity to failure," but even he, in *The Unnamable* anyway, cannot settle for entirely empty silence. *The Unnamable* ends: ". . . it will be

I, it will be the silence, where I am, I don't know, I'll never know, in the silence you don't know, you must go on, I can't go on, I'll go on."[28]

The "creative" freedom of the ironical genius is free-floating; it is everywhere and nowhere; nothing succeeds in answering to its radically unanchored subjectivity. Romantic irony in this sense is double: first, an effort to elevate inwardness into absoluteness; second, a resulting attitude that all otherness is as nothing in inevitably failing to meet the standard of absoluteness, fantasized by the ironical genius. It is interesting that here again selfhood must have attained a certain level of consciousness of itself, the immanent difference of inwardness, for this comedy of failure to be possible. Hegel will grant the risibility of the worthlessness that subjectivity here rightly sees. But he strenuously objects to the absolutizing of empty negativity in which the worthless and the worthy are lumped equally together and equally debunked. He sees this happening in Romantic irony, and traces the result to the vacuity of the subjectivity involved.

Hegel is willing to grant the promise of meaning in irony. His praise of Solger's emphasis on irony is warm, though he claims that Solger fails to see that the negativity of irony is not the totality. In relation to Hegel's own thinking, it may be ingredient in the Idea but it is but one moment within it. The point is that Hegel is a searching explorer of the territory of self-conscious subjectivity in relation to the ruses it employs to deal with failure, of the comedy of errors it perpetuates in not properly facing up to its failures, of the risk of absolutizing failure if the self does not see its own negating power in the appropriate light.

It seems to me that the discourse of deconstruction reveals a more textually sophisticated and self-conscious echo of a similar world of irony. Does not "eunuch irony," as I called it, help us explain why philosophical eros must be put "under erasure"? Here we find that sense of internal distance (say, from traditional thought) in which a skepticism germinates. There is the sense of the debunking powers of thought, indeed an intoxication with the will to overturn, subvert, dislocate the ancestors, all the while carried out with a deep anxiety of influence. A devastating irony here is that the champions of difference, too, often turn out to be the clones of Derrida. On the margins we do not find originals; we find crowds.

Francis Bacon once spoke of the skeptic as one who shows what he called a "giddiness" with regard to fixing a belief. Derrida strikes one sometimes as, let us say, a giddy Socratic gadfly, an ironist intoxicated with wordplay, a hovering, equivocal dialectician, philosophically everywhere and yet nowhere. Incidentally, Derrida's dialectical ability to be everywhere and nowhere, in fact, means, contra

Derrida himself: There are no margins of philosophy. Being everywhere and being nowhere stirs the uneasy sense that when all "presence" is deconstructed, when the hierarchy of traditional binary oppositions has been subverted, we may in fact be left with nothing.

Of course, this is all equivocal once more because we are left with something, not nothing; but this "something" seems to be the anti-philosophical philosopher who clings to the old skeptical license to say: "It is as nothing." Or contrariwise, within the mask of revolutionary rhetoric—to parody Wittgenstein—deconstruction after all might leave everything exactly as it is. One has to ask, as Hegel asked of Romantic irony, what is worthy to withstand and outlive the onslaught of its skepticism? What withstands is what is worthy from the past and present; what outlives is what is worthy for the future. Is anything worthy? Or is it all straw? Derrida says that Bataille opposes "Hegel's dialectic to gaiety and one who can say 'It is nothing'. . ."[29] But does not Derrida too say: "It is as nothing?" If so, *how* does he say it? Put otherwise: What does Derrida really *love*?

As I have said, "It is nothing" can be said in many ways, one of which is at work in dialectic.[30] Hegelian laughter intends to be a laughter with an outcome—speculative reconciliation with being beyond all logical folly. It is not clear what the outcome of Bataille/Derrida's laughter is. It certainly has one point: goading, infuriating the Hegelians with pointlessness. Maybe this is not so pointless, especially when Hegelians become oblivious to the comedy of a hubristic panlogism. Hegel recognizes that some forms of laughter can be ways of being-at-home with being even in failure. Laughter can be a being-at-home in not being-at-home. We laugh at failure; we come to nothing; the failure counts for nothing. And yet we still say Yes. In some respects comedy can be a more universal, more humane commentary on failure than tragedy. The comic experience of counting for nothing can be, as it were, metaphysically forgiving. If "It is nothing" can be said in many ways, one of the ways of philosophically laughing can open the promise of reconciliation.

I do not need to be reminded that the notion of being-at-home will be summarily dismissed as "nostalgia," but this dismissal is too cheaply bought. Nostalgia is a buzz word that ought itself to be deconstructed. Laughter may yield a consent even in absolute negativity. It may make us self-consciously aware of absurdity; but in the memorial inwardizing of the absurd, an affirmation may break out even in this accepting of absurdity. We might reread here the end of the *Phenomenology*, and instead of seeing there only the dialectical domination of being, rethink the traces there of a possible giving up, a surrender to otherness as other. Since the negative is the negative of itself, the Golgotha is inner, intimate. This is not what Hegel says, but in that innering of the Golgotha there may be just that breaking down of every closure of dialectical self-mediation and the breaking through of forms of otherness, even in inwardness itself, which are recalcitrant to complete mastery by dialectical self-mediation.

The point could be put in terms of religious *Vorstellung*, again by rethinking, beyond the closure of dialectical self-mediation, the meaning of the forgiveness of sin. Sin is the failure of the self in the sight of God, it is refusal that radically estranges one from the ground of being. But the self that hubristically wills to be the absolute eventually breaks. This very breakdown may occasion the manifestation of the absolute as *other*. This breakdown can become self-conscious, can be acknowledged. In the acknowledgement of breakdown, the promise of something other may break through. Forgiveness entails such a breakthrough beyond closed self-mediation. What does the forgiveness say? It says that the failure counts for nothing, it is set at nought. True forgiveness is an *agapeic* way to say: "It is as nothing." The failure is transfigured by this forgiveness. It is not that the radical failure is not real; it is that even in its reality as forgiven, we are given back our being. In the promise of agapeic community, we can begin to be at home with being again.

Dialectical logic cannot conceptually comprehend this transfiguration completely. Yet dialectic is a mode of philosophical naming that, suitably qualified against every closure of self-mediation, points us better towards this breakthrough than does deconstruction. This breakdown and breakthrough of every closure of self-mediation, even the dialectical self-mediation of the absolute Idea, makes us ask: Can we find, after all, a kind of Lutheran laugh in the Hegelian logos? Would this not be a grace and not just work? A gift from the other, not the production of one's own dialectically self-mediating power? A gift that laughs at our excessive seriousness about history as the labor of the concept? Would this festive laughter of the absolute not be a gracing of being, a sacred laughter not altogether unlike the sovereign laughter of Bataille, albeit an excess from above rather than from below? Does not Bataille's laughter really reject the absolute work of Marx/Kojève, and not this other, hidden, healing laughter?

Is there a laughter which it is impossible to say whence it comes, whether from above or below, since it seems to come from nowhere, and yet also from the heart of being?

Chapter 6

Can Philosophy Laugh at Itself?
On Hegel and Aristophanes—With a Bow to Plato

Between the Professor and the Comic Poet

Can philosophy laugh at itself? Like Houdini I weigh myself down with chains, the harder to test my virtuosity as an escape artist. I take the heaviest burden on myself: Hegel. If any philosopher was serious, Hegel was. But—to parody Nietzsche—here is the heaviest thought: Hegel had a sense of humor. My reader will think that already I am joking, but please do not laugh. I am deadly serious: Hegel had a sense of humor. I will proceed seriously to substantiate this audacity to the logical concept by looking at the relation of Hegel and Aristophanes. Let me dampen any suspicion of frivolity or outrage to logical respectability. So I slip back into the tone of scholarly sobriety and purr: To my best knowledge, this relation is one of the most overlooked by commentators. It is also one of the most interesting for the following reasons.

In asking if philosophy can laugh at itself, the limits of speculation are in question. The explosive energy of laughter seems to be outside system and to strain any logicist bias of speculation. I want to say that laughter is not so much outside philosophy as a mode of being between. Laughter erupts in the middle between speculation and its other, in this case, the earthy body and the originating energies of being that precede and exceed logic. Aristophanes was one of the most profound mockers of philosophy in his caricature of Socrates. Nor is this mockery devoid of religious concern, for there is a kind a sacred folly in some Aristophanic laughter. Hegel's attitude to Aristophanic mockery, a delight in it relative to Socratic dialectic, makes us think again about the caricature of Hegel himself as Dr. Panlogos.

Further, the relation of Hegel and Aristophanes may do some reparation for the Kierkegaardian slander that Hegel was the epitome of the dull, domesticated bourgeois professor (as we all know, bourgeois professors have no sense of humor). Nietzsche said: Homer *versus* Plato, this is one of life's fundamental antagonisms. But do we have to say: Aristophanes versus Hegel? Further still, Hegel's response to Aristophanes tells us something important about Hegel's attitude towards the comic as, in a sense, the acme of the aesthetic. Kierkegaard has already said more than the deconstructionists by saying less. He said: to escape Hegelianism all one needs is a little humor, common-sense and a bit of Greek *ataraxia*.[1] But does Hegel forget to laugh? If this duo, Hegel and Aristophanes, is not an odd couple, even if it is, together both make us ask if there is something comic about philosophy itself. Is there a laughter of the speculative? Does the comic spirit secretly gestate in philosophy? Simply put: Aristophanes is outrageous in the way he pillories Saint Socrates, so why then did Herr Doktor Professor Hegel love this outrageous poet? Does Hegel hint at philosophy's tolerance of its own debunking, its willingness to visit on itself its own comic ridicule, to find in itself something comically outrageous? Socrates was a perplexing enigma, a strange questionable thinker, not only for Hegel and Aristophanes, but also for Plato and Nietzsche.

I am not proposing a trivialization of speculation in the spirit of postmodern frivolity. I am asking about speculation in relation to the irreverent reverence of Aristophanic sacredness. Relative to this sacred folly, our themes of dialectic and its other, of the dialectical one and the metaxological double will surface again. Will Hegelian system finally be at a loss before a certain laughter that is other than, outside world–history, at a loss for a different speculative mindfulness to listen for this sacred laughter? In my view, speculative dialectic does not fully comprehend the agapeic energy of festive being that the metaxological allows us to acknowledge in laughter. There is an agapeic mindfulness out of which issues, in its festive celebration of being, a certain speculative laughter. This speculative yes to the community of being in no way subordinates the otherness of being to any conceptual whole constructed by the philosopher's mind. The yes of this laughter is a festive gesture towards the metaxological openness of agapeic being.

Though Hegel was a bourgeois professor, he did have a sense of humor. There is not much laughter to be found in Hölderlin or Heidegger, and Hegel is not as jocular as Nietzsche, but I do find a sardonic, self-deprecating sense of humor. I would characterize this as tending to black humor, sometimes earthy humor. There is also a bitter streak in Hegel, sometimes running to exasperation, intemperance, and sarcasm. Overall he is not devoid of readiness to debunk pretentiousness. This is evident in the *Letters* and I will return to a significant example, but there are many examples from his philosophical writings. I mentioned before his tart demolition of Schelling's position as the night in which all cows are black: this is laughable as logical argument but brilliant as a pithy debunking image. Nor is Hegel unaware of the incongruities of the body when he speaks of the identity of the organ of generation and of pissing (*Pissen*). There is bitter humor in comparing the cheapness of human life and its death in the French Revolution to gulping back a glass of water or slicing through a cabbage. Hegel even laughs at the confraternity of scholars. I think of Hegel debunking those scholars who hasten to a new *Sache*, like flies to freshly spilt milk. I think of his discussion of the spiritual animal kingdom (*das geistige Tierreich*). What is the voice of philosophy in "the conversation of mankind"? Suppose this conversation takes place in *das geistige Tierreich*? In this zoo of the spirit is the voice of the philosopher the speech-act of the speculative cow?[2]

In Aristophanes many of the jokes are lost on us because of their topicality. And admittedly Hegel is nothing compared to Aristophanes. There is certainly an earthiness about Aristophanes, a joy in debunking. I mean earthiness literally in that his laughter produces the experience of being brought down to earth. The home of the comic is the fleshed body in its contrast with the human being's soaring, transcending spirit (*The Birds* laughs somewhere between these extremes). The elemental energy of laughter breaks through in the between. It often feeds on a sense of incongruity between two worlds: on the one hand, the ideal that is dreamt about or ambitiously pursued; on the other hand, the actual place of dreaming, the grounding reality of what we are, in its variance with the ideal. Philosophical laughter can break through in the middle between speculative ideality and bodily reality. Incongruity can also be evident within one reality as at variance or in contradiction with itself. In either case, incongruity or internal instability generate a kind of open dialectic that dissolves contradiction and drives beyond it, in forcing us to stand outside the contradiction and see it as such, that is, as risible.

The earthiness of Aristophanic comedy can do more than debunk or deflate. It can bring us home to earth in a certain being-at-home with being. I think of the women in *Lysistrata* withholding sexual congress from their warrior males in the interest of forcing peace. (Is this the praxis of post-phallogocentric philosophy? Some hilarious possibilities of reversal are raised by the play *Ecclesiazusae*.) In *Lysistrata* there ensues the pathetic risibility of the sexually restless males: the bodies they use to kill remind them against their will of a fleshed order they cannot easily control or crush. The resulting erotic irritability is salutary comic reminder both of the bodily pleasures we crave and our inability to slough them off even for swelling martial goals. The elemental erotic body testifies to a concrete universality that transcends politics and the lust for power, a commonness beyond the division of male and female, Athenian and Spartan.

The incongruity played out in the middle here concerns the elemental lack of coincidence between abstract intellect and reality, speculation and the body, thinking and being. Comedy testifies to the joyful discordance of these two in the middle. It is relevant to remember that much comedy excites a certain joy in discordance: in the conflict of father and son, youth and age, the new and old, in the war of male and female, masters and slaves, mortals and gods, in the conflict of cleverness and simplicity, the rustic commonsense bumpkin and the sophisticated city slicker. We find most of these conflicts in Aristophanes' *Clouds*, as well as the "speculative" discordance of the Just and Unjust Logos. Even in the conflict, comedy still affords a celebration of being as festive.

The god of comedy, Comus, was a god of fertility, hence the association of comedy with plenty, with excess, with an agapeic over-abundance of being, as I would put it metaxologically. There is some speculation that even the emphasis on the obscenity of the body is supposedly connected with the *kōmos*: the procession of revellers at such religious festivals would make use of obscenity to ward off evil spirits. Gestures such as scatological speech and the display of oversize phalluses were connected with, let us say, the fertile equivocity of the power of genesis itself. Comic festivity laughs in the middle of the ambiguous excess of being as original power, an excess we cannot entirely master, and certainly not by thought alone, but which we can participate in and celebrate.

What of the speculative thinker and the joyful discordance of comedy. I suggest that Jonathan Swift in *Gulliver's Travels* is Aristophanes' modern twin who gives us great images of the abstracted, alienated thinker. In the voyage to Laputa, Gulliver comes across individuals, covered with Pythagorean mathematical symbols, with one eye turned inward, one eye upward. These discordant eyes call to mind a caricature of what Augustine describes as the movement of his thought: from the exterior to the interior (the eye turned inward), from the inferior to the superior (the eye turned upward). I have described the double mediation of metaxological mind as analogous to Augustine's twofold movement. What is funny here? Not only the danger of being cross-eyed, but also this: The Laputan mathematicians are so abstracted in thought that they have to be accompanied by *flappers*. These have a sort of inflated bladder, used to flap the thinker's mouth to remind him to talk and his ear to remind him to listen. What is the speculative meaning of *flappers? Flappers* are metaphorical embodiments of something like Peircian Secondness. In my terms, they are comic reminders of the *second* mediation of metaxological mind, namely, that thought must do more than think itself alone; it must think its other or others. Sometimes speculative mind has to be slapped on the face to be reminded of this.

Slapping is not the only form of this second movement. There are less violent forms of Secondness, more attuned to the elemental body in its rapport with the fleshed thereness of the other. Eros, whether speculative or bodily, brings us before this thereness. Swift was acutely aware of the place of the body in comedy. Hence the neglected women of the Laputan thinkers are always running away from the floating mathematical island, returning to the earth and having love affairs with servants, committing adultery even before the disengaged eyes of their cogitating husbands.

I mention in passing a group of philosophical comics who have escaped the flying mathematical island: Monty Python's Flying Circus. The members of this group are quite philosophically sophisticated. They have a hilarious monologue about logic and sex on the record (executive version) of *In Search of the Holy Grail.* A professor of logic proves to his adulterous wife that there is no *logically necessary* connection between her adultery with the milkman earlier in the day and the fact that, later in the day, she has no dinner ready for the professor when he comes home from school (Socrates' Thinkery, *Phrontistērion* in Aristophanes' *Clouds*; we will return to the comedy of the school of philosophy). The professor demonstrates that it is a logical fallacy on her part to connect her morning adultery with the absence of evening dinner. Logically speaking one can have *both* adultery in the morning and dinner ready in the evening. The validity of the logic does not impress the professor's neglected wife.[3]

Besides the comedy of the elemental body, there also are passages of lyrical lightness, soaring singing poetry in Aristophanes. There are philosophical counterparts to such passages in Plato and Nietzsche. Because both Plato and Nietzsche were poets as well as philosophers, because they were both plurivocal philosophers, they were especially capable of what in *Philosophy and its Others* I call thought singing its other. I can find no immediate analogue to such passages in Hegel, except perhaps moments of logical excitation where Hegel is carried away by the movement of the thought itself. Then it seems that Hegel is not thinking, but that Hegel is being thought.

Where does the comic sense of incongruity between speculative thought and being emerge in Hegel? Here I find it instructive to read his *Letters* in tandem with the *Science of Logic*. One result is an impression of disjunction between the everyday world and the rare ether of the *Begriff*. Moreover, and I think this is the important point, Hegel was very aware of this disjunction. Though his stated philosophical intention was to show the Idea in the everyday, one senses often in the *Letters* the recalcitrance of ordinary life to such logical manifestation. Hegel's project is to overcome any dualism of the appearing and essential, the commonsense and scientific, the everyday and philosophical. It is to articulate contradiction within the one dialectically self-mediating whole: the incongruity is interpreted as two sides in tension of a whole that from a more encompassing standpoint contains the two sides as clashing articulations necessary to the full unfolding of the whole's own self-development. The *Phenomenology* as a ladder to the absolute is, as it were, the mediating process between the *Letters* and the *Logic*.[4]

An important question with respect to the comic is whether the two in tension or contradiction can be contained in the dialectical one, or whether there is a two that tends to dissolve this dialectical one and indeed resists incorporation into a larger dialectical whole. As should be clear from the last chapter, the first option gives us a dialectical sense of laughter, the second a metaxological sense. In the latter we continue to live in the between, without reduction of the otherness of the extremes to a totalizing unity. This particular question, in this particular form, is not one that Hegel puts to himself. Below we will see an ambiguous mixture of the dialectical and the metaxological in Aristophanic laughter. The primary thrust of Hegel's logical thought is to incorporate the joyful discordance of laughter within a dialectical concordance. The comic comes within the embrace of the dialectic: dialectic is the logical comedy of contradiction. The comedy has a happy ending in the sense that the dialectical debunking of the incongruity in the middle serves a more embracing reconstitution of unity.

Yet we must not be too logical. To be too logical might be laughably illogical. And as I say, a reading of the *Letters* shows Hegel as a citizen of *many worlds*, with a sense of the complex tension rather than seamless harmony between them. Hegel reveals his solid commonsense, indicative, so to say, of his respect for the scoffing Thracian maid. And yet he is the thinker of the *Begriff* which, as he said himself, seems to ask commonsense to walk on its head. I do not find the collapse of this complex tension in Hegel. In fact, without this complex tension no sense of humor would be possible. It is only the repeated resurfacing of this tension in the between that gives birth to the repeated need of the comic.

For comedy is a way of living with the contradiction between two worlds that does not do away with the contradiction, but allows us to affirm both poles at once, that is, continue to live with and in the complex tension. Commonsense has to have a sense of its own absurdity; philosophy is particularly sensitive to this common nonsense. But philosophy has to be alive to its own potential for absurdity; otherwise it forgets its incongruity, its own nonsense vis-à-vis commonsense, which in fact provides the place of origination for its own questing thought. The comic, like the dialectical, can be one way of moving between poles in tension without simplistically collapsing their difference or blandly disarming their clash. To that extent the comic, like a properly open dialectic, is a form of justice: it gives to each its due, and what is due is sometimes mockery.

Consider this example gleaned from Hegel's *Letters*.[5] When Hegel was headmaster at the *Gymnasium* at Nuremberg, because of lack of funds the *Gymnasium* did not have toilets and the children had to make use of neighboring houses to relieve themselves. As headmaster Hegel had to make sure that the incoming children were properly toilet trained. Hegel, as it were, had to supervise the civility of their excretory functions. Note first this comic contrast: Hegel is the heroic thinker of absolute *Geist*, yet here as a man making a living in a disruptive interim of his academic career, he has to oversee the "lower" functions of young, unregulated bodies. The contrast is between the speculative exaltation of *Geist* and the human body at stool.

We have here an opposition that allows no dialectical *Aufhebung*: the way up is not the same as the way down, as Heraclitus held. Yet my reading of the *Letters* detects a tongue-in-cheek humor in Hegel's sly recounting of the affair. Hegel is laughing—laughing at himself. It is significant that this was around the time that Hegel, in his solitude, was working on the *Science of Logic*. I find no complaint in Hegel. I find no self-importance. I find no stiff pretense that the thinker of absolute *Geist* is beyond the elemental necessity of anal relief. I find self-deprecating chuckling at the contrast. Perhaps there is no logical *Aufhebung* of excrement and *Geist*, yet the comic response is a drawing together of extremes that are absolutely separated. The laugh is an energy of being that sparks across a gap of absurdity, that redeems the absurdity, that rescues *Geist* as pure spirit from its unreal abstractness, that lifts the excretory functions beyond the complete lowering of our dignity. And if one objects that this is beneath *philosophy's* dignity, I simply recall the lesson Parmenides delivered to Socrates on the *eidē* and dirt.

What does this lesson teach? First there is the movement up: this is the speculative exaltation. Hegel calls the *Parmenides* "the greatest work of art of ancient dialectic," a "true revelation and positive expression of the divine life."[6] But then there is the comic, speculative deflation: this is the movement down. Consider what, if understood properly, is one of the most startling passages in philosophical literature. In the *Parmenides* (130c7ff.), Parmenides asks the young Socrates if there are *eidē* of things like hair, mud, dirt, things he might consider *geloia*, risible. Risible is perhaps not a strong enough word to capture the possible implication of a philosophical recoil from disgusting otherness. *Geloia* is from the verb *gelao*, to laugh—what is *geloios* is laughable, absurd, something ridiculous to be sneered at. Socrates replies it would be absurd to think there were *eidē* of such things. He does admit that he often "is disturbed by the thought that what is true of one thing is true of all. Then when I have taken up this position, I run away for fear of falling into some abyss (*buthos*: the depths, deeps of the sea) of nonsense (*phluaria*: silly talk, nonsense, foolery) and perishing; so when I come to those things which we were saying do have *eidē*, I stay and busy myself with them." "Yes, for you are still young," said Parmenides, " and philosophy has not yet taken hold upon you, Socrates, as I think it will later. Then you will not despise them; but now you still consider people's opinions, on account of your youth."

This exchange with Parmenides follows the young Socrates' exchange with Zeno who, in turn, admits that his book, written while he was young, defended Parmenides' logos against those who would turn it into a comedy (128d1: *kōmodein*). The younger Zeno's book tried to show that more laughable results (the word *geloia* peppers the passage) follow from the hypothesis of "the many" rather than the hypothesis of "the one." As I pointed out in the last chapter, the *reductio ad absurdum*, fathered by Zeno, offers philosophy the opportunity for *logical mockery* of what is other to logos.

One notes a certain mirroring between the younger Zeno and the younger Socrates. One notes the latter's anxiety: fear of being laughed at by others, fear of falling into or perishing in an abyss. The young Socrates would dwell with the easier cases; the dirty cases unsettle him and make him afraid of drowning in nonsense; he is afraid of being taken for a fool. He still lacks the proper audacity of thought. A different courage is needed. One must be willing to drown in the absurd; one must not fear to be ridiculous; the opinions of the many make a coward of thought. The young Socrates does not yet have the greater daring of thought that will come with age. The older Socrates, as we know, did make the daring leap and was willing to seem a fool and idiot. He had to cease worrying what the others thought and their domesticated sense of true being, their cave metaphysics. He accepted the *bios xenikos* of thought. You have to overcome the fear of death to be able to philosophize about the excremental, and to laugh.

There is here hinted an extraordinary revelation of the enigmatic ground on which philosophy stands: it is not a static ground at all, it may be as unmasterable in its otherness as the sea. I take the passage to imply a genial, yet severe criticism of a certain, let us say, immature logicism. Logicism pretends to a supposed universality, but philosophically it cannot endure to face the hardest cases, namely, the seemingly most nonsensical, indeed filthy cases from which we recoil. Immature logicism is mind trying to secure itself in the circle of thought thinking itself alone; it withdraws from the challenge to its self-certainty that is posed by the thought of what is other to thought.

Plato puts the imputed criticism of the young Socrates in the mouth of Parmenides, and this is all the more unsettling. We are wont to think of Parmenides as the purest father of speculative mind, as the dweller in the pure ether of logos, far from the way of mortals and their risible illogicality. But he seems to say that the philosopher least of all can shun the ugly, dirty, excremental things. Parmenides, father of logic, implies to the younger Socrates, son of dialectic: Philosophy's great test is to consider the lowest things in terms of the highest principles; philosophical mind, whether dialectical or metaxological, must move between, must think in the tension of the between, must try to think together both extremes in order to be intellectually honest. This struggle to think together the extremes of the between expresses the double mediation of metaxological mind: thought thinking itself, thought thinking its other.

Lest this seem too solemn, too grave, I suggest that the passage as a whole makes us wonder if *Plato himself* was laughing all the time, trying to hint to us something about the potentially comic nature of philosophy itself. Parmenides' warning about hair, mud, and dirt reminds one of Hegel's bad conscience about Krug's pen. Krug's question about his pen is to Hegelian logic as Pascal's query about Cleopatra's nose is to Hegelian world-history: small embarrassments, but absolutely irritating. Does Krug's pen do the dirt on thought thinking itself? Krug's pen reminds us of the being there of a being as *being* and not just as thought, its being there as a this. How does Hegel deal with this dirt? What he does hardly amounts to more than *jeering* at Herr Doktor Professor Krug. Hegel's mockery is not much more than a mask for the impotence of thought thinking itself to deduce from itself the being of a this, its being as other to thought. This being as other, in its refusal to go away, in its silent stubbornness as a this, in its idiocy, mocks Hegel's mockery.

With Parmenides' caution in mind, I turn back to Hegel's daily lower duties as headmaster of the high school. I envisage a deconstructionist reading the headmaster incident differently. Here is a hypothetical reading which paints headmaster Hegel as the last child of Parmenides. I ask you: Is this reading silly? Here it is.

Hegel is the thinker of absolute identity and the thought of absolute identity is exclusive of otherness, of what resists the panlogist pretensions of the absolute Idea. Where is the home of thought, of the circular self-mediation of the concept? Why nowhere else but the school—the school is the metaphorical place of the totalitarianism of the concept. There the otherness of the human being is tamed and the dictatorship of civilization inscribes its taboos and prohibitions on the body. There the energies of the body are domesticated by the ontotheological tradition. Hence, the body is extruded from the school and forced to perform its elemental necessities on the margins of philosophy. Hegel's school is not *l'Ecole Normale Supérieure.* So: Hegel as headmaster is the master of sameness in supervising the bowel movements of his charges. Headmaster Hegel is master of the head. Through this headship the tyranny of logos extends its system of prohibitions even into the elemental necessities themselves. This only shows the all-pervasiveness of the taboo system of logocentrism or ontotheology.

Note again that the houses of relief are outside the school. Note that one has to be already toilet trained to come to school. So? Hegel the headmaster is an accomplice. Hegel only carries forward the process of training that is historically ongoing. A Heideggerian might say: as the completion of toilet training, Hegel is the completion of a tradition that in certain respects is only completing itself in Hegel. Hegel the head is the agent of a larger process of domestication that is not confined to any one particular thinker but is the destiny of spirit in the West. The school and the body have nothing to do with each other; and yet the otherness of the body cannot be entirely repressed, for as an elemental necessity, an unthought, it always returns to make its repeated demand. At best it can be contained in a system that periodically allows it its relief, in order for the system itself (I mean the system of logos, not only the body!) to continue its control. But in fact, these elemental necessities, as ever recurrent, reveal that the system's claim to total self-sufficiency is illusory. It is supported by a repression, an exclusion that in moments of bodily overload breaks down and something other than the head of pure thought has to be acknowledged.

As I pen this parody, I feel that I ought, like Socrates in the *Phaedrus*, to veil my shameful head with a cloth. I ask the reader to hear a voice that speaks a different respect, even in the irreverence. Let the reader forgive my shameless parody of deconstructive readings, I plead. I also plead that there is a justice of irony here: Many deconstructive readings make a hermeneutical virtue of their own parodic reading of the great thinkers. Long stretches of Derrida are such good parodies of Hegel that one is unsure which is the original, which the image, whether the voice of Derrida is the voice of Hegel gone a little haywire with parodic mimicry.

I grant that the above sort of interpretation has its strengths, *if* Hegel is *only* the thinker of pure thought, a thinker of thought that represses the body and its energies. Moreover, such an interpretation has a certain coherence, even inherent plausibility if one brings to bear a hermeneutic of suspicion on the headmaster incident and a desire to see there what one wants to see in the tradition of philosophy. Unfortunately, the whole interpretation, even in its plausibility, and despite appearances, forgets to laugh, forgets that Hegel in his own way was laughing, forgets to ask if maybe Hegel's laughter might extend beyond this headmaster incident and be secretly at work in other places in the Hegelian corpus (aha! let me save the deconstructionist the trouble of pouncing on the word *corpus*; we cannot get away from the body even when we discuss Hegel's thought itself as a totality).

This headmaster incident is more generally relevant in this respect. Much comedy returns us to the elemental necessities of the body. Many jokes concern eating, drinking, sex, often in their deformed aspects, in their absurd, exaggerated dimensions, hence in those aspects that resist easy incorporation into an entirely logical interpretation of being. I think of the crudities of Falstaff, comic hero (that is, utter rascal) in a world of comedy that has no heroes. His tavern is an asylum of Saturnalian festival in which the normal order is subverted. Falstaff himself is the Lord of Misrule. This Lord of Misrule of a topsy turvy world reminds us of the repressed or forgotten body, returns us to the celebrating body and risks even subverting the hierarchy of power vis-à-vis the king in waiting. Prince Hal is King Falstaff's attendant, though later this Lord of Misrule will be rejected: political power, through the cunning of reason, will reassert its sway over the laughing body. Nevertheless, the necessary rule of the energies of the body cannot be entirely repressed. Folly is the other of logos, but an intimate other, a dialectical other in Hegelian terms, a metaxological other I prefer to say.[7]

One must ask the modern philosopher: Can there be any jokes for the Cartesian *cogito*? The answer must be no. Let us take the *cogito* as a modern figure for thought thinking itself. The *cogito* claims to inhabit a region of pure self-transparency, of clear and distinct concepts. But laughter cannot germinate, much less live in the fleshless ether of this pure region. This region has extruded the body; indeed the body in its elemental flesh has been already denied by the Cartesian when it has been reduced to a lifeless *res extensa*. A disembodied mind cannot laugh at the body considered absolutely as a *res extensa*.[8] The body has to have some of the living energy of being emergent in it for such laughter to be possible. One can only laugh at a human body that *seems* to be, or *pretends* to be a mere *res extensa*. For then you have the absurdity of abstraction—the absurdity of the bodily energies playing ridiculously at being dead, at death—and death is one of the most profound and recurrent occasions of laughter.

Here is a profound Aristophanic instance. There is a laughter of the suffering body, even if we journey to the kingdom of the dead. Aristophanes' *Frogs* offers us this laughter in the underworld, comedy even in Hades. In this play, the identity of the *personae*, especially Dionysus and his slave Xantias, is not at all univocal or fixed. They lack—even the god lacks—the self-certainty of the Cartesian ego. The interplay of the god and slave is beyond univocity. There is a kind of metaxological fluidity and porosity between identities. Thus, one notes the interchangeable identities between gods and heroes: Dionysus masquerades as Heracles. One notes the interchangeable identities between gods and mortals/slaves: Dionysus masquerades as Xantias his slave, while Xantias in turn passes himself off as Heracles.

What happens when the question of *true identity* comes up. The question arises in the dismal region of shades: Who is the real god? A Cartesian might now start to purr at the thought of the self-certainty of true identity. The purr must quickly turn to a moan, for nothing like simple univocal identity is possible in the kingdom of the dead. To answer the question of identity, Aeacus *beats* Dionysus disguised as a slave, *beats* Xantias dressed as Heracles (625ff.). No gentle flapping here. Gods are not supposed to feel pain, while suffering is a marker of identity for mortals. But *both* the god and the slave experience the pain. Both the god and slave *pretend not to feel pain*, both *play dead*, as though beyond the suffering body—like pure, disembodied thought, thought thinking only itself. There results the comic scene of Dionysus trying to stifle his cry of pain. The god, too, suffers in the home of the dead, and is absurdly, paradoxically indistinguishable from the mortal slave. Their unexpected identity in shared pain makes us laugh. The suffering of the divine, as well as the mortal, makes us laugh, with a laughter streaked with pained compassion.

A consistent Cartesianism would really make not only sacred folly, but all laughter absolutely impossible. Since laughter will return regardless of our will to conceptual clarity and regardless of any theory of being we have, a consistent Cartesianism is thereby refuted, existentially, if not logically. Properly thought through, laughter shows that Cartesianism is itself risible; hence the effective refutation of Cartesianism is to joke at the unreality of the pure *cogito*. (I imagine a modern Diogenes doing something like this.) Cartesian dualism produces two severed worlds of mind and body, both sides differently comic from the standpoint of the elemental being there of the mindful body itself—the actual body that lives and thinks.

For an aesthetic analogue of the alienated abstraction of the Cartesian *cogito*, think of the humor of Samuel Beckett, a paradigm artist for some postmoderns. There is nausea, despair, disgust in Beckett; the human condition is affliction, distress; there is also compassion for suffering. Often Beckett's very black humor functions against a background of quasi-Cartesian presuppositions of body and mind. It is as if the Beautiful Soul had transposed the disembodied Cartesian mind from epistemology to aesthetics. But in the transposition, the abstracted Beautiful Soul learns progressively of the bankruptcy of the aesthetic, if it is divorced from the celebrating energy of the body. Eventually the Beautiful Soul deconstructs its own aestheticism. This happens in Beckett: An aesthetic Cartesian ghost vanishes into black absence—the "death of the self." In Beckett, as paradigmatic postmodern writer, the Cartesian mind becomes a parodist of its own abstraction; in a parody of the thought that thinks itself, this aesthetic parody parodies itself, and then parodies itself parodying itself. . . .The results are first comic, but parody that parodies itself breeds a dizzying dissolution, a mimicry that disseminates itself in mimicries of mimicries. . . .The quickest and most effective way out of this clever aesthetic hall of mirrors is a joke that reminds us of, recalls us, to the body. The living body is the great mocker of even the most brilliant virtuosity of formalistic cleverness. This point has an application to logic as well as to aesthetics.

In Aristophanes there is a tremendous amount of parody, not least, as we now shall see, the parody of philosophy itself in the *Clouds*. The unwitting comedy of the abstracted *cogito* is a modern version of a like comedy that Aristophanes saw in Socrates in the ancient world:

Socrates as a dangerous personification of abstracted, alienated thought. Aristophanes is full of lewd jokes, obscenities about the excretory functions, bawdiness about sex, and so on.[9] One notes the incongruity of two worlds in the *Clouds* between reason and sexual obscenity: whenever Socrates tries to communicate an idea to Strepsiades, the latter tends to inject a sexual or crude corporeal connotation into the matter. Socrates the soaring mind cannot get through to Strepsiades, the debunking, gross body.

Here Aristophanes gives us a better "deconstruction" of philosophy than contemporary deconstructionists. Aristophanes would say that the deconstructionists get it all wrong when they accuse *philosophy* of "phallogocentrism." As the *Clouds* make clear, it is not Socratic philosophy that is "phallogocentric" but commonsense. Socratic philosophy is sexless thinking, but the commonsense of *hoi polloi*, represented by Strepsiades, is obsessed with the phallus. In fact, a male character was represented on the Greek stage by an actor wearing a leather phallus. In the revised version of the *Clouds* that survives, Aristophanes queries why he was only given third prize the first time the play was produced. He claims that he wrote the most *clever* play and deliberately did not give the audience what it seems to have most wanted in the first version, namely, outsize phalluses. It is not philosophy that is "phallogocentric" but the people.

Aristophanes' irreverence extended fearlessly to the world-historical lords of politics, to an extent that many commentators have found astonishing. He pilloried these masters (Cleon in *Knights*) in a way that astonishes us about the tolerance of debunking shown by the politicians and the Greek people themselves. An extraordinary robustness of spirit is needed for a people and its rulers to so endure their own laughing negation. One must be strong to laugh at oneself with such wicked mercilessness. Socrates had this strength, it seems: a story has it that Socrates stood up at the *Clouds* and applauded his Mask for its likeness.[10] He showed himself a true Aristophanic Greek in being able to endure, even love the cruelty of self-debunking.

Let me offer an example from Aristophanes analogous to the high school affair from Hegel. As is well known, in the *Clouds* Socrates is presented as a sophist in the matter of argumentative technique. He is a virtuoso of logos, capable of making the weaker case appear the stronger, and the stronger the weaker. He is also presented as a "Presocratic" in speculative thought about the things above the earth and below it. This is part of the point about Socrates being suspended in the basket above the stage. Here is an unforgettable image of the free-floating thinker, uprooted from the earth, stranger to the energies of the body, an abstracted thinker who loses himself in the clouds of abstracted thought. It is believed that the contraption used to suspend Socrates was the machine employed to show heroes and gods flying through the air, beings supposedly immune from the grosser exigencies of concrete existence. From the comic sufferings of Dionysus in Hades, we know what Aristophanes thought of this immunity.

In an almost literal sense, Socrates the speculative philosopher is presented as a basket case. Celestial speculation coexists with the effort to measure "such high mysteries (*musteria*)" as the jump of a flea by dipping its feet in wax (144ff.). Pure disinterested theory worries if a gnat hums through its mouth or its bum (155ff.). The students have their eyes fixed on the ground, "searching into the darkness below Tartarus" (192), while their rumps are in the sky, taking private lessons on the stars (186ff.). A lizard defecates on Socrates' face as he muses on the moon (171ff.).

Socrates has this exchange with Strepsiades early in the play (367ff.). The Greek gods are at issue and Socrates appears in the guise of one totally devoid of a sense of the sacred otherness of being, a demythologizer, a logocentric enlightener who has no sense of the otherness of the Holy. The issue is the interpretation of rain (see Thales: water is the mother of all things; Strepsiades actually invokes Thales, 180). Socrates says that Zeus has been booted out and that Clouds, Chaos and Tongue are the new gods. Rain is now merely a precipitation from the clouds. Contrary to Strepsiades' vulgar mythological imagination, the rain is not Zeus pissing through a sieve (*dia koskinou ourein*, 373). Are we in the environs of Hegel's toilet again? And his school?

The laughter here evoked points to a crude conjunction of extremes: the gods and pissing. The comedy is the coupling of uranian divinity and urination. The joke involves a kind of gross *comic* demythologizing. There is something paradoxical here in that Aristophanes is known for his critique of Socratic demythologizing. Socratic demythologizing is rational, yet in laughing at rational demythologizing, Aristophanes risks a comic demythologizing. And yet, as we know, Aristophanes was conservative in that he abhorred the manner in which the sophists and "Presocratics" produced an undermining of the traditional grounds of the polis. These grounds were the gods. The gods shaped a people into a people. If the gods were mere clouds, there was no basis for the people, hence Socrates was a political as well as religious destroyer: impiety and treason intertwined. Yet in invoking the body of Zeus, Aristophanes himself also invokes the laughable nature of the gods, just the very thing he hated in the sophists and rational enlighteners. The common phrase well describes Aristophanes' laughter: Nothing seems sacred. Yet Aristophanes blamed the innovators for producing just that result.

If the gods are Clouds they are indeterminate, hence capable of taking on any shape, like Hamlet's chameleon. Everything seems possible, everything permitted. The result is a nihilism and the absence of any ground of ethical value. Similarly, rational thinking is the blowing of windbags, philosophy itself a puff of air, not even the dream of a thinking reed. It is noticeable, however, that even with respect to Clouds or Chaos or Tongue, the philosopher cannot avoid a certain *Gottesdienst*. Socrates is himself called a high priest by the Chorus (359) and he *initiates* Strepsiades into the inner sanctum of the *Phrontistērion*. Students refer to the mysteries within. This is a parody of initiation into a mystery religion. Moreover, in all this *parodia sacra* the new principle of Clouds tends to take on the powerful religious resonances of the old gods. This, too, is relevant to the later accusation against Socrates of inventing new gods. But it is also relevant to the impossibility of getting away from some "gods," even by those who strike the pose of being debunking demythologizers. New gods will seep in, and a new naiveté about the fact: the enlightener will take himself for an atheist, in ignorance of himself, smugly hypocritical. The skeptic of the other's gods will prove a dogmatist of his own; and he will not know or own he has gods; such is the inevitable self-deception.

How do we accommodate this tension: that in his defence of the gods Aristophanes had to allow us to laugh at the gods. The answer as I see it is: only by granting a certain metaxological togetherness of acceptance and debunking in Aristophanic laughter itself. That is, one debunks what one loves because one knows the frailty of the human. But just that very frailty points to the need for images that shape a sense of what lies beyond the human. Laughter occurs in the between; between consent and suspicion, between the absurdity of being human (whether in relation to the body, or alternatively in being high falutin') and the need for a beyond in some sense more ultimate than the human being. And yet every image of the beyond is derisory. Comedy here is a religious demythologizing: no image is *the* image.

Zeus is imagined as pissing, and we laugh; and yet in a sense without Zeus human life is impossible. Aristophanes, the defender of traditional gods, laughs at traditional gods mercilessly. He negates and yet he affirms. I think Aristophanes is aware of this aporia, but he does not have a dialectical *Aufhebung* to deal with it. He has laughter. This does not overcome the contradiction, or entirely heal its pain (sometimes it just masks it). Nevertheless, the explosion of energy that erupts with laughter allows us to live with and in the aporia. When Socrates in the *Republic* debunks the images of the gods, he looks at Zeus pissing in a less humorous way. He wants to wash clean the bodies of the gods, and rob the scoffers of the pretext of laughter. He does not want the gods to be objects of laughter at all— but this is already to court the death of the gods. In one sense, Aristophanes knew better: laughter keeps us alive in a contradiction by keeping us alive to the origin of the contradiction. And the justification for this is that the contradiction not only keeps thinking alive but that it also keeps us alive in keeping us closer to the elemental energies of bodily being there.

Hegel and the Comic Acme:
Between the Aristophanic and Socratic End of Antiquity

I revert to Hegel in relation to this theme, namely, that the comic is a certain acme of the aesthetic. It perhaps will surprise some readers that Hegel assigns an extremely high place to comedy in the economy of spirit. There should be less surprise if we remember that Hegel places art at the highest level of spirit along with philosophy and religion. I stress: art is placed at the level of absoluteness. If we put aside the complicated question of the interrelations of philosophy and art and the question of art's subordination, the startling fact, in tension with the panlogist Hegel, is that art is still given absolute status.

The added point now is that within the aesthetic, one can make the case that the comic is the fulfillment of the aesthetic as absolute. The comic reveals the absoluteness of the aesthetic as a form of absolute spirit. Contra Bataille and Derrida who claim that there is nothing of the comic in Hegel (see chapter 5), it is clear that consummating points in the ancient and modern worlds are in comic art. Comedy is explicitly mentioned at the end of the discussion of classical art, and the figure singled out for special note is Aristophanes. Comedy is mentioned in modern romantic art also, and the crowning figure here mentioned is Shakespeare. In both cases, there is both a completion, a dissolution, and the indication of a continuation. There is a completion: classical art has run through a plurality of forms from the primitive to the sophisticated, and now in comedy the moment of its own self-debunking appears. But that self-debunking is not born of simple exhaustion. To say this would be to ignore the agency of this self-debunking, Aristophanes. As we have seen, he is full of a light energy of destruction and creation that is at the opposite extreme to exhaustion.

At the end of classical art, at the end of the Greek world, Hegel calls attention to an opening up (which the Christian, Romantic era will develop and complete) of self-consciousness or inwardness. With this we find a growing sense of disjunction between the images of the mythic tradition and the inward act of assent to those images. This is my way of putting the matter. Aristophanic comedy is only possible for one who senses the threat involved in the sophistic skepticism regarding the traditional images of the gods. Hence there is actually a kinship with Socrates here. Socrates responds to this threat by further pursuing the path of logos; Aristophanes wants to defuse the threat by laughing at philosophical thought, debunking its pretensions, and hence calling a halt to its potential for cultural corrosion.

The difficulty is that Aristophanes must *already* be infected with the spirit of philosophical debunking in order to be able both to acknowledge its threat and fight against it. Aristophanes and Socrates are twin faces of alarmed response to this same threat of dissolution: the aesthetic and the reflective—though Aristophanes sees the philosophic response as merely a more masked way of continuing the threat. That there are arguments *at all*, whether for or against the gods, shows a *rupture* in the immediacy of belief in divinities. As a comic artist Aristophanes is already outside the immediacy of the religious. Inevitably more distanced, mediated thought, one form of which Socrates represents, must be taken into account. Yet Aristophanes tries to debunk thought—though he does so with thought. Aristophanes debunks Socratic thought with comic wit, which is itself a form of the comic skepticism of thought. I will return to this, for Hegel is, in some ways, in between Aristophanes and Socrates here.

If the comic is an acme of the aesthetic, just because it testifies to this developing inwardness, it also hints at the self-dissolution of the aesthetic. The aesthetic can only live with a certain naiveté in relation to the truth of the image. When a sense of separate inwardness appears, inevitably every image will be questioned as to its truth/untruth. But just this questioning means that we no longer live unself-consciously in the images. This is extremely significant when the images in question are those of the traditional gods. If we no longer live naively in those images, then the dying of the gods becomes possible, the traditional religion may go under, and in the case of the Greek world, the religious foundations of political communal life may be also undermined. Such is the destructive power of inwardness, its capacity for relentless negativity, perhaps known more deeply by Hegel than by any other philosopher, Nietzsche included.

This destructive energy comes to a kind of affirmative expression in the comic spirit. This is the thing about Aristophanes that seems to draw Hegel's attention: I call it this being-at-home in not being-at-home; this serene energy of being in the very debunking of all the forms of being, even those that carry the sacred images. Hegel sees this as *subjectivity* at home with itself even in all loss, hilarity in all the craziness. I return to Hegel's stress on subjectivity, but first I note that there is a genuine loss, a loss of meaning. I underline again that what is lost is the absolute meaning that is carried by the mythic images of the gods. Immediate immersion in those images is lost, a loss experienced as the loss of the world as meaningful. Let us not underestimate this loss. Aesthetic images can be carriers of the sense of being as a whole, carriers of a sense of world. This was especially true in the premodern world. Greek *Kunstreligion* is not art in the post-Kantian sense of a specialized realm of aesthetic experience. The aesthetic and the mythic, that is, the religious cannot be separated. To lose the aesthetic is to lose the absolute in so far as this is brought to mind and articulated by such images. Yet in this absolute loss the spirit can be at home with itself. This is one of the most enigmatic things, I believe.

Though we might not be able to take the divine images with the previous seriousness, by the incorporation of debunking into a celebrating comic order something can be preserved. This incorporation is both negative and positive. It is negative of naive consciousness. But even in that negation one can be affirmatively at home with being and oneself in all the debunking. Remember again that we are talking about the traditional gods who gave meaning to the totality of Greek life. Their debunking reveals a certain failure of the sacred, so there is nothing trivial about the laughter here. When Hegel cites Aristophanes with approval, the warmth of this approval springs partly, I think, from the affirmative joy permeating his most extreme debunking. This indicates something about Hegel's own spirit. What he approves in Aristophanes is a pure freedom in folly, a joy in absurdity. Hegel seems to think that this madness, this extreme levity about the most serious things is the highest aesthetic freedom.

I think here of Nietzsche's distinction between a base and noble nihilism. Aristophanic comedy recalls noble nihilism in that there is an affirmative intent in all its negativity. Base nihilism merely negates; noble nihilism affirms in negation. Aristophanes is a nihilist to the extent that he knows that *everything can be debunked.* And everything is debunked. Yet there is more than debunking going on. The philosophical analogue might be what Hegel calls noble skepticism: ancient skepticism is noble in so far as its debunking of the finite involves an opening to something other than the finite. Everything turns on how you say: "It is nothing." Aristotle said: *to on legetai pollachōs.* Comedy, by contrast, makes us say: *to mē on legetai pollachōs.* The nothing is said in many ways. A crucial way of affirmatively "saying" the nothing is the laughter of the comic. In this outburst or upsurgence of the energy of being, the negative is the negative of itself and hence affirmative. If "It is nothing" can be said in many ways, one of the ways opens the promise of reconciliation.

I will say little about modern comedy except that Hegel finds this same being-at-home in not being-at-home. Indeed in the modern world the principle of inwardness has reached a completion relative to which the end of the ancient world was only a beginning. The laughter at the end of the ancient world is the beginning of the inwardness of the modern. Hence Aristophanes (as the aesthetic twin of Socrates' reflective inwardness) is on the cusp between the end of the ancient world and the beginnings of the modern. Modern comedy takes places in a context of developed inwardness. We will see shortly that in the ancient world Hegel judges Aristophanes superior to Socrates in a certain sense. But what might be the analogue in the modern world? Who would be the Aristophanes of the epoch of Hegelian reason? Is there any comedy at the level of the Hegelian *Begriff?* Or does the modern completion of inwardness inevitably imply an inversion of Aristophanes' superiority to Socrates, such that no art, not even that of a modern Aristophanes, could be superior to Hegelian philosophizing?

A Nietzschean or post-Nietzschean will answer such questions by accusing Hegelian thought of a conceptual intolerance to art's possible superiority. The block nature of such a charge must be denied. This does not mean a block acquittal. I must ask again: Can philosophy laugh at itself? What can we glean from the fact that Hegel laughs with Aristophanes against Socrates? Does it mean that philosophy, too, can laugh at the absurdity it perennially risks, must risk: taking the abstraction for the fullness of actuality? When Aristophanes dangles Socrates over the stage, we have an image of abstracted, alienated thought, an aesthetic exemplification of Whitehead's fallacy of misplaced concreteness. That Hegel laughs here should surprise us; for in attacking Socrates, Aristophanes attacks philosophy itself.

The Socrates of the *Clouds* is a rationalistic demythologizer, devoid of poetic nuance. He is an exemplar of logicism, hence a destroyer of the religious and aesthetic. This coincides almost exactly with the received picture of Hegel; Hegel the panlogist swallows the religious and artistic, and proves himself void of imaginative vision and the sense of sacred mystery. So we should be severely jolted by Hegel's criticism of Socrates and praise for the justice of Aristophanes' pillory. More than most philosophers, Hegel wanted philosophically to overcome abstract thought—dialectic would move us to concrete thought beyond the comedy of derisory abstraction. The irony is that most of his critics see Hegel as dangling in his own basket of *Geist* above the real drama of concrete being.

Hegel's most extensive discussion of Aristophanes is not to be found, as one would expect, in the *Lectures on Aesthetics*, but in the *Lectures on the History of Philosophy*.[11] This fact itself is significant: the importance of Aristophanic laughter for *philosophy itself*, as well as the end of antiquity, is at stake. Laughter is not a merely "aestheticist" matter. The context of discussion concerns the accusations brought against Socrates. Hegel views the accusations as just; hence Aristophanes' picture is also just. An important matter is the shaking of the idea of law by the one-sided reflecting consciousness of Socrates. Aristophanes' sense of Socrates' one-sidedness is regarded as a prelude to his death. That Hegel sides with Aristophanes implies that the subjective freedom of a great comic artist reveals more concerning the complex truth of Greek *Sittlichkeit* than does the subjective freedom of the abstract thinker. In political terms Aristophanes, like Socrates, shows absolute, fearless freedom of spirit. But he is bound to his polis in a different way than Socrates. Aristophanes comically sees the contradiction between subjective freedom and the polis; Socrates tends to be less alert to the alienated dimensions of his own abstracted thought.

Of course, Aristophanes brought many great figures on the stage to pillory, Aeschylus, Pericles, Sophocles, Alcibiades, the gods themselves. Hegel admits that this irreverence to public and sacred figures would be intolerable to contemporary serious Germans. It is interesting that Hegel notes Aristophanes' mockery of Euripides both here and in the *Aesthetics*. I mention this to recall Nietzsche's coupling of Socrates and Euripides as together responsible (with their supposed totalizing insistence on clarity and transparency) for the destruction of the tragic acme of Greek life. So consider that in Aristophanes' *Frogs* Dionysus descends into Hades after the death of Euripides. Athens is now bereft of a worthy poet and Dionysus is intent on bringing Euripides back with him. In Hades there ensues a contest between Aeschylus and Euripides. But it is not to Euripides but to *Aeschylus* (1467ff.) that Aristophanes has Dionysus award the final victory. Nietzsche would approve.[12]

In siding with Aristophanes against Socrates, Hegel implies that Aristophanes is a justified defender of the richer depths of traditional Greek life, as against the subjectivizing thought of Socrates, which uproots abstracted reflection from the ground of a people's rich *Sittlichkeit*. One might say, Hegel criticizes Socrates for "logocentrism," that very sin the Nietzscheans and post-Nietzscheans charge against Hegel's thought as itself the *ne plus ultra* of logocentrism. He explicitly says that Socrates neglects the *alogical* (a charge also made by Aristotle, to which Hegel concurs). There is irony indeed that Hegel, through the eyes of Aristophanes, sees a profound loss in the dissolution of Greek *Sittlichkeit* because of the relentless debunking power of abstract thought, and the inwardness to which it gives rise. (Hegel is a critic of what Nietzsche in the *Birth of Tragedy* calls "Socratic man!")

Hegel says that Aristophanes' mockery of Socrates in *The Clouds* is not that of a shallow joker but has a deeper meaning than merely to mock. There is a contradiction in the matter itself, and (recall Hegel's distinction between *das Lächerliche* and *das Komische*)[13] true laughter is not directed at what is genuinely worthy but on what in itself presents the contradiction. Something or somebody preens itself as worthy but in fact that something or somebody is worthless; laughter exposes the disjunction between pretension and actuality. If the thing itself is not in contradiction, the comedy is superficial and groundless. We might say that comedy has a certain ontological dimension; it reveals something about the being of the matter in question. It is a dissolution that emerges from within the matter itself. It is the being of living contradiction in the revelation of its absurdity that generates the comedy of that matter.

One inevitably thinks of dialectic in relation to the two agons in the *Clouds*, the first between the Just and Unjust Logos, the second between Father and Son, Strepsiades and Pheidippides. Aristophanes was parodying the sophistic eristic and the legal agon of his day (the two Logoi on stage are said to have been dressed up as fighting cocks). As a virtuoso of argumentative technique in its polemical, eristic forms, Aristophanes might have been a sophist if he chose (at 520 he presents himself as a poet who is *sophos*), or indeed a Socratic, if he could have taken philosophy seriously.

The agon between the Just and Unjust Logos reminds us of the later problem of ancient skepticism with equipollence, and Hegel's own preoccupation with this in relation to Kant's antinomies, modern skepticism and dialectic (as we saw in chapter 5). Nor is it irrelevant to recall again that Hegel spends far more time on Zeno's dialectic than on Parmenides' One in his treatment of the history of philosophy. His interest in the former is in the logical agon of thought; to this agon the dialectic gives articulate form. It is also worth noting that ambiguity continues to hover over the agons of Aristophanes: it is not clear which side, if any, wins. This would delight deconstructionists who like to show something "undecidable" in every dialectic. This is their way of refusing Hegel's *Aufhebung*. Aristophanes could teach them a thing or two. In Aristophanes' play no character personifies the ideals of the Just Logos. This does not make Aristophanes a base nihilist. It may be a comment on the failure of human beings, rather than on the worth of the ethical ideal in question.

The at-homeness with self that Hegel finds in Aristophanes intimately reflects the ability of the Athenian people to be cheerfully at home with itself. In that sense, Aristophanes is closer to being the voice of the Athenian polis than is Socrates. This community with the polis does not exclude the negative (this is also clear with Socratic dialectic). Aristophanes attacks Athens for its failure to live up to itself. It is living pretentiousness that is debunked, yet for such debunking to be effective the people must already acknowledge the ideal that is being deformed in the living actuality. Such ideals constitute the spirit of the people at its richest. To usurp Socrates' own metaphor, it is Aristophanes who is the gadfly that tries to wake Athens up to its laughable stupidity. But the sting is not only painful; it is joyful violence. Hegel implies this when he sees in Aristophanes the free side of the Athenian people, which is capable of self-enjoyment in loss itself. Things come to grief and show themselves as absurd, but in just their coming to nothing the Greek spirit was able to exult comically.

Relevant to Aristophanes as the voice of Athens, consider this story: when asked by Dionysus of Syracuse about the Athenian people and institutions, Plato is said to have sent him the works of Aristophanes. Nietzsche mentions the story that when Plato died the works of Aristophanes were discovered under his pillow.[14] I think it is apposite to invoke Nietzsche here in that he laughed at all the other philosophers, not least at Plato, who here honors Aristophanes so highly. While the buffoonery in *Zarathustra* is sometimes uneven, among works by philosophers it is rare for its comic energy. If one reflects on the togetherness of comedy and suffering (see below on Plato's picture of Aristophanes), it will not be strange that Nietzsche, the defender of Attic tragedy, is yet a laughing philosopher.

Can one say that there permeates the Socratic way the same joy in being, even in debunking, such as we find in Aristophanic laughter? Hegel seems to say no. Socrates develops the dialectic but there is a certain emptiness in the results. The universal becomes empty through Socratic dialectic. Hegel does not deny that there is exaggeration in Aristophanes' portrait. But caricature can serve the revelation of truth; an essential tendency becomes visible in being magnified in caricature. I think that what Hegel dislikes about Socrates here is not his commitment to a life of thought, but that his thought was too focused individually on Socrates himself. Implicitly Socrates set himself up as judge of the people. The internal contingency of his own daimon usurps the external daimon of the people and their religious oracles. It is the contingency of subjective reflection that Hegel criticizes. In seeing Socrates as thus one-sided, Hegel—I suspect—was implicitly reacting to the one-sidedness of subjectivists in his own time, who in absolutizing their own subjectivity set themselves above tradition and the established law of the people. This is nowhere more evident than in Hegel's relentless criticism of the Romantic irony of his own day which, with suitable qualifications, we have seen to be a post-Kantian parallel to Socratic irony.

I do not think that this is the end of the matter. What I previously called the idiocy of the philosopher, the intimate thisness of the thinker as this thinker, is also at stake. Socrates himself says that if he had not lived as an idiot (*idiōteuein*, *Apology*, 32a3), he would not have survived to the age he did. There is also the question of philosophy as an idiot wisdom, that is to say, a metaxological mindfulness that stays true to the intimacy of being, while not being racked by dualistic opposition with being other than the self. There is an idiot wisdom in festive laughter too.[15]

It is Aristophanes' criticism of Socrates' relation to the people that Hegel endorses. The people were right to find him guilty of this accusation. But, Hegel says, his condemnation to death followed less from the accusation than from his refusal to acknowledge the right of the people in relation to the accused. Hegel acknowledges the tragic dimension of this, for Socrates' guilt was copartner with the people's guilt. In condemning subjective reflection, the Greek people was also condemning itself, for already the spirit of such reflection had infected it. In condemning Socrates it condemned itself. The fate of their world was dissolution, and out of the ashes of dissolution, the very principle of condemned inwardness becomes the basis for the construction of a new spiritual and cultural world. That this spirit of inwardness is already at work in Socrates' antagonists is evident in the contradiction I noted above in Aristophanes himself: to debunk the debunkers, Aristophanes must already have stepped beyond the naiveté of unreflecting *Sittlichkeit,* and hence already be in the same world of *Geist* as Socrates and the Sophists. His laughter is precisely a weapon to take the sting of destruction out of the gadfly of abstract reflection; but in that defensive weapon the same sting of complex inwardness, unnaive presence in *Sittlichkeit,* is already producing its *pharmakon* in the double sense Derrida exploits: poison and medicine.

In an important regard one must modify Hegel's position and say that the modern world begins with the defeat of Aristophanes. His comic defense measure failed. And the seeming failure of the executed Socrates provided only martyr's blood to nourish the soil of the new emergent sense of *Geist* as subjective inwardness that was to determine the shape of the world subsequent to classical antiquity, whether in religious form in Christian culture, or in secular form in post-Cartesian thought. Socrates won. The spirit of the comic becomes secondary to the seriousness of progressively self-emancipating rational inwardness. Indeed we must modify Heidegger and those in his shadow and say: the charge against the Western tradition should not be "logocentrism," but not enough laughter.

Again I do not mean clever postmodern frivolity but Aristophanic laughter that comes out of alogical, rather metalogical depths: reverent irreverence or irreverent reverence. Laughter can be mad or nihilistic or disgusted with being. It can also be generous: a festive celebration in the dismemberment of negativity itself. The *joy* in being in laughter can be a being-at-home in the metaxological community of being, even though negation, stupidity, arrogance, brutality, evil, despair, rancor, banality also make one not to be at home. What here looks like a contradiction to an unripe logicism need not be invidious contradiction to the largess of a mature speculative mindfulness: a being-at-home in not being-at-home. The laughter of speculative mind would be the laughter of the gods—a reconciliation with being in folly, beyond folly. Hegel might not be entirely averse to this suggestion, though inevitably he would interpret the metalogical depths in terms of the unarticulated immediacy of *Geist*. Then he would go on to articulate the metalogical conceptually by means of his speculative dialectic. This would risk turning the interrupting, elemental energy of laughter, its being-at-home in not being-at-home, into a dialectically domesticated other.

Who Laughs Last?
Between Hegelian Self-Certainty and Plato's Silence

I close by bowing towards another great philosopher's picture of Aristophanes, namely Plato's in the *Symposium*. The contrast suggested by the two pictures will bring out some of the tensions between the Aristophanic and Hegelian spirits, indeed their discordant mutuality. It will also bring out the discordant mutuality between these two and Socrates and Plato. This will raise again the question of the one and the double, and the tension between the dialectical and the metaxological. What I say about the *Symposium* will relate to the theme of philosophy and laughter, though much more might be said on other themes.

In Plato's *Symposium* we are presented with a drinking party, a festive celebration with plurivocal promise. Aristophanes delivers his speech, and there is more than one speech. Moreover, the theme of the speeches, eros, lends itself to a plurality of articulations. I mean this not only in the evident sense that a plurality of speakers give different speeches, each accentuating something distinctive, but also in the deeper regard that eros articulates itself in a plurivocal manner. Thus, Diotima reminds us that eros, like poiesis, has in itself a more embracing sense with a plural promise, even though one particular sense is taken to usurp the whole: eros is contracted to sexual eros, poiesis to poetry in the more specialized sense (205b–d). We philosophers have to remember the "more" that is not encapsulated in the specialized sense.

Moreover, because there is a certain incompleteness to each speech, we need a plurality of logoi. The plurivocal promise of the banquet is also evident in that each speech has a plurality of listeners. We must remember that as Aristophanes speaks, Socrates is right there with him, alert, attentive. The *Symposium* is a *sunousia*, a being with, a philosophical intercourse with erotic possibilities and agapeic promise. It is an agapē in the sense of a feast, a celebrating meal where a community of selves and others think and rejoice, philosophize and joke. So, too, the logoi of both Aristophanes and Socrates are beyond univocity. They show a significant doubleness, as we shall see. This is sometimes equivocal and duplicitous. But there is more. Plato himself is more than all the determinate speeches. Not only the plurivocal setting of the work, but also Plato's very work itself, is inherently metaxological.

There is the following link with the *Clouds*. The imputation of blasphemy to Socrates in the *Clouds* also shadows the *Symposium*. The occasion of this gathering was proximate to the mutilation of the Hermes and the profaning of the Eleusinian mysteries, blamed on Alcibiades and his cohorts. Indirectly, Socrates was suspect as the alleged corrupting teacher of Alcibiades. Mirroring Pheidippides, Alcibiades seemed to be one more impious son produced by Socrates. If there is philosophical laughter in the *Symposium*, it will raise suspicions of impiety: if nothing is sacred to philosophical laughter, if everything can be debunked, all is allowed, even the imprudent, impudent, desecration of the Hermes. The Hermes were originally phallic stones yes, and the thought of aroused flesh as hermeneutically divine may now arouse only a smile. Nevertheless, the Hermes figures were markers (Roman: *Terminus*) of the essential boundary between life and death, mortals and gods, essential mediators between these two. If philosophical laughter leads to a nihilistic desecration of the Hermes, then the medium between mortals and gods is destroyed. Being ethical and being religious in the middle collapses into a joke—a bad joke.

Before Aristophanes begins his speech he says that he is not afraid to utter foolishness, for folly is native to his muse. The word he uses for folly is *geloia*, the same word used by the younger Socrates in running away from the hair, mud and dirt. Aristophanes the comic poet is not afraid of these (189a–b). There will be laughter, and it will be laughter with a negative, even violent side. Yet it will have profound spiritual seriousness. Laughter will be a response to the ultimacy of suffering.

Aristophanes' speech about eros puts the emphasis on the *origin*, the original condition of the whole human being. The stress is on a primal plenitude that will be split, thus initiating the human quest for its own other and its reconstituted wholeness. One is inevitably reminded of Hegel's triadic movement from the immediacy of the original unity through the necessary self-differentiation of this unity, to the reconstituted unity that overcomes the estrangement of dualistic opposition. The original one gives rise to a double, but the double turns out to be two sides of the split original. The wholeness at the end reconstitutes the original unity but at a further level of differentiated articulation.

Aristophanes' story is well-known: the original nature (*archaia phusis*, 192e) of human beings was one of a spherical whole (*holon*), a globular double of what we now are, with four legs, four hands, two-faced head, doubled genitals, and so on. . . . Because of our powerfulness and hubris, Zeus split us in half. Henceforth we are the broken half (*sumbolon* is Aristophanes' word, 191d) of an original whole, always in search of our lost half. That search is simply eros. Aristophanes' tale is a myth of origins: the origin is the whole, while life in the middle is the effort to reconstitute the lost, now broken whole. This is a funny myth, brilliantly imaginative, but it is full of pain and suffering. One sees the comedy of the doubled body, first spherical, then halved, then threatened with being quartered, such that we will have to hop around on one leg. The comedy of eros is also evident in the humorous yet painful efforts of the half-humans to reunite, or again in the threat of their being further reduced to quarter spheres with sliced genitals.

Clearly Aristophanes' view is as deeply tragic as comic. One telling image is of an egg being sliced by a hair (190d): the egg might be the image of fertility, the original seed or source of genesis, but the pain of sundering, of splitting, is very palpable. There is the image of the quartered wholes as like the profiles on tombs (193a): a flat mask that memorializes loss. In this threat of the further wrath of Zeus, death haunts eros. Underneath the joking is suffering and violence. Its energy is by no means blandly serene. In part it is the violence of being that makes us, forces us to laugh. If laughter does not heal the rift, at least it may help us forget it, for a time.

One does see affinities with Hegel, in that for Aristophanes the original whole is guilty of the original sin, conspiring against the gods, launching an assault on the heavens (*eis ton ouranon*, 190c), threatening to assault the gods. The impious Giants are recalled (190c), and their implication in the origin of evil, according to Orphic myth.[16] The hubristic self-assertion of the origin leads to the fall into evil and difference and the initiation of the human quest for its completing other. Aristophanes bespeaks the pain of difference in this quest in a very sharp and moving way. Yet his sense of the origin in itself is not erotic, though it relates to the erotic, in that the erotic quest is the search to reconstitute the original one. The origin itself is first a kind of plenitude. But it is not an agapeic plenitude. It is a plenitude of power in the form of hubristic self-assertion.

Though we are in search of the whole, Aristophanes implies we will never be reunited in a seamless fashion with our lost counterpart—our other self, ourself as other. The scar of the first splitting is inerasable, imaged in the navel, where Apollo the divine surgeon has stitched together the torn skin of the original whole. The navel is where we are joined and held together but that very tucked center is a memorial of our original sundering (*mnēmeion einai tou palaiou pathous*, 191a). Nor is there any absolute reconstitution of the lost whole. After the origin, in a painful sense, being is loss. What is regained is done so only episodically. We fall back into suffering difference once more. Because of the pathos of suffering in this quest for wholeness, no insipid harmony is implied or possible. There is always a scar of otherness or difference that will be recalcitrant to overcoming. I would say that Aristophanes' double, doubling, is not the affirmative sense of the double that I articulated in previous chapters, precisely because it is not fully thought through as metaxological. It is perhaps close to the self-doubling of Hegel's unhappy consciousness. The latter inevitably comes to mind in that the wound to the original one will never be completely healed. We are condemned to separateness.

Socrates' account of eros turns from the origin to the end in a different sense. Eros is not for the half or the whole simply, except in so far as they are good: finally and simply, it is the good that we love (205e–206a). This turn to the end reminds us of Hegel's teleological thrust, though we will find in Socrates, as in Aristophanes, a strong stress on the episodic, hence finally unmasterable, revelation of the telos. I note that Socrates, in contrast to Aristophanes, is initially afraid to look ridiculous or to be made a laughing stock, at least so he says (199b2–3). But the older Socrates is slyer than his younger self. Any laughter will be deflected in advance in that he will tell of the instruction of this younger self by *another*, Diotima. If he recounts anything ridiculous, he will be recounting, and hence not the sole present butt of the joke. Of course, this instruction by another recalls the instruction of the younger Socrates by Parmenides. In the present case, an older Socrates will tell of the instruction of the younger Socrates by a female sage, a stranger woman (*xenē anakrinousa*, 201e4) beyond sex because of age, perhaps like the aged Parmenides.

The ignorance and callowness of the younger Socrates is implied; he must submit to an older other, and in this submission he must learn to take the intermediate, the *metaxu*, with philosophical seriousness (see 204b). An older woman will free him from the fear of being laughed at by the younger woman, the Thracian maid. The younger Socrates is often perplexed and uncomprehending in his response to Diotima. He is still too much of a pre-Socratic cosmologist or physiologist, a Thales absorbed in the skies, a follower of Anaxagoras (see *Phaedo*, 96a–99e) for whom the sun is a stone (*Apology*, 26d), the caricature of which Aristophanes gives us in *Clouds*, more at home with the non-human than the human, not yet mature enough for the between. Parmenides' rebuke turned, too, on the inability of the younger Socrates to take the middle with proper philosophical mindfulness.

Against the hubristic plenitude of the Aristophanic original whole, Socrates stresses that eros begins in lack, without initially asking about the archē of this lack. But there is an ambiguity in the story told (203aff.) in that eros, as a between, is a mingling of his father, contrivance, resource, *Poros* (the son of cunning, *Mētis*) and his mother, poverty, *Penia*. I take this to imply that for us mortals in the middle, eros as lack always contains the promise of something more than lack. *Poros* has connotations of a "way," a "way across," as in crossing a stream. *Poros* might imply: An other than lacking way lets us cross a gap of emptiness. Into this way across, this intermediating power of crossing, is ingrained the memory of a certain *plenty*, in a sense other than the hubristic plenitude.

This is what I mean: Diotima presents *Poros* as a god who is drunk with nectar at the gods' celebration of the birth of Aphrodite; he stumbles from the feast of the table of the gods, and sleeps in the garden of Zeus. *Penia*, the mother of eros, sleeps with *Poros* in his drunken, divine slumber. Eros is born of their union. The wakefulness of indigent eros is born of the intoxicated sleep of overfull divinity. The resourcefulness of eros is not just the cunning of reason. The trace of divine drunkenness and festivity, agapeic plenty, is embodied in the genesis of eros; the memory of that trace might subsequently be reactivated in the thrust of eros beyond its own lack. This is why later there will be talk of the deathless element to the mortal being in its becoming; death and the deathless mingle in the originative process of becoming (203e). Death is not simply correlated with the threatened wrath of Zeus, as with Aristophanes. Rather it coexists in tension with the memory of the deathless (*to athanatos*) that comes to us in sudden moments of divine intoxication, when we do not know if we wake or sleep, live or die, see into the heart of things or dream.

Eros as simply lacking makes no sense; at work in eros, already from the origin, from its genesis, is the original power of being in becoming itself, what I name in terms of the plenitude of agapeic being.[17] The importance of plenty beyond lack I also take to be consistent with the stress on *generation beyond ourselves*, whether in children or works or speeches, or political communities. The plenitude of being overcomes the lack within the self, not simply for the self, but for the generation of an other or others, beyond the self.

Eros is not a drive to the complete dialectical self-mediation of the human being; it is certainly a self-mediation of the human, but that self-mediation of desire drives beyond the human to what is other than it. Desire's self-mediation is driven beyond self-mediation to metaxological intermediation with the other, named in its absolute form by Diotima as absolute beauty or good. This other to the human self, just in its otherness, gives a ballast and directionality to human eros, otherwise unstable and equivocal. The promise of plenty, not only in terms of the beauty of being, but its inherent goodness, is inscribed into the Socratic notion of erotic lack. I take this as an indication that the lack of eros itself would never drive forward, even to its own self-mediated satisfaction, were it not underpinned and excitated by an affirmative energy of being that cannot be described in purely lacking terms.

So too in Socrates' account, the lack itself is ultimately oriented to an other that is beyond the self in an even more ultimate sense: an other that is not generated beyond eros through eros, but an other that draws out the promise of eros, while itself remaining finally other even in that drawing out, other than human self-generation and human generation beyond self. It hardly needs to be said that eros is here described as a daimon that is *metaxu*, between earth and heaven, mortals and divinities. The articulation of eros takes places in the *metaxu,* and so in a sense binds up the whole. There is a *Gottesdienst* in this middle, too: the power of daimonic eros is to interpret (*hermēneuon*) and transport human things to the gods and divine things to man (202e). I note that Socrates' speech recounts his own *initiation* into the mysteries of eros by the Mantinean priestess. This is especially true of Diotima's final revelation (210aff.), during which Socrates is completely silent, surrendering to the revelation, though perhaps not fully understanding all that is said. I find the promise of a double mediation between mortals and divinities in Socrates' account of the *metaxu.*

What do we make of this strong assertion: God with man does not mingle (*theos de anthrōpōi ou mignutai,* 203a)? This seems to rule out any mediation at all, and give us a dualism of man and God that is unbridgeable. It seems to give us the equivocal difference of the unhappy consciousness, between the changing eros of the mortal self and the unchangeable beyond of the God. Such an oppositional dualism is not the point at all, I think. I think it is a strong affirmation of the otherness of transcendence as other. I take it as an affirmation of the otherness of transcendence as ultimately beyond all anthropomorphic reductions. That this need not be fixated into a dualistic opposition is evident when immediately the mediation of eros from both sides is asserted: eros as a daimon is the means whereby the intercourse and dialogue of men and gods (*hē homilia kai hē dialektos theois pros anthrōpous* 203a) is made possible. The metaxological makes the ultimate dialectic, diologue possible. The metaxological double is affirmed, but it is affirmed as in itself affirmative, not as a to-be-negated dualism. Sometimes the promise of this affirmative double is communicated to mortals by the gods through gifted daimonic selves—let us say a divinely inspired poet or philosopher or statesman—whose lives or work embody the call of the double mediation.

Here we can ask the question: How does the erotic drive of the philosopher finally relate to the other? I suggest that the telos of this drive indicates a reversal of directionality right at the end. Eros would seem to insist on *self-mediation* in wanting to possess the other, hence making the other *for me* as the means, medium of my self-fulfillment. But as Diotima describes the unfolding of philosophical eros, there is a progressive divestment of the sense of any "for-the-self" that is self-enclosed. Quite to the contrary, in finding its own self-mediation more energetically and mindfully activated, the philosopher discovers the opening of this self-mediation beyond self-mediation: openness to the other becomes more accentuated the more deep or high erotic self-mediation becomes.

I mentioned Socrates' silence during the final revelation. But we easily forget that this silence is no simple immediacy. We forget because of the brilliance of Plato's philosophical artistry. Socrates' silence is no blank but is multiply mediated, plurivocally mediated. Here is the intricacy: Plato writes of the older Socrates speaking of the younger Socrates listening, silently listening to the speech of another, Diotima, whose speech, in turn, reveals or mediates the ultimate revelation of an other beyond all speech, the beautiful itself. *For us* readers the final revelation is mediated in at least a fourfold way! In fact, the telling and retelling is even more complex; the entire written dialogue tells of Appolodorus retelling to a friend a retelling of Aristodemus of the different speeches at the banquet! But for all of us—readers, writer, *personae* of the dialogue—at the limit of the middle, there is a limit of logos, the sense of which is itself mediated by a plurality of logoi, both philosophical and other than philosophical, logoi that mingle with the listening silences of the reader and the writer and the *personae*. This is just a hint of the intricate richness of Plato's plurivocity as a philosophical writer.

Thus, there is a speculative silence of being shown and seeing at the heart of speech, a complex yet simple silence that is plurivocally mediated and woven into the attempted saying of desire's origin or end. Diotima turns to what she calls the "vast sea of beauty" (210d). Not earth, not heaven, but sea; at this height we are all at sea. The vast ocean reminds us of the abundant indeterminate matrix of being, the overdetermined waters of the agapeic mother of all. Thales haunts us again. We cannot absolutely name this mother, for every saying is a determination of the indeterminate, hence not the name of this overdetermined other. Yet in contemplation of it, beautiful logoi and a plentiful harvest of philosophy may be generated (210d). Plato's own work as a plurivocal logos itself offers such a harvest of plenty.

Socrates is counseled to give his very best attention to the revelation of the highest beauty. If we cannot absolutely say it, it may at least show itself to our patient silence. This patient knowing is implied by the power of beauty itself as astonishing (*thaumaston*, 210e). The beautiful is a show of the good. Hence at the highest point there is this *reversal* from the side of the other: suddenly, *exaiphnēs,* philosophical vision is offered as a gift from the otherness of absolute beauty or the absolute good. We are reminded of the blinding vision of the Sun in the *Republic* (see, 515c6; 516e5) which also comes *exaiphnēs*; also the spark of illumination that suddenly (*exaiphnēs*) passes in dialogue between philosophers (*Seventh Letter*, 341c–d). In this blinding vision of excess, we do not fly like the Hegelian owl at twilight but flutter in some disorientation, more like the Aristotelian bat in sunlight.

We ought not to underestimate the stunning power of the metaphysical astonishment here named. This is something very strange. The reversal is an astounding and startling revelation. From the standpoint of a purely self-mediating dialectic, it makes no sense. It stuns such a dialectic into silence. If philosophical mind is identified with dialectical self-mediation, it is beyond such a mind. We may repeat the Platonic letter here, but if the spirit of astonishment is lacking, this very repetition will dull our sense of the strangeness of the startling reversal. As coming from the other, the sudden reversal inflicts a violent wrenching out of any closed self-mediation. In the opening of self-mediating eros, the directionality of mediation is reversed as the good gives itself to the philosophical self out of its otherness. The reversal is a rupture and hence *exaiphnēs*, for there is no way in which the second mediation from the otherness of the good can be reduced to the self-mediation of the erotic philosopher. The blinding sight is like a kind of death. It extinguishes our vile self-insistence; the self is not (as Hegel will say below) the absolute being or *Wesen*. The end of eros is beyond eros; it comes to erotic striving as a gift of the good beyond eros.

The affirmation of transcendence recalls: God with man does not mingle. The ambiguity here, of course, is that there is a mingling after vision: a certain community of friendship between man and God can come to be (see 212a; *huparchei theophilei genesthai*). There is also mingling in the sense of a divine gift offered. Here I think we must take seriously Plato's repeated assertion that philosophy itself is a divine gift. In the rupture of the *exaiphnēs*, the reversal of direction offers mania to the philosopher, offers the gift of divine madness. As we saw in previous chapters, Hegel would reduce this double directionality to two sides of a singular process of dialectical self-mediation. I reject this. Plato would reject it, I think. The rupture of the *exaiphnēs* names a difference or otherness that will not be bridged completely by any process of singular self-mediation, least of all our self-mediation. In the rupture, a gift of divine energy sparks across the gap. We are reminded of divine laughter. This gift of divine madness offers the dark generosity of a sacred folly. Aristophanes knew the darkness of the sacred folly. His laughter celebrated its generosity. Plato both knew and celebrated philosophically this generosity.

But let us return for a while to the comparison of Aristophanes' and Hegel's view of the origin and end. For Hegel the origin is the undeveloped; but the origin develops itself, mediates with itself. Its *telos* is the reconstitution of the original whole but after having passed through the mediation of difference. Hence, the *telos* reconstitutes the original whole at a higher level of self-differentiated appropriation. My question is: Do we find the same pain of first splitting in Hegel, as we find in Aristophanes? The Hegelian middle is essentially self-mediating. There is a likeness and unlikeness to Aristophanes: in the latter the middle could be said to be self-mediating, but none of us is ever a whole self, and thus the self-mediation shows an element of futility, certainly in this life. Moreover, Aristophanic "self-mediation" can never achieve the conceptual self-transparency of Hegelian self-mediation: the lovers in search of their other self, their self as other, proceed by intimation and divination (*manteuetai*, 192d), not by lucid conceptual self-consciousness.

Can we see here an anticipation of Sartre's view: man is a useless passion? Sartre's man wants to be Sartre's God, a logically impossible unity of the in-itself and the for-itself, the undifferentiated, self-identical plenitude of being and the differentiated identity of desire as lack, as nothing. Sartre's dualism of being and nothingness reduplicates the despairing opposition of the unchangeable and the changing of the unhappy consciousness. In Aristophanes' speech in the *Symposium* the hope of a reconstituted whole in the *next* life is not entirely ruled out (193d). And as already suggested, one does find anticipations of the unhappy consciousness, and in the "Hegelian" language of the one splitting itself in two. In Hegel the image of the circle is pervasive, and also the implication that he has managed to reconstitute in thought the absolute circular, that is, dialectically self-mediating whole.[18] We are reminded again of Parmenides' *eukukleos Alētheia*, well-rounded truth. But though the call of wholeness is named by Aristophanes, the attainment of absolute closure is denied. The truth is a wounded circle. We will never here be entire again. Hegel's commitment to the attainment of the whole makes him see more happiness in the comic than may be there, at least in the form of complete self-mediation. This would help account for his finally forward looking glance; also his vindication of Socrates *in the long run* (though not in a form that Socrates and Plato, as portrayed above, would accept); also the final superiority of Hegelian philosophy itself vis-à-vis the aesthetic and religious.

Hegel's reference to the comic consciousness towards the end of the *Phenomenology* is relevant here.[19] Hegel's discussion does not involve an explicit identification of Aristophanes but there is a reference to the Greek gods becoming clouds. The emphasis is on comedy exhibiting the fate of the gods: the gods want to be something on their own account as individuals but this pretension is uncovered; the mask is dropped. Part of what Hegel is getting at is what I called

Aristophanes' comic demythologizing. But for Hegel the real lesson is the *self-certainty of consciousness at home with itself,* while everything other, even the divine, is at its mercy. "What this self-consciousness beholds is that whatever assumes the form of essentiality over against it, is instead dissolved in it—in its thinking, its existence, and its action—and is at its mercy. It is the return of everything universal into the certainty of itself which, in consequence, is this complete loss of fear and of essential being on the part of all that is alien. This self-certainty is a state of spiritual well-being and repose therein, such as is not to be found anywhere outside of this Comedy."[20] Hegel goes on to say: "The proposition that expresses this levity runs: The Self is absolute Being [*Wesen*]."[21]

This proposition is folly for Platonic eros, the folly that must be extinguished at the sudden moment of reversal. Extinguished by laughter: I find it hard to suppress the image of Aristophanes saying in reply to Hegel—Absolute *Wesen*? Nonsense! The self is absolute nonsense! I do not see him as quite saying with Pascal: *le moi est haïssable*. If one could repeat Pascal with the proper lightheartedness, it would be right—*keine Rache*, as Nietzsche might say. The levity of Aristophanes laughs at a pretense to absoluteness, sharply but without hatred. In Hegel's pretense, the dominance of dialectical *self-mediation* comes out comically; the entire result of Aristophanic comedy is the return of the self to itself. One shakes one's head at the final Hegelian outcome, for it leaves one with the uneasy feeling that Hegel somehow missed the whole point, just when the point was revealed. Hegel is laughing, but he is laughing at the wrong thing!

While the Hegelian return to self is extremely complicated, all otherness is viewed as finally a subordinate moment in the self-mediation of consciousness certain of itself. You will raise the objection: Did not Hegel take negativity more fully into account? A few pages later in the *Phenomenology* he again mentions the comic consciousness in connection with the unhappy consciousness—the acme of torn consciousness. "[T]his Unhappy Consciousness constitutes the counterpart and the completion of the comic consciousness that is perfectly happy within itself. Into the latter, all divine being returns, or it is the complete *alienation* of *substance*. The Unhappy Consciousness, on the other hand, is, conversely, the tragic fate of the certainty of self that aims to be absolute."[22] Subsequently he deals with the "death of God"; there is also the famous passage on the demise of the ancient world. Hegel certainly is full of pathos, a sense of the suffering of loss. But total loss is not total since it turns around into "the birthplace of *Geist* as it becomes self-consciousness." The new emergence is "the simplicity of the pure *Begriff* which contains these forms as its moments."[23] Laughter and grief cause *Geist* to pause briefly. Then we are off to the races again in terms of dialectical self-mediation and its conceptual subordination of otherness as a moment in the unfolding of the self-appropriating whole.

I think the claim to absolute self-mediation here would cause Aristophanes to howl with both execration and glee. It is to Plato's credit that he lets Aristophanes name the pain of sundering as an otherness that resists incorporation into self-mediation. This shows a philosophical willingness to let otherness be as other, an otherness the suffering of which is not "healed" by being renamed as the repose of self-certain consciousness. Even relative to our being healed, there is also the crucial fact that (in Plato's account of Socratic initiation) the sudden moment of illumination is episodic. The absolute is briefly, enigmatically revealed, and we fall back into finitude, back into the middle, where there is no complete self-mediation that can absolutely encompass the middle or its extremes. It is in our joyful and suffering passage through the interstices of the middle that the episodic glimpse of the ultimate is offered. Our task is mindfully to move in these interstices and to remember what is given.

Against Hegel's too simplistic vision of serene self-certainty, recall the end of the *Clouds* which follows the agon between the son and the father. This does not give us the agony of evil when a father kills a son, or a son a father. It does show us the human comedy in the son's proof that it is logically right to beat the father, and to justify this beating in terms of imitating Zeus. Socrates seems to have taught Pheidippides only too well. The son's logical success in sophistic fast talking drives the cunning, loutish father to rage. In the father there is the upsurgence of anger, passion, more elemental energies than abstract thought. Strepsiades, the buffoon, repents the folly of his impiety. The fool sees the folly of "wise" sophistry. The irrepressible idiot triumphs over the cunning of powerful abstraction.

Also against Hegel's vision of Aristophanic serenity as dialectically self-mediating, there is the ominous fact that the *Clouds* does not end in the usual feast or marriage banquet or comic celebration. It ends in *destruction and wreck*. Strepsiades asks Hermes for counsel (1480), and seeming to get his answer, proceeds to revenge the philosophical blasphemy against the gods by *burning down* Socrates' *Phrontistērion*. Does the resourceful father have the last laugh, in setting fire to the *Phrontistērion*? Can we laugh at this immolation of the school, this burning of the books, this deconstruction of speculation? The play does not end with the serene self-certainty of consciousness dialectically at home with itself, but the fiery immolation of the house of Socratic thought. All hell breaks loose. To this the Chorus in conclusion simply says: Let us go. . . . The laughing ends in disturbingly equivocal violence.

Against Hegel's finally forward-looking glance to the origin, against his vindication of Socrates *in the long run*, against the final superiority of Hegelian philosophy itself vis-à-vis the aesthetic and religious, Aristophanes' glance to the origin makes it impossible for him to be an optimist. It is as if he said—our business is not to worry about a world-historical future that may never come but to live in the present in the light of the great exemplars of the past and with respect for what is elemental in our humanness. The latter in part explains, I think, Aristophanes' political concerns: his vision of politicians as repeatedly selling out our elemental humanity in pursuit of ultimately vain visions of empire.

As a philosopher of the world-historical, Hegel pays more attention to empires than to the elemental. The laughter which says "It is nothing" is strangely muted at the level of the world-historical. Granted, Hegel is again ineradicably ambiguous, if not plurivocal, despite himself. The famous Owl of Minerva passage says: When philosophy paints its grey on grey, then has a shape of life grown old. By philosophy's grey in grey it cannot be rejuvenated but only understood. The Owl of Minerva spreads its wings only with the falling of the dusk. This passage can be seen as streaked with strains of this Aristophanic "pessimism." Where in these grey streaks are the green shoots of reinvigorating comedy? Can philosophy fly at night (I did not say: fly by night), just as a certain agapeic comedy can laugh in the face of dissolution and death? If we fly at night, do we take wing into the ether or into clouds, or do we tumble to the earth again, like that foolhardy son, Icarus? On the earth itself, what color is the rose in the cross of the present? Grey? Red? Black? Green? Green of a shoot that will not die on the wooden cross, because its sap of being is sunk deep in life's golden tree?

I asked before and I ask again: Is Hegel's logos ever graced by something like a Lutheran laugh, a gift from the agapeic other beyond dialectical self-mediation? Hegel is equivocal between the darker humor and the sometimes bland confidence that *Geist* will drive forward to its higher reconstitution of unity. We cannot attribute to him the naive optimism of dialectics that Nietzsche sees in Socrates. His joy in Aristophanes shows him the comedy of the dark side, which the negativity of dialectic must itself embrace. And what of the other bird of philosophy, the Socratic swan, the song bird of Apollo who tried to sing on the eve of death? Socrates did sing and called the music of mind philosophy. But you say: An owl hoots, neither sings, nor laughs. Might one conceive the owl's hoot as a discordant laugh at the night? What kind of laugh? A laugh that would sing but instead comes out as a hoot, because its tries to choke its own incomprehensible levity?

I do not find in Hegel this final levity at the limit of comprehension. The *Anstrengung des Begriffs*, the strenuousness of the concept cannot let go of its own seriousness. It cannot abandon itself to the final "It is nothing." Suppose we compare the end of philosophy in *Clouds* to the end of the *Symposium*, all the while keeping in mind the self-certainty of Hegelian absolute knowing. In both endings we find the comic disruption of philosophical thinking, a disruption provocative and recalcitrant to any smooth self-mediation of pure concepts. In Plato's work one might think than the philosopher, having flown speculatively so high up, having had the sudden vision of the highest, the beautiful itself, would now shun the mortal trash of the lower life of the body, of boys, of eating, of drinking (see 211d–e). What more is there, when we have seen the faceless, fleshless beauty (211a7–8), beauty beyond suffering (211b6), beauty pure, whole, unmixed (211e2)? What then does Plato, the philosopher, the poet, do to us?

After we have flown so high above the body, he joyfully brings us crashing down to earth again. He brings us back comically to the flesh of being. After Socrates' speech—which is greeted equivocally, with Aristophanes trying to register a protest—there is a knocking on the outer door. The outside breaks in. The loud bawl of the drunken Alcibiades is the voice that violently wrenches us back to earth. There is the intrusion of less restrained revelry. Alcibiades enters, crowned with ivy like Dionysus, surrounded by a group of revellers (*kōmastai*, 212c). The moderated leisure, *skolē*, of the previous logoi is dissolved; school is over. The appearance of Alcibiades is said to be rupturing, sudden, *exaiphnēs* (212c6). This is the fleshed, sensuous suddenness of a living self to counterpart the suddenness of the supersensuous appearance to noetic vision of the beautiful itself (210e4). This is a Bacchanalian revelry, but the song of Alcibiades shows that Socrates is not particularly erotic at all. Socrates will accuse him of trying to take revenge in his speech, a dissatisfied, corrupt student/son that inevitably for us recalls the discontented student/father Strepsiades. Plato tells of the unrestrained drinking (214a–b): First of Alcibiades, then of Socrates, quickly, without protest...

We are not given a logos of Socrates' soul; his self must be revealed through images (*di eikonōn*, 215a8). The *metaxu* demands images, not just conceptual self-mediation. There is frankness, a satyr play (*saturikon*) on Socrates, praise and marveling at his strangeness: the seeming equivocality, duplicity of his Silenus-like nature. There is a different double here to the sliced eggs of Aristophanes or Hegel's unhappy consciousness: when the two halves of the Silenus figures are separated by being opened, we find statues of the god within (215a). The double does not diminish the integrity of selfhood, but harbors the god in inwardness.

This affirmative doubleness of the Silenus also marked Socrates' logoi: at first they seemed most laughable (*geloioi*), but if opened they are "most divine," and full of rich images of excellence (221e-222a). Remember, too, that the Silenus was also a companion of Dionysus; remember that the satyr is a figure for what is other to, and outside, a more domesticated civility. Socrates' identity is other to his manifest identity, he has no univocal identity. Socrates even warns Alcibiades to beware (remember Spinoza's *Caute!*) lest he hide from him that he, Socrates is nothing, counts for nothing (*mē se lanthanō ouden ōn*, 219a). His inward otherness is manifested in the mask, but also withdrawn. He is a harmony of opposites in the middle, beauty in the ugly, hubris in irony, wise in foolishness.

In feasting, Alcibiades says, Socrates alone could enjoy himself to the hilt, though, most astonishingly, no one ever saw him drunk (220a). Alcibiades tells us of another feast—a feast within the feast of the *Symposium*, obverse of the feast of the gods within the feast, for it does not celebrate the birth of Aphrodite or the conception of eros, but recounts the night of Alcibiades' attempted seduction of Socrates. In that night nothing happens. Alcibiades laments and accuses. Again the end of his speech is greeted with laughter, exactly what kind is not clear, perhaps at the comedy of failed seduction. Socrates makes Alcibiades look like a fool. Alcibiades' frankness is noted. Where will all this end, we wonder.

But now Plato surprises us with yet another ending, beyond all the previous ends. Suddenly, *exaiphnēs*, another crowd of revellers, *kōmastai*, comes through the open doors (223b). Instead of closure at the end, there is an opening and yet another opening. Instead of blessedness on the speculative heights of absolute knowing, there is a descent and a further descent, a descent lower than the flawed, drunken genius of Alcibiades. Plato brings us through the middle in reverse, down and down, closer and closer to hair, mud and dirt, from beauty itself, to a flawed beautiful self, to drunks, to shouting, to singing. Finally, at the opposite extreme to logical order, the whole place becomes full of hubbub. Nothing is in order (*ouketi en kosmōi oudeni: kosmos*—an aesthetic term in the Greek sense of *aisthetikos*, a sensuous show, with ontological, theological, ethical, cosmological resonances); it becomes necessary to drink a vast amount of wine (223b–d).

We are not quite at the end yet. There is no one, univocal end. The ends of *Clouds* and *Symposium* conclude with images of disorder. The cosmos seems to fall apart. In one, thought is burned to the ground; the disorder is destructive; the suddenness brings to an end the laughter. In the other, unrestrained revelry breaks out; not a one is sober at this Bacchanalian revel, except Socrates, who drinks as much as, if not more than anyone. The Dionysian disorder seems to destroy the conditions of philosophy in favor of festive being as elemental. The cosmos seems to fall apart, but does the middle somehow hold?

The night of revelry that seems so other to philosophy is not the final scene. The final scene is not twilight, not night, but dawn. Not the flight of the owl, but cock crow; and Socrates bending Aristophanes and Agathon to the view that the same person could write comedy and tragedy. Aristophanes first falls asleep, then Agathon. Socrates rises and goes about his normal day. Socrates passes through the seductive and the intoxicated night. In Alcibiades' earlier recounting, Socrates previously had passed, wrapped in contemplation, through day and night, returning to normal with a prayer to the Sun (see 220c). But who, beyond night and day, can compose tragedy and comedy? Who is the writer who is thus plurivocal? Is it not Plato the philosophical poet?

I will end now, shortly. One more word before I go—a word about what remains wordless. We must remember Plato again, the silence of Plato. It is Plato here who is a true plurivocal thinker, a real metaxological philosopher. Bear in mind that the plurivocal situation in his work is not just in the content of what is said. The implicit promise of the metaxological also lies in the dramatic situation of the philosopher and poet in interplay. Plato gives us a philosophical image of a philosophical/poetic interplay between a philosopher and a comic poet. In the philosophic image he inscribes the communivocity of the poet and the philosopher.

In one sense Plato is nothing or nobody—for he never appears directly in his dialogues, except to be mentioned on occasion, for instance, as too sick to attend Socrates on the vigil of his death. In another sense, he is everyone and each of his personae. He says everything and he says nothing. He appears in none of his characters, and yet he appears in all of them. Even more than Socrates, he has no univocal identity; but he is not merely equivocal. For there is a mediation of the different identities and *personae* he images for us. This imagistic intermediation is the philosophical dialogue itself. The movement of thought in the dialogue cannot be reduced to the voice of just one of the participants, not even that of Socrates, hence the movement of thought in the Platonic dialogue could not be captured by dialectical self-mediation.

Plato could never be a Hegelian. It is not merely that there is no absolute logos of conceptual self-certainty, but that to seek one is a speculative failure—failure to acknowledge the agapeic surplus of being in its otherness, the excess that precedes, sustains, and surpasses every dialectical circle of self-mediating thought. Plato is metaxological: he "is" and "is not" all the others. He offers us philosophical images of a community of plurality in interplay, yet as irreducible others even in their intermediation. He metaxologically offers us the gathered plurality of others, and his saying leaves off with a certain silence about himself. Philosophical reticence leaves the plurality of others be as other. In that sense Plato exhibits what I call agapeic mind.

A last irony: If Plato exhibits an agapeic mind, he is absolutely misidentified when he is charged with the secret will to power of logocentrism or metaphysics of presence. Agapeic mind slips through the toils of every deconstruction of philosophy. How can one overcome metaphysics then? Impossible, if metaphysics is metaxological. Impossible, if the philosophical or speculative mind is agapeic. Who last laughs? Socrates? Hegel? Nietzsche? Heidegger? Derrida? None of these. Who, what laughs last? Aristophanes? Or is it, after all, this silence of Plato?

I end at last by changing my question at the beginning. Now it is: Can *philosophers* laugh at themselves? Answer: Socrates? Very much so. Aristotle? Not much. Descartes? Not at all. Kant? Not at all. Hegel? Now and then. Nietzsche? An astonishing buffoon—I repeat his own word, with some admiration. Husserl? Not at all. Heidegger? I cannot find it. Derrida? At others, yes. At himself? No, not at all.

Most of these are brothers of Spinoza when he said of his philosophizing: Not to laugh, not to weep, neither to curse, but to understand (*non ridere, non lugere, neque detestari, sed intelligere*). Such an understanding seems to desert the between and make philosophy inhuman. But this is too simple, too simplifying of philosophy's greatness. Is there possible *another* laughter, another weeping, another detesting, another loving, beyond the first laughter and grief and contempt, another agapē that comes *after* the first understanding? But this would ask of us a kind of afterlife of philosophical understanding, a second, doubled mindfulness, what in another place I call a posthumous mindfulness.[24] This would be an asking we can barely answer, exceeding, as it does, all our dialectical self-mediations.

And the divine Plato? If we give credence to the story—and I think it is perfectly in character—that Aristophanes' works were found under the pillow of the dead Plato, we are left with the astonishing image of Plato dying laughingly, laughing towards death, lovingly savoring the joyful discordance, the irreverent reverence of Aristophanes, but after the first understanding. This is a laughing at the last, a festive celebration of being, in its highs and lows, even on the eve of death, an agapeic yes to the plenitude of being, the fullness of life, dirt and divinity, all as imaged and affirmed in Aristophanes' words. This is the last laugh: a last yes, as if from beyond comedy and tragedy, redoubled, as if from beyond death itself.

Notes

Preface

1. A version of some material in sections III and IV, chapter 1 appeared in "Hegel, History and Philosophical Contemporaneity," *Filosofia Oggi*, 4, 1981, No. 2, 211–226; a version of some material in sections III, IV, and VI, chapter 2 appeared in "Hegel, Philosophy and Worship," *Cithara*, 19:1, 1979, 3–20; a version of sections V, VI, VII, chapter 3, appeared as "Hegel and the Problem of Religious Representation," *Philosophical Studies*, (Ireland), 30, 1984, 9–22; a version of sections I and II, chapter 6 appeared as "Can Philosophy Laugh at Itself: On Hegel and Aristophanes," in *The Owl of Minerva*, vol. 20, No. 2, Spring 1989, 131–149.

Introduction

1. The model of the philosopher as scientist has been acceptable to many thinkers due to the success and prestige of modern science. Now the scientific and technicist models of philosophy seem to have reached their limit. Other models, related to the poet, for instance, have begun to reassert a sway that is not new at all but actually continuous with the great tradition of metaphysics. In the light of this new willingness to be nondogmatic about the nature of philosophy itself, it is opportune to ask about the ideal of philosophical thinking. The proximity of art and religion to philosophy also might make Hegel a contemporary in quite interesting, perhaps startling ways. For a treatment of the different self-images of the philosophy, the scholar, scientist, technician, poet, priest, revolutionary, hero and sage, see my *Philosophy and its Others: Ways of Being and Mind* (Albany: SUNY Press, 1990), chapter 1. For the major ambiguous oppositions (between scientism and aestheticism, religion and atheism, foundationalism and historicism, panlogism and irrationalism) that have defined reaction to and interpretation of Hegel, see my introduction to *Hegel and His Critics: Philosophy in the Aftermath of Hegel*, ed. William Desmond (Albany: SUNY Press, 1989).

2. *Art and the Absolute: A Study of Hegel's Aesthetics* (Albany: SUNY Press, 1986).

3. In *Philosophy and its Others*, and in *Desire, Dialectic, and Otherness: An Essay on Origins* (New Haven: Yale University Press, 1987).

4. For a fuller account of the self-deconstruction of logic in post-idealistic philosophy in relation to the fourfold sense of being involved in the metaxological, see my meditation on being mindful and logic in *Philosophy and its Others*, pp. 212–229.

5. See *Art and the Absolute*, chapters 4 and 5. Here again I read Hegel with a less suspicious hermeneutics than the post-structuralists, et al. The charges against him are not always directed at the right place. The metaxological understanding tries to avoid misdirected accusation; as I say, in the notion of an open wholeness it includes a defense and recovery of a dialectical self-mediation that is sufficiently qualified to avoid closure. There is an inward *otherness* to the self that is beyond encapsulation. The matter is more complicated and less amenable to closure if we acknowledge the other as other in a sense irreducible to the self in its own otherness (Hegel's sense). The metaxological sense of the other and the open sense of wholeness that permeate the present reflections, these allow me to read Hegel as *other* to more standard interpretations. See the issue of *CLIO*, 20: 4, Summer 1991, devoted to the theme "William Desmond: Beyond Hegel? - Discussion and Response." I explain my relation to Hegel in an essay in intellectual auto-biography ("Being Between") and an essay ("In Reply") responding to the questions raised by Clark Butler, Brian Martine, Merold Westphal and Stephen Houlgate.

6. On the agapeic absolute, see *Desire, Dialectic, and Otherness*, chapter 8. On the intentional infinitude of self, see ibid., passim; on the self's inward otherness, see *Philosophy and its Others*, e.g. pp. 54–55, 90ff., 141ff., 184ff., 231ff. In the present work I will return to the matter of the agapeic absolute.

7. In discussing the Absolute Idea Hegel, in passing, suggests that the third might also be considered a fourth [*Science of Logic*, trans. A.V. Miller (New York: Humanities Press, 1969), p. 836]. This is not the fourfold of which I talk. What Hegel says is complex, but the following gives some sense of his meaning. He says ". . . now as the first negative is already the second term, the term reckoned as *third* can also be reckoned as *fourth*, and instead of a *triplicity*, the abstract form may be taken as a *quadruplicity*; in this way, the negative or the difference is counted as a *duality*. The third or fourth is in general the unity of the first and second moments, of the immediate and the mediated. That it is this *unity*, as that the whole form of the method is a *triplicity*, is, it is true, merely the superficial external side of the mode of cognition. . ." The passage perhaps makes little sense to the uninitiated. It *does* make sense as a very abstract articulation of dialectical self-mediation. But I cannot see how one can take this reference to quadruplicity as anything other than merely incidental. Taken in any stronger sense—and Hegel gives us no reasons here, or in his system generally—it would be impossible to integrate into his system. Hegel disparages mere counting as an external

formalism. The quadruplicity mentioned is that of an "abstract form"; moreover, the fourth here is a reckoning of the third, not finally other than it; hence Hegel's counting to four here would in the end be still counting to one, taken in four ways. Hegel's whole stress is on the *self-sublating* movement between unity and triplicity, which as "the course of cognition at the same time returns into itself" [ibid.]. This is what I refer to under the rubric of dialectical self-mediation. This is very evident from Hegel's full discussion in the passages cited.

Chapter 1

1. G. W. F. Hegel, *Philosophy of Right*, trans. T. M. Knox (Oxford: Clarendon Press, 1952), p. 11; hereafter PR. See my "Hermeneutics and Hegel's Aesthetics," *The Irish Journal of Philosophy*, 2, 1985, pp. 94–104.

2. Marx, *Early Writings*, trans. and ed. T. B. Bottomore (McGraw-Hill: New York, 1963), p. 44.

3. Ibid., pp. 200, 201–202.

4. See ibid., pp. 202, 44, 216.

5. Ibid., p. 198.

6. Ibid., p. 49.

7. Ibid.; see pp. 51ff. I return to the instrumentalizing of reason below in terms of work, but see Marx's praise of industry, e.g. in the *Communist Manifesto*. In that historicism is tied the view that we only know what we make, it offers an interpretation of Vico's saying that *verum et factum convertuntur*, a dictum Marx liked to cite. Vico's historicism is balanced by an affirmation that nature is God's fact, *factum*. So the truth of nature is only properly accessible to God. We cannot hope to exhaust nature's richness; it is the human world, as made by man, that is the proper object of our cognition. Subsequent thinkers play down nature as God's fact; finally all facts will be seen as human facts, man's power replacing divine providence.

8. See Stanley Rosen, "Hegel and Historicism," *CLIO*, 7:1 (1977), pp. 33–51.

9. G. W. F. Hegel, *Enzyklopädie der Philosophischen Wissenschaften*, in *Werke*, ed. Eva Moldenhauer and Karl Markus Michel (Frankfurt: Suhrkamp Verlag, 1969–1971), §246, *Zusatz*; *Hegel's Philosophy of Nature: Being Part II of the Encyclopedia of the Philosophical Sciences*. trans. A. V. Miller (Oxford: Oxford University Press, 1970), p. 13.

10. On the erotic and agapeic absolute see *Desire, Dialectic, and Otherness*, chapter 8.

11. "Schopenhauer, Art and the Dark Origin," in *Schopenhauer*, ed. Eric von der Luft (Mellen Press: Lewistown, NY, 1988), pp. 101–122.

12. Aristotle, *Politics*, 1254b3–5; Aquinas, *Selected Writings of St. Thomas Aquinas*, trans. R. P. Goodwin (Macmillan: New York, 1965), p. 83.

13. On mindfulness, and not necessarily identified with Hegelian reason, see *Philosophy and its Others*, especially chapters 5 and 6.

14. For Croce's statement, see Victor Farias, *Heidegger and Nazism*, eds. J. Margolis and T. Rockmore, trans. P. Burrell, D. Di Bernardi, G. Ricci (Philadelphia: Temple University Press, 1989), p. 111.

15. See *Heidegger and Nazism*, p. 104. One notes the revolutionary fervor in Heidegger's writing from this period; there is the same kind of rhetoric (philosophy as war, combat, violence) that we find on the revolutionary Left in Marx's critique of Hegel (see, for instance, *Early Writings*, pp. 43, 46, 47, 59). See *Philosophy and its Others*, pp. 43–48 on philosophy and revolution.

16. In a 1936 conversation with Karl Löwith, and in response to the latter's suggestion that Heidegger's Nazism was essentially related to his philosophy, "Heidegger agreed with me without reservation" and explained how his concept of historicity provided the basis of his political engagements; Karl Löwith, *Mein Leben in Deutschland vor und nach 1933* (Stuttgart: Metzler, 1986), p. 57. An English translation of these passages is to be found in *Martin Heidegger and National Socialism: Questions and Answers*, eds. Gunther Neske and Emil Kettering, trans. Lisa Harries, intro. Karsten Harries (New York: Paragon House, 1990), p. 158. Löwith also says there: "He also left no doubt about his belief in Hitler. According to him, Hitler had underestimated only two things: the vitality of the Christian churches and the obstacles to the Anschluss of Austria." Over twenty years ago Stanley Rosen explored the connection of historicity and political nihilism in Heidegger in *Nihilism* (New Haven: Yale University Press, 1969), pp. 119ff.

17. Martin Heidegger, *Basic Writings*, ed. David Krell (New York: Harper and Row, 1977), p. 386.

18. Ibid., p. 374.

19. Ibid.

20. In *Philosophy as a Rigorous Science* [in *Phenomenology and the Crisis of Philosophy*, trans. with introduction by Quentin Lauer (New York: Harper and Row, 1965)], Husserl asserts that the decision of science "bears the stamp of eternity" (p. 142). He warns (p. 141): "For the sake of time we must not sacrifice eternity." In *Philosophy and the Crisis of European Man* (also translated in the above volume), his view of the *telos* of philosophy in relation to Europe is very reminiscent of Hegel, though Husserl offers a progress of spirit to infinity, an unending task. Philosophy is connected to a new humanity. One is reminded of Plato's description of the philosopher as the spectator of all time and eternity. Should we say: As Hegel was to Marx, Husserl was to Heidegger? In the move from the first to the second, we observe an analogous transition from transcendental logic to historical praxis and existence. There is here a dialectical irony regarding Husserl and historicism, namely, that his own lectures on internal time consciousness, which Heidegger

edited, nurtured Heidegger's own distancing from phenomenology as a transcendental version of metaphysics of presence (Derrida simply repeats this move). Logic and eternal essence are then deconstructed. Of course, in Hegel there was always the problem of the move from logic to nature and history. Husserl blames Hegel for a slide from philosophy as systematic science into romantic reaction (pp. 76–78). But Hegel was already more deeply aware than Husserl of the *two sides* of the problem. It was never a problem of just one side. See Tom Rockmore "Husserl's Critique of Hegel," in *Hegel and His Critics*, chapter XI.

21. *Basic Writings*, pp. 387, 392.

22. This is again evident from Farias' book. See Heidegger's *Introduction to Metaphysics*, trans. R. Manheim (Garden City, NY: Anchor Books, 1961), pp. 38–39, where he talks with distaste of the degradation of spirit to intelligence, a manipulative tool in the service of others—he singles out Marxism and positivism for mention. Yet Heidegger as Nazi degraded philosophy into a tool of National Socialism, albeit in the service of its "inner truth and greatness." I cannot see this as anything other than a world-historical instrumentalizing of the philosopher.

23. Farias, *Heidegger and Nazism*, p. 282.

24. PR, p. 10.

25. *Phänomenologie des Geistes*, ed. J. Hoffmeister (Hamburg: Felix Meiner, 1952), p. 558; *Phenomenology of Spirit*, trans. A. V. Miller (Oxford: Clarendon Press, 1977), p. 487: hereafter PhG and PS.

26. G. W. F. Hegel, *Lectures on the History of Philosophy*, trans. E. S. Haldane and F. H. Simson (London: Kegan Paul, Trench, Trubner and Co., 1892), I, pp. 87ff.; hereafter LHP.

27. LHP, I, p. 30.

28. LHP, I, pp. 38–39; see p. 36 on the *Weltgeist's* freedom from hurry. In *Encyclopedia*, § 258 Hegel says: "Time. . .has no power over the Concept, nor is the Concept in time or temporal; on the contrary, *it* is the power over time, which is this negativity only *qua* externality." And in the *Zusatz*: ". . .the Idea, Spirit, transcends time because it is itself the Concept of time; it is eternal, in and for itself, and is not dragged into the time-process because it does not lose itself in one side of the process."

29. LHP, I, p. 39.

30. LHP, I, p. 45.

31. G. W. F. Hegel, *Vorlesungen über die Ästhetik* in *Werke* (eds. Molderhauer and Michel), I, pp. 22–23; *Hegel's Aesthetics*, trans. T. M. Knox (Oxford; Clarendon Press, 1975), I, p. 9; hereafter VA and HA. See my "Art, Origins, Otherness: Hegel and Aesthetic Self-Mediation," in *Philosophy and Art*, ed. Daniel Dahlstrom (Washington: Catholic University of America Press, 1991).

32. On the subjective, objective and political work of art, see *The Philosophy of History*, trans. J. Sibree (New York: Dover, 1956), pp. 241–274.

33. See my "Hegel, Legal Status and Otherness," in *The Cardozo Law Review*, vol. 10, Nos. 5–6, pp. 1713–1726.

34. "The Positivity of the Christian Religion," in *Early Theological Writings*, trans. T. M. Knox (Philadelphia: University of Pennsylvania Press, 1971), p. 159.

35. I am not denying that the *Phenomenology* and the *Logic* are essays in transcendental philosophy. I am saying that the transcendental conditions of knowing, being, and intelligibility must be more than purely formal, hence must appear, and this inevitably raises the relation of the transcendental and the historical. On Husserl's attack on psychologism and historicism, see note 20 above.

36. The Hegelian state in *The Philosophy of Right* is an internally differentiated organism; but see the article listed in note 33 relative to freedom and organic metaphors.

37. See LHP, III, p. 423.

38. PhG, p. 558; PS, p. 487; see PhG. p. 38, PS, p. 97: "*. . . die Zeit. . . ist sie der daseiende Begriff selbst.*" The first citation goes on to speak of the canceling of time; as mentioned at the beginning of section VII, this is relevant to the question of the double intention. See *Encyclopedia*, § 258, *Zusatz*: "Time itself in its concept, is eternal (*Die Zeit selbst ist in ihrem Begriffe ewig*)."

39. On "earthly divinity" see PR, § 272, *Zusatz*; Knox, p. 285.

40. See *Desire, Dialectic, and Otherness*, chapter 8 on the absolute original; also chapter 4 on the critique of static eternity relative to univocity and relative to becoming reduced to a merely equivocal process. The issue here relates to time itself as an "open whole" in metaxological intermediation with eternity; becoming as self-mediating and intermediating with the other of becoming. The view is too complex to reconstruct here.

41. See note 10 above; also previous note.

42. There are basic issues here, some of which I mention in the introduction. In particular I mention the relation of wholeness and infinitude, and their reinterpretation in a more than dialectical way; see *Desire, Dialectic, and Otherness*. In *Art and the Absolute* I use the term "open whole" in relation to the art work; such a term suggests wholeness without imputing any false closure. Peter Hodgson, *God in History* (Nashville: Abingdon Press, 1989) makes an interesting and very intelligent use of this notion to offer a qualified Hegelian view of God in history.

Chapter 2

1. On this, see *Philosophy and its Others*.

2. G. W. F. Hegel, *Vorlesungen über die Philosophie der Religion*, ed. Walter Jaeschke (Hamburg: Felix Meiner, 1983–1985), 1, 1827 series, pp. 63–64; *Lectures on the Philosophy of Religion*, ed. Peter C. Hodgson, trans. R. F. Brown, P. C. Hodgson, J. M. Stewart, with the assistance of H. S. Harris (Berkeley: University of California, 1984–1987), 1, 1827 series, p. 153. Hereafter VPR and LPR.

3. On this see *Art and the Absolute*.

4. Alexandre Kojève, *Introduction to the Reading of Hegel*, trans. James H. Nichols, Jr., and ed. Allan Bloom (New York: Basic Books, 1969), chapter 4.

5. Cf. Karl Popper, *The Open Society and its Enemies* (London: Routledge and Kegan Paul, 1945), vol. II. Cf. Albert Camus, *The Rebel: An Essay on Man in Revolt*. trans. Anthony Bower (New York: Vintage Books, 1956), pp. 133–148.

6. F. Nietzsche, *On the Genealogy of Morals*, trans. Walter Kaufmann and R. J. Hollingdale (New York: Random House, 1969), p. 23.

7. We find the first of these statements in *Science of Logic*, p. 25; the second in PhG, p. 57, PS, p. 43—the sarcasm here is equivocal; relative to the third, see *Science of Logic*, p. 26 where Hegel speaks of "those solitary souls who were sacrificed by their people and exiled from the world to the end that the eternal should be contemplated and served by lives devoted solely thereto—not for any practical gain but for the sake of blessedness..."

8. See note 2 above; also *The Difference Between Fichte's and Schelling's System of Philosophy*, trans. H. S. Harris and Walter Cerf (Albany: State University of New York Press, 1977), p. 172; also VA, I, p. 139; HA, I, p. 101.

9. See *Twilight of the Idols and the Antichrist*, trans. R. J. Hollingdale (Baltimore: Penguin, 1968), the section on "Reason" in Philosophy, 1 and 2; the title of the book is itself relevant; the sections mention dialectic and the ahistoricist worship of the philosophers; Heraclitus is exempted from the idolatry.

10. F. Nietzsche, *The Birth of Tragedy from the Spirit of Music*, trans. Walter Kaufmann (New York: Random House, 1967), section 2. On aesthetic theodicy in Nietzsche and Hegel, see *Art and the Absolute*, chapter 6.

11. On Aquinas and natural sacrament, see the citation in Louis Dupré, *The Other Dimension* (Garden City, New York: Doubleday, 1972), p. 181; on nature as the body of god, the aesthetic presencing of divinity, see *Philosophy and its Others*, chapter 3.

12. *Philosophy of History*, pp. 377–378; but on the Eucharist see also *Early Theological Writings*, pp. 89–91.

13. Heidegger, *Introduction to Metaphysics*, p. 6.

14. *Philosophy and its Others*, pp. 260–261, 282–284, 303ff., 309–311.

15. G. Bataille, *Visions of Excess: Selected Writings, 1927–1939*, ed. with intro. by Allan Stoekl, trans. A. Stoekl, C. R. Lovitt and D. M. Leslie, Jr. (Minneapolis: University of Minnesota Press, 1985), pp. 116ff.

16. E. Levinas, *Totality and Infinity*, trans. A. Lingis (Pittsburg: Duquesne University Press, 1969), p. 295 on philosophy and liturgy; on p. 80 he refers to religion as "the ultimate structure." "For the relation between the being here below and the transcendent being that results in no community of concept or totality—a relation without relation—we reserve the term religion." See also "The Trace of the Other," trans. A. Lingis, *Tijdschrift voor Philosophie*, September, 1963, pp. 605–623. See R. Kearney, *Dialogues with Contemporary Continental Thinkers* (Manchester: Manchester University Press, 1984); the theme of *Athens and Jerusalem* figures in his conversation with both Derrida and Levinas. See Lev Shestov's *Athens and Jerusalem*, trans. B. Martin (Athens: Ohio University Press, 1966).

17. See R. Girard, *Violence and the Sacred*, trans. P. Gregory (Baltimore: Johns Hopkins Press, 1977); also G. Bataille, *op. cit.*

18. Hegel subscribes to this old idea of Plato and Aristotle, connecting it with the claim that all religion entails some notion of revelation: *Encyclopedia*, § 564; *Hegel's Philosophy of Mind: Being Part Three of the Encyclopedia of the Philosophical Sciences*. trans. William Wallace (Oxford: Oxford University Press, 1971), pp. 297–298.

19. See, VPR, 1, pp. 278ff.

20. On being as festive agapē, see *Philosophy and its Others*, chapter 6.

21. Ibid. Hegel himself lays a strong emphasis on the festival and the meal in his discussion of Greek cultus in the *Phenomenology*.

22. On the absorbing god, *Desire, Dialectic, and Otherness*, chapter 1, chapter 8.

23. PhG, pp. 501–502; PS, p. 435.

24. Eric Voegelin, "On Hegel—A Study in Sorcery," *Studium Generale* 24 (1971), pp. 335–368. Even though Voegelin tends to overstate the case, this is a very thought-provoking study, in the main because Voegelin is deeply attentive to the metaxu.

25. PhG, p. 163; PS, p. 131.

26. Cf. PhG, p. 164; PS, p. 131 where Hegel says that this "beyond" cannot be found where it is sought: for it is meant to be just a "beyond," that which cannot be found.

27. PhG, pp. 168–169; PS, pp. 135–136.

28. PhG, p. 163; PS, p. 131.

29. Ibid; cf. also PhG, pp. 164–165; PS, p. 132, and the section on the *schöne Seele*.

30. PhG, p. 161; PS, p. 129: "The remote "beyond" is fixed in its opposition to the individual, so any hope of becoming one with it must remain a hope: without fulfillment, without present fruition." But such a hope is an empty hope, that is, a hopeless hope.

31. Cf. PhG, p. 127; PS, pp. 159–160.

32. Cf. PhG, p. 158; PS, p. 126, where Hegel tells us that concentrated *within* the unhappy consciousness is both the slave and slavemaster.

33. Cf. PhG, p. 148; PS, p. 117 on death as sovereign master; cf. also PhG, p. 324; PS, pp. 272–273 where in connection with death as lord and master Hegel speaks of war as shaking man out of his absorption in finite existence.

34. PhG, pp. 168–170; PS, pp. 135–137.

35. Alienation here in a sense related to the political one of giving over one's rights to the sovereign.

36. PhG, p. 160; PS, p. 127.

37. The alienation of the unhappy consciousness makes its attitude to be one of "struggle against an enemy" (PhG, p. 159; PS, p. 126): initially this enmity is directed to itself, but it is merely a continuation of this to redirect this enmity towards what is other. So it is not insignificant that for Hegel the resignation of the will of the unhappy consciousness is not really a full surrender (PhG, pp. 167, 170; PS, pp. 136, 137).

38. Cf. *Being and Nothingness.* trans. Hazel E. Barnes (New York: Washington Square Press, 1966), p. 140. For Hegel, of course, the final point is neither to swing between mastery and slavery, nor to concentrate them together in the unhappy consciousness. It is a travesty of Hegel's view to reduce all relations, including that between the human being and God, to the dialectic of master and slave.

39. Cf. PhG, p. 140; PS, p. 110: "Self-consciousness attains its satisfaction only in another self-consciousness." Also ibid. where Hegel talks about the "we" of spirit, of *Geist: "Ich,* das *Wir,* und *Wir* das *Ich* ist." On the struggle for recognition, cf. Kojève, *op. cit.*; also Hans-Georg Gadamer, *Hegel's Dialectic: Five Hermeneutical Studies.* trans. P. Christopher Smith (New Haven and London: Yale University Press, 1976), chapter 3.

40. PhG, p. 523; PS, p. 455; also PhG, p. 546; PS, p. 476.

41. PhG, p. 525; PS, p. 456.

42. This trial of negation recalls the "trial by death" that Hegel speaks of in relation to the dialectic of master and slave (PhG, pp. 144ff.; PS, pp. 113ff.)

43. *Der erscheinende Gott* (PhG, p. 473; PS, p. 409; see below, note 2, chapter 4) appears at the end of the section on evil and forgiveness, in transition to religion; the yea, yea here is later echoed (PhG, p. 547; PS, p. 477); even the unhappy consciousness, much earlier, cannot absolutely escape some affirmative stance, for reality to it is "only in one respect essentially null, but in another sense also a sanctified world (*eine geheiligte Welt)*" PhG, p. 165; PS, pp. 132–133.

44. "...*das* unglückliche Bewusstsein *ist das Bewusstsein seiner als des gedoppelten nur widersprechenden Wesens.*" PhG, p. 158; PS, p. 126; cf. PhG, p. 165; PS, p. 132, where its doubling, *Entzweiung* is named.

45. On posthumous mind as intricately doubled and thought singing its other, see *Philosophy and its Others*, pp. 278ff., 300, 304, 368–369.

46. On static eternity etc., see *Desire, Dialectic, and Otherness*; also chapter 1 above.

47. *The Difference Between Fichte's and Schelling's System of Philosophy*, p. 89.

48. Cf. PhG, p. 67; PS, p. 49, where Hegel speaks of the ascent to philosophical knowing as a "path of doubt, or more properly a highway of despair."

49. Cf. *Difference*, p. 96.

50. Cf. PhG, p. 313; PS, p. 263: "*Die Vernunft ist Geist, indem die Gewissheit, alle Realität zu sein, zur Wahrheit erhoben, und sie sich ihrer selbst als ihrer Welt, und der Welt als ihrer selbst bewusst ist.*"

51. *Cf. Difference*, pp. 96, 106.

52. Again see *Desire, Dialectic, and Otherness* on the absorbing god and the absolute original.

53. Cf. PhG, pp. 63ff.; PS, pp. 46ff.

54. *Nicomachean Ethics*, X, 7, 1177b. If there is a work comparable to philosophy, this for Hegel is the work of art. But the work of art is not finite, instrumental toil. It is neither a means to an end, nor calculative, nor serving animal desire. It is an activity which is an end in itself, a celebration that is whole within itself. On the question of philosophy and leisure, cf. Josef Pieper, *Leisure: The Basis of Culture*, trans. Alexander Dru (New York: Pantheon Books, 1952). Pieper rightly asserts that leisure is not mere idleness (p. 27): rather it must be tied with festive affirmation and celebration (pp. 29–20). Appropriately for our purposes here, he finds that the basis of leisure is ultimately worship (pp. 40ff.).

55. PhG, p. 45; PS, p. 32.

56. Cf. introduction to *Phenomenology*.

57. Nietzsche's claim that God is the deification of the will to nothingness in *Antichrist, #* 18.

58. Cf. Kojève's comment on this, *op. cit.*, p. 168.

59. Heidegger tells us that authentic selfness begins only with anguish before one's finitude and nothingness in death. On the necessity that philosophy, to be liberated, face death, cf. PhG, pp. 29–30; PS, p. 19. Cf. also Stanley Rosen, *G. W. F. Hegel: An Introduction to the Science of Wisdom* (New Haven: Yale University Press, 1974), p. 164. The issue relates to what I have called "posthumous mind"; see note 45 above.

60. Cf. the last pages of Hegel's discussion of the unhappy consciousness, where he speaks of moments of giving up (*Momente des Aufgebens*, PhG, p. 170; PS, p. 137), of surrender, before the emergence of reason.

61. On theoretical activity as blessed in most resembling divine activity, cf. Aristotle's *Metaphysics*, 1072b25; also *Ethics*, X, 7; *Politics*, VII, 2–3. Cf. *Science of Logic*, pp. 33–34, where Hegel, in Aristotle's words, reminds us of the connection between philosophy and leisure. There is also the passage cited at the outset: a nation without a metaphysics is like a temple without a holy of holies (p. 25).

62. PhG, p. 39; PS, p. 27: "*Das Wahre ist so der bacchantische Taumel...*"

Chapter 3

1. Emil Fackenheim, *The Religious Dimensions in Hegel's Thought* (Bloomington: Indiana University Press, 1967), p. 178 note. Here Fackenheim points out that in "naive ancient theology" God is the "object," one object among others; whereas in modern reflexive theology, the focus is on "the religious divine-human relationship." It is unfair to describe ancient theology as naive. Nor must one forget Hegel's contempt for those unwilling to talk about God.

2. On the anthropological versus the speculative reading of Hegel's position, see Walter Jaeschke's, "Speculative and Anthropological Criticism of Religion: A Theological Orientation to Hegel and Feuerbach," *Journal of the American Academy of Religion*, XLVII/3, pp. 345–364. Jaeschke grants the difficulty of reconciling Hegel with more orthodox views, yet notes that Hegel's speculative treatment has to be kept apart from the anthropological reduction, à la Feuerbach and other Young Hegelians.

3. Peter Winch, D. L. Phillips, W. D. Hudson have been among those who have held to "Wittgensteinian fideism." See, for instance, W. D. Hudson, *Ludwig Wittgenstein—The Bearing of his Philosophy upon Religious Belief* (Richmond: John Knox Press, 1968). See also Kai Nielsen's criticism, "Wittgensteinian Fideism," *Philosophy*, 42 (1967), pp. 191–209.

4. Some representative studies of Hegel's philosophy of religion include Fackenheim, *op. cit.;* Quentin Lauer S. J., *Hegel's Concept of God* (Albany: State University of New York Press, 1982); Bernard Reardon, *Hegel's Philosophy of Religion* (New York: Harper and Row, 1977); Darrell Christensen, ed., *Hegel and the Philosophy of Religion* (The Hague: Nijhoff, 1970).

5. The saying is attributed to Pascal; see *Pensées*, trans. A. J. Krailsheimer (Baltimore: Penguin, 1966), p. 355.

6. *The Philosophy of History*, p. 439.

7. On the place of representation in Hegel's system, see Malcolm Clark's, *Logic and System: A Study of the Transition from "Vorstellung" to Thought in the Philosophy of Hegel* (The Hague: Nijhoff, 1971).

8. On the proofs of God's existence as presenting this "elevation" in a more abstract way, see Lauer, *op. cit.*, pp. 216–217, 226–227.

9. See, for instance, *Encyclopedia*, § 573. Philosophic knowing is "the recognition of this content and of its forms; it is the *liberation* from the one-sidedness of the forms [i.e., of art and religion], the elevation of them to the absolute form which determines itself as content, remaining identical with the content...."

10. Quentin Lauer insists, however: "...philosophical knowing neither swallows up nor dispenses with faith; it simply transforms faith into an explicit awareness of its own implications." *op. cit.*, p. 288.

11. See Lawrence S. Stepelevich, ed., *The Young Hegelians: An Anthology* (New York and Cambridge: Cambridge University Press, 1983). Also, David McLellan, *The Young Hegelians and Karl Marx* (London: Macmillan, 1969); Sidney Hook, *From Hegel to Marx* (New York: Humanities Press, 1958).

12. On literalism, and its metaxological transformation, see *Philosophy and its Others*, chapter 3. On "demythologization" and "symbols" see, for instance, Paul Tillich, *Dynamics of Faith* (New York: Harper and Row, 1957), pp. 48–54.

13. See Henri De Lubac, *The Drama of Atheist Humanism*, trans. E. M. Riley (Cleveland and New York: World Publishing Co., 1963).

14. See Tillich's remark, *op. cit.*, p. 52: "In the last analysis it is not rational criticism of the myth which is decisive but the inner religious criticism."

15. See *Encyclopedia*, § 573: "Philosophy indeed can recognize its own forms in the categories of religious consciousness, and even its own teaching in the doctrine of religion—which therefore it does not disparage. But the converse is not true: the religious consciousness does not apply the criticism of thought to itself, does not comprehend itself, and is therefore, as it stands, exclusive."

16. See John MacQuarrie's remark in *God-Talk* (New York: Harper and Row, 1967), p. 176: Jews and Christians have decisively revolted "against the idea that the divine can be objectified, so as to manifest itself in sensible phenomena." Hegel also is cognizant of what he speaks of as "the more highly cultivated consciousness" in *Berliner Schriften*, ed. Johannes Hoffmeister (Hamburg: Meiner Verlag, 1956), p. 15. There still remains the ambiguity on the question of form, as is indicated by what he says in section 573 of the *Encyclopedia*, cited in note 15. At a deeper level there is the question of the different forms of mediation.

17. *Encyclopedia*, § 82, *Zusatz*; see also PhG, p. 503; PS. p. 437: "For the mystical (*das Mystische*) is not concealment of a secret (*ist nicht Verborgenheit eines Geheimnisses*), or ignorance, but consists in the self knowing itself to be one with the divine being and that this, therefore, is revealed. Only the self is manifest to itself. . . ."

18. In addition to the citations in note 17 see also the following which deepens the suspicion of Hegel's somewhat disingenuous use of "mystery," "mystical": "The Trinity is called the *mystery* of God (*das Mysterium Gottes*); its content is mystical (*der Inhalt ist mystisch*), that is, speculative. But what is for reason is not a secret (*ist kein Geheimnis*). In the Christian religion one *knows*, and this is a secret only for the finite understanding, and for the thought that is based on sense experience." VPR, 3, 1824, p. 125; LPR 3, 1824, p. 192.

19. See *Philosophy and its Others*, pp. 135–143.

20. Ibid., p. 141; I will say something more about the heart in the next chapter on evil.

Chapter 4

1. S. Kierkegaard, *Sickness unto Death*, ed. and trans. H. V. Hong and E. H. Hong (Princeton: Princeton University Press, 1980), p. 119. Kierkegaard is talking about the impossibility of explaining sin speculatively.

2. PhG, p. 473, PS, p. 409; see above note 43, chapter two: "For this antithesis is rather the *indiscrete continuity* and *identity* of "I"="I"; and each, through the very contradiction of its pure universality, which at the same time still strives against its identity with the other, and cuts itself off from it, *explicitly* supersedes itself within its own self. Through this externalization, this knowledge which in its existence is self-discordant returns into the unity of the self. It is the *actual* "I," the universal knowledge of *itself* in its *absolute opposite*, in the knowledge which remains *internal*, and which, on account of the purity of its separated *being-within-self*, is itself completely universal. The reconciling *Yea*, in which the two "I"s let go their antithetical *existence*, is the *existence* of the "I" which has expanded into a duality, and therein

remains identical with itself, and, in its complete externalization and opposite, possesses the certainty of itself: it is God manifested in the midst of those who know themselves in the form of pure knowledge."

3. *Philosophy and its Others*, chapter 6.

4. In the rest of this chapter, I will refer to the lecture series of 1827, unless otherwise stated. VPR, 3, p. 218; LPR, 3, p. 293.

5. VPR, 3, p. 222; LPR, 3, pp. 297–298.

6. Ibid.

7. VPR, 3, p. 223; LPR, 3, p. 299.

8. VPR, 3, p. 224; LPR, 3, p. 299.

9. VPR, 3, p. 224; LPR, 3, p. 300.

10. There is a reversal of the second and third sections between 1824 and 1827; the story of the Fall is second in the 1827 series.

11. VPR, 3, p. 226; LPR, 3, p. 302.

12. Ibid.

13. In PhG, p. 538; PS, p. 468, Hegel says that "the becoming of Evil can be shifted further back out of the existent world even into the primary world of Thought (*Denken*). It can therefore be said that it is the very first-born Son of Light himself who fell because he withdrew into himself or became self-centred. . ." Here we have the emphasis on knowledge that distances us from the representation (*Vorstellung*) of evil. See also *Encyclopedia*, § 248, *Zusatz*, where Hegel assents to Jacob Boehme's account of creation in terms of Lucifer as God's first born Son of Light. In VPR, 3, p. 218, LPR, 3, p. 293, Hegel mentions Jacob Boehme relative to the same point.

14. VPR, 3, p. 227–228; LPR, 3, p. 304.

15. VPR, 3, p. 229; LPR, 3, p. 305. As translating *Schmerz*, "anguish" might be misleading, since we now readily think of *Angst* in Kierkegaard, Freud, Heidegger. In Kierkegaard *Angst* is bound up with sin and the leap from innocence to guilty possibility. See *The Concept of Dread*, trans. Walter Lowrie, 2nd ed. (Princeton: Princeton University Press, 1957). There are some interesting affinities with Hegel here.

16. See VPR, 3, p. 224; LPR, 3, p. 300.

17. See *Difference*, p. 89; see chapter 2 above on doubling with respect to the unhappy consciousness.

18. See *Philosophy and its Others*, pp. 203–205. On goodwill and agapeic otherness, see *Desire, Dialectic, and Otherness*, chapter 7.

19. VPR, 3, p. 229; LPR, 3, p. 306.

20. VPR, 3, p. 230; LPR, 3, p. 307.

21. VPR, 3, p. 232; LPR, 3, p. 308; see my "Hegel, Legal Status and Otherness."

22. VPR, 3, p. 232; LPR, 3, p. 308.

23. See, VPR, 3, pp. 231–233; LPR, 3, pp. 308–309.

24. On "aesthetic theodicy" see *Art and the Absolute*, pp. 150–159.

25. Stalin: you can't make omelettes without breaking some eggs—repeated by the worshippers of *Realpolitik* who have struggled with their consciences and lost, a loss confessed with a peculiar satisfaction. See Bertolt Brecht, expressing a common attitude on the revolutionary Left:

> With whom would the right-minded man not sit
> To help the right?
> What medicine would taste too bad
> To the dying man?
> What baseness would you not commit
> To root out baseness?
> If finally you could change the world
> What task would you be too good for?
> Sink down in the filth
> Embrace the butcher,
> But change the world: it needs it.

From "The Measures Taken," in *The Jewish Wife and Other Short Plays* (New York: Grove Press, 1965), pp. 96–97.

26. On the Nazi murderers as "desk killers," see A. Rosenberg and P. Marcus "The Holocaust as a Test of Philosophy," in *Echoes of the Holocaust: Philosophical Reflections on a Dark Time*, ed. A. Rosenberg and G. E. Myers (Philadelphia: Temple University Press, 1988), pp. 213–215. In his essay ("Holocaust: Moral Indifference as the Form of Modern Evil") in this book, Rainer Baum points out about the commanders of the SS (p. 71): "Products of German universities, 43 percent with a doctorate, they were among the most highly educated of all the leaders of the Third Reich."

27. See *Philosophy and its Others*, pp. 201–205 on the "wolf man" and the refusing will as a wild, lawless otherness.

28. Hegel does acknowledge the heart (VPR, 1, 1827, pp. 285–291); but he reduces it the level of mere subjective feeling; as the mere feeling of self-particularity, it reveals the undeveloped indefiniteness of immediacy; Hegel says it is a source or "seed" only in this barest sense of implicit immediacy, with all the dangers of subjective caprice. Hegel reduces the heart to a moment of equivocal immediacy within a logic of explicit dialectical self-mediation. I do not disagree with Hegel's view that the "heart" may call for mediated

articulation; the whole issue is the nature of the mediation, whether there are mediations other than the dialectical, whether an essential elemental remains recalcitrant to dialectical self-mediation. On the elemental, see *Philosophy and its Others*, e.g. pp. 269ff.; on Hegel and the elemental, p. 367.

29. On idiot wisdom, see *Philosophy and its Others*, chapter 6. See also "Being at a Loss: Reflections on Philosophy and the Tragic," to appear in a volume on philosophy and tragedy, Nenos Georgopoulis, ed. (London: Macmillan, 1992).

30. I have developed these ideas more fully in "Being at a Loss: Reflections on Philosophy and the Tragic," cited in note 29.

31. VA, I, p. 265; HA, I, p. 202.

32. VA, III, p. 51; HA, II, p. 824.

33. VA, III, p. 53; HA, II, p. 826.

34. *Hegel: The Letters*, trans. C. Butler and C. Seiler (Bloomington: Indiana University Press, 1984), pp. 270–272.

35. PhG, p. 67; PS, p. 49.

Chapter 5

1. J. Derrida, *Of Grammatology*, trans. G. Spivak (Baltimore: Johns Hopkins, 1974), p. 26.

2. J. Derrida, *Positions*, trans. A. Bass (Chicago: University of Chicago Press, 1981), p. 77.

3. I have discussed some of these affinities in *Art and the Absolute*, chapter 5.

4. J. Derrida, *Writing and Difference*, trans. A. Bass (Chicago: University of Chicago Press, 1978), p. 252.

5. Ibid., p. 261. I note my debt to Joseph Flay's paper, "Hegel, Derrida and Batille's Laughter," and to Judith Butler's commentary, in *Hegel and his Critics*.

6. *Writing and Difference*. pp. 255, 256.

7. Ibid., p. 256.

8. Ibid., p. 257.

9. See Levinas "The Trace of the Other"; also *Totality and Infinity*; also Richard Kearney's interview with Levinas in *Dialogues with Contemporary Continental Thinkers*; also *The Levinas Reader*. ed. Seán Hand (Cambridge: Blackwell, 1989), p. 172: philosophy is almost all but identified with

Husserlian transcendentalism; in Levinas' essays many of his characterizations of "philosophy" might be acceptable as characterizations of Husserl's
views but tend to flatten the pluralism of the philosophical tradition, the
plurivocity of philosophers themselves.

10. On metaphysics and ontology, see *Totality and Infinity*, also "Trace
of the Other"; on infinitude and wholeness, see *Desire, Dialectic, and
Otherness*, chapters 7 and 8; on erotic equivocation and wanton laughter
mentioned above, see *Totality and Infinity*, pp. 263ff.

11. Derrida, *Margins*, p. 247; on totalizing descriptions, see Paul De Man's
essay on Derrida, "The Rhetoric of Blindness," in *Blindness and Insight*, 2nd
ed. rev. (Minneapolis: University of Minnesota Press, 1983), p. 114, where he
says that the "metaphysics of presence" is a "tradition that defines Western
thought in its entirety. . ."

12. Kearney, *Dialogues*, p. 108.

13. *Philosophy and its Others*, pp. 298ff.

14. VA, III, p. 527; HA, II, p. 1199.

15. *Birth Of Tragedy*, section 7, last paragraph.

16. On failure see *Philosophy and its Others*, pp. 242–258; on breakdown
and breakthrough, chapters 5 and 6.

17. J. Derrida "Like the Sound of the Deep Sea within a Shell: Paul de
Man's War," in *Critical Inquiry*, 14, Spring 1988, pp. 590–652.

18. VA, III, p. 528; HA, II, p. 1200.

19. In "On the Relationship of Skepticism to Philosophy," trans. H. S.
Harris in *Between Kant and Hegel* (Albany: SUNY Press, 1985), p. 325,
Hegel himself quotes this statement of Sextus Empiricus; on self-
accomplishing skepticism, PhG, p. 67; PS, p. 50. See Michael N. Forster, *Hegel
and Skepticism* (Cambridge: Harvard University Press, 1989).

20. In the *Will to Power* Nietzsche says in connection with Socrates: "It
is the slave that triumphs in the dialectic. . . .The dialectic can only serve
as a defensive weapon." See G. Deleuze, *Nietzsche and Philosophy*, trans. H.
Tomlinson (New York: Columbia University Press, 1983), p. 121: "The man
of *ressentiment* needs to conceive a non-ego, then to oppose himself to this
non-ego in order finally to posit himself as self. This is the strange syllogism
of the slave: he needs two negations in order to produce the appearance of
affirmation. We already sense the form in which the syllogism of the slave
has been so successful in philosophy: *the dialectic*. The dialectic, as the ideology
of *ressentiment*."

21. On posthumous mind, see *Philosophy and its Others*; see "Being at
a Loss: Reflections on Philosophy and the Tragic."

22. PhG, p. 24; PS, p. 14.

23. PhG, p. 30; PS, p. 19; See Voegelin on Hegel's sorcery, above chapter 2, note 24.

24. Just one example: Luc Ferry and Alain Renaut in *French Philosophy in the Sixties*, trans. M. H. S. Cattani (Amherst: University of Massachusetts Press, 1990), p. 13, report Derrida's answer to their question at the colloquium at Cerisy in 1980 concerning his demands for "another coherence" that would not be "logicometaphysical." Derrida's answer was: "I cannot tell you what it is."

25. *Writing and Difference*, p. 89.

26. See W. and M. Kneale, *The Development of Logic* (Oxford: Clarendon Press, 1962), p. 10.

27. In *Philosophy and its Others*, chapter 3.

28. One could see the development from romanticism to modernism to postmodernism as involving a progressive radicalization of the ironical posture, culminating in the pervasiveness of parody. This point requires elaboration too extensive to be undertaken here. But see *Art and the Absolute*, chapters 5 and 6. See Richard Kearney, *The Wake of Imagination* (Minneapolis: University of Minnesota Press, 1988).

29. See *Writing and Difference*, p. 258.

30. On the possibility of saying "It is nothing" differently, see the meditation on philosophy and failure, *Philosophy and its Others*, pp. 242–258. A different affirmative response to coming to nothing follows in chapter 6 under the rubric of thought singing its other.

Chapter 6

1. S. Kierkegaard, *Concluding Unscientific Postscript*, trans. David F. Swenson and Walter Lowrie (Princeton: Princeton University Press, 1941), p. 34.

2. All of these familiar examples are from the *Phenomenology*.

3. Monty Python's Flying Circus, *In Search of the Holy Grail* (New York: Arista Records, 1975).

4. See my review of *Hegel: The Letters* in *The Owl of Minerva*, vol. 17, no. 2, 1986, pp. 204–208.

5. *Hegel: The Letters*, pp. 189ff. That the matter was on Hegel's mind is indicated by the fact that he mentions the toilets in three different letters to Niethammer (12 and 20 February, 7 May, 1809; *Letters*, pp. 189ff., 195, 197). One finds, on the one hand, Hegel's exasperation with the failure of officials to provide proper funds and, on the other hand, an inability to shake off the temptation to laugh.

6. PhG, p. 57; PS, p. 44.

7. See *Philosophy and its Others.* pp. 257–258, 273, 303ff., on folly and the metaxological.

8. In *Clavis Fichtiana* (1804) Jean Paul satirized the comic discrepancy between the speculative *Ich* of Fichte and our consciousness of ourselves as bodily beings. Hegel liked Jean Paul's humor very much, as we know from the *Aesthetics*; see VA, II, pp. 230–231; HA, I, pp. 601–602.

9. See Jeffrey Henderson, *The Maculate Muse: Obscene Language in Attic Comedy* (New Haven: Yale University Press, 1975).

10. Plutarch, *Moralia, Book I. The Education of Children*, 10c–d.

11. LHP, I, pp. 426ff.

12. See *Birth of Tragedy*, § 11 where Nietzsche speaks of the death of tragedy through the new comedy of Euripides; he refers to what Euripides says in Aristophanes' *Frogs*.

13. VA, II, p. 527; HA, II, p. 1199.

14. F. Nietzsche, *Beyond Good and Evil*, trans. M. Cowan (Chicago: Regnery, 1955), § 28; also in the *Nachlass*, Fall 1885–Spring 1886.

15. On idiocy, see my discussion of evil in chapter 4; also note 7 above on festive folly; also my "Being at a Loss: Reflections on Philosophy and the Tragic."

16. On the Orphic myth of the origin of evil, see Paul Ricoeur, *The Symbolism of Evil*, trans. E. Buchanan (Boston: Beacon Press, 1967), pp. 282, 290ff.

17. On desire and lack, see *Desire, Dialectic, and Otherness*, especially chapter 1.

18. See Tom Rockmore, *Hegel's Circular Epistemology* (Bloomington: Indiana University Press, 1986).

19. PhG, pp. 517ff.; PS, pp. 450ff.

20. PhG, p. 520; PS, pp. 452–53.

21. PhG, p. 521; PS, p. 453.

22. PhG, p. 523; PS, pp. 454–55.

23. PhG, p. 525; PS, pp. 456, 457. Hegel's subsequent discussion is essentially transitional to Christianity as revealed religion; there questions relative to the "death of God," Jesus, evil and particularity are all relevant. I have said something about these issues in previous chapters.

24. On posthumous mind, see *Philosophy and its Others*, pp. 278ff., 300, 304, 368–369. See my remarks on Lear above in chapter 4; also "Being at a Loss."

Index

Absolute: erotic and agapeic, 36, 54, 77ff., 115ff., 135ff., 181ff.
Absolute Spirit, 2, 29, 85, 151ff., 166ff., 271–272
Adorno, T., 20, 116, 248, 267, 269, 288
Aeschylus, 321
Agapeic being, 17, 77ff., 128ff., 175–176, 223; and evil, 244
Alcibiades, 321, 326, 338–339
Anaxagoras, 329
Anaximander, 200–201
Aquinas, Thomas, 12, 91, 159ff., 251, 290
Arendt, H., 226
Aristophanes, 17, 146, 148, 295, chapter 6 *passim*
Aristotle, 8, 11, 31, 117, 121, 127, 131, 137, 140, 155, 232, 242, 244, 246, 254–255, 269, 284, 289, 319
Anthropomorphism, 171ff.
Aufhebung, 13, 61, 67, 75–77, 83, 91, 172, 177, 207, 211, 240, 290, 307
Augustine, St., 12, 54, 121, 156, 157, 175, 196, 201, 222, 304

Bataille, G., 93, 103, 209–212, 263–264, 266, 290, 300, 317
Beautiful Soul, 198–199, 229–230, 296ff., 313
Beckett, S., 297–298, 313
Body and comedy, 311ff., 338

Catholicism, 65, 70–71, 74–75, 106, 108, 116, 245
Chaplin, Charlie, 54, 287

Cogito, 21, 139; and laughter, 312ff.
Comedy, 113, chapter 5 *passim*, chapter 6 *passim*
Croce, B., 24
Cult, chapter 2 *passim*

Death of God, 14, 111–112, 133, 215, 280, 335; *see* God
Deconstruction, 17, 32, 56, chapter 5 *passim*
Derrida, J., 12, 56, 93, 139, chapter 5 *passim*, 311, 317, 324, 341
Descartes, R., 9, 21, 37, 49, 70, 121–122, 156, 157, 191–92, 230, 245, 246
Dialectic, 2, 5, 6, 11ff., 22–23, 45, 50, 56, 60–61, 63, 65, 71–72, 74ff., 80, 95, 101, 105, 110, 113ff., 120, 126ff., 143, 153, 165, 182, 185–187; and evil, chapter 4 *passim*, 263, 266, 278, 282, 284ff., 292, 294, 300, 306, 337, 341; *see* equivocity, mediation, metaxological, univocity
Diogenes, 13, 313
Diotima, 329ff.
Dostoevski, F., 30, 230
Double, 8, 10, 12; double vision, 52, 74ff., 80–82, 94, 113ff.; in philosophy 126ff.; and religion chapter 3 *passim*; and evil will, 209, 213; and Aristophanes, 327–328; *see* dualism
Dualism, 7, 31ff., 62–63, 65–66, 69, 74ff., 80, 96, 99, 106, 108, 110, 115–117, 119–120, 150, 200, 212; *see* double